Teaching to Learn

NEW DIRECTIONS IN MATHEMATICS AND SCIENCE EDUCATION
Volume 4

Scope
Mathematics and science education are in a state of change. Received models of teaching, curriculum, and researching in the two fields are adopting and developing new ways of thinking about how people of all ages know, learn, and develop. The recent literature in both fields includes contributions focusing on issues and using theoretical frames that were unthinkable a decade ago. For example, we see an increase in the use of conceptual and methodological tools from anthropology and semiotics to understand how different forms of knowledge are interconnected, how students learn, how textbooks are written, etcetera. Science and mathematics educators also have turned to issues such as identity and emotion as salient to the way in which people of all ages display and develop knowledge and skills. And they use dialectical or phenomenological approaches to answer ever arising questions about learning and development in science and mathematics.

The purpose of this series is to encourage the publication of books that are close to the cutting edge of both fields. The series aims at becoming a leader in providing refreshing and bold new work—rather than out-of-date reproductions of past states of the art—shaping both fields more than reproducing them, thereby closing the traditional gap that exists between journal articles and books in terms of their salience about what is new. The series is intended not only to foster books concerned with knowing, learning, and teaching in school but also with doing and learning mathematics and science across the whole lifespan (e.g., science in kindergarten; mathematics at work); and it is to be a vehicle for publishing books that fall between the two domains—such as when scientists learn about graphs and graphing as part of their work.

Teaching to Learn
A View from the Field

Kenneth Tobin
The Graduate Center, City University of New York, USA
&
Wolff-Michael Roth
University of Victoria, Canada

SENSE PUBLISHERS
ROTTERDAM / TAIPEI

A C.I.P. record for this book is available from the Library of Congress.

Paperback ISBN: 90-77874-81-X
Hardback ISBN: 90-77874-91-7

Published by: Sense Publishers,
P.O. Box 21858, 3001 AW
Rotterdam, The Netherlands

Printed on acid-free paper

CONTENTS

PREFACE

This book, as any book, is the result of a historical process that we, as any individual, produce and are subjected to. This book has long been coming; or, to express it differently, we have wanted to write the book for a considerable time, ever since we engaged in extended investigations aimed at better understanding what it means to learn to teach from the perspective of the teacher. More so, we wanted to articulate what it really means to participate in coteaching and cogenerative dialoguing—not just thinking about or theorizing these forms of activity but really to experience them in flesh and blood. In his book *Toward a Philosophy of the Act*, Mikhail Bakhtin (1993) points out that the very essence of knowing and learning *only* reveals itself when persons are acting in praxis, as it is only here that their participative thinking deals with the once-occurrent nature of every act. As soon as we theorize actions, we think about them as something possible, as entities of a certain type, which we may find in other situations, too. We think abstractly and no longer have the perspective *from* the inside of praxis. This sense that we ought to write a book *from the inside of praxis* led us to formulate the subtitle of this book, *A Perspective from the Field*. Although we have written about coteaching and cogenerative dialoguing before, and although we have written as coteachers and as participants in cogenerative dialoguing, this book more than any other text we have written in the past—see the annotated bibliography on coteaching and cogenerative dialoguing in the appendix—was written as a text *from the field*. More so than theoretical understanding, we intended to provide our readers with a *feel*, a sense of what it is like to be part of a group of teachers who, in solidarity with one another, enact collective responsibility together *with* their students.

As the prefix *co-* indicates, coteaching and cogenerative dialoguing centrally are concerned with the social aspects of teaching and learning—the prefix *co-* also is found in its expanded form *col-* in the terms collective and collaborate. This focus on the collective expressed by the prefix *co-* contrasts the predominant ethos of many industrialized nations. In fact, our Western culture generally and the North American culture more specifically is so concerned with individuality and individualism that most of its members are concerned only with themselves thereby forgetting that the generalized other, the *Other*, is the condition for each of us; and each of us is part of the condition for all the other Selves that make our culture. This means that the relation denoted by the term *with* constitutes the very possibility for being *human* rather than being just another animal (e.g., Nancy, 2000). Being (in the world) means being *with* others. When the Other is absent, because contact and interchange with others is truncated—such as is the case for blind and deaf children or for persons with severe forms of autism—then those aspects of our being that make us specifically human—a sense of Self, knowledgeability, interactional knowledge—are greatly diminished in the person. As if we could not escape the *with*, the terms "condition," "contact," and "constitute" that we just used, too, use the modified prefix *co-*. This book, therefore, is a reaffirmation of the *with*—as in *being with*—that grounds knowing and learning, whether I am a student of science, an experienced science teacher, or a new science teacher. I am what and who I am *because* of the other; and in coteaching and cogenerative dialoguing, this relation between Self and others is actively exploited, as we learn with and from others even in those moments when we neither are conscious—derived from Lat. *con-* , with, and *scire*, to know—of it nor do reflect on what we do and learn.

A project such as this never succeeds without the support of those close to the authors, the agencies that provide grants, the institutions that give authors leave, and everybody else who contributes (the *con-*!) to making society what it is and thereby provides professors with the space to do research and write books. But there are also some organizations and individuals who contribute more directly and immediately to making a project possible—without grants, it would have been much more difficult for Michael to travel as frequently as he did from the Canadian West Coast to the U.S. East Coast to participate in coteaching and cogenerative dialoguing in the schools where Ken did his research, where the new teachers in his program enacted coteaching and cogenerative dialoguing, and where he taught for extended periods of time day in and day out. We want to thank specifically those agencies relevant to our work on the current book. The research in this book is supported in part by the National Science Foundation under Grant Numbers DUE-0427570 and REC-0107022. Any opinions, findings, and conclusions or recommendations expressed in the book are those of the authors and do not necessarily reflect the views of the National Science Foundation.

We also want to thank all those teachers who willingly hosted us in their classrooms, with whom we taught and enacted cogenerative dialogues, and with whom, therefore, we learned so much about teaching and learning. We thank all those new teachers who, despite their rather recent participation in the field of science teaching, were open to our presence in their classrooms, which, as we can say with confidence, contributed not only to our but also to their own learning: to teach and to talk about teaching. We are grateful to the students, who participated in this research, a rather unimportant issue in their lives considering the enormously precarious conditions that they faced in their everyday lives at home and in the streets. Finally, to Sylvie and Barb, who support our professional and private selves so selflessly—we dedicate this volume to them.

New York, USA
Victoria, Canada
July 2006

TOWARD A PRAXIS PERSPECTIVE ON COTEACHING AND COGENERATIVE DIALOGUING

The relative lack of impact that educational research has had on classroom practice and educational policy is often attributed to the lack of relevance of our research to the lives of classroom teachers and/or how we "package" our findings and recommendations. Overall, this manuscript/research report has little more to add than a reiteration of the importance of context in learning to teach, supervision of teaching, the assessment of teaching, and research on teaching. For quite some time both teachers and researchers have understood that there exists no single set of skills and approaches that apply generically across teaching situations. Unfortunately, these authors have reiterated this point, but have chosen to "package" it rather awkwardly in a theoretical framework that will have little meaning to teacher educators and teachers, let alone those researchers who value practicality. The introduction of new terminology/jargon is not inherently negative if it adds new insight and meaning to phenomena of concern. However, the introduction of constructs such as *habitus* and *Mitsein* do little more than obscure some rather intuitive notions that have been recognized more directly by both teachers and researchers. This manuscript, unfortunately, is an exemplar of what is wrong with the direction educational research has taken with regard to the improvement of teaching. (Excerpt from reviewer comments, January 2000)

When we sat down to write about our collective experiences with coteaching we knew we were onto something. We were excited at the practical impact of coteaching and especially intrigued by the potential of collaborating to push the theoretical boundaries. As the words flowed to produce a quite lengthy manuscript, the rich potential of the emerging theory was evident to us. We had a rationale for using coteaching and theoretical lenses to guide what would be an extended research program that took the form of a series of design experiments—we enacted coteaching, studied it, and, based on what we learned from the research, redesigned coteaching. In this process our theory expanded and revealed further potential for increasing opportunities to learn to teach science.

The above excerpt from the editors of a leading science education journal was a shock to us. Clearly the editors and the peers they chose to review our paper were on a different wavelength than we were. Nevertheless, as senior scholars we did not allow either the tone of the review or its central message to deter us. Instead we resolved to expand the manuscript and publish it as a book—*At the Elbow of Another* (Roth & Tobin, 2002) eventually received a *Choice Book Award*, given to books "selected for their excellence in scholarship and presentation, the significance of their contribution to the field, and their value as important often the first treatment of their subject." Since then we have continued our research, expanded the theoretical underpinnings for learning to teach, and greatly expanded the models of coteaching. Now, after many publications in peer-reviewed journals and two books (see the annotated list of relevant publications in the appendix), we begin this third book on coteaching.

It seems as if almost everybody is an expert on what constitutes effective teaching and how problems in teacher education can be solved. For example, in the United States the National Science Foundation has taken a stance that effective approaches to science teacher preparation and enhancement should involve collaborative partnerships between scientists (usually from colleges of science), science educators (usually from the colleges of education), and school district personnel. Many models have emerged from such collaborations, often featuring the type and amount of science subject matter needed by teachers and the ways in which the science is learned. A good example of an innovation of this sort is the Master's degree in chemistry education, developed by the Department of Chemistry and the Graduate School of Education at the University of Pennsylvania. This degree comprises ten new courses designed to educate science teachers with relatively little background in chemistry to teach chemistry, especially in urban high schools. Eight of the courses are in chemistry and two are in chemistry education. A feature of the program is that each chemistry course incorporates an inquiry model that the professors use in teaching the science teachers need to know to teach high school chemistry. The chemistry education courses focus on what the teachers do when they teach, requiring them to do research and curriculum design for their own classes. Since the degree is for practicing teachers it is offered on a part-time basis with courses offered in three concentrated summer sessions and two Saturdays a month over two academic years.

The chemistry education degree addresses the science achievement crisis, as it is perceived by scientists and their construction of core problems—insufficient Americans majoring in science and then entering graduate school—problems they attribute to high school science teachers having less than optimal knowledge of science. Recognizing the professional and personal commitments that might deter teachers from participating, the degree is offered at times when teachers can attend and tuition is waived for twenty participants a year. Now in its sixth year the program is judged a success because of the number of teachers who apply, pass, and continue to teach. We have no problem with this approach to professional development and programs like it—especially if the participants undertake research on teaching and learning in their classrooms. However, we do have queries. Do the participating teachers learn to teach and do they enact praxis in ways that afford their students' learning? Also, do students of the participants and graduates from the program enjoy enhanced learning environments, increase their understandings of science, and join the pipeline of would-be scientists?

Of course not all collaborative ventures between scientists, science educators, and teachers are built from the ground up in ways that cohere with values such as inquiry and respect for what can be offered by scholarship in education. For example, in chapter 5 we explore ways in which coteaching and cogenerative dialogues were salient in a professional development project designed mainly by chemists in collaboration with an urban school district in the United States. In this project a primary assumption seemed to be that students would do well on high stakes achievement tests if they received intensive instruction on the subject matter most likely to be tested and participated in the minimum number of laboratory activities needed to meet state requirements. The approach was supported by weekly practice on tests given in previous years. Our research explores how, even within this framework, teachers and students participated in forms of coteaching and cogenerative dialoguing, which, when recognized as such, can be fine-tuned to produce more productive learning environments.

Numerous science teacher education programs involve reading and understanding research and theory about teaching and learning, field experiences and associated discussions and written analyses—reflections on practice, thereby connecting theory and research to practice. However, many of these approaches make assumptions about teaching that imply that it is an entirely rational process that involves teachers summing up what needs to be done and consciously making choices about how to initiate, structure and react. Learning to teach is seen as a conscious process that is best understood through psychological models, including processes often referred to as reflection in action, metacognition, and rational decision-making. Our perspective, which we develop throughout the book, is that psychological models have failed to deliver and in large part may be at the base of the problems we encountered with colleagues. These colleagues often failed to see the advantages of what we were proposing as a teacher education model involving coteaching and cogenerative dialoguing.

In the following section, we ground coteaching and cogenerative dialoguing in being-with, that is, in an analytic of coexistence.

BEING-*WITH*: TOWARD A COEXISTENTIAL ANALYTIC

Both of our key terms, *coteaching* and *cogenerative dialoguing* have been constructed using the prefix *co-*. We originally constructed the term coteaching to distinguish what we were doing from *team teaching*, a term essentially used to denote a practice where teachers enact a particular form of division of labor, whereby participants split up the tasks at hand according to competency and inclination. Such arrangements frequently lead to situations where the participating teachers work on their own, the sole difference with other teaching situation being that they work in their areas of strength. In contrast, coteaching was constructed analogous to copiloting, a work situation in which both pilots take full responsibility for all aspects of work. In doing so, they learn from each other. That is, pilots learn to fly by working as copilots; and although they never fly without copilots, their knowledgeability in praxis is recognized in the promotion to pilot. While pilots pilot together, they do more than get their passengers from city A to city B and learn to fly: they essentially develop shared understanding of the situation in which they are together. But shared understanding—contrary to the way some scholars articulate the term—does not mean sharing explicit forms of knowledge, representations, or theory. Rather, we use the term *understanding* in the way phenomenological and hermeneutic philosophers employ it, as an implicit form of knowledgeability: knowing our way around the world and knowing how the world works even without explicit theories and concepts. Tennis players, for example, have an understanding of physics that by far transcends their explicit knowledge of the physics of motion. They know what to do to get the ball to a particular spot on the opponent's side of the court even though they may not know any physics at all.

Being-*with* creates exactly this kind of understanding, knowing how the world works even though none of the participants may be able to theorize the events in which they participate. It is a world that we are conscious of, that is, that we know (Lat. *scire*) together with (Lat. *co-*) others. More importantly, by being-with others we come to understand even without "appropriating" or "constructing" "meaning." This is so because in being with, we come to understand the situation and ourselves; but in "understanding ourselves, we understand that there is nothing to understand; more precisely, this means that there is no appropriation of meaning, because "'meaning' *is the sharing of Being*" (Nancy, 2000, p. 98, our emphasis). Coteaching and cogenerative dialoguing both are forms of praxis that set up and expose participants to learn and understand in and through the sharing of being in the classroom. "In being-with and as being with, *we* have always already begun to understand meaning, to understand ourselves and the world as meaning. And this understanding is always already completed, full, whole, and infinite" (p. 98, original emphasis).

How can it be, some readers may ask themselves, that others are implicated in our understanding? How can it be that the Other—all the ones other than "I" in the *we* of collective understanding—is implicated in and a source of the practical understanding of how the world works and of knowing one's way around the world? This is so, because the Other is the very condition of individual being; without the Other, there is no sense to actions, words, language, objects, or Being. Thus, "the Other presides over the organization of the world into objects and over the transitive relations of these objects. These objects exist only through the possibilities with which Others filled up the world" (Deleuze, 1969/1990, p. 312). Or again, "co-appearance consists in its appearance to itself and to one another, all at once. There is no appearing to oneself except as appearing to one another" (Nancy, 2000, p. 67). That is, the world itself, filled with objects and events, is known to us only in and through our relations with others. The emergence of consciousness at the individual level and its integral relation *being-with* has been demonstrated in a series of experiments conducted by the Russian psychologist Alexander Meshcheryakov.

Meshcheryakov worked with deaf-blind children, who frequently did not achieve mental development and failed to learn to walk, eat, drink and so on, developed as any other children when they were allowed to find (become conscious of) themselves in activities with other children and adults. They did not *know* objects like spoons or forks but gorged themselves with food stuffing it into their mouths. They began to become aware of things as things and of others as others through the mediation of an Other, initially some teacher. For example, the teacher might lead one of the deaf-blind children to other children already playing, allowing the former to feel the latter's movements and objects they were playing with. Furthermore, the teachers also allowed these deaf-blind children to discover themselves, their own bodies, by interacting with dolls and leading the children to discover resemblances (correspondences) between other bodies and their own. It is in the process of hundreds of such learning episodes that the children discovered that there is signification separate from particular signifiers.

Ultimately, then, we come to know and understand in and through our relation to others—being is always being-*with*. It is because of this relation to others that each action comes to have a sense; and because we produce actions in and through our bodies, sense comes to be grounded in our embodied experience. *Coteaching*, that is, teaching with someone else provides the opportunity to develop understanding grounded in the being-with an Other; and *cogenerative dialoguing* is the place where this understanding can be articulated in language. But language, as Being, *presupposes* the Other: "Language is the element of the with *as such*; it is the space of its declaration" (Nancy, 2000, p. 88, original emphasis). At the very moment a (pre)human individual produced an utterance for another, he or she *presupposed* its intelligibility, that is, presupposed a shared understanding not only of the situation that they found themselves and to which the utterance referred but also of the utterance ("word") itself.

Grounding teaching in this way leads us to an understanding of the dialectic of teaching, in other words, the relationship of teaching as praxis—where actions occur only once and cannot ever be taken back—and teaching as ethos (culture), which is constitutive of the sense and intersubjectivity of each act of teaching. But grounding teaching in this way, that is, in being-with, also obliterates the difference between the ethical and the ontological. Because the Other is the condition for my being and because I am the condition for everyone else, I am also responsible not only for my own actions but also for those of the Other (Levinas, 1978/1998). This is so because action possibilities exist at a collective level; and actions are account-able, we can always say what we did and why we did something. I am therefore part of the condition that allows an Other to act with the presupposition that his or her action is intelligible to me, therefore possible. This means, that his or her action inherently is enabled by me and all the other Selves that together constitute the condition for his or her being. Coteaching and cogenerative dialoguing are in line with the ethics that arises from being-with, coresponsibility.

Coresponsibility means being responsible together rather than you are responsible for some things and I am responsible for others. If the latter situation was the case, I can always blame the Other when something has not happened according to our plans. It is a situation where individuals can divest themselves of their responsibilities shifting them to others; such divestment of responsibilities is rampant in individualistic societies, and, as the frequency and extent of litigation cases shows, it is particularly rampant in the US. On the other hand, collective responsibility or coresponsibility means that at any moment each and every individual is responsible for the situation as a whole. Thus coteachers are responsible for all aspects of some lesson, even though one person may take the lead and another more of a backseat. But at any moment, if someone—lead or backseat teacher—sees that something requires action or remediation, then he or she begins to act accordingly. If the plans had been that the Other was to have taken care of the issue, then cogenerative dialoguing after or a huddle during the lesson is a situation where this can be brought up and talked about.

Being-with and coresponsibility therefore also mean *solidarity*, a term that denotes the fact or quality of being (perfectly) at one with someone else with respect to interests, sympathies, aspirations, understanding, and so on. Functioning coteaching and cogenerative dialoguing praxis not only presuppose solidarity—without alignment, we cannot teach in concert, as without alignment, we cannot participate in a jam session or be a member of a team—but also produce solidarity. The more we work together in solidarity, the more solidarity we produce, that is, the more our interests, sympathies, aspirations, understanding, and so on converge and come to be shared.

OVERVIEW

This book essentially articulates coteaching and cogenerative dialoguing, two forms of praxis that coevolved in our work, from the perspective of praxis itself. Our intent has been to articulate the two forms of praxis in a way that allows readers to develop a sense of what it means to be there, in the classroom, to experience others and oneself, including moments of more central participation and moments of reflective consideration of the actions of others.

In chapter 1, we lay the ground for the remainder of the book, articulating the course our inquiries have taken. More specifically, we ground the remainder of the book in our understanding of teaching as *praxis*—in contrast to teaching practice, which means teaching as articulated in discourse—and teaching as culture (*ethos*). We provide a first articulation of coteaching and then describe how this praxis came to emerge from what we each were doing before. We introduce issues concerning the mutuality and the key features of coteaching and we discuss (literally) the role of theory in building conceptual models of and for what we do.

As we point out in the preface, Bakhtin exhorts us to clearly differentiate the once-occurrent nature of lived experience from talking about and theorizing this experience. In chapter 2, we provide a description of coteaching from the inside in the attempt to communicate the sense of what it means to coteach. We use one particular biology lesson on monohybrids and dihybrids that we cotaught with Chuck, a resident teacher, and Andrea, a new teacher currently enrolled in a master's level certification program. The predominant view is through Michael's eyes; but we reflect together about the shared events in metalogues that follow the descriptions. We then take a look at the peripheral roles participants may take and exemplify this aspect with episodes from a lesson Ken cotaught with Aaron, a resident physics teacher in the same school where Chuck taught.

In chapter 3 we take up where we left off in the preceding chapter with an effort to bring further insights into coteaching through first hand accounts and analyses of videotape of a cotaught lesson—in this case involving several coteachers with experience of teaching a chemistry class for an extended period of time. Our motive is to introduce possibilities that emerged from a cotaught lesson, taking up issues that pertain to learning to teach, teacher education and professional development. In an ethnographic study of coteaching we explore two questions: What happens during cotaught lessons? and Why does this happen? Our approach is to describe the roles of teachers and students as they are enacted in a year in which coteaching was a vehicle for learning to teach science in an urban high school. Our descriptions, analyses, and interpretations of what happens provide readers with examples of how to do research on coteaching and emphasize the wealth of roles and the associated potential for learning that is associated with coteaching.

In the first three chapters we examine coteaching as a means of learning to teach. We see that coteachers teach together and become like the other in numerous ways, thereby reproducing certain teaching practices. Coteachers become like one another in the ways in which they talk, gesture, observe the class, use space and time, access materials, and interact with one another and students. Depending on the situation, teachers may (not) be aware of what they have learned. Furthermore, changes in teaching and prevailing practices may not benefit all learners. As a precaution against teaching being enacted in ways that are not optimal, it is desirable for teachers and students to use *cogenerative dialogues* to identify and review what seems to work and what does not, especially practices and schema that disadvantage participants. In chapter 4, we articulate ways of getting started with cogenerative dialogues. Good starting points are discussions about any resistance participants encounter in their efforts to learn, contradictions they experience, and concerns they have about the roles and associated divisions of labor among participants, the rule structures for the class, and their access to the resources available to support learning. We describe how we got started with cogenerative dialogues, how they evolved, and how we structured them—not by first theorizing and then implementing them, but by evolving them together with teachers and students. We show how cogenerative dialogues constitute a context for producing and building new levels of solidarity.

In chapter 5 we articulate the nature of cogenerative dialogues by examining in greater detail a cogenerative dialogue that followed the cotaught lesson presented in chapter 3. Our account shows that students can be valuable contributors to the understanding of classroom events and participants in planning teaching strategies, learning approaches, and curriculum. Although cogenerative dialogues have evolved a great deal since this one took place, the analysis provides insights into the topics that arose and how they unfolded. Importantly, the transcripts provide insights into the ways in which the participants view classroom events and their personal roles in relation to the collective of the class. Both of the student participants have struggled with science in the recent past and could easily be regarded as students at risk of not proceeding with further education beyond high school; yet the ways in which they speak about complex topics show that they have deep insights into education and ways in which it can be changed to better serve their needs. They also show that they are cooperative with their teachers and resolute in making suggestions, especially when they feel enacted curricula are not challenging and therefore do not meet their needs.

Professional development approaches and needs can be mediated, and perhaps contorted, by macrostructures such as high stakes testing. In such circumstances well-intended educators, and especially people from funding agencies, might focus resources on improving the performance levels on high stakes tests. In chapter 6 we are explicit about some of the issues inherent in planning and enacting effective professional development programs planned to address the needs of disadvantaged high school youth in New York City. This context is salient because there is a significant focus on learning subject matter and holding students, teachers, and schools accountable for high levels of academic achievement through performance on state-level examinations referred to as *Regents* examinations.

As is evident from the earlier chapters, coteaching and cogenerative dialogues are more than methods for learning to teach and improving the quality of teaching and learning. Increasingly, researchers have employed coteaching and cogenerative dialogues as research methods, forms of participant observation that create opportunities for coteachers (as researchers) to experience directly the praxis of teachers and learners. In chapter 7, we articulate some of the key issues involved in using coteaching and cogenerative dialoguing as research method. This includes considerations of possible ethical implications. We describe and exemplify how different stakeholders contribute to making the two methods work, how analyses unfold, how data are generated, and how analyses are written. Concerning cogenerative dialoguing, we provide descriptions how they allow us to do recursive analysis of data that begins during sessions designed for understanding and changing the curriculum and end with how to continue these voice-preserving dialogues right into the manuscript.

Teaching is evaluated in numerous ways and, depending on the purposes of evaluation, the validity of the performance measures on which decisions are made may be crucial to the teacher and the institution in which the teacher practices. In chapter 8, we describe and explain how coteaching and cogenerative dialoguing are forms of assessment and evaluation praxis that differ from the received ways of doing assessment and evaluation. We are concerned with questions such as, "Are measures of teaching performance dependable for the purposes of their intended use?" "Are the data on the basis of which decisions are made trustworthy, credible and dependable?" "Can the measures be used to differentiate individuals for decision-making purposes?" "Can the performance of individuals be dependably compared to given criteria and judged to have surpassed or fallen short of given benchmarks?"

In the epilogue, we use the metalogue form for reflecting on the various aspects of coteaching and cogenerative dialoguing, we articulate what we have learned from our studies, including the analyses presented here.

Over the years, we have conducted extensive research on coteaching and cogenerative dialoguing and thereby established a field of research that did not exist—despite the claims of some reviewers of our early work. Though the claims were easy to refute on the basis of our searches in the ISI database, some editors of science education journals have used them as resources to reject our early work. In the appendix, we provide an annotated bibliography with brief descriptions of the various studies we conducted and published; this will give readers an idea about the ground that this now extensive research agenda has prepared and covered. We thought that constructing this annotated bibliography will provide our readers with a resource for better understanding the history and evolution of coteaching and cogenerative dialoguing praxis.

NARRATIVE GENRES

Throughout this book, we employ a variety of narrative genres chosen in each situation to provide a best match between content and form. Thus, we use field-notes, transcripts, and narrative first-person accounts to bring readers as close as possible to the events as seen from different points of view. Thus, a transcript renders what has been captured on camera; enhanced fieldnotes are descriptions that an ethnographer makes in the field subsequently enhanced to turn it into *thick* descriptions; and we use narrative first-person accounts to render how a participant has experienced some event or to express our personal perspectives on a particular issue (e.g., evaluation). We draw on more traditional expository style for articulating theory or theoretical explanations of events; or we draw on metalogues— conversations between the authors—to learn from what we have learned and articulated before. Sometimes the metalogues appear at the end of a chapter, at other times, they appear at the end of a section; and sometimes they appear repeatedly throughout a section. In each situation, our sense of the most appropriate way of presenting the issues at hand mediated which format we chose; this sense a sense of the game and cannot be further ground and argued for. Pertaining to the conversational format of the metalogues: One advantage of articulating issues in terms of conversations is that we are not forced to take the same position on some issue but that we can present our (slightly) varying stances and allow our personal voices to come to the fore.

DIALECTICS

We are fundamentally committed to a dialectical approach to understanding to culture including the pertinent issues of knowing, learning, teaching, and learning to teach science. In dialectical approaches, situations are approached in a holistic fashion paying heed to the recommendation that if one were to structure such systems into parts, these would always mutually presuppose each other. To take a concrete example, let us look at structure and agency, which in cultural sociology and cultural-historical activity theory underlying this book are thought in dialectical terms. Thus, what a teacher or student can do in a classroom is mediated by the structures they find therein: a number of whiteboards spread throughout a science classroom provide different opportunities for what can be done than a single overhead projector, especially when the school makes available only one 8.5 inch by 11 inch transparency available (which is the case in the classroom featured in chapter

2). A classroom with laboratory facilities in the back provides a different set of resources than not having laboratory facilities at all (a case of which is described in chapter 6). Thus, what can be done and therefore agency depends on the material (and conceptual) structures. Simultaneously, structures make no sense apart from agency: what salient structure is depends on the participants in a situation, their past experiences, the schemas that have been developed, and so on. Thus, even though there may be several whiteboards available in a science room, it may not be apparent to a teacher that this constitutes a resource for enacting science lessons in a different way, for example, in the way described in chapter 3. This means that agency and structure presuppose each other—they cannot be considered to be independent theoretical categories that at times *inter*act. To make salient the mutual codependence of particular concepts, we have chosen some time ago to turn them into *one* concept by collating them separated by a vertical line. Thus, because agency and structure are codependent and mutually presupposing concepts, we combine them to form the new *structure|agency* concept, which we also denote as structure|agency dialectic. Throughout the book, we draw on other dialectical pairs that have shown to be useful in understanding coteaching and cogenerative dialoguing.

CHAPTER 1

GETTING STARTED WITH COTEACHING

In this chapter we introduce the methodology of coteaching and describe some of its history—providing theoretical and empirical rationale and our perspectives, which are grounded in our experiences with coteaching and teacher education. We lay the ground for the remainder of the book, articulating the course our inquiries have taken. More specifically, we ground the remainder of the book in our understanding of teaching as *praxis*—in contrast to teaching practice, which means teaching as articulated in discourse—and teaching as culture (*ethos*). We provide a first articulation of coteaching and then describe how this praxis came to emerge from what we each were doing before. We introduce issues concerning the mutuality and the key features of coteaching and we discuss (literally) the role of theory in building conceptual models of and for what we do.

TEACHING AS PRAXIS

What are productive ways to think about teaching? In many teacher education courses there is separation between learning about teaching by reading books and journals; participating in lectures, workshops and tutorials; and observing and teaching peers and K–12 children in small groups and whole classes. These different contexts, in which individuals are expected to learn about teaching, can be thought of as fields, allowing for particular forms of learning to occur—but is any of what is learned accurately described as teaching? What is teaching? How does someone learn to teach? How can individuals represent or reproduce what they know about teaching? We consider questions such as these to be central to teacher education and the ideas we discuss in this chapter. In an endeavor to unpack what we mean by teaching we begin with what is learned from reading books and journals, including what is read in this chapter. If the focus is on teaching, then what is read is about teaching; but what is learned is not teaching per se but are descriptions of teaching. Similarly, if a person writes about what she knows of teaching, perhaps reflecting on a recent teaching experience, what is inscribed in the words and the thoughts associated with those inscriptions are not teaching, but are *about* teaching. Hence the fields of reading and writing about teaching do not require a person to teach and what can be written and read are not proxies for how well a person can teach. Similarly, talking about what a person knows about teaching is not teaching, but is *talk about* teaching. Reading, writing and talking about teaching are useful activities that allow a person to create foci for thinking about teaching in much the same way that a person thinks about teaching when she watches someone else teach.

In all of the examples given in the previous paragraph, the learning that occurs is *about* teaching, allowing for the creation of conceptual objects that are useful referents for further thought, discussion, and writing. These conceptual objects can be foci for negotiating agreements about possible learning environments, teacher and learner roles, and criteria for judging whether or not enacted curricula are effective. However, in none of the mentioned instances is the knowledge accurately thought of as knowledgeable teaching. In fact, knowledge is considered from a theoretical or skills perspective, that which contributes to practical wisdom is effectively excluded—this is because practical wisdom is intimately tied to the singularity of a practical act, which inherently only occurs once (Bakhtin, 1993). Theoretically considered, actions can be played over and over again and the different results can be evaluated against this or that set of norms. Real everyday teaching, as all forms of praxis, is constituted by actions that are aspects of once-occurrent events; we may be able to apologize for something we have done but we cannot undo it. Each act inherently is a historical act.

Teaching is something that is done. The knowledge that is accurately referred to as teaching is enacted as a practical activity, which we describe as praxis—knowledge in action or knowledgeability. So that we can highlight the main features of praxis we present the following vignette that describes the teaching of chemistry in an urban high school class consisting mainly of tenth grade students. The vignette involves Victoria, a *new teacher*—our term for teachers in training—who learns to teach alongside Alex, a regular chemistry teacher in an urban school in a metropolitan on the American east coast.

> Victoria was reviewing chemical valence, preparing students for the end of topic quiz. Her chief goal for the lesson was to ensure that the students could use the periodic table to figure out the valence for a group of elements, focusing especially on elements having a valence of 1 through 4. She had planned on revising what she referred to as a trick for figuring out the valence from the position on the periodic table and then moving on to an exercise in which students would write the correct formula for given chemical compounds. As Victoria explains to the class to "Look at the placement on the table of the elements. So that's the trick for figuring out the valence electrons." Mirabelle raises her hand just as Victoria finishes saying "the." Victoria finishes her utterance and then calls on Mirabelle, who says, "I figured out a system way you can remember (0.8 s) how many valence electrons." Just as Mirabelle starts to say "how," following a pause of almost a second, Victoria speaks simultaneously—so for a time there is overlapping speech "Yeah. So this is the trick. The placement on the table is how you can remember how many electrons there are."

In this vignette Victoria and Mirabelle both enact culture as human praxis. Their actions are partly conscious and partly (perhaps mainly) unconscious. Victoria has set out to review how students could use the periodic table to quickly find the valence for an element. However, Mirabelle raises her hand and when called upon breaches the flow of Victoria's teaching. The opportunity to resume speaking presents itself with a pause of 0.8 seconds, as Mirabelle appears to gather her thoughts before completing her utterance. In the interaction Mirabelle and Victoria both enact praxis fluently—enactment being anticipatory, timely and appropriate. What is teaching in the vignette? Victoria's teaching consists of her actions as they are distributed through time and space. When she commences her explanation she is close to the periodic table and as she starts to speak "Look at the placement on the table . . ." she moves toward the periodic table and gestures to the second row of elements. Just as Victoria commences the word valence, Mirabelle raises her hand and is called on without a discernible pause immediately after Victoria states the word "electrons." The exchanges between Victoria and Mirabelle especially, involve verbal and nonverbal interactions, the place (including its resources), and the histories of Victoria, Mirabelle and others in the class, school and school district (to mention but a few). The interactions between Victoria and Mirabelle show conviction, persistence, passion, empathy, frustration, annoyance, and the motives of the collective. As time unfolds, signs of emotion are evident in the body movements, gestures, facial expressions and prosody of the speakers. Emotions are part of praxis and so too are the practices of all participants, including interactions with resources (i.e., social, material and symbolic).

A key issue about praxis is that it is dynamic—human praxis structures the fields in which it is enacted, and is structured by them. What we mean by this is that praxis is mediated by what is usually done in a given field (i.e., its history) and the resources of the field, including other participants, the materials available to support action (e.g., teaching aids like the periodic table, equipment, furniture, space, time), and symbols (e.g., schema associated with the field, like rules, ideology and signs associated with artifacts, people and practices). A teacher's schemas are only part of a classroom's structure, which is dynamic and includes the schemas and practices of all participants, the presence and absence of material and temporal resources, and the human resources that can be accessed and appropriated. If a teacher or student acts in some way, the outcomes of this action become resources for the actions of all participants in the classroom. Whether they are appropriated depends on the agencies of all participants, which are dialectically related to the structures of the field, including participants' practices.

While reviewing a videotape of this lesson other students from the class identified this vignette as a contradiction to what normally happens in their science class. They felt that Mirabelle's suggestion of a different way of finding valence was a good example of a student showing inquiry, a phenomenon that was rare. During the vignette, first Victoria and then Mirabelle may have experienced resistance to their fluent enactment of praxis. For example, as Victoria sets out to review how the valence of an element could be obtained from the periodic table, Mirabelle's raised hand might not have been anticipated, in which case she may have experienced the raised hand as resistance. Even so, she has encountered similar interruptions before and completes her utterance before calling on Mirabelle and giving her the go ahead to speak. Similarly, after just one utterance, as Mirabelle seemingly pauses to gather her argument, she is interrupted by Victoria. Just as Victoria commences her utterance, Mirabelle continues as well and for a moment they speak at the same time. Mirabelle may experience Victoria's interruption as resistance and it is interesting that as the interaction sequence unfolds, both speakers use gesture, prosody (especially high pitch and increased amplitude) to express emotions such as conviction.

Because teaching is praxis, it seems self-evident that field (internship) experiences are a central activity in learning to teach; that is learning to teach by teaching while, to the extent possible, bringing together all relevant knowledge forms. However, even though most of our teacher education colleagues readily accept the centrality of field experiences, it is a struggle to get consensus on what should happen in the field. Many educators believe that field experiences should commence with a relatively lengthy period of observing others teach. New teachers are required to observe and take notes on the teaching of a designated resident teacher and extra observations of other teachers in the building prior to them beginning to teach. There is an expectation that the resident teacher and those to be observed would be exemplary teachers, thereby allowing new teachers to learn about teaching by observing the best and interacting with them about what they do and why they do what they do. Regular conversations about the observations are scheduled, a goal for new teachers being to build images of teaching, and through reflective dialogues with others, to associate images of practice with rationale provided by experienced participants, including a resident teacher and a university supervisor.

The purpose of having experienced others look over planning notes and participate in dialogues with new teachers is to provide interpretations of teaching and learning that are informed by their own teaching experiences, knowledge of the university coursework, and theories to illuminate the practices deemed salient to an observed lesson. However, although conversations like these are useful they are limited because, unless coteaching occurs, they may lack the lived experience of teaching *these* students in *this* place and at *this* time. Most important, in teaching praxis, actions are intimately tied to and not understandable apart from emotional-volitional and ethico-moral dimensions. These dimensions are not external mediators of practical action but central to their very constitution (Varela & Depraz, 2005). That is, our momentary and long-term emotional makeup shapes what we do—we have good, bad days, so-so, and just everyday normal days; and what we do has outcomes that shape and are resources for the actions of others, which gives what we do an ethico-moral dimension.

If coteaching does not occur the activities of the observer and the observed are stridently different since one teacher teaches while the other watches and writes notes about events and interactions she considers salient. Talk *about* teaching differs ontologically from teaching praxis and there are no guarantees that rationales provided, even by experts who are sincere about what they say, have any connections to what is done and why it is done. Hence, interactive dialogues add to the repertoire of talk about teaching without contributing directly to what and how to teach. Presumably all participants have opportunities to refine their teaching schemas, including values, beliefs, and metaphors for effective and less effective teaching practices. From the perspective of both the resident teacher and the observing new teacher, such discussions can lead to resolutions to adopt certain practices in the future and to discontinue others. However, teaching practices are enacted as praxis; nothing that is said, written, or resolved can do more than change discourses related to teaching and learning. Practices consistent with those schemas might be created in praxis if the structures of the classroom facilitate their development and enactment.

TEACHING AS CULTURE

We view teaching as a form of *cultural enactment* (Sewell, 1999). Culture comes to be enacted in the form of practices and associated schema that members bring to salient issues. In the process, they exercise their agency (i.e., power to act) as part of which they appropriate the structures of a field to simultaneously meet their personal goals (teaching a science concept) and the collective's motives (the schooling of new generations). The structures of the field and the relevant schema are dialectically related, that is, they presuppose each other. For example, what members perceive in a particular field, such as a science classroom, depends on their schema; but a schema comes to be active only because the material structures of the field call for it.

In a productive field culture is enacted fluently, with flow between participants who are able to anticipate one another's practices, respond appropriately and in a timely way. Culture is invisible when those in a field engage productively, accept what happens, and take it in stride (Swidler, 1986). Such occasions are "settled." Participants experience themselves as having some room to maneuver, while interacting in the pursuit of individual goals and collective motives. Thus, when classroom situations are settled, teachers teach in an anticipatory way in which their actions flow in synchrony with others' actions. In contrast, during unsettled times, flow is breached because enactment either is not anticipated, untimely, or inappropriate. On such occasions culture becomes visible, that is, participants become conscious as they step out of action to review what happened and what should happen next. They then exhibit those aspects of cultural practices that normally are invisible. Hence, when individuals experience resistance, or at a collective level, as contradictions arise in a class, culture becomes visible and parts of it are enacted consciously and deliberately. Lack of anticipation can breach the flow of teaching and learning and contribute to dysfunctional learning environments. If students know what a teacher is attempting to change, and if they have a hand in agreeing to the changes, then it may be easier for them to support and anticipate what is to happen and interact appropriately.

Because of the ways in which they are structured, fields usually support particular forms of culture that characterize them; in fact, the structures of the field contain culture in a crystallized form. For example, the culture that is appropriate for a church is quite different than the culture enacted in a sports field. The structure of the church—arrangement and orientation of pews, altar, walkways, and so on enables some actions while constraining others; the structure of a sports field— soccer, tennis, basketball—afford different sets of actions and therefore a different culture characteristic of each particular game. However, a key feature of the way we view culture is that the boundaries around fields are porous, allowing participants to enact culture from other fields in a given field such as a science classroom. For example, in the vignette involving Mirabelle's suggestion of an alternative way to use the periodic table to find the valence of an element, students from the class volunteered that Mirabelle typically spoke like this while on the basketball court, where they described her as a bully. That is, on this occasion, features of Mirabelle's classroom talk were similar in form to the ways in which she argued on a basketball court. If this is the case, then it serves as an example of culture from the field of the basketball court being enacted in the field of the science classroom. When culture from a different field is enacted in a science classroom it might be unexpected, breach cultural fluency, and be experienced by participants as resistance.

An analysis of teaching, as a central part of teacher education, necessarily involves teachers who step back from teaching to review what has been happening, or as often happens, stepping back after a breach to figure out what to do next. After a lesson, a teacher might make entries in a reflective journal, speak to students about how the lesson went, or systematically analyze what happens using videotape. We view the contradictions that underlie such breaches as a normal part of social life and important in the sense that they become foci for critical dialogues, potential seeds for improving social life in a given field (such as achievement in a science classroom). Contradictions are a necessary part of cultural enactment, not sources of error to be explained away. They are in fact opportunities to articulate understanding and provide occasions for developing such understanding through explanation-seeking interpretation. Seeking out moments of weak coherence in and across cultural fields allows identifying associated contradictions, the analysis of which constitutes an opportunity for professional growth.

When teaching is considered as cultural enactment, learning to teach is regarded as cultural *production*, where production involves *reproduction* and *transformation* of existing forms of culture. In this way, cultural production is both preserving past practices *and* generating new ones at the same time. If teachers produce the culture of teaching, in the process of learning to teach, they would exercise agency as they appropriate resources in the fields in which learning occurs. We embrace the articulated agency|structure dialectic, which we use throughout the book to develop key ideas about cultural production (i.e., learning) and identity. The term dialectic here means that structure and agency mutually presuppose each other: without agency there is no structure and without structure there is no agency.

COTEACHING

For some time now we have employed coteaching and cogenerative dialogues as models for learning to teach and for doing research and evaluation. In a research program that has been ongoing in urban schools for ten years we have learned a great deal about teaching, learning to teach, and the theoretical frameworks that can be used fruitfully to illuminate teaching and learning to teach. We also have learned a considerable amount about the methodologies to enact coteaching and cogenerative dialogues in contexts that include initial teacher education programs, professional development for teachers, research, and evaluation.

Coteaching occurs when two or more persons teach a group of students with a dual purpose: providing more opportunities for students to learn and providing opportunities to the persons to grow as teachers. First, the presence of multiple teachers provides a greater array of dynamic structures than is possible when only one teacher is present. Accordingly, the students in a class experience expanded agency and associated opportunities for learning and creating new identities. Second, a higher incidence of teaching in cotaught classrooms is not only experienced by students, but also the teachers, who can appropriate the enacted teaching of others, learn, and expand their own repertoire of teaching practices and schema. By being in a class with other teachers, and coteaching with them, all coteachers experience many more interactions between teachers and students than would occur in a classroom with just one teacher and they also experience teacher–teacher interactions. The observation is made from the vantage point of a participant, which thereby is characterized by the same emotional-volitional and ethico-moral dimensions as those of other participants. The increased experience with interactions is a foundation for learning to teach and constitutes a framework for learning to teach through coteaching.

We use the term *coteaching* rather than team teaching because the emphasis in our approach is on learning from one another and the historically constituted decision of those who designed and enacted our approach to field experience to call it coteaching. Thus, very early in this work, while sitting in an airport next to a copilot Michael had the idea that one could think of learning to teach in the same way that pilots practice learning to fly—from copilot came coteaching. A review of team teaching and academic achievement described four organizational patterns in team teaching, each focusing on leadership and none considering that power relationships among team teachers would be equally distributed—that they could learn from one another irrespective of their experience as teachers and that they could also serve as teachers for one another (Armstrong, 1977). Similarly, our approach contrasts with team teaching, involving large teams of up to eight teachers in a high school that mainly involves coplanning. There are studies that show that coteaching was not essential or central to the success. Teaching at one another's elbows is central to our approach, which is similar to peer teaching, although this is not our preferred term because in our model those who coteach are not necessarily peers in terms of their teaching or other professional experience.

Coteaching is premised on the idea that by working with one or more colleagues in all phases of teaching (planning, conducting lessons, debriefing, grading), teachers learn from others without having to stop and reflect on what they are doing at the moment and why they are doing what they are doing. This led us to coin what has become our central motto: *coteaching is colearning in praxis*. As coteaching partners enact teaching, what each does serves as a resource for others to learn to teach—by virtue of what is done, as it is done. During the process of learning to teach in this way, some of what is learned is or can be made explicit; but in most cases learning occurs unconsciously. This learning environment has a further and crucial advantage in that the resources available in the classroom for students to learn are increased because teachers' actions synergistically build on each other. That is, when coteaching occurs, students experience more teaching and have increased opportunities to appropriate the enacted teaching practices and increase their learning. Hence, coteaching is a form of praxis that can be used in programs leading to initial certification and then in the first few years of teaching; coteaching can also be used for professional development and perhaps to overcome the lack of mentoring so many beginning teachers experience, especially in urban schools. By coteaching with others, teachers transcend the experience of isolation. Throughout this book we explore different ways in which coteaching can be enacted in programs for initial certification and in professional development programs—especially, but not limited to, those undertaken within a school.

Although we began to experiment with coteaching in different countries and in different years, we independently found out that two teachers planning, teaching, and debriefing all lessons together allowed them to learn about science teaching, both in explicit and in tacit ways. Upon learning about our common interests and research, we began to collaborate in conducting research on learning to teach by coteaching in the context of an urban science teacher preparation program in the northeastern USA. In the following two sections we reflect on the beginnings of our work on coteaching—research on professional development in Canada, initiated by Michael.

Getting Started

Michael: Coteaching began for me when, between 1989 and 1992, I developed a professional development program while teaching and being a department head of science at a private high school. Until that moment, the practice at the school was that the department head would visit a teacher two or three times a year and then write a report about the teaching. I thought that this arrangement put too much power into the hands of the department head, emphasized evaluation too much, and too little valued continuous development. I then designed a four-step program to address these shortcomings. One of the four steps consisted of teaching with another, explicitly designed to learn to teach while doing the real thing, as distinct from another component, which consisted of peer observation and evaluation. But for each teacher, there were only four to six days per year when he taught with another.

After my move to the university, I began research in elementary schools. I was interested in finding out how students learn in curricula designed according to social constructivist principles. But whereas the teachers were willing to participate in the project, they hesitated because they did not feel confident enough in teaching science and in teaching through open inquiry. Recognizing that these elementary teachers knew the children, school culture, and had tremendous experience establishing a culture of learning in their classrooms, I proposed to teach together with them. In this way, so I explained, their competencies and experience could be brought to the teaching, whereas I brought my own experience and subject matter competence in science. The explicit purpose was to teach with another person so that the expertise of both teachers would come to bear on the enacted curriculum. Thus, we not only planned together but also taught together; we agreed before that sitting in the back of or leaving the classroom was not a viable option for participant teachers.

In my first study, however, and although I had taught with the regular classroom teacher (Christina) for some time, I stepped back to let one of my graduate students (Bridget) teach, because she was also a professional curriculum developer who had developed and taught the engineering curriculum we wanted to employ. As we began to watch the videotapes of the lessons, we noted in particular how Christina, who initially only asked right–wrong and yes–no questions, began to ask the productive questions that characterized Bridget's teaching. We also noted how in many ways Bridget began to interact with the children like Christina. Thus, the learning was mutual. For me the most interesting aspect was that the learning occurred without either Bridget's or Christina's awareness of it. That is, it was not through reflection on practice that these teachers learned but by participating in real, once-occurrent praxis. It became evident to me that teaching with someone else not only enhances the opportunities for children to learn but also provides teachers with opportunities to learn to teach.

When I began to write about it in 1994, I was seeking a theoretical framework. I came across *A Theory of Practice* (Bourdieu, 1990), and began to think about knowing and learning not in terms of knowledge in the head but in terms of participation in the real, concrete praxis of science education. From this perspective, learning was observable as changing participation: We did not have to get into the head of the teachers but were concerned only with teaching as it was made available by and to the coteachers; and in this way, relevant aspects of teaching were made available to researchers, too. I was then seeking a name for what we were doing. Team-teaching was a possibility that I discarded, because I knew what others were doing when they team-taught: much like in team sports, where individuals take different positions according to their abilities—in soccer, e.g., there are goalies, defenders, midfielders, (center) forwards, each requiring their own forms of knowledgeability, skill, schemas—teachers were splitting the work so that each teacher was doing only what fell into her area of strength, often not even teaching with the other at the same time.

At about the same time, I happened to travel somewhere by plane. While talking about our professions, another passenger, a pilot, told me about his training and learning. He talked about his experience as a copilot, which made me think of other situations where two people took on joint responsibility, such as co-PI of a research program or co-chair of a committee. It was then that the name coteaching was born for me. (I now checked the publications in the Web of Science: prior to that moment, there is only one study from the medical field that is associated with the search term coteaching.)

The Urban Context

Ken: Coteaching arose in urban schools as a response to a critical problem. The challenges of teaching in urban classrooms in the United States were so great that regular classroom teachers were reluctant to surrender their classes to new teachers assigned for field experiences in their classes. At the university involved in pioneering coteaching in the USA, science teacher certification was earned in a graduate degree in which science graduates participated in a full time program of study that included a one-year field experience. Classes were taken at the university in the evening and students taught in neighborhood high schools in the day. The intention was that new teachers would gradually assume responsibility for teaching to the point that a few weeks into the semester they would be teaching for a half a day each day and then in the second semester they would teach full time. A problem arose when most of the new teachers in one school had not been given a chance to teach even one class by the end of the first semester. The resident teachers were reluctant to give up their classes because they felt the new teachers would be unable to maintain control and effective learning environments.

The school principal recognized this problem and offered the suggestion that we create special classes for two new teachers, obtain emergency certification for them since they already had undergraduate degrees, and let them teach as a pair, without having a resident teacher act as a mentor. The principal was confident that this would be a better deal for the students and would afford the new teachers opportunities to learn to teach. Although we were reluctant to do this, we agreed as long as we studied what happened and were willing to make changes if events turned sour.

The coteaching experiment was a resounding success. The coteachers earned the respect of students and enacted an inquiry-oriented biology program that captured the attention of science teachers throughout the school and even brought parents into the school to see their students' work. We were surprised by the success of the coteaching activity and expanded the incidence of coteaching, taking the time to figure out theoretically what was happening (this process is described in *At the Elbows of Another* [Roth & Tobin, 2002]). With a solid theoretical frame we would be able to tweak the system to afford greater opportunities to learn to teach. Over the years coteaching and the associated cogenerative dialogues evolved to be complementary activities with great potential for transforming pedagogy and practice in schools.

Because of the success in placing two new teachers together to coteach during their field experience we continued this practice in the following year. All new teachers were assigned in pairs to undertake a field experience with a resident teacher in an urban high school. We left it to the three teachers to decide how the teaching assignments were arranged, with an expectation that coteaching would occur in conjunction with some opportunities to teach solo. When it was not possible to assign two new teachers to a resident teacher we opted for the more traditional assignment practice of one new teacher to one resident teacher, modified with an expectation that the two would coteach for a significant proportion of their time together. The enactment of coteaching showed considerable diversity. There were examples of four, three, and two coteachers teaching together, sometimes including and at other times not including the resident teacher. These numbers swelled considerably when university supervisors and school administrators visited the classroom. Rather than observing from the side or back of the classroom, perhaps taking notes on the teachers' strengths and weaknesses, we encouraged all participants to coteach, usually enacting peripheral roles. Accordingly, we frequently had configurations in which four or five coteachers cotaught a class.

The biggest problems we experienced in the initial years of enacting coteaching stemmed from a lack of experience of what to expect. Personal differences among coteachers were encountered frequently and we had a tendency to let coteachers work out the kinks as they unfolded. However, differences in personality sometimes led to failures of coteachers interacting successfully and the production of forms of negative emotions such as frustration, disappointment, resentment, and anger. In one instance a clash involved a new teacher assigned to coteach with a peer seeking certification in physics and mathematics. One of the new teachers complained: "I was married to a guy like this for several years and we got a divorce. This is just not going to work out." We made a switch almost immediately based on an assumption that the male should move to another class even though this resulted in three new teachers coteaching with a resident teacher. This arrangement allowed for many possibilities, including four coteachers teaching together at the elbows of one another. An irony is that the new teacher who had requested the switch then proceeded to have a conflict-ridden coteaching experience with her resident teacher, who eventually filed a complaint against her. The essence of this problem was a failure of the new teacher to respect the resident teacher and her refusal to acknowledge that she could learn from her. In such circumstances (with hindsight) it may have been preferable not to proceed with the coteaching assignment.

In another instance, four new teachers, three female and one male, were assigned to a resident teacher to teach science to a grade nine class. The three females shared similar perspectives on the role of planning in teaching and on the need to specify roles for each of the coteachers ahead of time. In contrast, the male was more laid back about the need to plan in advance and wanted more flexibility to enact roles that were responsive to the unfolding dynamic structures of urban classrooms. He did not see a need for lengthy planning sessions and did not regard it as a priority to participate in them. In contrast, the female coteachers wanted to be well prepared and participated in extensive planning activities. When the male teacher did not enact their plans, the coteachers regarded him as unprepared and unprofessional. Before long the female coteachers requested that the male be removed from the coteaching group and he was reassigned to coteach with another resident teacher. The reassignment worked well in the sense that all coteachers then worked effectively together, to the benefit of improved learning environments for more students.

Other problems appeared to arise in the enactment of coteaching, leading to unsuccessful interactions and the production of negative emotional energy. Typical of these problems is a scenario in which a teacher poses a question with the idea that the students would benefit from thinking about the question for some time before a conversation about the answer. If the coteacher steps in and provides the answer there is a possibility that the other teacher will feel disappointed and even resentful. Similarly if a student asks a question and a coteacher chooses not to answer to allow others in the class to think about an answer, there can be a build up of negative emotional energy that might eventually manifest in anger. Rather than reassignment of coteachers it is possible that problems such as these, which occur as coteaching is enacted, are best resolved in cogenerative dialogues.

* * *

Michael: Immediately prior to the participation in the work at City High School in Philadelphia, I had cotaught with one new teacher, Nadely Boyd. During her internship at a local middle school, we cotaught a four-month unit on water and the environment. The most salient aspect, again, was asking productive questions. As in other situations, Nadely was asking yes–no questions. While coteaching, I was ready to take over a whole-class session when I felt that the students could be asked to think through some of the issues themselves. I then signaled that I wanted to move in; when Nadely acceded to my request, I asked questions that encouraged individual students to respond at length, and also allowed many students to answer.

Ken: That is a good example of coteaching expanding the structures to support student agency and learning. Did you have evidence that Nadely benefited from the experience too?

Michael: In our debriefing sessions, Nadely often said that while stepping back, she was thinking that I must have so many good questions at the tip of my tongue, whereas she could not think of any good questions to ask. But as we worked together, while stepping back in whole-class sessions to let me engage students through productive questions, or by trailing me for a little while when students were pursuing small-group tasks, her questioning became more like mine.

Ken: When I first began to teach in urban high schools, as a professor wanting to experience urban science teaching at first hand, I was quite unsuccessful. I struggled to succeed for several months and then when I returned from some national meetings the regular class teacher had resumed teaching the class and rather than have him relinquish control, as he had done previously, we began to coteach. Although I was not aware of the changes in my teaching, video analysis reveals that the changes were dramatic and immediate. My coteacher's presence provided me with structures that allowed for different forms of teaching to be enacted and a higher degree of fluency. Essentially I was unaware of the improvements until I did the research at a much later time.

Michael: I am sure that there are many things I learned while coteaching. I cannot put many of the things into words, for example, the ways of being in the classroom with elementary students. Until the early 1990s, most of my experience was in middle and high schools. Being in the elementary classroom with another teacher allowed me to act in ways appropriate for this age group. The most important aspect for me was that I came to deal with my own presuppositions about teaching. I repeatedly found myself in situations where, while stepping back from teaching, I thought by myself, "Why did she [my coteacher] do such and such? This is stupid?" But almost simultaneously, another question emerged in my mind, "What is it in my experiences that makes me look at these actions of the other teacher as 'stupid'."

Ken: I suppose you have those thoughts when the collective teaching breaks down—does not work as you anticipated and the breach in flow creates a moment to reflect on what did not work. In this case the problem is something the other teacher did that either was inappropriate, not timely, or perhaps unanticipated by you or the students. In your case, the breach gave you a chance to step back, out of action, and reflect on action.

Michael: It was the difference between what I would have had the tendency to do and what the other did at that moment—that is, there were different schemas brought to the situation, which expressed themselves in the differences between the action I observed and the one I expected. But I learned from these situations: As I was experiencing the teacher, I found myself confronted with my own judgments. While analyzing these judgments, I came to understand my presuppositions, my pre-understandings on which my own teaching was based. In experiencing another, my own understanding became the object of reflection, and in this, changed itself.

Ken: The focus in my auto/ethnographies of coteaching have been on my own (re)learning to teach. It is clear that I learned to enact teaching with more bodily movement, greater verve, and a higher degree of oral fluency through greater intonation of my voice, changes in the amplitude of speaking, and speeding up of delivery. These characteristics were central to success with African American youth in West Philadelphia and I no doubt learned them from coteaching with Alex, an experienced Black science teacher. I have not explored what others may have learned by coteaching with me, as you have done in your research.

Michael: Among the many possible things that others may have learned from coteaching with me are: subject matter and questioning were the two aspects of my teaching that often became the focus of our joint inquiry. In coplanning, I often explicated the subject matter underlying the topic we were to teach together, and the associated pedagogies. For example, in a unit on simple machines, I explicated to the different teachers the physics underlying simple machines. We then moved to considering pedagogies that would allow students to participate in framing the object of activity, and in framing what they needed to know in the process. Others learned from me how to use particular questioning techniques during whole-class interactions, which allowed students to explore certain issues at length, and use similar techniques during the work with small groups.

Ken: Did you see evidence of learning in the students you and your coteachers were teaching?

Michael: As part of our research, we were able to document learning using very different evaluation techniques, which included written test, individual interviews, discussions students had in pairs, and hands-on tasks. But perhaps the most important evidence of a more widespread effect of coteaching was when we realized that not only the coteachers learned to ask productive questions, but also students picked up on productive questions. During discussions, they asked each other for additional evidence, elaborations, and justifications. That is, the questions students asked of their peers came to resemble the ways in which I questioned from the beginning, a way that was then appropriated by the coteacher, and eventually adopted in the class more widely. We also observed this effect in other coteaching configurations, for example, in the class that Christina and Bridget taught together. The effect was so evident that they took notice of it even before I became aware of the changing ways in which Christina's fourth and fifth graders asked each other questions.

Ken: Even though we started to use coteaching as a response to problems, the benefits were soon very evident and we expanded our uses in initial certification programs. The mode was to assign new teachers in pairs to resident teachers. What was interesting to me was that any time a pairing was not possible and we assigned one new teacher to a resident teacher the student protested that this practice was unfair. They valued the presence of a coteaching peer as much as having a resident teacher. Our research, undertaken over a period of about six years, strongly supports the use of coteaching in initial teacher certification programs.

Michael: My sense is that the model has tremendous possibilities for learning to teach. Teaching is a practice where you interact with others in real time. In this aspect, it is unlike writing, for example, where you have all the time to deliberate what you want to say and how to say it. Thus, the rationalist model of knowing does not fit well, for there is no time in teaching to think about what to do. It is therefore better to think of teaching in terms of knowledge-ability, knowing in praxis. To be a good teacher means that you act appropriately without thinking about what to do next, that you enact principles although you have no time to think about an explicit formulation of them. I am thinking of the teacher in the way the French philosopher Paul Ricœur (1992) thinks of the person of wise judgment who determines at the same time the general rule and the particular case by grasping a situation in its singularity.

Acting appropriately cannot be learned by watching someone else teaching, like watching professional team sports does not make you a better athlete. Being with another teacher, experiencing *this* action of the other in *this* situation provides an opportunity to learn to act appropriately without necessarily knowing what makes the action more appropriate than any other. This is so because participation leads to, as Mikhail Bakhtin (1993) suggests, the same or similar emotional-volitional and ethico-moral toning of actions, including perceptions. This does not mean that new teachers cannot reflect on their actions—especially when there is time and an appropriate forum.

Ken: Yes. As we have seen, teachers become like the other by being in and coparticipating in a field with the other—for better or for worse. For that reason it makes sense to participate in cogenerative dialogues to explore the extent to which teaching produces desirable structures to benefit all.

Michael: As we explore in subsequent chapters, coteaching is useful in professional development, too. There are two experiences that really highlighted for me the suitability of coteaching for professional development. In the latter part of the 1980s, I obtained a State of Indiana grant to conduct professional development of science teachers during a two-week summer workshop. The workshop for about twenty teachers cost the equivalent of more than two yearly salaries of a mid-career science teacher. At the end, although the teachers were pleased having attended the workshop, I felt that very little had changed in their teaching. A few years later, after coteaching for two months, Christina said that in this period she learned more than she would have in three or more university courses. I began to think that if I had bought out two science teachers for one year, I could have achieved some real change in one or two Indiana schools. Each teacher would have cotaught with three different teachers for a period of about three months, then shifted to teach with three other teachers for three months, and then have another iteration of the model. That is, at the end of nine months, each resident teacher would have cotaught with nine teachers, so that at the end of the year, twenty teachers would have had a tremendous and ongoing professional development.

Ken: As we show in chapter 6, coteaching is a wonderful approach to professional development programs that involve different stakeholders in summer programs, for example. In this instance, university scientists cotaught with high school science teachers, new teachers, and undergraduate cadets to assist underachieving urban youth to succeed on a high stakes science test. There is more than a hint that coteaching was useful not only in expanding the learning opportunities for the youth but also for all teachers to learn to teach urban youth more effectively.

MUTUALITY OF ROLES IN COTEACHING

Coteachers cannot act as if they were alone. The presence of another teacher mediates their roles. Thus, coteaching participants adopt complementary roles and the coordination of the step forward, step back routine is important. From one lesson to the next it is often the case that one teacher assumes more time in a central role in whole-class activities than her coteachers. However, in small-group and individualized activities the roles are symmetrical and in many cases what one teacher does bears a strong family resemblance to what the coteachers are doing. The key to success is to focus on the learning of students and the complementarity of roles adopted in support of that goal. The following fieldnote provides an example of coteaching; it shows how roles may be enacted in a whole-class teaching and learning situation.

> Lisa and Jeannie are biology graduates, both in their first semester of teaching. Lisa is certified and Jeannie is seeking certification to teach biology. They coteach biology in a double sized room in which a partition between two separate classrooms is pushed back. In this coteaching classroom, the students sit at fixed lab stations to which stools are attached. Hence it is virtually impossible for them to see the chalkboard from any of the available seating in the room. Accordingly, Lisa has found a small portable chalkboard and placed it centrally to allow students to see illustrative diagrams and notes. To compensate for a lack of chalkboard space the coteachers produce daily handouts that contain summaries of the key points to be learned, questions for students to answer, and homework to be completed.
>
> In a lesson on the sequencing of amino acids to form proteins Lisa assumes a central role in reviewing key concepts, writing the main ideas on a centrally located chalkboard, and walking students through the daily handout. Lisa moves among the students and with shrill voice and animated gestures, she asks questions that require students to locate information in the summary handout and call out the answers in a chorus. The lesson segment is lively, noisy, and most students are continuously involved. Jeannie moves around the classroom, assisting to refocus inattentive students and, as necessary, clarifying any of Lisa's explanations and questions before confusion arises. Occasionally Jeannie steps forward to emphasize and elaborate content she regards as important. Jeannie's roles complement Lisa's and together they provide students access to teaching that is coordinated and mutually enhancing.
>
> After the review is completed Lisa hands the lesson over to Jeannie who explains the students' roles in a simulation of protein synthesis. As Jeannie quietly explains the goals and roles of participants Lisa writes the key ideas and procedures on the chalkboard. These inscriptions then become resources for students to access in support of their learning and for Jeannie to refer to as she continues to teach. Just as Jeannie did in the previous part of the lesson, Lisa gives explanations and asks questions of the whole class as it becomes necessary. There are no examples of one teacher interrupting the flow of teaching and learning, although at times Lisa steps forward to participate and quickly steps back if Jeannie continues to teach. The request for a turn at teaching is signaled from one coteacher to the

other verbally or non verbally, often through hand gestures, facial expressions, head nods, and eye contact.

During the simulation the students are to obtain genetic information from cards dispersed around the classroom. Although some students show urgency in obtaining the information and making sense of it, many use the time to socialize and take a break. The two coteachers and Ken move around the classroom, providing assistance and encouraging students to stay actively involved. Since as a trained physics teacher Ken is far out of field, he acknowledges that he does not have a strong grasp of the science and advises students to get assistance from either of the coteachers or from peers such as Abdul. His roles as a researcher are similar to those that might be undertaken by university supervisors, resident teachers, and school administrators. More can be learned about teaching these students in this class at this time by coteaching with the purpose of facilitating their learning. He regards his roles in this lesson as legitimate, peripheral, and aligned with the motive of maximizing the learning of all students. It is not in Ken's, the students', or the coteachers' interests that he masquerades as an expert on protein synthesis or biology. However, Ken does have important roles in being helpful to students and encouraging their active participation.

When the data collecting part of the activity concludes, Lisa directs students to return to their small groups, interpret the data, and answer the questions on a worksheet. The coteachers usher the students to their groups and then move from group to group to provide substantive assistance as necessary. A feature of the interactions between the coteachers and the students is that the coteachers stay with students who request help for as long as it takes to provide substantive assistance.

KEY FEATURES OF COTEACHING

Our extended research suggests that new teachers should not remain on the side observing others teach and taking notes for too long. As soon as feasible, a new teacher can begin to coteach as a peripheral participant, stepping forward to interact with students and the resident teacher with the purpose of increasing the learning opportunities for students without disrupting the flow of teaching or the plans of a resident teacher.

Although it is highly desirable for coteachers to plan together this may not happen in many cases because of time constraints. Often one teacher plans the lesson, is central, and the coteacher knows what is to be done in broad terms but not in fine detail. Examples of this arrangement occur initially when a new teacher is assigned to participate in a field experience of coteaching with a resident teacher. Initially the resident teacher might do most planning while the new teacher assumes legitimate peripheral teaching roles. Later the new teacher can do most of the planning and the resident teacher can enact peripheral teaching roles. As the coteachers become tuned to one another's teaching both can assume central roles, a critical agreement being that they have a shared responsibility to enhance the students' learning. The concept *legitimate peripheral participation* (Lave & Wenger, 1991) assists us in conceptualizing the attendant division of labor.

Legitimate peripheral participation was coined as a dialectical concept such that participation always is legitimate peripheral. Legitimacy is thought along a scale from less to more legitimate; and peripherality is thought in terms of a margin|center dialectic according to which each moment of participation is both marginal and central (Roth, Hwang, Lee, & Goulart, 2005). This dialectic allows us to consider each moment of praxis as simultaneously marginal and central to the ongoing event—not just as a reflection of the different perspectives that exist in a classroom but inherently, as an expression of the contradictory nature of participation as such. Thus, in having stepped back to provide another teacher with an opportunity to enact the lead role, a coteacher is both marginal—not in the lead—and central—actively shaping the present condition in the way it is, for example, by not vying for a turn at talk.

The roles available as a legitimate peripheral participant depend on the structure of a lesson, such as whether the central teacher is enacting whole-class episodes in which she is lecturing with the aid of material resources such as a chalkboard and a periodic table. In such cases the coteachers would monitor all participants' practices for signs of wanting to get involved in the lesson. In addition, the supporting coteacher would closely monitor the verbal interaction, including gestures and any signs of uncertainty or inattentiveness from the students. When coteachers sense that one of them wants to step forward to teach the whole class, the central teacher can complete what she is doing and then step back and transfer whole-class teaching to the coteacher. The step back, step forward, step back cycle can be repeated many times and some of the teaching turns can be brief and others long. A common example of this is when a coteacher provides an alternative explanation or clarifies a point that might be a potential source of confusion. As coteachers grow accustomed to one another's ways of teaching the interactions that occur when one steps forward and the other steps back can be anticipated and become smoother and less conscious.

A role that usually does not need to be negotiated is for the peripheral teacher to assist students as needs emerge. As questions arise for a student they can be resolved non-obtrusively by a coteacher while the central teacher continues to teach, not disrupted by the quiet interaction between a needy student and a coteacher. In such cases a coteacher moves close to a student who has requested assistance and, either by sitting next to that student or by crouching down close to her, the coteacher is able to interact quietly and thereby become a resource for that student's learning. This teacher's participation is both marginal—with respect to the learning of some students—and central—with respect to the learning of others.

The coteaching arrangements that have worked best in teacher certification programs have involved one to three new teachers being assigned to a resident teacher. As long as all coteachers are committed to coplanning the benefits from coteaching are maximized. The common problems we have dealt with include clashes about values and commitments to teaching, differences in the role of the teacher in mediating the learning of students, and the failure of one or more of the coteachers to fully participate in coplanning. The roles of all participants can be negotiated and agreed to from the outset of a decision to participate in coteaching, with the understanding that agreements reached about roles will be revisited regularly in a context of the lived experiences and the goal of maximizing the learning of students. When agreements are reached on roles and motives, there is a need for all participants to understand that plans and commitments are only part of the structure of a classroom field. As a lesson unfolds it is important for all participants to be flexible and appropriate and produce structures in ways that afford not only their own learning, but also the goals of the whole class. This necessitates real-time fine-tuning of roles as the dynamics of a classroom unfold. Even though a coteacher's roles might not be as originally planned, the criteria for judging success are whether or not learning opportunities are maximized for all. Deviations from a plan can be regarded as contradictions, and as such, they can be discussed in cogenerative dialogues so that in the future such contradictions can be anticipated in planning and become part of the agreed-to approach.

THE ROLE OF THEORY IN MODEL BUILDING

Ken: As praxis, coteaching is enacted in a field and as such structures the field and is structured by it. The main issue for me is how can praxis be improved in as much as it affords higher learning for students and more opportunities for coteachers to learn to teach effectively by coteaching?

Michael: In the past, the predominant approach to the improvement of praxis was to have researchers come in, generate some knowledge or theory, then develop workshops to tell teachers about findings, and then ask teachers to apply what they have heard about in their own classrooms. Teaching and learning to teach were practiced as two different forms of activity. The approach presupposes general and generalizable knowledge to be valid for all teachers under all circumstances—as if they were computers or robots doing whatever the program specifies them to do and drawing on whatever facts are stored in memory. Coteaching is based on a different epistemology, one that privileges concrete human praxis as the site where knowing and learning are exhibited to be learned, studied, and learned from.

Ken: Prior to beginning coteaching I was searching for ways to make sense of the connections between teacher learning and teaching. As a person who had been involved in research on teaching since 1973, this issue had been a high priority as my research program moved from Piagetian theory to radical behaviorism, to neo-Piagetian theory, to radical constructivism, to social constructivism, and ultimately to a plethora of sociocultural theories.

Michael: I have had similar experiences, moving through a similar set of theories in search of a way of understanding what I was doing that is more consistent with the actual experience of teaching and learning to teach. It was this tension between the two forms of activity—teaching and theorizing teaching—

29

that continuously pushed me to seek for better ways of explaining and, in the process, understanding teaching.

Ken: Pierre Bourdieu's ideas about habitus were prominent in my research through the 1990s, however, they were never more salient than in my auto/ethnography of (re)learning to teach science in urban high schools. As I struggled to be successful you pointed out to me that my habitus was in breakdown and I was enacting praxis in ways that were not fluent—inappropriate, not anticipatory and too late. Your suggestion was not welcomed at a personal level, but the insights from interpreting my experiences as a breakdown of habitus were central to learning from my research.

Michael: Today I think that my understanding of habitus was rather un- and underdeveloped. But it did give me a starting point in what later became an understanding of dialectical approaches to knowing and learning, that is, to a variety of approaches also salient in cultural sociology.

Ken: As my research group has learned about cultural sociology and the sociology of emotions we have had to examine the parsimony of the theoretical constructs. The continual review of constructs and their meanings within our own research has resulted in us not using ideas that initially were regarded as powerful. These include some very powerful ideas such as *praxeology*, *Spielraum*, *strategies of action*, and *institutional node*. The constructs are still part of the platform, it is just that we have kept the terms to a minimum—the result being that we have a framework that is coherent, parsimonious, and— while being grounded in the work of others—is distinctive in the ways we use the constituent frameworks in our research.

Michael: One difficult aspect of changing the ways in which we talk about our research objects in theoretical terms is that we need to rupture with our previous ways of talking all the while making sure that any new conceptual notions do not make reading our work too difficult. Thus, taken out of context, the term *praxeology* may sound arcane to some—when it is just a way of denoting theory as talk. In ancient Greek, talk was called *logos*; in our situation, the talk was about *praxis*. *Praxeology* then is a construction that parallels the denotations constructed for other sciences, including biology, physiology, or sociology. The advantage of the term praxeology is that it directs our attention to praxis and its central role in knowing and understanding that cannot be captured in any form of theoretical reduction.

Ken: Theoretical frameworks illuminate issues as salient while obscuring others. The importance of this is to use the theory predictably to consider ways to improve desired forms of production and eliminate contradictions—while realizing that the introduction of changes will produce additional contradictions. The obscuring function of theoretical frameworks argues for an active realization that social theories are not master narratives and to search for other viable frameworks that may illuminate social life in different and yet equally important ways.

Michael: Your point about the role of theory is well taken. The notion of praxeology orients us to think of theory not as a master narrative but as a locally relevant explanation that takes full account of the contextual specifics. It is a way of theorizing each instance as a concrete realization of the general. Each action is both *singular*, concretely enacted by this person in this situation, and *plural*, a possibility for acting in this culture generally. In this way, we are not merely concerned with praxis in all its singularity but rather with the dialectic of praxis—concrete, once-occurrent action—and ethos—actions as cultural possibility. In this way, we keep variance within theory rather than discarding it as an unwanted aspect from which we cannot learn anything. Through this work on coteaching I have come to realize that what matters in concrete praxis is attention to precisely the variance that many forms of theory consider to be noise or unexplained variance. One of these forms of variation arise from the emotional state and valences that orient and determine human beings at every moment of their life.

Ken: Emotions are central to Randall Collins' theory of interaction ritual chains. His theory draws attention to the importance of interaction rituals and the emotional buildups associated with success and failure. The framework also addresses *solidarity*, which links to our research on the individual and collective dialectic and identity formation in relation to agency|structure relationships in particular fields.

Michael: This co or mutual determination of agency and structure has proven to be a fruitful way of thinking about what people do and how they do it. Because of its reflexive nature—it is to be applied not only to the research object but also to the theory itself—this dialectical theory inherently lends itself to development.

Ken: So, in closing this conversation, let us return to the critical review of our initial empirical and theoretical work on coteaching. I feel strongly that the excerpt from the review that we cite at the beginning of the introduction fails to see the dialectical link between schema and practice. Our studies of coteaching produce understandings that allow us to adapt the ways in which we plan to enact coteaching and at the same time to change the theoretical lenses used to make sense of our experiences with coteaching. The identification and efforts to remove contradictions fuel cycles of production that transform practices and schema—and hence, what we learn involves new models and new ways of looking at and making sense of them.

Michael: I think of the reviewers' comments as an attempt to reproduce older forms of the culture of science education and therefore as a reproduction of the status quo. The reviewers evidently were unprepared to appreciate the theoretical and practical possibilities that our approach offered.

Ken: The reviewers' critique can be interpreted as their resistance to our ways of producing culture. If we step back, as you suggest we do when we encounter resistance (as a personal experience), the phenomenon of the critical review is replete with contradictions that we met by disseminating our work continuously in myriad ways; making efforts to more clearly reach out to stakeholders in the hope that practices in the international community will be mediated by our scholarship.

Michael: To this day, I am not sure whether the reviewers' comments cited at the beginning of the introduction with were truly made on intellectual grounds, which would testify to the lack of understanding on their part, or whether they were motivated by personal differences they had with you and me. In any case, the success of our work since then—a glimpse of which can be taken from the history of our publications (see appendix)—has shown that we were onto something.

COTEACHING AS LIVED EXPERIENCE

It is difficult to imagine what coteaching is like without having been in a coteaching situation. It is difficult to imagine, because coteaching, like all teaching, is something one lives; and this lived experience is difficult to communicate by means of text. Whenever we talk *about* what we have experienced, we already enact an interpretive reduction in which this or that aspect of the fullness that we have lived is accounted for in what we say (Figure 2.1). We mean, any text, even the most elaborate *thick* description, even the most interpretive text—and precisely those—constitute a reduction of praxis, a reduction from the once-occurrent, history making because irretractable events we live. This first interpretive reduction, in which our testimony is reduced to an account, is prelogic and preconscious. Such observations captured in one or the other account further can be reduced by explicitly applying concepts and theory; because we actively *choose* the concepts, this *logical* reduction, which leads us to structural accounts and statistics, therefore is conscious (Figure 2.1).

When an author talks about some events after the fact, from a retrospective; it is no longer the experience as it is at the moment we are there, caught up in the unfolding events, without a way out. Any decisions have to be made on the spot; and whatever we do, we cannot take back. But our actions change the world so that what we do becomes resource and constraint to the Other, that is, the other in general. This once-occurrent nature of everyday praxis has a particular emotional-volitional and ethico-moral character that constitutes the radical difference incompatibility between "the world of culture and the world of life, the only world in which we create, cognize, contemplate, live our lives and die" (Bakhtin, 1993, p. 2). This world in which we live—as contrasted with the world we reflect and talk about—is the "world in which the acts of our activity are objectified and the world in which these acts actually proceed and are actually accomplished once and only

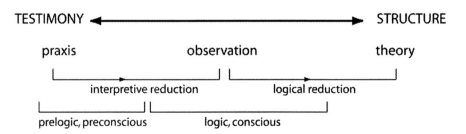

Figure 2.1. Relationship between praxis, in which events are once-occurrent, observation, which may involve accounts of praxis in everyday language, and theory.

once" (p. 2). We recognize that anything we can do here to communicate what it means to coteach already constitutes a reduction and therefore cannot capture the richness of the events that we have experienced while coteaching. Nevertheless, we attempt in the next two chapters to give readers a better sense of what coteaching feels like when one is living it than one might get from reading many research articles.

Many teachers have noted the gap that exists between their daily experience in and of the classroom, on the one hand, and the kinds of things that are being said and done at the university. This gap, as can be seen from Figure 2.1, is produced by the (single, double) reduction that stands between the lived event and its characteristic participative thinking, on the one hand, and the interpretive or logical account, on the other hand. This makes apparent the disconnection between knowledgeability of teaching, which we experience, and the factual statements and theories generally propounded in academe. In addition to being a fundamental gap, the experience of a gap is further mediated by the lack of grounding of academic language in the experiences of the teachers that the academic language was created to describe and communicate. But this statement does not articulate the problem precisely enough, because we have not yet distinguished between the language of the classroom, the language teachers use to talk about their experiences in the classroom, and the language professors and other scholars use when they talk and write about classroom teaching and what teachers say about what they do when they teach. In fact, we can think of a continuum of interpretive discourses about the praxis of teaching that reaches from thick descriptions in auto/biographical accounts by participants (far left in the scale of interpretive reductions [Figure 2.1]) to the most abstract and perhaps esoteric statistical discourse about the correlation between, for example, teacher subject matter knowledge and knowledge of the nature of science or beliefs (far right in the logical reduction [Figure 2.1]). For the present purposes, let us briefly take a look at three types of language from this spectrum and how they relate to each other.

Language can be thought of as a tool that allows us to get our work done; we can also think of it as a resource or artifact that we draw on in our actions as teachers just as we draw on other resources, including textbooks, chalkboards, curriculum statements, labs, lab materials, and schedules. We consider the following activities to be different: the praxis of teaching, talking about teaching as we are sitting around in the staffroom, and, for professors or teacher-researchers, writing about teaching and talk about teaching. Each activity has its own core objects of interest, so that the language we use differs, more or less perfectly adapted to do what we intend to do. Each activity is located along the continuum between testimony and structure (Figure 2.1). In the science classroom, the language we use as part of praxis may be suitable to teaching a biology lesson, so that the language is adapted to teaching biology. Language here serves as a primary artifact, it allows us to do the work of teaching—it is the language *of* teaching.

Now, when we get together with other science teachers in staff- or lunchrooms, we talk *about* our teaching. In this, we are already making an interpretive reduction by *accounting for* our experiences and the events we have witnessed. We may talk about our intents, about specific students and events, and about teaching strategies. The language now is *about* some other situation in which we used a different language: the language of teaching biology is different from the language used in talking about the teaching of biology. So we may refer to this new language as a secondary tool or artifact (Wartofsky, 1979). It is true that at some level, it is a primary artifact, too, namely when we think about the work of talking about teaching strategies or talking about students.

As soon as we step back from the lunchroom situation and think about the conversation we had with other teachers or researchers, trying to find patterns in this talk, we are at a new level. At this level, we now talk *about* the lunchroom talk. Language about teaching is now a tertiary artifact, with which we do our theorizing. The fundamental question is whether and how the three types of language are related. This, to us, is an empirical question that cannot be presupposed. That is, what the relation is between theorizing teachers' lunchroom talk and the language and behavior of teaching biology has to be shown in and through research. We *must not* assume that the two types of language are inherently consistent, that is, characterized by strong coherence. Rather, weak coherence between the two situations—teaching biology and theorizing teacher lunchroom talk about teaching biology—should be taken as the norm. What then needs to be explained is the presence of strong coherence, including an explanation of those aspects of sociocultural reality that mediate such coherence.

Teachers' lunchroom language is *grounded* in their experience, which we recognize from the fact that other teachers understand what we are talking about. We recognize our own similar experiences, similar interactions with particular students, and so on. In this point, the lunchroom language differs from the language many academics and researchers write about school life. This language is no longer grounded in the lived experience of the people who spend their daily life in the classroom. In our work, we have attempted to bridge that gap between language *of* and *about* teaching, that is, the differences between first, secondary, and tertiary functions of language. One of the drawbacks of the lack of grounding of tertiary artifacts in the lived experience of teachers is that teachers no longer recognize themselves—if some article is about them—or the type of experience they have in the research accounts. So in coteaching, we have grounded our writing about what we are doing in the conversations with our fellow teachers who have witnessed the experience together with us from a similar position. That is, we have grounded our theoretical accounts in the language that we have used with teachers in schools to talk about what we were doing with them.

Another problem that crops up when we talk about teaching in the lunchroom or write about it in journals is that even if we use language as a secondary tool, we are already removed from the situation. We know the beginning and the end of the story, but not the details of what occurred in between—so that the temporal aspects of experiencing the teaching get flattened. Actions no longer have the character of once-occurrent events but, denoted as specific kinds of objects by means of categories, are cultural possibilities and therefore generic and general. Each action, from the perspective of *ethos*, is related not just to one but a multiplicity of actualiza-

35

tions, each of which is brought about in concrete *praxis* (Deleuze, 1968/1994). With this flattening, teaching appears to be much more rational and driven by intentions than it is when we teach, where what we do is better described as getting into and being in tune with the events as they unfold. In these events, we are not masters who direct the movement of each participant; rather, we coproduce enacted classrooms together with the students. In teaching, we are therefore subject to both agency and passivity, we contribute to making the enacted curriculum as much as being subject to the actions of others and therefore to the events globally. What happens surpasses our intentions. More so, even when we act, we are not totally in control of what we do, knowing what we have done only after the action has condensed (has been objectified) in the completed act. Most frequently, for example, we do not precisely know what words we use in the question that we just began to ask of students. The question frequently has not been formulated in the head to be spoken in a second moment so that others can hear it. In addition to our words, we orient our bodies, use gesture, modulate our voice—and all of this we do without being conscious of what we produce to make particular aspects of the situation stand out as resources and thereby mark their salience for others to attend to. The precise question we ask, therefore, is known even to us only once it has been completed.

It is similar with other aspects of interacting with students and peers. Because we respond in situated ways to what they are saying, we cannot stop to reflect about what they just have said, because doing such reflecting would take much more time than our conversational partners would be willing to give us. Rather, we talk the talk as we walk the walk, in real time, without time out. When the words do not come forth, we stutter, mutter, correct ourselves, and restart until the sentence or question is finally out. Our *sense* of language and grammar are resources for deciding whether what we have said so far is sufficiently complete or correct. Because we do not have time for much thinking, we cobble together our actions drawing on the resources we have, making the time to find a frame for talking—in so doing we make the lesson as our actions unfold over time. That is, even in our talking that constitutes the teaching, there are both intentional-volitional and passive elements. Furthermore, emotional coloring pervades these elements: how we feel shapes what we do and our intentions are colored by the long-term payoffs and by the considerations of ethical principles, such as equality of learning opportunities for male and female students, or equality of learning opportunities for students of all race, culture, socioeconomic status, and so on.

Now the difference between teachers lies in part in their professional experiences, which allows a more experienced person to anticipate possible future developments and to position herself such that negative events are less likely to happen. Furthermore, more experienced teachers have a greater *room to maneuver* (we also denote this concept by the term *Spielraum*), they have, without requiring deliberation, multiple options available for acting; new teachers do not have this room to maneuver and then have to stop and consciously think about what to do next, or simply abandon themselves to the lesson even if it does not go at all the way they had planned. That is, an experienced practitioner has a greater range of actions, more possibilities for doing what is right at the moment, than a new practitioner, who may have to stop and reflect on what to do next.

In coteaching, teachers learn to be attuned to the lesson as a whole, that is, to what other teachers are contributing and what the students do. Unless they want to create conflict, all coteachers submit to the lesson that is the outcome of the interaction of all participating teachers and students.

COTEACHING FROM THE INSIDE: MICHAEL

Let us take a look now at two episodes from a tenth-grade biology lesson at City High School, cotaught by four teachers. Chuck was the regular teacher of the class, who had accepted two new teachers as his companions so that they can learn to teach while teaching with him and with one another. On this particular day, Andrea, one of the two new teachers, and her peer decided to use the separating wall of the classroom to divide it and teach two separate lessons. In addition to Andrea and Chuck, there are the two of us. Ken was Andrea's university supervisor and conducted research on coteaching in the school; Ken was also the instructor of the science methods course in which Andrea had enrolled. Michael was a researcher visiting the school to participate in and research coteaching and cogenerative dialoguing. The episodes are written from Michael's perspective, which is also reflected in the video offprints, as he was standing right next to the camera during that part of the lesson.

Coteaching the Monohybrid Cross

"Tell me the difference between genotype and phenotype," I hear Andrea's voice project into this part of the tenth-grade classroom, which I share with half of the class, Ken, and Chuck. We have proceeded a few minutes into this part of the lesson, which Andrea has formulated as a review. "Uh," producing a sound while projecting her hand into the air, unmistakably articulating Natasia's intent to answer. But Andrea points to her right calling on Judy. "Phenotypes is a," the student begins, while looking for something in her notebook as a resource for producing the answer. "Say it in your own words," encourages Andrea. Judy responds
– Expression of genes.
– Phenotype is the expression of genes. Could you give me an example of a phenotype?
– Well like the eyes, one student begins.
– Like the color of your eyes, Andrea elaborates.
– Hair, another student calls out.
– The color of your hair, Andrea reformulates.
– And the geno- is the make up of the cell.
– The genetic make up, Andrea reformulates and then continues, I want you to tell me the percentages of the offspring for genotypes *and* for phenotypes.

A student utters something but with such a voice that it cannot be heard. "Say it," Chuck encourages her. "Recessive," the student repeats. Andrea takes a turn,

Figure 2.2. Chuck has entered the interactional floor articulating an easy way to remember the difference between genotype and phenotype. As he speaks, he "writes" the letters "p" and "g" into the air.

"Homozygous recessive th*at* me*a*ns . . .? that there are two recessive . . ." Before she finishes her sentence, a student calls out, "Blue eyes." And then Chuck picks up, "A good way of remembering the difference between genotype and phenotype– An easy way to remember it is, just think of the first letter. A *p*," he makes a gesture as if writing the letter *p* (Figure 2.2) as he continues, "for physical expression, or physical appearance. And *g* is for the *g*enes. So if you ever get confused, *g* is genotype and *p* physical expression, phenotype."

Until this moment, I am tuned into the unfolding lesson, trying to make sure I do not miss an opportunity to make a useful contribution. As I do not know how the lesson will unfold, just as anyone else does not know it, I simply trust my professional instincts that I can add at an appropriate moment. But here I am hanging on to an idea for a moment. The German word "Eselsbrücke" surges into my consciousness and comes with a sense of critique, which constitutes an emotional valence. Critique, disapproval, is a stance of lower valence than approval, which is *more desirable*. The German word literally means "bridge of an ass"; English speakers actually use a Latin expression, *pons asinorum*. As the lesson goes on, Chuck's advice appears to me as a pons asinorum, a way to assist students in the rote recognition of the difference between genotype and phenotype, and a sense of critique and disapproval rises within me. But there is no time to dwell on it, as the lesson continues to unfold and sweeps me away.

Andrea calls on Keisha to put a Punnett square on the overhead transparency. While the student does this, there is some chatter. Andrea walks over to Ken and exchanges some words, the student next to him flipping through her notebook. I do not and cannot know what is going on, and really, I am attuned to the classroom as a whole. Currently I am watching Keisha. As she gets done, Andrea again turns to Keisha asking about the percentages of the genotypes and phenotypes. "You did a wonderful job there with your Punnett Square. So what percent are going to have blue eyes, and what percent are going to have brown eyes?" Keisha responds, but I can't hear what she is saying. But Andrea nods, "Good. All right, sit down." I am following the unfolding lesson, having a sense that there must be other ways of dealing with, and especially reviewing this subject matter. "You know what another name for that is," Chuck's voice enters my consciousness disrupting me dwelling on curriculum alternatives. "When you really get into genetics? When you take a homozygous recessive and," he turns away from me and I don't understand. I only catch the end of his sentence, "test cross." "What's it?," Ken asks holding his hand behind the ears; he too did not hear Chuck. "Test cross," Andrea and Chuck respond in unison. "Test cross, you start determining the genotypes."

At this moment, I have a sense of being surpassed by the events. I have no clue what they are talking about—I am not a biology teacher. I feel I have to ask Chuck afterwards, for when I taught genetics some fifteen years earlier, there was no textbook entry on test crosses. But another idea is displacing anything else I am attending to at the moment. I have the sense that I ought to ask a puzzle about my family and have the students answer, doing something like the forensic anthropologist in the novels my wife loves to read. It is not that the idea is clear to me at the moment in the way it is clear when I write it down, name it. It was more an orientation, something fleeting. I also sense a bit of criticism, as Chuck's comment appears to be a throw away. But then I also sense that I need to sit down later and investigate my criticism; I sense it is more an expression of the presupposition I have about teaching than it is a reflection of what Chuck has been doing. I need to get a handle on this, and better understand my own ideology.

All of this passes in but a few seconds, not really taking up my thoughts, because I am focusing on getting in on the action. But this sense colors what I am doing, and I also sense that I want to contribute in a way that supports student learning and provides a good example that we can discuss later. As Chuck finishes, I attempt to get a turn at talk, "I," but the events seem to unfold without me, as Andrea is in the process of moving on, "All right." I see Ken looking toward Chuck, pointing at me (Figure 2.3). He says, "A question!" and Chuck, who turns in my direction, utters, "Uh, someone, have a question?" I respond, "Yea, I have," and, as I now have the turn at talk, try to orient myself in the space, "Uh."

It is my turn and I do not have the question as a whole in my mind, though I have a sense of what I want to do and a sense of anticipation that an interesting discussion might come about. That is, unlike the way in which researchers describe the relationship between knowing and, for example, questioning, what I am about to ask is not already formulated. I have not gone to my memory store to look up my scientific knowledge and then embody it into a question that I will ask of students. Rather, I have this sense of having to ask a question the nature of which I am aware of, but which is a question that I do not know yet precisely, as its exact shape is in the process of emerging. I begin to talk, laying the question in talking in the same manner that I would lay a garden path in walking there, where there is not yet known. "I wonder whether anyone can figure out a little bit about my family." Andrea invites me, "Okay."

Figure 2.3. Ken is pointing at me uttering, "A question," which alerts Chuck who provides me with the space for entering the interactional floor.

"So I have blue eyes, and my wife has blue eyes. I wonder if anyone can figure out what my son Niels' eyes are?" There is a pause—the students did not seem to have understood. "Why would they be . . .?"

Without being called upon, Natasia begins, "You have blue eyes, she has blue eyes." A fleeting image rushes through my mind: Niels is the son from my first marriage. But I sense that introducing this only complicates the real story I am after here; I also know Natasia's name because it is the name of Niels' mother. I cannot even say that I am thinking, it's just an awareness, unformulated, and therefore nothing I can reflect upon, something I do not even *have* the time to reflect upon, because this would take me out of the lesson, away from following Natasia in the unfolding of her answer. As I focus on the lesson, I am swept away again and don't know that these thoughts that had just been present already had disappeared again.

Natasia continues, but I can't quite make out what she is saying. She does not speak loud enough for me, and for a moment I am aware of my hearing problems, but the thought disappears as Andrea comments, "A good question." Natasia enters the interactional floor again, "You have blue eyes, and she has blue eyes, you both have recessive genes." "Uh um," I go, but Andrea takes over.

"Let's think about this," she says and continues, "Let's list the possible–" she stops and then comments, "Excellent, excellent point. I am glad you brought that up."

"It makes him have recessive genes," Natasia says.

Andrea comments, "Natasia makes a good point. Recessive." She continues, "Let's think of *all* the possible genotypes, okay. He has blue eyes; the expression, phenotype is blue. But what are the possible genotypes that they have? What are the possible genotypes they may have?" Natasia again is the student who answers—even without being called upon.

"He would have t'be recessive." She turns to me, "The both of you have blue eyes?" "Uh," I make some time, and then find my stance, "My wife and I we both have blue eyes."

Andrea comments, "The phenotypic expression is . . . ," but Natasia counters, "Yea, but both of them have recessive genes." The two now seem to engage in a two-way conversation.

– Okay.
– A dark color dominates the gene pool.
– Okay.
– Like brown eyes will dominate over blue eyes.
– Okay. So he would have to have?

"Recessive," Natasia goes and pauses, and then says "genes." "And so?" Andrea asks with a long, drawn-out final syllable. Natasia responds, "All the genes are recessive."

Andrea has been noting something, and as Natasia, Ken, and others turn to me having raised my hand again, "I have another question." "He has an*other* question!" Andrea comments, but it sounds to me like, "Oh no, not yet another one." Again, this is but a sense, a coloring that pervades my awareness and my actions. But I am too caught up getting ready for my question, which I frame as I go along. I simply have the sense that I want to pose another problem, adding to the lesson, but in a different way than asking students to regurgitate what they have heard during some previous lesson. There is a latent sense that problems that resemble "Who done it?" or "Who's the murderer given some genetic information?" is a better and perhaps more interesting way of reviewing the biological concepts underlying hybrid crosses. But there is no time to try to understand what is going on, we have to talk about this during the cogenerative dialogue session that we have planned for the following lunch break. I have taken the interactional floor and I have to move on, being sensitive to the unfolding context that is in part constituted by the question I am posing without knowing what the question will ultimately look like. Again, the events sweep me away.

– I have two brothers and a sister. My brother Ulrich has brown eyes. My brother Axel has brown eyes. My sister Sabine has brown eyes. I have blue eyes. What are the eye colors, the *pos*sible eye colors my parents have?

There is a moment of silence. There is bit of shuffling, students and the other teachers looking around at each other. Andrea orients to the overhead projector. Did my question pose too great of a challenge. Then, a student begins to respond. I note that it is not Natasia. "Your dad might have brown eyes, and your mom has blue." I go, "Or?" and hear Chuck querying at the same time, "*Or?*" Several students get in, uttering as if my question was stupid, "Or your mom has brown eyes and your dad has blue eyes." For a moment there is more movement and excitement than there has been in this entire review episode. And then Natasia shouts; drowning out everyone else, her right arm stretched out pointing toward me commanding a turn at talk, "Or they both have brown eyes but they be heterozygous." "Um," I go with what the video recording attests to being an approving and positively astonished tone of voice.

Andrea praises with a drawn out "Gooood!" and I add, "Yea, both of my parents have brown eyes." Natasia leans back with a broad smile, and Andrea acknowledges the contribution once more, "I love it." I continue, "Um, so what kind of brown eyes do they have." I later realize that Natasia already has provided the answer to the question I am currently asking, but I am unaware of it. I later will ask myself, "How could I have missed that aspect of Natasia's contribution?" I must have been so caught up getting ready for the next question that I no longer am attuned to what *exactly* she is saying.

Several students shout out, "Light brown." I am stunned, but sense that I have asked a stupid non-productive question. I do not have the time to think about what has happened here because the lesson relentlessly continues. As Natasia calls out, I am caught up in the events as if swimming in a river, leaving me no time to reflect, but seek to cope all the while contributing to making this lesson happen. "One dark one light!" "Yea but," I begin to respond in trying to find my composure, "What genotype will they be?"

"Heterozygous," Natasia responds so quickly as she almost overlaps my question.

– Heterozygous, why?

– Or have one heterozygous and one homozygous. She stops, looks into the air, hesitates, and continuous, "No heterozygous." And then Chuck steps in and takes a turn at talk.

– What are the genotypes? What genotype can his mother have? What are the genotypes? Several students have turned around, as Chuck stands in the back of the classroom, behind the back of many. Natasia feels to be the designated next speaker, but Chuck interrupts the attempt to think aloud about an answer.

– Um.

– When you think genotype, which letter has she? What are the *geno*types?

– Um.

– Gimme the letters!

There is a pause, Natasia mutters a bit. The pause gets longer. A sense surfaces within me that I need to step in. "Could, could–" but before I find my stance and utter a question, Natasia beings shouting out again, "One of them had–." I get another "could" in, but Natasia is on a roll now, and I take a step back, passively following what she says rather than attempting to talk. Natasia says, "One or both have big B's." She holds up two fingers of her left hand. Chuck chimes in, "Think about it." He continues, "One or both parents have to have big B's, what would that? Let's say his mom. What would they have to have?" Natasia responds, "It couldn't be." I try to help.

– Could it be–? Can one of them be homozygous dominant?

– NO!, Natasha says shaking her head.

– If I have blue eyes? Natasia turns her head toward Chuck, but I continue, "I have blue eyes and both of my parents have brown." Natasia shakes her head with a broad smile on her face. "No, because you are recessive blue." The student next to her also shakes her head and others look at me. Mixed in with my feeling that there are some interesting things happening here, there is also a feeling of helplessness

Figure 2.4. I (Michael) am standing in one of the front corners of the classroom, just to the left of the video camera so that it records me whenever I move a bit forward. As I am participating with Andrea and Chuck in teaching the monohybrid cross, I am vaguely aware that Ken frequently turns to the student on his right. "Is he talking about genetics, or about the lesson? Perhaps he is just chattering about something else on his mind right now."

mixed in, for I feel I cannot ask other students to contribute for lack of knowing their names. So Natasia dominates the conversation on the student side, whereas on the teachers' side at least Chuck and Andrea are part of the game. I noticed that Ken frequently is turning to the student next to him, but I have no sense whether they talk about genetics or about something else. It is a strange feeling, is he just like an inattentive student?

– So you can figure out a lot about my family just by knowing what eye colors they have. I hear Andrea comment.

– Very good. Do you all understand that? Several students answer with "Yea." "Very good," Andrea continues in the attempt of finding a stance for continuing the lesson, as my stepping back gives her the space to step forward and continue. "All right, now, what kind of cross is the cross we just did?" But I am now coming to have some other thoughts. Throughout this episode, Ken has been turning toward the student to his right, talking (Figure 2.4). Has he been bored with what I have contributed? Were they having a side conversation? Or has the student said something that I, being hard of hearing, have not heard and he is simply doing the kind of coteaching that he has been writing about?

* * *

Ken: When you joined the coteaching in a central way, it is without prior approval or buy-in of the class. These were early days in our work on coteaching and we had not realized how important it was to negotiate and reach agreement on either of us assuming a central role. Hence, your intervention was unexpected and in some senses a breach to the flow of the lesson. It was not clear to the coteachers or students that you were a teacher and so it took them some time to adjust, and then you had a chance to earn that status of teacher—which you did relatively quickly.

Michael: When I now reflect on this moment, in particular the fact that I have been able to follow the lesson and contribute despite my novice status in the school, Bakhtin's notion of *participative thinking* comes to mind, which, although it has little to do with reflection, describes a practitioner's relation to the present situation quite well. Truly coteaching with another means knowing what is going on even without cogitation. This form of thinking allows us to participate, take on the lead role in a whole-class interactive session, and then fade into the background again. But you are right: although we all had taught in the laboratory session, Andrea may not have expected me to participate during the whole-class session. In this situation, I felt comfortable to move from the sideline into the central role.

Ken: I regarded my role as identifying students who may have need of additional structure and supporting them as coteaching proceeds. When there are more than two coteachers, such as in this case, one-on-one teaching can be a very effective way of engaging students. In this case I was trying to get this student engaged in a high-energy way.

Michael: I guess there is also the question of cost–benefit. If there is more than one teacher in a classroom, you want to maximize the teaching each person can do, and therefore, maximize learning on the student part. Whole-class situations, unless conceived in the way you present it, do not lend themselves as easily to the distributed nature of teaching where each teacher works both extensively and intensively with students in need of mediation.

Ken: One-on-one teaching during a cotaught lesson can be distracting to other coteachers and students in the vicinity. Given your discomfort, it underlines the importance of understanding and accepting one another's roles. Perhaps what we take from this scenario is that when one-on-one teaching is distracting to others they can legitimately ask for quiet or a temporary cessation of one-on-one participation. Issues such as these are contradictions, perhaps experienced by you as resistance, to be taken up in cogenerative dialogues.

Michael: I am not sure I was experiencing discomfort—in the account I attempt to present again, in narrative form, the fleeting nature of our perceptions, the things we note without making them salient to hang on to them. We notice it as an event in the background and it may be that we forget this aspect as quickly as it passes. There is no transition of the presentation of the moment into a representation—and that is what for me participative thinking is about, a sense of the praxis situation as a whole, though in any instance, only some aspects, like the story about my son's eye color, stick out and constitute my main concerns.

Ken: Okay, I accept that in your case. But more generally, my one-on-one interactions are structures that could easily be regarded by a coteacher as resistance to the flow of what she is trying to accomplish. As such she may experience a build up of negative emotions that could detract from the solidarity between the two of us and lead to less productive coteaching. The takeaway message for me is for an understanding to be established that one or other of the coteachers can call for complete attention at any time without others regarding this as a sign of disrespect. If such a call were inappropriate the issue could be taken up in a subsequent huddle or cogenerative dialogue.

Michael: I may be a bit over sensitive, or more sensitive than others, but to me teaching, as researching, fundamentally involves a certain amount of solicitude in the very constitution of acting. By solicitude I mean to cover both being concerned and being affected, disquietude and concern that come with care and responsibility *for* the other. I have a sense of not only being exposed to the other but also affecting the other through my action, and this effect on the other, in a moment of countertransference, affects me in turn.

Ken: Classes have complex social arrangements and our early decision to give priority to the learning of the students is salient—rather than the new teachers learning to teach. If all coteachers concur with that motive and strive to attain it then the moral and emotional aspects of enacting coteaching can adaptively align to benefit student learning. Having said that, I regard it as important for teachers to participate in ways that expand the agency of coteachers and students. This necessarily involves ethical concerns, especially caring for the others and not being too imperialistic in insisting on one course of action over another. As coteaching is enacted, the necessity is to be adaptive in ways that allow others to participate in ways that lead toward productive outcomes.

Michael: The most important aspect for me from this account of coteaching concerns the narrative itself, which is very different from the accounts of teaching one can find in the literature. Teaching is something lived, we do it with and through our bodies, and we experience it with and because of our bodies, which are exposed to the situation as a whole, including the actions of others, students and coteachers alike. Finding ways of talking and writing about teaching that move away from the silly accounts that articulate what we do as if we were computers implementing a program and drawing on stored knowledge that someone can elicit using an interview. The praxis perspective I am aiming at here means giving reason to the way in which we experience ourselves as knowing persons, interacting with others in our care.

Ken: I agree. Models of teaching that assume that teaching consists of sets of conscious decisions may inadvertently lead to inappropriate ways of planning and then enacting teaching. In contrast, the coteaching model we have explored here highlights praxis, not just of teachers, but of all participants, fluently enacting appropriate forms of culture in ways that lead to the attainment of collective outcomes, including science knowledgeability and solidarity among the participants (across the teacher student boundaries).

Michael: This way of describing teaching, *participative thinking* and solicitude, is a way of escaping the means-end model that characterizes other theoretical models and conceptual frameworks. Our way of thinking also includes an essentially passive component in that we take into account the fact that we are affected by the actions of others and the concrete structures they produce for

Figure 2.5. I have tuned out of following Andrea and the lesson, attending for the moment to a student who appeared to be sleeping. I wanted to find out what was going on.

our own actions. That is, coteaching, as teaching, is not only about agency, it is also about the passivity of being affected and in turn, about affecting others. *This* we can learn only by coteaching, as participative thinking expresses itself only in praxis.

Coteaching the Dihybrid Cross

Andrea has completed the review of the monohybrid. She begins, "We are getting into the dihybrid cross. We are getting into the big league. So why don't you help me out here?" I see a student with the head on the desk. I am thinking, perhaps she had to work all night and now feels so tired. I walk over to her, no longer attending to what Andrea was saying, asking whether she had been up late working or watching television (Figure 2.5). She responds saying that she is not feeling well. I do not have to reflect, well knowing from my longtime teaching experience that some girls have a difficult time coping with hormonal changes in their bodies. A thought flashes through my mind, "Would she be pretending." But I am already backing off again. As I turn away from the student, I tune into Andrea's voice again, which for the moment had been in the background. She says, "Let's think of something that we can cross." Natasia calls out, "eyes and hair." Ken looks at Natasia, then looks toward Andrea and says, "Weight . . . weight and height." There are two other students who call out something, but it was not sufficiently loud for me to hear it. "Alright," Andrea then continues again, "So we can do eyes and hair."

"We could do that brown is dominant over blue, and black hair is dominant over blond." "There are traits that appear to be linked. Anyone remember what linked traits are?"

"Alright, we are going to do a dihybrid cross." And then, turning her body in the direction of Chuck (Figure 2.6), reaching the pen out toward Chuck asks, "You

Figure 2.6. The classroom from my perspective during a major change over in the lesson, from Andrea (left), who has just reviewed simple crosses, to Chuck (right), who will review the more complicated dihybrid cross. (Image is split at the juncture of two images from the roving camera.)

want to teach that to them?" Chuck responds, "If you don't mind." He then continues while walking toward the front passing close by me, "First of all, when you do a dihybrid cross, I tell you right now, without even– looking at this, it's gonna be a nine-three-three-one ratio.

I have stepped back metaphorically for a split moment, thinking about transitions between two coteachers and how they achieve them. Ken and I have written about how in efficient coteaching, one coteacher makes space for another to come in and take over, while the other in stepping in displays willingness to step forward and take over. They do so without planning, but accomplish these transitions as part of the lesson itself. For example, Andrea has reached forward holding the pen, literally inviting him to take it and use it as part of his teaching; I know without reflecting that we have written about this, too. And we have written about the seamlessness with which such transitions occur. But I am already attending to the lesson again. As quickly as these thoughts are occurring to me they have also disappeared again. They are perhaps not even thoughts, for I am aware of what is going on right now; they are but fleeting images, like what we see out of the corner of our eyes all the while being focused on something else. It is not well characterized by the word *thinking* if it is used to denote *reflection*; rather, this is the sort of thinking that has been denoted by the term *participative thinking*, which is more of a sense of what is going on and which allows me to do the right thing at the right time without having to reflect. It is a fleeting sense, too, that colors the way I am participating, but fading in and out as we go along. It is a sense integrally characterized by an emotional and ethico-moral toning. Here, too, I do not *follow* (moral) norms as if I were going step by step through a recipe, but rather, what I do inherently is characterized by ethico-moral dimensions. As for any accomplished practitioner, acting wisely means simultaneously determining "the rule and the case by grasping the situation in its singularity" (Ricœur, 1992, p. 175).

Together with the students, Chuck begins to fill in four-letter combinations into each square. He asks, "What can you have this large B hook up with?" One student calls out, "Everything" and Natasia suggests, "The other large B." Chuck continues, always writing down the letters that he utters, "A large B with a large B. What else? A large B with?" Chuck continues, with single and double letter responses from the students to fill his square. A little later, Andrea suggests a different way of finding the solution. "Right, but one way you can do it is, because the allele . . . the allele on one side of the condition and then the condition on the other, and then you bring this together and cross."

All of a sudden I notice myself hanging onto an idea rather than letting it pass away as so many ideas and images that therefore are only fleeting—Natasia is so interested in genetics, just as I was interested in genetics in college. I am thinking about my final presentation that I have given one semester, concerning the invention of the structure of DNA. I had focused on the physical structure of the molecules involved and the different kinds of chemical relations they were able to form. I do not remember the details, but I clearly do remember how my biology teacher notes that he really liked the presentation but that the chemistry of the bases was way over his head. I am thinking, "I bet Natasia could be like this in another year or two, she is really keen on understanding biology rather than just rote memorizing it."

My thoughts begin to veer off to another topic. I notice that I am developing a critical perspective on Chuck's teaching. Chuck is using letters. It's formulaic; he is just using letters and not working toward understanding. I know that my presupposition is that teaching means working for and toward understanding. Chuck does something that I feel is different, he develops mnemonics so that students can do well on the tests. I appreciate what he is doing to help *these* students to be more successful on examinations that are used to weed them out of college trajectories. And yet, I have the sense that we teachers can both work toward understanding and toward being successful on high-stakes examinations. But the lesson is sweeping me away as I have become more appreciative of Chuck's actions and tune back into what he is doing.

Chuck acknowledges Andrea's contribution with a "Yeah" and continues. After completing the square with the four-letter combinations, he explains, "Since this is the genotype possible combinations of one parent, the other parent would have the same and you bring it down here and then you recombine them." He suggests that students should do that on their own and then gives them a hint for checking their work, "If you do it right, you can always check this block right here." Chuck points to the bottom right square and continues, "Because there you are going to get a homozygous recessive. One-sixteenth, in other words, when you combine, you get the answer in the sixteenth block small b small b, small h small h." Natasia suggests, "We already know that" but Chuck does not seem to take note of this comment.

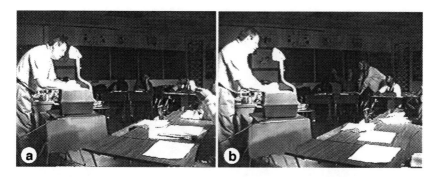

Figure 2.7. a. Ken proposes a different way of figuring out the offspring combinations for a dihybrid cross. b. Now the earlier situation flashed through my mind when Ken and Andrea were talking, and Ken gestured toward the Punnett square on the screen, moving his hand first from left to right, then from top to bottom.

As Chuck moves on through the lesson, he interacts with Natasia. I see Ken wiggle back and forth on his chair, as if he wanted to get in and contribute to the lesson. Some time later, while Chuck is setting up a task for the students (Figure 2.7.a), Ken calls out, "Can't you write the hair across the top and the height down the side and get the same?" Now the image of a moment about three minutes before flashes up in my mind, where he was talking to Andrea and gestured toward the Punnett square, moving his hand from left to right, then wiggled it suggesting writing; he then moves his hand downward, followed by some wiggling movement as if he is writing (Figure 2.7.b). Before I can pursue this idea, which requires me to stop and reflect and thereby disconnect with the lesson, Chuck responds to Ken without looking up from drawing another square responds with a drawn out "No!" I realize what I am saying in the same moment that I am saying it: "You have to have one parent on the top and one on the side."

My response has come from my innermost depth, some place that I cannot see and have no control over. In the moment I could probably not articulate why I was saying what I was saying. But later on, while reflecting upon the instant, I know that I have acted in this way because of some schema or disposition, which is not available to conscious reflection. But I know that the dispositions are not just there, they are in fact a reflection of my participation in science. They are sedimentations of science culture that have developed over years of engagement with doing Punnett Squares and teaching them to middle school students. I have been saying "You have to have one parent on the top and one on the side" in the same way I might jump across a puddle without even spending a flick of thought about how to move my feet and legs, how to generate momentum using my arms, how to lift myself off the ground to get carried across the water without having my feet touch the water. I might not even be conscious of the fact that I have avoided a puddle. More so, if asked about it, I might have to do some thinking, analyzing what is behind all of it in the same way that Chuck might have to think about his little b's and big B's if

Figure 2.8. I am talking to Ken about the dihybrid cross problem. He has figured out what Ken was saying earlier in the lesson, but also tell him what the accepted way of doing the dihybrid cross was within the biology community.

someone asked a question like "Why a little b?" and "How come recessive genes are denoted by little bs rather than big Bs or big Cs?"

Chuck is completing his presentation and provides students with the assignment to do a dihybrid on their own. He walks off to the side so that he can work with students individually, just as he had announced, "Why don't you do it and we come around to work with you individually." Andrea responds, "Actually, we only have two minutes left." She takes over, beginning to bring the lesson to a close. It is an opportunity for me to walk over to Ken and make some remarks about the solution to the dihybrid cross and how I think that his and Chuck's solutions are linked (Figure 2.8). It is only now that I can explain to him that he had been correct, but that biologists have a standard way of setting up the Punnett Squares, namely having the genes of one parent written across and those for the other parent down on the side. I know, though, that at other times in similar situations, we might have had the opportunity to talk about it while the lesson was going on, just as he has talked during this lesson to the student next to him, to Chuck, and even Andrea. But I have been at the opposite side of the classroom, and also so involved and interested in contributing that I have never thought about crossing over to touch base with him.

* * *

Ken: Looking back at my practices, my two main roles appear to have been to re-engage students who showed evidence of losing focus and, when Andrea stepped back, to interact with her about aspects of the lesson—much as we denote as *huddles*, brief meetings during a lesson in which coteachers align each other concerning what to do next.

Michael: As I was writing my account and again as I worked through the text, I was thinking that coteaching provides these resources for assisting new teachers in learning by reflecting as the lesson goes on. That is, in this situation Chuck had taken the lead and there now was a space for you to talk to Andrea, which means, you were able to address issues without too much of a remove from when the events actually happen. In this sense, this is similar to a cogenerative huddle two coteachers might engage in as part of the ongoing lesson to reflect on the best way to deal with some situation.

Ken: Chuck's approach was confusing to students. He was "winging it" in the sense that he and Andrea had not pre-planned the dihybrid cross. Accordingly, he was relying on the fact that he had done this exercise many times before and knew to set it up to get four lower case letters in the sixteenth square. As you noted, his approach was technical and devoid of associated biology, at least in an explicit sense.

Michael: He was not only confusing students, he was confusing me as well. I was asking myself why he put the gene combinations on the outside of the Punnett square in the way he did. But I was also hesitant in the sense that at that moment of the event I am not quite acquainted with him and do not know how he would experience not only being interrupted but also questioned about the content of what he was doing as well.

Ken: Though I did not intend it as such, my suggestion is a wonderful segue from a technical approach, where my suggestion to set up the cross is legitimate, to a correct solution that makes sense biologically. Chuck might have used my suggestion as a structure to move from a technical solution to one involving the necessity to show what each parent contributes genetically.

Michael: I was also thinking that this could have been an ideal situation to discuss the difficulties as part of the lesson, thereby providing students with the opportunity to see trained scientists struggle with an issue that they do not know well at the moment. Natasia, too, turns out to have an understanding. Articulating the troubles for and with students could have constituted a very interesting and very different lesson. This would have been an opportunity to see that science is about process, about doubt, and about clarifying rather than about regurgitating facts. But then, the needs of these students may have been different, such as when the instability of their own home lives were to lead them to need more certainty with respect to what to know and how to know it.

PERIPHERAL ROLES IN COTAUGHT LESSONS: KEN

Before accounting for my own experience of this lesson and reflecting on it, I want to briefly contextualize the present coteaching experience within my biographical experience. My initial experiences with coteaching, as a coteacher, were not so productive because my coteachers failed to coteach with me. When I first negotiated to coteach with Aaron at City High School he agreed. But when the time came he handed over the reins to me, preferring to take a break, sitting at his desk observing as I struggled to teach solo. Similarly, a new teacher and one of my doctoral students also preferred to observe from the periphery, only getting involved in small-group and individualized activities. At the time I was preoccupied with my relative lack of success and with all the issues to be resolved I did not assign high priority to learning to teach through coteaching. Instead I felt I could figure it out for myself, adapt what I knew and could do to these students in this urban school, and learn from student researchers I had enlisted to advise me.

After three months of struggle I had to participate in the spring professional meetings for researchers, thereby returning the classes to Aaron for the two weeks I was away. He agreed to follow our curriculum plan, which was to relate the science they were learning to local circumstances and especially to their interests. When I returned I had taken the time to review what had happened earlier and suggested we coteach the new topic on the science of music. Although I took a lead in many lessons, Aaron did too and together we cotaught the unit, with regular involvement of a doctoral student who was an experienced urban science teacher.

As I reviewed videotapes of the three of us coteaching a lesson on resonance, using oscillating pendulums as a hands-on activity, it is apparent that I am very relaxed in the ways I interact with students and coteachers. When horseplay occurred among students my tendency was to walk away and let the students self-regulate their participation, there was very little time spent on controlling student misbehavior or redirecting students. Also, there was an opportunity to spend quality time with students who wanted assistance and check back with them. There were numerous examples of all three teachers participating with students in some of their investigations. Although we were not using *emotional energy* as a theoretical framework at that time, it is evident that there was widespread evidence of success in the pendulum activities, and indicators of enjoyment, interest and challenge were widespread. Instances of frustration and anger were few in number, short lived, and resolved by the students themselves. This has changed over the course of the years that I was coteaching with others at City High School so that my relationship to students and teachers at the time of the present biology lesson was quite different to my initial experiences at coteaching.

At the time I enter this lesson, which turns out to include a laboratory hands-on task and a teaching sequence about mono and dihybrid crosses, I, a university supervisor and researcher, have earned the trust and respect of the new and resident teachers at City High. The students know who I am and accept me as a teacher. The resident teachers make it clear that students are to regard me as their teacher and treat me with respect. Accordingly, when I join a class I routinely begin to look to see who needs my assistance, individually or in small groups. Only occasionally do I step forward to interact with the whole class, although this happens by invitation and when I feel I can contribute to the learning of the class. (The next chapter presents some data from a class in which I was a coteacher. Deeper insights into my roles can be gleaned from these analyses.)

As I enter this lesson, which I have not planned together with the teachers, I am looking for a place to place myself, where I could be of assistance to students on an as needed basis. This genetics lesson is no different than many others in which I have participated. On this occasion I feel I have two obvious choices, to place my-self near to Natasia, a student with a passion for biology who often loses interest because she is not challenged by the knowledge demands of the course, or sit next to a female with her head on the desk. I opt to try to persuade the student with her head down to get involved in the lesson. Initially my interactions with her are about getting involved and as the lesson progress I interact with her as if in a tutoring session, providing additional structures to augment the unfolding structures of the classroom interactions, which she is not following. Today I am not surprised that Michael may have regarded me as off task and even disruptive because to get this student involved I have to be light hearted and interact in a high energy way. Im-portantly, my peripheral roles are understood by the teacher and students and are familiar to them since I was a regular coteacher in their classroom.

Like Michael I am quite concerned with Chuck's ways of teaching the students, as if to memorize facts and tables for reproduction on examinations. Though well intentioned his approach is against the grain as far as my preferences are concerned and my frustration spills over once or twice in the lesson when I suggest at one time that the students be left to complete the matrix for a dihybrid cross them-selves. My suggestion arises when it becomes clear that Chuck has no idea how to teach this on the fly and his efforts are muddled and confusing to the students. It is also apparent that students like Natasia know how to create the matrix and signs of frustration are cropping up. This is typical about emotions: they are not just there within us, raging passions that we feel in our bodies, but they are observable here as elsewhere in interactions. In fact, we only know and know about emotions be-cause we experience and talk about them in the course of growing up. Without the mediation of others, our parents, siblings, friends, and teachers, we would not know *emotions* as such; we would know only instinctive drives that we are unable to control.

In this situation, however, Chuck perseveres, even though the attention of the students dies off and the intellectual puzzles are left to be picked up in a cogenera-tive dialogue right after the class and then in the forthcoming weeks and months when the lesson will become the object for serious research involving the coteach-ers and Natasia. As we have surmised, it will turn out that Natasia not only knows how to solve the dihybrid cross, but also reconstructs the matrix rather quickly sev-eral months after the lesson. Also, it will turn out that she finds Michael's ques-tions salient and years later will remember him asking them and her responses. Hence, I point out that Michael's stepping forward in the lesson, though unplanned, is an example of cultural fluency, being timely, appropriate and anticipatory in at least several senses. First, the coteachers and the students pick up on his question and numerous successful interactions occur in the moments after Michael's inter-vention. Second, the question allows the coteachers and students to connect with earlier parts of the lesson and then to build further to continue their planned review in a way that was more engaging and high energy for all participants. Finally, as the lesson unfolds, Michael's peripheral roles continue and his subsequent interac-tions afford ongoing participation of several students, including Natasia and both coteachers.

* * *

Michael: What appears to be important in understanding coteaching and the different roles we might take is the idea of *legitimate peripheral participation*. When we coteach, the extent and intensity of our participation depends on whether we have actually participated in the planning of the lesson, the degree to which we are familiar and knowledgeable about the content being taught, the level of ease we have with the other participants. Thus, your participation is different than mine given that you have been in this school and this classroom repeatedly over an extended period of time. I have come to know these students and teachers (Chuck, Andrea) on this day. Nevertheless, coteaching is built on the idea that all our participation is legitimate peripheral. Here, I do not mean to say that participation is more or less legitimate, but participation inherently is legitimate. Furthermore, participation is not more or less peripheral: all participation is peripheral, simultaneously at the core and at the fringe of the events. In other words, all participation is to be understood in terms of the margin|center dialectic, as each act is central—reproducing the practices of the field—and marginal—producing new cultural practices at the very moment of reproducing them.

Ken: You make an important point. If we think theoretically about the classroom as a field of cultural production—as participants enact practices they simultaneously reproduce and transform culture (i.e., reproduce|transform). In this way, through participation, each person changes the structures of the field and the agencies of others. This is clear when you consider that my practices were distracting you, structuring your participation in the lesson, albeit momentarily. Presumably Chuck, Andrea, and many of the students were aware of those same practices.

Michael: One of the most difficult aspects about coteaching for some teacher is the fact that they not only have to get used to the idea of the curriculum as an event that is enacted collectively with students but also involves the participation of other teachers, who apparently enact intentions different from our own. Coteaching actually brings out these differences better than any other form of research, as we constitute the same event together, positioned not identically—because all position also is *dis*position—though at one another's elbows. As practitioners, our participation involves *participative thinking*, and if the actions of others are different from the ones our participative thinking (not reflection!) wants us to enact, a contradiction emerges. This contradiction, when taken up in cogenerative dialoguing sessions following the lessons, are possible kernels for the evolution of better understanding arising from the collective interpretive processes of those sessions.

CODA

In this chapter, we provide a description of coteaching that allows readers to develop a sense of what it means to teach with someone else. Our account here shows that as teachers, we are not like robots, merely implementing the actions that some computer in our heads figures outs and then makes our bodies enact. Rather, in the classroom, we are whole persons who get caught up in the flow of events, which we both contribute to producing and to which we are subject. Even if we had set particular goals, the realization of goals in concrete praxis is a creative act (e.g., Suchman, 1987) and therefore inherently full of surprises. As in any other social situation, we are not in control. This lack of (total) control expresses itself in the inherent and always present difference between planned and enacted curriculum. It is the same gap that others articulated as existing between plans and situated actions.

In coteaching, in addition to being attuned to the actions of students, we are also attuned to the actions of fellow teachers. Their actions are as legitimate as our own, even though there are situations where we are perplexed because of the differences between what we might have done and what one or the other teaching partner has done. However, despite the differences between the concrete action of the other and the possible action of a coteacher, there is an inherent comprehension. We know and understand what the other has done as something we could have done but for some reason would not have done. Being there in the same situation, subject to the same contingent possibilities and constraints, we are in a position to articulate the reasons for our actions and our preferences; and these stand a much better chance of corresponding to the needs of the situation than if an outside observer—the fly-on-the-wall educational ethnographer—were to say what had to be done.

In the converse situation, when the actions of the others appear just right, we actually learn by participating. Such learning frequently occurs without our conscious awareness, though this does not prohibit us from further reflecting after the fact about the events and to learn in the process of attempting to explain what has happened. Such attempts of explaining, which require us to first make the moment present again and then to interpret it are possible only because we already have a practical understanding. We cannot interpret something that we do not already have a practical comprehension of—the interpretive reduction articulated in Figure 2.1 requires practical understanding. But this practical understanding requires interpretative explanation for its development (Ricœur, 1991). In other words, any effort in explaining coteaching specifically but any form of practice generally, is preceded, accompanied, and concluded by practical understanding. Yet our practical understanding expands at the very moment we attempt to articulate and explain it. All of this takes time, which is not available in the moment of teaching, unfolding as it does in time, without time-out to reflect on events. That is, the idea of a process of reflection *in* practice is inherently flawed, as any reflection requires the making present again of something that becomes the object of reflection; and it requires language and other signs as tools to work on the object of reflection. This reflection, as we point out at the beginning of this chapter, is a different form of activity, using discourses that are very different from those that characterize our teaching. All reflection concerning some event requires us to abstract ourselves from the event, make it an object of reflection—which inherently makes the episode we reflect upon something completed. In this chapter, we attempt to provide a description of a different kind of thinking, participative thinking, which is more like a sense of the event that we participate in constituting, and a more or less vague awareness of what else is going on in the surrounding world. It is against this vague awareness as a background that anything specifically attended to in the here and now comes to take on salience. To deepen our understanding, we further explore the roles of coteachers in greater depth in the next chapter, this time with a first person experience of Ken with interpretive analyses from Michael.

WHAT HAPPENS DURING COTEACHING?

In this chapter we take up where we left off in chapter 2, with an effort to bring further insights into coteaching through first hand accounts and analyses of videotape of a cotaught lesson—in this case involving several coteachers with experience of teaching a chemistry class for an extended period of time. Our motive is to introduce possibilities that emerged from a cotaught lesson, taking up issues that pertain to learning to teach, teacher education and professional development. In an ethnographic study of coteaching we explore two questions: What happens during cotaught lessons? and Why does this happen? Our approach is to describe the roles of teachers and students as they are enacted in a year in which coteaching was a vehicle for learning to teach science in an urban high school. Our descriptions, analyses, and interpretations of what happens provide readers with examples of how to do research on coteaching and emphasize the wealth of roles and the associated potential for learning that is associated with coteaching.

Three distinctive fields—whole-class, small-group, and individualized—are apparent in our ethnographic analyses of the data sources, each with its own characteristic structures and associated culture. These fields were identified and labeled in terms of the interactions that arise in relation to the organization of students. Since each field is nested within the classroom, the boundaries between the different fields are weak, transitions between fields are frequent, and culture originating in one field is enacted readily in others. In each of the noticeably distinct fields we explore agency|structure relationships, that is, the mutually constitutive nature of actions and the structures at hand. What we accomplish with these analyses are illustrative examples of roles, rules and practices associated with coteaching. These are considered as points of departure for those planning to enact coteaching. We begin by reviewing what we know about different aspects of coteaching and then move into an account of coteaching in different fields through the eyes of Ken, who cotaught the lessons analyzed.

FIELDS AND STRUCTURES OF COTEACHING

In this section, we review pertinent results of our research on the different fields in and enactments of coteaching. We focus on the changeover that occurs when one teacher takes the lead from another without "dropping the baton [ball]," on the potential pitfalls of coteaching, the complementary nature of roles, and on the phenomenon of becoming like the other that can be observed both at the mesolevel and microlevel when two or more individuals coteach for extended periods of time.

Exchanging the Baton

Whole-class interactive fields are common in all of the classes in which we have undertaken research on coteaching—when two or more coteachers collaborate with the goal of improving the learning of their students all the while creating learning opportunities for themselves. Initially we directed most attention to this organizational structure because it requires coordination between the two teachers to be effective and there are chances for breakdown if any of the coteachers is not willing to collaborate and step forward and step back as necessary. Since in a whole-class setting the coteachers are often center stage, it was a priority for early studies to describe what happens; and it was necessary to develop a heuristic to guide individuals new to coteaching. The heuristic, which is described in detail elsewhere (Roth & Tobin, 2002, p. 189), contains a check list of items such as "Is willing and shows willingness to step forward" and "Is willing and shows willingness to step back."

Whole-class structures were common in most of the lessons these teachers cotaught and they tended to be used to inform students of long and short term plans, introduce new content, elaborate and clarify science content and procedures, and review and re-teach subject matter regarded as important and difficult to learn. In an effort to explore the fields and associated cultural enactment nested within the whole-class field, we analyze resources from the coteaching of chemistry by Alex, a resident science teacher and two new teachers, Victoria and Jessica. The data sources, which are in fact resources to the researchers' actions that produce new (theoretical, textual) structures, consist of ten hours of digitized videotapes, ethnographic fieldnotes, and informal interviews. In whole-class fields we can identify numerous categories in which agency|structure relationships were sufficiently different to warrant a distinctive label. These are described, analyzed and interpreted below.

Often one of the coteachers takes a lead in a lesson, frequently involving explanations of subject matter and procedures. When this occurs the other coteachers provide support through monitoring, scanning, tutoring, inscribing, demonstrating, and attending. A key feature of the whole-class field is the preparedness of all coteachers to step forward and step back as it becomes appropriate or necessary. What exactly makes stepping forward or backward appropriate cannot be determined from the outside, but depends on the present moment and on the demands and constraints that *are experienced* only *in concrete praxis.* It is only *in* and *from* praxis that its nature can become apparent; outside researchers cannot but see the lifeless patterns in the actions of the acting individuals and the artifacts they employ (Bakhtin, 1993). That is, for example, in the monohybrid episode described in chapter 2, it cannot be determined from the outside when another teacher may enter the ongoing teacher–student exchanges. The ultimate idea is to bring about smooth exchanges of the baton so that from a student perspective, the lesson simply continues as if the changeover between teachers had been planned ahead of time. When smooth baton exchanges occur between coteachers the verbal structuring that occurs can include multiple coteachers.

Our research shows that there are different nonverbal signs used, usually in a nonconscious manner, in the process of exchanging the baton. Signs used to signal transitions among coteachers include voice inflections, gestures, and body movement, orientation, and positioning. As coteachers gain experience of teaching together the transitions from one person teaching the whole class to another teaching the whole class can become anticipatory, smooth, and timely and can be enacted without conscious awareness. That is, for example, one can observe an individual to make a head nod or move a hand just slightly, and then the other teacher takes over. When asked subsequently, the teacher who has given up the lead to the other frequently is not even aware of the signs she has produced and which characterizes the moment of transition. Thus, in the head nod, the teacher has signaled willingness to step back; in other words, the head nod is a resource for the other individual to step forward and step into the lead teacher role. For coteachers familiar with one another and the class, these transitions are smooth and do not require conscious attention. These transitions are fluid and feel normal to all participants, and in fact, talking about these transitions as something special is for experienced coteachers like talking about something that is self-evident. However, smooth transitions should not be considered the norm but an achievement in and through the ongoing activity that requires conscious and nonconscious work in addition to a disposition to make coteaching work.

When successive transitions between coteachers occur a form of interactive coteaching unfolds, during which two or more coteachers provide resources for each other and the whole class. Coteachers build on each other's drawings; make reference to what another teacher has said, or exchange roles of speaker and (chalkboard) note taker. Teaching practices emerge as a dynamic structure that expands the agency of students. Commonly students listen attentively and copy notes. Frequently they also get involved orally, interacting with teachers in a chorus of voices, asking and providing answers to questions. Indeed a very common form of whole-class interaction involves one or more coteachers explaining subject matter and procedures and then testing student understanding by asking questions. Frequently more than one student speaks at a time as answers are provided and questions are posed to the coteachers. In these cases the interaction chains involving students are consistent with the dispositions characteristic of African American culture (Boykin, 1986): students preferring to participate orally and in so doing to show verve, fluency, and expressive individualism.

As one coteacher speaks to the students it is common for other coteachers to inscribe notes and keywords, diagrams, pictures and symbols such as formulae and equations on to the chalkboard, often using gesture to support what the other teacher is saying (pointing to salient inscriptions or using gestures iconically). The effect of such a division of labor is that students come to be presented with multiple, different resources for sense making—spoken discourse and inscriptions. Similarly, the coteachers often provide an aid to learning by pointing to salient artifacts such as part of the periodic table. In much the same vein, though not as common, coteachers perform a demonstration as an illustration of what is being explained or raised as a question.

Potential Pitfalls

In our ongoing research on coteaching we have described the different ways in which coteaching unfolds when two or more coteachers teach at one another's elbows. Some of the pitfalls involve "dropping the baton in an exchange," that is, actions that breach the flow of teaching as one or the other teacher does not step forward as expected, steps forward at an inappropriate time, and refuses to yield the floor when a coteacher endeavors to teach. At the center of these problems is a lack of the continued production and reproduction of rapport between the teachers, often driven by a failure to respect the potential of the others to contribute through coteaching. Failure to co-plan also can be a problem that manifests in breaches in the classroom as teaching is enacted. A critical problem we encountered is when one teacher provides inquiry structures, such as unanswered questions and time for thought, only to find these structures being appropriated by a coteacher to enact a more expository style of teaching. In such a moment, the means espoused by one teacher to realize the goal of the lesson (allowing students to learn an aspect of chemistry), that is, open-ended questions, do not correspond to the goals of the other, who wants to draw on direct teaching as the means to achieve the goal. When this occurs frustration can build between teachers and it is essential that the issue be discussed cogeneratively. In some instances, this discussion may occur in a brief huddle close to when and where the event occurs; but in other instances the issues are more complex and may need to be addressed outside of the class and when there is sufficient time to reflect on the problem as a whole.

Complementary Roles

Coteachers also enact roles that focus on assisting students as one of them provides verbal structure while the others enact roles that include *attending* to what is being said, *scanning* the students for signs of confusion or requests for assistance, and *monitoring* the participation of students. These relatively unobtrusive roles often transition into the field of *tutoring,* especially then when a teacher realizes that one or several students exhibit or articulate a need for one-on-one or small-group teaching. Tutoring is provided on an as-needed basis and it is therefore essential that all coteachers accept tutoring as an acceptable and desirable form of structure that occurs within the same space and simultaneously with whole-class interactions in which one teacher (or a student) is speaking to the whole class.

When tutoring occurs with larger groups of students we describe the structure as *zoning,* since each coteacher teaches a large group of students simultaneously. In this case students often have options to tune into a coteacher who is teaching in a different zone of the room. When zoning occurs, we see evidence of students benefiting from teachers in another zone and also instances where contradictions have to be resolved because two teachers are teaching simultaneously. Chuck, the biology teacher in chapter 2, occasionally uses zoning—placing a partition between the two parts of a large classroom and oscillating between the two halves, coteaching in each with one new teacher. Here, the respective new teacher working with the students ascertains continuity of the lesson and discourse in each half of the class-room, whereas Chuck constitutes an additional resource person oscillating between the two classroom halves.

As is evident from the breakout of different roles of coteachers in whole-class settings, there is ample scope for peripheral participation among coteachers. By being in the class with other teachers there are many opportunities to learn science subject matter and procedures from other coteachers. As a coteacher becomes more knowledgeable the possibilities expand for more central forms of participation in assisting students to learn. In some of our earlier research we explored the ways in which coteachers who were out-of-field could learn science (in this case genetics) by coteaching with in-field colleagues such as in the lessons with Andrea and Chuck featured in the previous chapter. In that situation, the contradictions emerg-ing from the conversations about the dihybrid cross led us to reflect, together with students (e.g., Natasia), on how this subject matter might be taught better. In the process, the understandings of all participants were articulated and further elabo-rated.

Becoming Like the Other

A striking feature of coteaching in whole-class settings is that the coteachers be-come like the other by being in the same class with other coteachers. As we show in other chapters the teachers become like one another in the ways in which they appropriate space, time, and materials and use them as resources for acting. Al-though we have had personal experiences of becoming like the other in the way our dialects and accents have changed as we moved between countries, cultures, and speech communities, this knowledge about nonconscious changes in the way we act and speak had not become salient aspects of our research until we began to no-tice these features at multiple fronts—speech patterns, movements, and gestures—in our coteaching research.

As coteachers work together for a while, they become like the other in terms of how they move in the classroom, gesture, and orient their bodies. Because they use and build on each other's resources—e.g., a diagram on the chalkboard begun by one and completed by another teacher—they also become like each other in using resources in similar ways. And they become like one another in the ways in which they interact with one another and students, especially in how they speak. Similari-ties include the pauses in speech, voice intonation and inflection, and the amplitude and pitch of talk. Much of the process of becoming like the other is nonconscious and it is a good idea to focus on the salient features of teaching, including contra-dictions, in cogenerative dialogues to articulate what has been nonconscious and thereby become aware of it. Though nonconscious, these features nevertheless are resources in the actions of others. This became quite apparent during one of our collective research periods when Michael pointed out to Ken how conversation participants produce signs that contribute to making the interaction unfold smoothly. For example, listeners nod slightly, thereby signaling to the speaker that they hear and also that the other may continue speaking. From that moment on,

Ken began to notice the pervasiveness of this phenomenon that is so central to the interactive work conversation participants accomplish.

We can understand this phenomenon of becoming like the other as the result of a number of processes. First, Aristotle described the process of *mimesis*, which means copying another's behavior in a nonconscious or unconscious way. Recent neurophysiological work points out the existence of mirror neurons, which are active both in the production of some behavior (e.g., hand movement, head nod) and in the perception of the same behavior of others. Our ability to see particular movements and our ability to enact the same movements are tightly connected. Second, our research has shown that the pitch levels of two or more speakers in functioning, conflict-free interactions tend to adjust to one another whereas the pitch levels of speakers who differ (sharply) over some point tend to diverge dramatically, leading to doubling and even tripling of the pitch levels. Physicists long have known about the alignment of frequency-based phenomena: two pendulum (clocks) hanging close to each other from the same wall tend to adjust to each other in frequency—corresponding to pitch in human speech phenomena—and period. Sociologists have come to denote the alignment between two or more people using the same notion as physicists: *entrainment*. Of course, in social situations two or more people do not have to hang on a wall but rather entrainment occurs because the participants in any situation have to cooperate to produce it for what it is: a successful lesson is not the result of the actions of a "knowledgeable" teacher but rather the product of a successful cooperation and coordination involving teacher and students; a successful cogenerative dialoguing session is not *determined* by the actions of a particularly gifted researcher but is the result of a successful cooperation involving the stakeholders present. Third, because two or more teachers cannot use the same physical space while coteaching, for example, whole-class sessions, their movements frequently are *complementary* both in spatial and temporal ways. That is, the stepping forward and speaking by one teacher is associated with the stepping back and being silent of the other. Again, there is an alignment through *entrainment*, but this time involving a phase shift. Thus, when Andrea had finished the review of the monohybrid, she stepped back associated with the simultaneous stepping forward of Chuck; and when he steps back, Andrea may step forward. As a new teacher, she may become entrained into the successful practices and structures that the experienced teacher and his class bring forth.

FIRST-PERSON PERSPECTIVE OF COTEACHING FIELDS: SETTING THE STAGE

In the following sections, Ken describes a particular coteaching experience in a chemistry class normally taught by the experienced teacher Alex. Ken's narrative provides us with an account of how coteaching looks like from the perspective of one coteacher, who simultaneously focuses on teaching those who seem to need or express a need for assistance. In writing this chapter we use personal pronouns such as *I* and *my* to represent Ken's voice and *we* when Michael and Ken speak collectively. If there is a possibility of confusion we use Michael or Ken to denote the applicable voice.

The research is situated at City High School, a pseudonym for a relatively large comprehensive neighborhood high school in inner city Philadelphia in the USA. The school, which has been a site for our ongoing research on the teaching and learning of science for more than seven years, consists of about 2,000 students, nearly all of whom are of African American origin, from home circumstances that are economically challenging. This particular study was undertaken in the fall of 2002 and the spring of 2003, when City High School was in a transition decreasing the number of small learning communities—i.e., schools within the school, each containing about 300 to 350 students—from ten to six. As part of the transition the resident science teacher in this study had relocated from a low performing small learning community to one consisting of students who had the goal of attending college. In my roles as researcher and teacher educator I (Ken) began coteaching at the school in the spring of 1998 and continued an intensive presence through the spring of 2003.

When I undertook research at City High School I carried a small digital video camera in my hand and left it in record mode as I moved about the classroom in which I worked. Although my movement sometimes led to rapid movements of the camera and off-centered video, the mobility of the camera was a decided advantage. When I was asked to teach an individual or small group, as occurred frequently, I rested the camera on a desk and taught while the camera continued to record both video and sound.

On a particular day in December I visited a class in which Alex was coteaching chemistry with Victoria and Jessica, the two new teachers that I was supervising. As it was usual for me, I cotaught in a peripheral way with Alex, Jessica, and Victoria, who were coteaching each day. On this particular day the three regular coteachers had decided to assign students a series of exercises on limiting reagents in a chemical reaction that they were to work through. The exercises were written on the front board and initially students worked alone or with those adjacent to them to obtain a solution. The exercises were graded, each building on the other and the first stemming from a recent lab.

The first exercise required students to describe the reaction and the products when 4.7 moles of sodium were made to react with 1.7 moles of chlorine. The chemical reaction between sodium and chlorine is captured in the corresponding chemical equation:

$$2\,Na + Cl_2 \rightarrow 2\,NaCl \tag{3.1}$$

Students had to write and balance the equation (3.1) and then understand that two moles of sodium would combine chemically with one mole of chlorine (gas) to produce two moles of sodium chloride. As a consequence, only 3.4 moles of sodium would react with the chlorine, using up all of the latter but leaving 1.3 moles of sodium unused. Chlorine therefore is the limiting agent of this reaction.

After a short introduction the students began to work on the exercises and the four coteachers moved around the class to interact with students if and when it was desirable. Because I was holding the camera while being actively involved as a coteacher, much of the audio concerns my teaching and associated interactions with students. However, at any time one or more of the other coteachers also can be seen and heard on the videotape, as can many students in addition to those directly interacting with me.

The availability of so many coteachers allows a variety of teaching roles to evolve in response to the unfolding needs of the learners. Hence as one coteacher takes a lead, others can be on the lookout to interact with students on an as-needed basis. As we show in chapter 2, it is essential that all coteachers understand that this is expected when coteaching occurs and if distractions occur, our commitment to collective responsibility requires anyone noticing a distraction to make others aware of it. The following scenarios include examples of the coteachers interacting with individuals and small groups to afford learning. In some instances the coteachers initiated the interactions and in others they were called to provide assistance.

BREAKING CONVENTIONS

Alex invited a student to present her solution to the first problem on the front whiteboard, a break from the convention of the whiteboard being a resource used by the teacher to focus attention on what is to be learned (Figure 3.1). The student's use of the whiteboard, therefore, led to another configuration for the production and reproduction of resources—e.g., equations and other inscriptions on the chalkboard that others may use subsequently—and patterned actions.

When one or more of the coteachers break conventions the resulting structures can expand the agency of all coteachers and the students. For example, the chalkboard, or in this case the whiteboard, is a resource that is mainly used by teachers in whole-class settings. However, Victoria, Alex and I were involved in a master's

Figure 3.1. In a break from convention a student presents her solution to the first exercise and receives peer review.

degree program in which part of an inquiry model involves students' use of the chalkboard as a means to afford peer review of solutions to exercises. Accordingly, it was no surprise when Alex asked one of the students to write her solution on the whiteboard. The student did this after arriving at a solution and then when called on by Alex she explained and justified her solution. In this instance a peer made one suggestion for change and the student gladly accepted the suggestion. Later in this lesson other students spontaneously used the whiteboard to present their solutions and then Alex obtained and distributed a set of small square whiteboards so that each group could use one to write out a solution and then present it to the class. In both of these examples, the agency of students was expanded by the provision of material structures that would allow them to present solutions in ways that encouraged discussion among peers and corrections and elaborations to occur. Hence, Alex's break from the conventional use of the whiteboard had ripple effects as other coteachers and students used the resource in a similar way; and then Alex expanded the idea for all groups to use portable white boards to afford peer review.

ZONING—MEETING THE NEEDS OF STUDENTS

In an example of *zoning*, Victoria gathered together a group of students who had recently been absent and tutored them on how to solve this problem, taking them through step by step (Figure 3.2). Immediately students began to call on the other coteachers to assist them with the exercise. The students were to identify which of the reactants was the limiting one, what was produced, and what was remaining from the initial materials. Marisole, the first student I worked with in a one-on-one fashion, seemed to know sufficient standard chemistry to engage with the task and I provided scaffolds in somewhat lengthy explanations that connected the equation, which she had balanced, back to the details of the exercise. She was quick to note

Figure 3.2. Alex and Victoria teach one-on-one in a highly focused way—crouching in Victoria's case to have eye contact with a student.

65

Figure 3.3. Arlene speaks to the absentee group, who are focused, as is Jessica. To the right of Jessica a student records the group proceedings on a white board.

that sodium was in excess and understood that 1.7 moles of chlorine would chemically combine with 3.4 moles of sodium.

Later in the lesson I accompanied Marisole to her group. However, Victoria began to interact with students in that zone of the classroom and when a student from the other side of the classroom called my name, I moved to help him. After a minute or so I approached the group of students Victoria had worked with earlier. This group consisted of students who had recently missed one or more lessons and needed special assistance. I was impressed with the ways in which Victoria had interacted with this group and was interested to see how they could fare with this more difficult exercise.

As I approached the "absentee" group, the tape shows that Arlene, a female, was firmly in charge of the group (Figure 3.3). She and the others in the group were writing down formulae for the reactants. Arlene kept events moving and when they had gotten the formulae down, she explained what was to be done in a procedural sense, emphasizing that the first task for the group was to balance the equation. My presence was a structure—and therefore a resource for action—that Arlene soon appropriated to help them balance the equation. This form of structure, evidently, arises from the new forms of social relation made available in and for the group through my presence. The following exchanges between Arlene, other students, and me are indicative of a group that had a shared focus and was willing to collaborate to get the task accomplished while learning chemistry.

Episode 3.1

Time	Name	Utterance	Actions
12:18	Arlene	Now. Doctor Tobin. Please help balance this.	
12:20	Tobin	Yeah. Sure.	Audible conversa-

		I always start from the left	tion in the back-
12:27	Arlene	Hmm. Hm.	ground from an-
12:28	Tobin	=Yeah	other group.
12:29	Arlene	You got one. Hmm. It go right here.	
12:32	Victoria	So, I fully expect an answer in thirteen minutes	
12:36	Rachel	In how many minutes?	
12:39	Arlene	That's not for us. That's for um ...	
	Markist	=That group.	
	Arlene	=Hmm. Hm.	
12:48	Arlene	That's right. Right?	
12:49	Tobin	=Yeah. See the thing you've got here is two lots of NH_4. So you're probably gonna need two lots of NH_3. Just to get you started. Okay?	Victoria asks the group (13:08): "Heh. When you guys are ready? Rachel says
13:00	Tobin	So. That's lookin' . . . that's lookin' pretty good right now. So what's the next thing you're going to look at? Hydrogens. No. Hydrogens. [whistles faintly] Over to the left. There you go.	"Mm," and reaches out to accept a white-board (13:21) onto which she will eventually write the solution to the problem.
13:09	Arlene	Six.	
13:10	Tobin	Six plus	
13:13	Arlene	Huh	
13:13:15	Rachel	You forgot [one	
13:14	Tobin	[Six plus	
13:14:15	Arlene	Another two	
13:15	Tobin	=Is eight. Add two. What've you got over here?	
13:18	Arlene	Two and awright. You got . . . only. You add two right? Two and five?	
13:22:15	Tobin	=Right	
13:25	Arlene	And two here. Awright. That's balanced.	
13:27	Tobin	So. You've got the hydrogens [sorted out	
13:28	Arlene	[it's balanced. Right?	
13:30	Tobin	So. Now what about sulfates?	

13:31	Arlene	They fine
13:32	Tobin	Yep. You're fine then.
13:33:15	Rachel	Can I see?
13:35	Tobin	You're set to trot.

As I left the group for a moment I encouraged them not to just write the balanced equation onto the whiteboard but to ensure that everyone in the group understood the chemistry involved as well as Arlene. My comments acknowledged Arlene's role in this situation as a leader who understood what she was doing and supported her role as a peer tutor. Arlene quickly stepped forward and began to explain what she had done to her peers who leaned forward to listen. As Arlene explained, Rachel inscribed the equation on to the whiteboard and the group moved on to solve the exercise concerning limiting reagents.

The interactions of these students with me are an example of several important features of this cotaught lesson. As I had noted from earlier studies in urban science classrooms, sporadic attendance of urban youth is a challenge for teachers and learners that often cannot be addressed without significant rupturing of fluent enactment of the curriculum. Victoria's initiative in creating a separate group for these students allowed her to catch them up on what they needed to know in order to be productive and then the group showed its persistence, mutual focus and solidarity in collaborating to solve all problems. They requested my presence and then used the available relation as a scaffold to correctly balance an equation. Even though there were inputs from adjacent fields, they processed them, responded orally, and yet maintained focus on balancing the equation. In so doing they shared the turns at talk and showed their knowledgeability of chemistry in their written solutions to the problem and nonverbal actions as they followed the flow of the coordinated verbal interactions and inscriptions.

CHECKING UNDERSTANDING

My analysis of the videotape showed that, as I moved across the front of the classroom, Victoria, Alex, and Jessica enacted similar roles to mine. Each was interacting one on one with students, explaining the details of the exercise in relation to the equation, making sure that students knew how to read the equation in terms of the molar ratios involved in a chemical reaction. There was a high incidence of the coteachers moving about the classroom and being recruited by students to lend a hand with the chemistry associated with the task. Commonly the assistance was preceded by a brief interaction with the student who needed help, several short verbal exchanges to identify the focus for the help, and a lengthy explanation of an aspect of chemistry. The one-on-one nature of the structure allowed students to listen attentively and when appropriate to test their understandings with an extended explanation to the teacher.

When I reached Darnel, he expressed confidence in understanding the chemistry in a standard way and explained his solution to the exercise (Figure 3.4). As it happened, I noticed that his answer was not consistent with standard chemistry and I quickly interacted with him in a process that allowed him to obtain and understand the answer that we coteachers wanted him to arrive at.

Episode 3.2

Time (s)	Name	Utterance
08.0	Darnel	I said that Na salt is in excess.
10.0	Tobin	Right
11.0	Darnel	=Cl is limiting.
12.0	Tobin	=You got it.
12.5	Darnel	=and then we had the Cl . . .
13.5	Tobin	=can you do the reasoning okay?
16.0	Darnel	Yeah.
17.0	Darnel	Then we had to, um, how many moles are produced of NaCl. And we started with four point seven moles of Na . . .
24.0	Tobin	=right.
25.0	Darnel	U::m. And then we had a conversion.
27.0	Tobin	But this was limiting ((points to Cl_2 in the equation)).
28.5	Darnel	Yeah.
29.0	Tobin	=Yeah. Right.
29.5	Darnel	This, this u::m chloride was limiting so I did that. So I put chloride with chlorine.
37.0	Tobin	No::hohoho.
38.5	Darnel	=No.
39.0	Tobin	No::hoohoohoo.
40.0	Darnel	=no!
43.5	Tobin	No. If the other one's limiting. (2.0) If the other one's limiting then that's what you're gonna get. Right?
48.0	Darnel	(2.0) Oh. It surely is. Yeah. Yeah. Yeah.
50.0	Tobin	=Not. Not one point seven. Twice one point seven moles. So three point four moles of sodium chloride. Now do you get that?
62	Tobin	(5.0) Well . . .
62	Darnel	=Ye::ah [coz I understand what you sayin'. I understand. I understand.
63	Tobin	[No. You can figure it out.

The interaction with Darnell is salient because when I approached him he was confident that he had the correct answer. However in the coteaching setup I was able to probe to see the extent to which he understood his answer. I assumed that since Darnell was the student in the class who best understood chemistry, he would articulate the standard answer; therefore, I assumed that when he claimed to have

Figure 3.4. Darnell provides a rationale for his solution to the first exercise while Ken and his peers follow closely.

the correct answer he probably did. However, he had the wrong idea and his faulty understandings were revealed in the analysis of the tape. When I first approached Darnell he was looking bored with the class and during the interaction with me his facial features showed interest, engagement and attentiveness. He was focused on the exercise and wanted to understand the chemistry and get the right answer. His interactions with me were short, poignant, and successful. The above transcription shows that the interactions were even handed in the sense that Darnell and I shared the turns at talk and the amount of talk. It was apparent from his positive demeanor and facial expressions that Darnell enjoyed the intellectual engagement in this interaction and as I left him he looked very immersed in making entries in his notebook to reflect the conversation.

MANAGING TRANSITIONS

During the individualized and small-group structures and the associated transitions there was ample evidence of students setting a pace that was less than any of the coteachers might have wanted and occasional examples of students fooling around and distracting others. With only two exceptions none of the coteachers took time to discipline students. In each instance the coteachers were not emotionally worked up, as their prosody reveals: the interactions were brief, fluent, and there was no disruption to the flow of the lesson. For example, Alex took a little over two seconds of a transition to state "Now listen Joseph, stay with us or you can go someplace else." In other examples where students distracted others there was evidence of the students moderating the events in light-hearted ways that did not create widespread disturbance. In no instance was there a sustained period of disturbance due to off task behavior. As the coteachers moved about the classroom during the individualized and small-group structures they encouraged students to complete the exercise quickly and as necessary suggested alternative foci. In this class the students had primary responsibility for their participation and the efforts of the coteachers were directed toward managing the flow of participation and providing assistance to those who requested it.

EXPRESSIVE INDIVIDUALISM

Alex is a down to earth, let's get it done, high-energy teacher. He moves briskly about the classroom, gets to the point quickly, and provides many examples of expressive independence through his verve—body movements, including gestures, wiggles, sways and head movements. Also, he code switches frequently, using standard English and what the students fondly refer to as "hoodlish"—a form of expression that consists of a mix of English, some of the students' terms and metaphors, and his own crazy talk that almost has a childish flavor to it. The following transcription provides insights into these features of Alex's teaching as he finished up some whole-class teaching and asked for a change from whole-class to small-group structures.

Episode 3.3

Time (min)	Name	Utterance	Actions
6:28	Alex	What do I do first?	
6:29	Female	Change it to [moles.	
6:29:15	Class chorus	[moles.	
6:30	Alex	=Right. We can all do boompty boom and then we just go. Right? Let me write down now. Do me a favor. No. Let's . . . Yeah. Let's work in groups. Okay. So, mess up the chairs . . . you know, make the little islands of groupy group things. Right?	Alex points and motions with his hands to show the ways in which groups should be distributed in the room and arranged in a circle.

The above dialogue segued from the previous whole-class structure to one that became an impromptu small-group structure. The students initially showed their understanding of the process to follow and then Alex made an on the spot decision to allow them to work with others rather than have another individualized structure. Part of his plan in putting the students into small groups was that they would write their final solutions onto a small whiteboard, which then could be used in presenting the group solution to the whole class. In so doing he expanded the roles of students using a whiteboard to communicate their solutions to the rest of the class. His colloquial style (e.g., "islands of groupy group things") of addressing the students was a source of amusement and fun for the class and consolidated the student perspective concerning Alex: "he be cool" and "Alex, he the man." Alex's use of voice, verve, and gesture created enjoyment, which was visible on the faces of students who gave one another knowing looks and may have increased positive emotional energy and a sense of solidarity among class members. Alex exuded signs of affiliation with this class, signs that aligned him with students and thereby produced solidarity among the students and in this sense it is salient that he acted in ways to sustain his high-energy image of teacher many times in every lesson.

As the students moved into groups, Alex and Victoria wrote additional exercises on the board, and the other coteachers encouraged the students to quickly form their groups and start work. Although it is a small point, a striking feature on the videotape is just how alike Alex and Victoria appeared as they wrote the exercise on the board. The transition from the whole-class field to small groups also was an opportunity for the coteachers to interact with students, and in my case to check whether Marisole understood how conservation of mass was an important principle to invoke in her solution to the limiting reagents exercise. As Marisole moved to her group I asked her about it, and she replied affirmatively.

RESPECTING STUDENTS

As I moved about the classroom I encouraged students to remain involved and in cases when students had not finished the exercise or did not have their own copy, I pressed them to complete the task. On one occasion I put my hand on the shoulder of a male student. He cringed and I immediately remembered other instances where males did not like to be touched. Instead of avoiding the incident I apologized to the youth and said "You don't like me putting my hand on your shoulder do you. I am sorry." He replied in an agitated way and I briefly replied: "I'm cool. I didn't mean to offend you." My goal was to show I did not mean to be offensive, minimize the time spent on negative interactions—and move on quickly. I explained that I wanted to make sure that he also had a copy of the solution to the limiting reagents exercise. He pointed out that the written solution was his, making it clear to me that he had done his work. I said some encouraging words and quickly moved to encourage Marisole to design an exercise to test her knowledge of limiting reagents.

There are several salient aspects about this event, the first being that I knew that some students, especially African American males, do not like to be touched. When I had done so despite my previous experience, then it was because of a habitus in other cultural fields. That is, the present field was weakly bounded, allowing me to enact a different form of culture—with all the perils that this can give rise to, as we can see from the reaction of this youth. Second, from our research I had learned the folly of interacting in ways that produce asynchrony and negative emotions in students; touching African American youth is one of those forms of behavior that can lead to negative emotion and the associated asynchrony. Hence, I cut short the interactions about touching, offering an apology and expressly addressing respect, which operates within the African American urban community as akin to a currency. In this instance it is just as well that I did these things. He had satisfactorily completed his work and had assumed leadership within the group. If I had alienated him, the costs may have been more widespread than just his own disadvantage.

CHALLENGING STUDENTS

As we show in chapter 2, so much of what goes on in urban science classrooms involves technical approaches to getting correct answers. We do understand this to be the result of schooling, where grades are valued throughout the system at the expense of real understanding. It does not really matter what you know and how deeply you know it as long as you get a good grade. In the present case there was a real danger of learning how to balance equations and figure out how to find which reactant was limiting—without learning much chemistry. Accordingly, as I monitored what students had accomplished I was on the lookout for chances to see if they understood what they had done in terms of the chemistry and if there were ways to expand their knowledgeability through follow up exercises. Of course when I managed to steer students along different pathways I was sure to inform my coteachers so that they would support changes in direction and perhaps learn from my ways of doing and speaking about teaching.

Marisole had no idea what I meant by design a problem like the one you have just done. Accordingly, I created an exercise, which I referred to as the "Tobin challenge," in which hydrogen reacted with oxygen to produce water. As I explained the problem I talked about mixing the two gases and igniting them to produce a big boom. In describing the boom I raised my voice and threw up my hands in a clear example of expressive individualism. The bodily demonstration amused many students. As I did this I was reminded of Alex who often used his voice, verve, and gestures to produce forms of teaching that others experience as expressing a lot of energy. The exercise I developed was intentionally more difficult than the first one. Instead of answering in terms of moles I included an extra step of calculating the mass of the excess reagents and the products of the chemical reaction. After some cajoling Marisole and her adjacent peers got engaged intensively and I moved away to interact with others about the solution to the original exercise and encourage those who had finished to take a shot at the Tobin challenge (Figure 3.5).

Marisole was keen to finish solving the Tobin challenge and as soon as she had a solution she called my name and beckoned me to her desk. The following interactions resulted in a twenty-second episode.

Episode 3.4

Time (min)	Name	Utterance
2:39	Marisole	Here it is right here.
2:41	Tobin	Did you tell me what mass?
2:44	Marisole	Six point seven moles,

Figure 3.5. Marisole and her peers on either side accept the "Tobin challenge" and begin collaborating to produce a suitable answer.

2:45	Tobin	That's moles.
2:46	Marisole	Moles?
2:47	Tobin	Yeah. You gotta tell me what mass.
2:51	Marisole	(3.0) What mass?
2:52	Tobin	What is the mass of water?
2:54.5	Marisole	In grams or what?
2:56	Tobin	Yeah. What mass in grams?
2:56.6	Marisole	Change it from moles to grams.
2:58	Tobin	=Yeah. You've gotta now go from moles to gram. Yeah.

Just as Darnell seemed comfortable with the chemistry until I engaged him in an interaction, so too did Marisole seem adept at what she was doing until we talked about her solution. At this time it was apparent to me that she needed some scaffolding to have the resources needed to solve the exercise. I had a strong (professional) sense that she had the discrete knowledge but could not draw on it fluently to reach a solution that she felt comfortable with. Marisole knew that she had to translate the number of moles into mass. That is, she had a solution, but had not put it to the test to ascertain whether it met the specifics of the exercise nor whether it was viable. In part, this is the crux in teaching generally—students need act in order to see from success and failure whether they understand. But the tools available to them—e.g., a notebook or whiteboard—do not respond to an answer, leaving the students in limbo with respect to the correctness of their work. This is the reason why having two or more coteachers in the same class constitutes a form of social resource allowing to address the needs in the sense that there is someone who can assist them in evaluating the correctness of their solutions to tasks. Thus, in his *Designing Communities* (Roth, 1998), Michael writes about a fourth-grader who has filled in a page on a task requiring him to make equivalent fractions. But every answer was wrong. Michael gave him a computer with a mathematical modeling tool, which he had set up such that the student could test his answers. After a little while, the boy, who had used simple differences to answer a question such as

$$\frac{2}{3} = \frac{4}{?} \tag{3.2}$$

with 5 rather than the appropriate 6, the boy returned saying, "I figured it out. Whenever I double on top, I also need to double on the bottom." So the computer had talked back. In the present situation involving Marisole, my questions and explanations allowed her to retrieve relevant chemistry knowledge and arrive at a solution to the problem. However, without me being present, she would not have proceeded beyond the first stage of the solution, identifying the number of moles of water produced.

HUDDLING WITH COLLEAGUES

During my interactions with Marisole, just prior to her successfully coming up with the correct mass of water, Alex joined me at her desk. We huddled, leaving Marisole for a moment to reflect on her solution, as I quickly explained to Alex what we were doing and why we were doing it. As I had done previously with Jessica I explained in depth with the hope that Alex would at some later stage create a challenge to more fully engage all students in the class. During this particular huddle we addressed the "Tobin challenge," why the first exercise took the form it did, and what we would accomplish in the next exercise. However, the next exercise had not yet been assigned.

The other coteachers noticed what I was doing too. Later in the lesson Victoria issued a similar challenge to some students. She adapted the idea I had used earlier and even had a hint of my humor as she challenged the students to complete the first exercise and then address the *Victoria challenge* all within a short period of time. Her appropriation of the challenge idea is an example of how a teaching move disseminated to a coteacher within the same lesson, just as her innovation in creating the absentee group was a structure that expanded my coteaching roles. While students on my side of the classroom had engaged in the "Tobin challenge," others in the class had attempted "Victoria's challenge."

PEER TUTORING

A feature of cotaught lessons is an increased incidence of students teaching their peers. As they receive help, similar to the assistance received by Marisole and Darnell, there is a willingness to share what they have learned with peers and for peers to seek help from those who appear to have the knowledgeability. Based on what Darnell said about peer tutoring in a cogenerative dialogue (chapter 5), it appears as if he and others in the class enjoy peer tutoring and regard it as a way to not only

Figure 3.6. Darnell acts as a peer tutor for Abdul, pointing out a flaw in his logic.

assist those who need help but also to help themselves by learning science in deeper ways. This was not the first time we have found out about this particular cultural feature among African American students. Natasia and her peers from the biology class featured in chapter 2 have told us about the value they draw from peer tutoring and peer interactions.

Soon after my interactions with Darnell (described previously) the camera shows him interacting seriously with Abdul—explaining to him where Abdul had slipped up in his reasoning to a problem (Figure 3.6). Significantly, Darnell became a peer tutor to one of his peers who, like him, was among the higher achieving chemistry students in the class. This was a familiar pattern in the one-on-one interactions of this classroom. As one of the coteachers interacted with a student, others eavesdropped and occasionally contributed to the interaction. After the coteacher moved away it was common for one or more students to interact with the student who had been engaged with a coteacher, to learn what he or she could from a peer. Hence, in individualized structures, tutoring was a common role undertaken by the coteachers and the students, especially those who had been the recipients of help.

A feature of the individualized field was the amount of tutoring that occurred. At the far end of the classroom Marisole was tutoring the student adjacent to her. She had finished the exercise and so too had most students in this part of the room, with the exception of Esther, who was experiencing significant difficulties in balancing the equation. After I had assisted her to arrive at a solution to the exercise, Esther reluctantly admitted she was lost. She had limited proficiency in English and was struggling with making sense of the English and the chemistry. I asked if she would like Darnell to assist her to understand and when she nodded in approval, I asked him to be her peer teacher. As Darnell tutored Esther I briefly huddled with Jessica (one of the new teachers [see Figure 3.3]), explaining how and why I suggested that Darnell tutor Esther and reviewing the difficulty I had in explaining limiting reagents to her. As her university supervisor, my goal was for Jessica to understand the rationale for peer tutors and perhaps to use tutors in a similar way when opportunities arose. My belief was that both the tutee and the tutor benefit from peer tutoring.

METALOGUE ABOUT COTEACHING

Metalogue literally means a speech *between* two acts of a play; Gregory Bateson appropriated the term to denote explanatory conversations that in form, structure, or manner convey not only something about the problem being discussed but also transcend the problem leading to new forms of understanding. In turn, we have appropriated the term to describe the conversations that make sense of research situations but do not force us to take a singular authorial position. Rather, metalogues, like cogenerative dialogues, allow us to theorize events that we have experienced together all the while providing a resource for articulating the plurality of descriptions and theories different individuals evolve in and through the singularity of lived experience.

Michael: In this account of coteaching from your perspective, I can see the classroom through the eyes of a teacher familiar with students and his fellow teachers. It is the perspective of someone who is sure of himself and who does not wobble because of insecurities. You move from situation to situation, from one field to another, apparently without trepidation. You appear to know what a teacher needs to know—that a student knows or does not know some chemistry or that a student needs help and what appropriate help looks like. Others might classify such knowledge as pedagogical knowledge and content pedagogical knowledge, through which your apparent content knowledge comes to be enacted in situationally relevant ways.

Ken: As you are well aware, my teaching of urban students floundered during my initial "solo" attempts. As I explain in chapter 2, coteaching provides me with structures to re-learn how to teach *these* students in *this* place. Over many semesters of coteaching I learned to teach fluently and address the needs of learners, recognizing what they knew and could do, and creating structures to expand individual and collective agency. I think we do well not to think of this as pedagogical content knowledge because, as cultural enactment, good teaching is not something that a teacher "possesses" in some way that is disconnected from the field and its structures . . .

Michael: so that good teaching, in part, comes from and is embodied in the arrangement of the field and its structures, a form of distributed cognition of teaching.

Ken: To me, effective teaching involves a collective and shared responsibility for acting in ways that sustain dynamic structures that expand the agency of the self and others.

Michael: I agree with your hesitation to ascribe positive classroom learning environments to knowledge somehow lodged between the ears of a teacher. Lessons always involve the cooperation of teacher(s) and students. The fallacy of the concepts of content pedagogical knowledge and pedagogical knowledge is that they seek explanations for events in teachers as if they were the cause of what happens in a classroom. One of the things I noted while initially reading your account of the lesson is the quite different tone it has when compared to my account of the monohybrid and dihybrid lesson. Thus, your account is "forward," clearly agential, apparently without the hesitations and trepidations that are apparent in my own account. Although you suggest in the previous chapter that this may be the result of my unfamiliarity with situation, students, and teacher, it may actually go beyond that. It may be that my way of being is marked to a greater degree by the hesitations that come with solicitude and the fragility of social life. I am saying this, because while doing research interviews, I experience similar trepidations, which, as I write in chapter 2, may be the result of transference and countertransference, where I read my own anxieties in the way others act toward me.

Ken: You certainly have a good point, though I wonder how things would be if you were in the class day after day as I have been. These students would realize what a wonderful resource you are, how well intentioned you actions are and that you are there for them. You would become a sign of a committed teacher who is knowledgeable and willing to learn from the students and their perspectives on how well the science lessons, as they are enacted, meet their unfolding needs. My experience suggests they would accept you as their teacher and in a reciprocal way, assign you the respect you assign to them. At the heart of what it takes to be successful is a level of awareness that you cannot have control over these students, and that building a sense of collective and an affiliation with the class are central to good teaching and learning.

Michael: As I reflect on this lesson, it comes to my mind that science education researchers rarely if ever talk about, describe, and theorize the various emotional states and stances that we experience while coteaching specifically and teaching generally. In fact, one of the positive aspects of coteaching is the sense of being in it *with* another person, which decreases the fear of failure and lost opportunities. Because we know that there is someone else who may pick up when there is an opportunity for enriching students' learning experiences, we are less hesitant and concerned with making mistakes; and the less hesitant and concerned with mistakes we are, the more we tend to act appropriately and the fewer mistakes we tend to make. This, in turn, may foster a self-confident stance, which mediates what we do to lead to fewer mishaps, oversights, and breakdowns issuing from our actions. That is, there is a production–reproduction cycle at work concerning self-confidence, according to self-confident productions lead to the reproduction of self-confidence.

Ken: In the vignettes included in this chapter there are numerous coteachers and as such the agencies of the coteachers and students are greatly expanded, as are the action possibilities. Hence, some of the coteachers could look for signs of students either breaking down or faltering in some ways. Being able to provide teaching on an as needed basis allows students to feel successful, stay focused, and receive support for appropriate action. The incidence of misbe-havior was less than occurs in solo lessons and there was no anxiety (that I experienced) that things would get out of hand. Accordingly, the coteachers could act in ways to create solidarity through successful interactions, focus and fluency.

Michael: I am also reflecting about the coteaching in Philadelphia from the begin-ning, when I trailed you to live appropriate behavior at your elbow. I did not know how to behave in the hallways of the inner-city schools we were visit-ing and teaching, and I did not know how to interact with the students, many of whom were towering over me. But as I trailed you, I began to interact with the same individuals: it was as if I could see that one can interact with this student and how to best interact with him or her. Over time I felt more at ease and was able to interact with students even without having been introduced to them by you. This, then, shows how coteaching allows us to become familiar with a teaching situation without having a fear of failure and, as a result, to be more confident about one's interactions.

Ken: I am glad you raised this. That day helped me to understand that a person can learn from another by trailing them. I had taken a stance that the best way to learn to teach was through peripheral coteaching from the very outset. You helped me to understand that close watching was an important way to see what gets done in this place and how it is sometimes done. Before getting started you had to experience praxis close up. Trailing is far different that sit-ting on the side and jotting down notes into a yellow notepad. By trailing you were part of the lesson, and your presence allowed you to experience the field as a legitimate, yet quite peripheral participant—setting the stage for more central ways of being involved as the unfolding structures allowed.

Michael: Your descriptions also make it clear how important familiarity with con-tent and content pedagogy is. In chapter 2, when Chuck and Andrea use some term I am unfamiliar with or cannot clearly hear what they say, I immediately and without reflection move into a more cautious stance. That is, I end up acting cautiously, because I do not want to step forward and break the flow; I become hesitant not only when the concept is unfamiliar but also when I do not clearly hear and where asking to have the term rearticulated might be ex-perienced as a break—though there are situations where such asking is quite normal and not experienced as an interruption.

Ken: Some of the salient differences in the vignettes here compared to those in chapter 2 are that the coteachers were all welcomed overtly by Alex, the resi-dent teacher and his students. There was no hesitance on the parts of any of the coteachers to acknowledge the legitimacy of the others. It would have been exactly the same had you been there. Alex and the class wanted more coteachers and never questioned their unfolding practices—though from time to time huddles were needed for regrouping. Also, we all were in field to a greater extent with chemistry than we were in the biology classes.

Michael: The episodes you articulate for us in this chapter provide evidence that coteaching, above all, means dynamically interacting with the situation as a whole, drawing on the always contingent, historically emerging possibilities for acting. There is a potential danger in this, namely when an individual teacher interprets coteaching to mean laissez faire and relying on others. Coteaching requires being flexible all the while enacting co-responsibility for the lesson as a whole, even in the event that another teacher does something that I—singular plural—presently disagree with. In chapter 2, this occurs when I step forward at precisely the moment when the lesson appears to me emphasizing rote learning rather than conceptual understanding.

GETTING STARTED WITH COGENERATIVE DIALOGUES

In the first three chapters we examine coteaching as a means of learning to teach. We see that coteachers teach together and become like the other in numerous ways, thereby reproducing certain teaching practices. Coteachers become like one another in the ways in which they talk, gesture, observe the class, use space and time, access materials, and interact with one another and students. Depending on what it is that is learned, teachers may or may not be aware of what they have learned. Furthermore, changes in teaching and prevailing practices may not benefit all learners. For example, coteachers may learn from one another to shout at students to maintain their attention; even though teachers shouting might intimidate some students and truncate their participation. As a precaution against teaching being enacted in ways that are non-optimal, it is desirable for teachers and students to use cogenerative dialogues to identify and review what seems to work and what does not, especially practices and schema that disadvantage participants. Good starting points are discussions about any resistance participants encounter in their efforts to learn, contradictions they experience, and concerns they have about the roles and associated divisions of labor among participants, the rule structures for the class, and their access to the resources available to support learning. For example, in this chapter we describe how two coteachers regrouped the students to improve their classroom management. In a cogenerative dialogue Abdul points out how his new group was dysfunctional. An agreement was then reached to allow Abdul to rejoin the peers with whom he had previously worked productively.

Teachers can benefit from participation in cogenerative dialogues by hearing from others about their teaching—what works and what does not, and especially identifying practices about which the teacher is not aware. The perspectives of others become objects for reflection on what happens and possible ways to improve learning environments. It is not just the descriptions of teaching and learning practices that are of value to teachers but also the interpretive frameworks associated with them. As others explain what happens and whether what happens supports learning, teachers become aware of the schema used by participants in making sense of their lifeworlds. Furthermore, in small groups, teachers can listen attentively to others, thereby showing them the respect of dealing with what they have to say substantively. When teachers listen and make substantive comments they exhibit signs of respect for students and of being caring and responsive. In this way teachers not only show their respect for others but also earn their respect. Furthermore, by listening carefully and interacting about what is said substantively the teachers and students produce chains of successful interactions and synchrony among the interaction participants. If there is a focus on making interactions synchronous and successful, then it is more likely that a cogenerative dialogue will yield cogenerated outcomes in the form of resolutions about changes to be made in the enacted curriculum and responsibilities for enacting these changes in the classroom. Hence, the outcomes of cogenerative dialogues can be shared commitments to changing the structures of the classroom and thereby expanding individual and collective agency of participants. If those who participate in a cogenerative dialogue can negotiate a shared commitment to all resolutions then there seems a greater likelihood that the unfolding practices in a classroom will be anticipated by them, become part of successful interaction chains, and enhance progress toward enacting desired changes.

Although cogenerative dialogues originated in the context of coteaching, the most common form now involves a resident teacher meeting with two to three students from her class for the purpose of identifying and resolving contradictions. In this chapter we describe the different ways in which cogenerative dialogues have been used, beginning with their historical origins, and the underlying theoretical frameworks we have used to develop this particular type of field. We begin with a conversation in which we lay out the historical development of cogenerative dialogues.

THE EMERGENCE OF COGENERATIVE DIALOGUES

Ken: When I came to the University of Pennsylvania in 1997 I inherited a project that Fred Erickson had commenced whereby each new teacher was assigned two students from the urban high school classes in which they were teaching to help them to answer the question "how to better teach students like me." Based on the contingent selection advocated by Egon Guba and Yvonna Lincoln (1989) in *Fourth Generation Evaluation*, I required new teachers to identify a student from whom they felt they could learn most and then to select as the second student one who is as different from the first as possible. At the end of a lesson the students would meet with the new teacher and others who might have experienced the lesson (e.g., the resident teacher, university supervisor, school administrator) to discuss what had happened and how to improve the quality of teaching.

Michael: It is interesting how we ground the origins of some praxis in different ways, that is, how we begin our narratives of a beginning in very different ways. I began this project by rifling through old files to see when I had used the term cogenerative for the first time. I know that at some point in time, I read a chapter on participatory action research (Eldon & Levin, 1991). It was there that I had read the term "cogenerative dialogue" for the first time. However, when I began using the term later, it was somehow linked to the work we were doing in the context of coteaching. After teaching lessons together with elementary school teachers, I sat down with them for a debriefing about the events we had just lived and witnessed. At some point, I began to talk and write about coteaching. Searching for a term describing debriefing (which always occurred in a collegial way) accompanying the practice of coteaching, encompassing the collective and generative nature of theorizing praxis together, the term "cogenerative" must have emerged. I vaguely recall that I had tossed around the term "praxeology" (literally "talk about praxis") for denoting theory about practice generated by practitioners. But I did not want these praxeology sessions to be asymmetrical with respect to whose descriptions and explanations were valued. If the practitioner knows praxis differently, researchers interested in understanding why practitioners act in the way they do have to participate in praxis; praxeology then requires the input of all participants otherwise it will fail to account for how they experience praxis.

Ken: We definitely got the term from you—but first came praxeology. Following my visit to your research group in Canada we began to write about praxeology and when I returned to the University of Pennsylvania we used that term to describe the group discussions over practice. Later, when you were again at Penn you introduced me to the term cogenerative dialogue and for a while we used both terms in our descriptions of coteaching.

Michael: My records show that the earliest mention of cogenerative dialogues dates back to an article that you and I published. That piece actually carried the name for our method in its title: "{Coteaching|Cogenerative Dialoguing} as Praxis of Dialectic Method." That is, already around 1998, we must have had the sense that the two fields, coteaching and cogenerative dialoguing, stand in a dialectical relationship and have the potential to enhance each other.

Ken: Over time cogenerative dialogue was preferred and we rarely use praxeology these days. Even though first-time hearers might regard both terms as jargon, new teachers accepted cogenerative dialogues and understood their purposes to a greater extent than praxeology. After a lesson conversations involving the coteachers and selected students occurred. There was a tendency to regard the students as experts, listen carefully to their advice, and act on it.

Michael: This is probably to be expected since you started with a motto that was something like, "How do you teach kids like me?" The evolution from that point to one in which all voices are heard is one we can learn from.

Ken: The move toward building collective agreements for what needs to change in the classroom and responsibility for enacting agreed-to changes began when our research in urban science classes occurred in the same schools as the two in which the new teachers in the teacher education program at the University of Pennsylvania were assigned to. As a researcher you joined the regularly scheduled after class discussion and applied a theoretical lens of activity theory to our practices. In response to me asking Andrea Zimmermann why she had permitted a transition between activities to be so long you retorted: "If it was so long why didn't you shorten it?" It was at that moment that I realized the centrality of collective responsibility for the coteaching and also for the outcomes of discussion in the cogenerative dialogues.

Michael: I remember the incident clearly (see chapter 2), because we reflected a lot on the experience in Andrea's classroom and even wrote several articles involving different stakeholders such as Andrea, Natasia, and the resident teacher Chuck. I made the comment and then felt bad because it could easily be heard (interpreted) as a snide remark.

Ken: Others in the group may have thought of it in this way, however, you and I have a long history of scholarship and I am on the lookout to listen and learn when we interact in forums such as this. I was enacting praxis in ways that reflected traditional asymmetries between university professors, resident teachers, and new teachers. Traditionally it was the university professor who claimed authority in discussions such as this debriefing—a forerunner to cogenerative dialogues.

Michael: We talked a lot about the fact that if coteaching was to be symmetric, that is, if we had committed to concretely realize a collective responsibility for the learning of the students through our individual actions, we needed to act when we saw that something did not work and talk about the incident later.

Ken: This is an important point. We have now fine tuned the goals and roles of participants in cogenerative dialogues to emphasize the cogeneration of collective agreements on what is happening, contradictions that occur, and ways in which contradictions can be removed—either by eliminating them or increasing their incidence.

Michael: Then, of course, once we reified our practice through the denotation of cogenerative dialoguing, there was a need to theorize this practice itself.

Ken: The use of theory to make sense of cogenerative dialogues enabled us to iteratively consider an expanded array of potential outcomes and to explore relationships between individuals in relation to the collective and the manner in which agency|structure relationships unfolded. We realized many different possible outcomes from cogenerative dialogues and expanded the range of applications so that cogenerative dialogues could occur within lessons, immediately after lessons, and could actually involve whole classes or small subsets of the participants in a class.

Michael: It is a powerful idea that participants from different stakeholder groups can identify and discuss contradictions, leading to agreed-to ways to reduce the contradictions and assume a share in the responsibility for enacting agreed-to-changes. Varying the spaces and times of occurrence, and the numbers of participants provides different forms of structure for cogenerative dialogues; including different motives for holding them in the first place.

Ken: Initially the changes were minimal. For example, we had observed that *huddles* occurred routinely as a part of coteaching, that is, teachers got together during the lesson to have a brief exchange about what to do next. Coteachers would come together to touch base with one another and check in on what was to be done next. It reminded us of the huddle in American football—hence the name. We recognized these as a form of cogenerative dialogue that occurred within a science lesson. Initially huddles involved coteachers, but now we were able to see the wisdom of convening cogenerative dialogues within lessons and expanding the number and types of participant. At first our extensions were to the idea of huddles and there was an increased incidence of huddles that occurred for short periods of time, usually while students were involved in small-group or individualized tasks. Huddles were quite short and typically, though not always, did not involve students. However, a new form of cogenerative dialogue that did involve students occurred within class time and took the place of the regular curriculum.

Michael: In a sense, you pushed the idea of cogenerative dialoguing to make a version of it part of the coteaching praxis itself. The idea then was to no longer wait for talking about what to do next, but to get together when there was a need to make sense of what was going on and what ought to happen next right then and there. In this sense, then, this form of cogenerative dialoguing is a collective version of what educators have come to know as "reflection *in* practice," though it would have been better to denote reflection *on* practice because all reflection requires a removal from the praxis of teaching itself. Even if termed to be *in* practice, this reflection is very different from what I now think of as *participative thinking* to denote what and how practitioners think while doing what the ongoing activity calls for. In a huddle, my participative thinking is typical for reflection *on* the lesson rather than being thinking *for* the lesson. But then in our work, we extended cogenerative dialoguing from involving teachers and a small number of student representatives (usually two or three), to involving the teachers and the entire class.

Ken: Whole-class cogenerative dialogues began as an extension of the more traditional form in which two student researchers met with coteachers to identify and resolve contradictions and cogenerate new rules, roles and resolutions. We decided that the two students could bring the cogenerative dialogue to the whole class, using a computer and projector to present video vignettes that showed the contradictions and then allowing whole-class discussion to afford all participants considering what the small group had considered and decided. The whole-class conversations then became a field for collective decisions to emerge within a context in which respectful interactions can occur, with an understanding that no voice is privileged and it is safe to make critical statements about others as long as the interactions are respectful and free of malicious intent; the goal being to improve the quality of science education.

Michael: So cogenerative dialoguing really has become a particular form of praxis of method in a triple sense. First, and perhaps most importantly, it has become a means for all stakeholders in a situation to deal with contradiction and conflict and to design changes themselves rather than waiting for policies and recommendations from researchers. Second, it constitutes an alternative to interviewing teachers about their experiences; that is, we generate data first by coteaching and then together by discursively evolving understandings of what happened. Third, it constitutes a concrete situation in which to generate theory as part of research.

Ken: Cogenerative dialogues also can be thought of as a central component of Ann Brown's (1992) *design experiment*, in which an experimental design is changed, even while it is being executed, for the purpose of providing the best education possible. What is unique about cogenerative dialogue as a curriculum evaluation and improvement tool is that the responsibility for improving a curriculum and enacting it successfully is collectively assumed and when the curriculum is enacted the students "have the back" of the teacher and vice versa. Accordingly, following each cogenerative dialogue agreed-to changes are enacted—subsequently; the extent to which the enacted curriculum produces successful learning outcomes is reviewed in cogenerative dialogues. As I see it, the infusion of cogenerative dialogues into design experiments increases the potential of design experiments to catalyze and sustain curricular improvements.

STRUCTURING COGENERATIVE DIALOGUES

We consider the setting of cogenerative dialogues as a field, a site for particular forms of cultural enactment. The boundaries of fields are porous, allowing culture produced in other fields to be enacted during cogenerative dialogues, and for culture produced in cogenerative dialogues to be enacted in the classroom field and elsewhere. Fields are structured; that is, they contain resources (social, symbolic, material, and cultural) that are appropriated and used as participants interact to meet individual and collective goals. The structures are dynamic, reflecting the membership of the cogenerative dialogue group, the rules and goals established by participants, and the practices enacted by participants. The agency, or power to act, of participants is dialectically related to the structure of the field. For example, if the participants in cogenerative dialogue decide to draw on a video clip from a previously shared lesson, this clip is a resource that structures what the participants say and do, and this is likely different from a session involving the same participants when they do not have the clip available. Each description or explanation offered by one of the participants becomes a resource for others, who react to, act on, or reinterpret what has been said. These actions and interpretations, in turn, become resources for the next speaker and other participants, both offering new possibilities for interpretive comments and constraining what can be said. For example, most readers will have heard someone say during a meeting, "I can't follow this act" and then say what he or she says. In this situation, the participant actively articulates the constraint experienced in the face of the previous speaker's comments. Accordingly, as participants enact practices, what they do expands and truncates the agency of others. Hence an important motto for participants in a cogenerative dialogue is to act in the interest of others. That is, as coteaching, cogenerative dialoguing is built not only on the ontology of the *with the other* but also on an ontology of the *for the other*—in both instances, the production and reproduction of solidarity is an outcome and objective.

Membership

Since the purpose of cogenerative dialogues is to listen and learn from the participants it is important to have a small enough group to permit all participants to speak and be heard. Accordingly, the number of student participants was initially set at two or three. We identify student participants who differ significantly from

Figure 4.1. Michael, Andrea, Shawan, Chuck, Ken, and Natasia (from front left around the table) participate in the cogenerative dialoguing session following the lesson on monohybrids and dihybrids (chapter 2).

one another in ways that are salient to the class. For example, in a diverse urban class the salient factors might be achievement level, race, and gender. Selecting to maintain diversity among the cogenerative dialogue participants is an important criterion. In this case, if the first selected student is a low achieving, White female we might consider selecting as the second participant a high achieving Black male. Often the selection is constrained by availability since we schedule cogenerative dialogues to occur as soon after class as possible, when some of the students we would most like to interact with have limited availability. In selecting particular students, we also want to be certain that students do not feel obligated but want to participate for the greater good of improving learning and teaching in their classrooms. All participants need to feel that participating in cogenerative dialogue sessions provide opportunities for actively changing their life conditions rather than merely being subject to them. To be useful and to be experienced as such requires participants to be and feel in control over their life condition, specifically schooling in the cases we are concerned with here. The experience of control over life conditions and the experience of the expansion of this control both have high emotional valence, which in turn is important for how students participate in producing and reproducing schooling. It is also a central component of the identity they come to enact situationally and of the identity narratives that they can build as a consequence to articulate images of self.

If university personnel, such as teacher educators or researchers, are involved in the class, they are invited to participate in the cogenerative dialogues (e.g., Figure 4.1). Similarly, we encourage school administrators to coteach, rather then observe and evaluate from the side, and when they do, we encourage them to participate in cogenerative dialogues. When conversations occur about shared experiences a greater number of stakeholders is involved—new teachers, resident teachers, university supervisors, and the (self-) selected students. The advantages of including stakeholders such as school administrators and university professors is that they are well placed institutionally to act in ways that mitigate some of the contradictions identified in cogenerative dialogues. Teachers and students can get frustrated when they agree to remove contradictions and then find they cannot produce the structures needed to do so—because the practices of others, from other fields (e.g., principal, school board), are structuring the classroom field. Policies and rules are good examples of structures that can be produced in fields such as the main office or in a university and then obligate participants in a classroom to enact curricula in ways that produce contradictions (e.g., requiring a test to be administered before a given unit of study is completed).

Christopher Emdin and Ed Lehner (2006) describe how the solidarity associated with participation in cogenerative dialogues spreads through successive grade levels of a school—producing a school-level solidarity theorized in the term of *cosmopolitanism*. The emergence of cosmopolitanism relates to the presence of multiple cogenerative dialogue groups throughout a school and across grade levels. This opens up the possibility for cogenerative dialogues about the shared experience of improving curricula through the use of cogenerative dialogues.

Since the participants in cogenerative dialogue are representatives of stakeholder groups it seems important to examine issues such as report back and dissemination to others about what is agreed-to in cogenerative dialogues. Accordingly, there was a trend in our work to create larger half-class and whole-class cogenerative dialogues. The students report to their peers on what was discussed and agreed-to in the smaller scale cogenerative dialogues. Video vignettes are used to project evidence of the patterns and contradictions and obtain buy-in from the class on the need to change. The most important issue we learned from these initial attempts is that cogenerative dialogue require collective buy-in and the realization that the ways in which participants in the cogenerative dialogue can assist each other in the classroom when efforts are made to enact changes. Just as cosmopolitanism involved scaling up solidarity to the whole-school level, the use of half-class and whole-class groups afford the emergence of commitment and affiliation within a larger collective. However, we find that scaling up is not the only productive way to go with cogenerative dialogues. There also is merit in reducing the size of cogenerative dialogues. Before exploring this issue in depth, we first address the ways in which rules structured cogenerative dialogues and expanded the individual and collective agencies of participants.

Rules

A key motive of cogenerative dialogues is to enact forms of culture that expand the agency of all participants and produce agreements on how to enact curricula differently in a classroom so as to afford improvements in the quality of teaching and learning. Hence in setting up cogenerative dialogues a rule structure is established to create forms of enactment that have a strong likelihood of producing the desired outcomes, in this case collective agreements and a sense of responsibility for enact-

GETTING STARTED WITH COGENERATIVE DIALOGUES

ing agreed-to changes in such events and phenomena as rules, roles, goals and access to resources. Since the participants tend to be different from one another in terms of how they are positioned in the classroom, we anticipate that on most issues there will be differences in perspective, which we do not regard as sources of error. In fact, because each individual is positioned differently—e.g., spatially (my physical space cannot be taken up by another person), institutionally, socially—he or she also is *dis*positioned, a term that we understand both literally and metaphorically. Accordingly, there is no intention to search for central tendencies in our research on cogenerative dialogues. We are interested in mapping individual trajectories over time and exploring the emergence of solidarity. On the basis of the agency|structure dialectic we know that to expand agency we should address the structure and after setting rules for the selection of participants we set other key rules, each with the purpose of expanding the agency of individuals and the collective. These rules both afford and constrain actions, whereby the constraints themselves are to be seen positively in the sense that they provide a resource for temporal continuity of the cogenerative dialogue field itself. The rules are designed such that they preserve the cogenerative nature of the praxis rather than allowing it to be dominated by any one individual or stakeholder group. In fact, the central idea of cogenerative dialoguing is to arrive at the articulation of common goals that reflect *common* interests rather than the formation of *partial* interests that inherently do not reflect the collective as a whole.

The first rule is that the talk should be shared among the participants. There are several aspects to this rule. The talk should be distributed equally among all participants in terms of the amount spoken and the number of turns of talk. Also, the sorts of talk should be similar—for example, equity should be evident in asking and answering questions, suggesting foci for discussion, and reacting to the suggestions of others. During cogenerative dialogues all participants have a shared responsibility for ensuring that the rules are enacted as intended. Hence when a person speaks, she should ensure that what she says relates to what was previously said, is pithy, and brings others into the conversation. That is, when a person takes a turn at talk the purpose is not just to be right or to compete with others—but it is to afford the participation of others and push toward common interests—i.e., the interests common to *all*—and a collective agreement. When verbal interaction occurs it should be successful in including others and edging toward consensus.

Part of successful interaction is to be an active listener, ensuring that by listening and interacting nonverbally in a synchronous way the speaker feels encouraged and develops a sense of contributing towards the collective motives of the group. Active listening can involve questions of the speaker to elaborate, clarify, and justify. In addition, a person from the group can sum up what she thought the previous speaker was saying—in effect seeking verification that she has it right. To reflect a common interest and common goal, no person should dominate conversation, successive turns at talking should be directly related to one another, and exchanges should be courteous. The main theme always should be "what is in it *for the other?*," a question as important as "What is in it for me?" In our praxis it became clear that if these conversations were to catalyze productive changes in the classroom, the participants would have to create new roles and an associated rule structure to support the new roles.

If cogenerative dialogues are to be productive it is important that a mutual focus is established from the outset. This is a role that can be shared from one cogenerative dialogue to the next—assuming responsibility for identifying some of the topics to be discussed and resolved collectively. Hence two participants can be identified to come prepared to create the foci for initial discussion during a cogenerative dialogue. One place to start is always whether or not what was tried in class as a result of the last cogenerative dialogue was successful—or at least the extent to which it was successful. Then any consequential contradictions arising from agreements from earlier cogenerative dialogues can be identified and efforts made to resolve them. One way we have tried to stimulate conversation is to use videotape to capture contradictions that become the starting points for cogenerative dialogues. These videotapes serve as objects of mutual focus. If one or two of the participants assume responsibility to bring some short video vignettes to focus discussion on contradictions encapsulated in the vignettes then there is a basis for consequential talk and the production of entrainment and solidarity. The contents of these videotapes thereby become both topic of talk and a ground that speakers can use to hold each other accountable for; they constitute a form of unavoidable and undeniable evidence. If such objects of mutual focus are absent, conversations can veer all over the place without an apparent goal for what is to be accomplished.

Power—the extent to which individuals can appropriate the resources of a field to impose their personal goals against the wishes of others (Kemper & Collins, 1990)—is an important concern in cogenerative dialogues. We do not understand power as an a priori category or resource, but a descriptive term that articulates a particular form of relation. Power is not inherent in a person—the same teacher may be deemed to be powerful in one class but powerless with respect to the events in another. One of the key rules we establish is to make it explicit that the playing field is flat during cogenerative dialogue, meaning that established hierarchies, such as those that apply to the classroom, do not apply here. Any participant can initiate and participate to attain collective motives and individual goals, as long as in so doing, she is respectful of others (i.e., while earning respect she shows respect to others), is aware of the need to afford others' active participation, and does not turn-shark or truncate others' participation. Because one of the purposes of cogenerative dialogue is to critically review the experiences of a shared lesson, the identification and dialoguing over sources of inequity in the classroom are salient; that is, participants make explicit when institutional differences between individuals are used as resources to produce power differentials; and possible changes to cultural enactment are explored. Accordingly, the dialogue should capture descriptions of what happens and associated contradictions of social life in classrooms, from the perspectives of each of the participants in a cogenerative dialogue. Theoretically, patterns and contradictions are regarded as coexisting and there is a realization that efforts to create and strengthen patterns by removing contradictions will also create fresh contradictions.

The search for contradictions can be enabled by awareness that, within a field, individuals will experience resistance as they enact culture, pursuing individual goals and collective motives. Resistance can be thought of in terms of breaches to fluent enactment of culture, truncation of agency, and failure to produce structures that would, if present, optimize fluent cultural enactment. Hence, the identification of examples of resistance and the associated contradictions are key steps in becoming aware of inequities and cogenerating suggestions for alternative structures (i.e., rules, roles, goals, structures).

The *dialectical relationship* between individual and collective can be explicit in cogenerative dialogues, because the relatively small size makes it more feasible to keep in mind the participation of others and their goals in relation to group motives. Saying that a relationship is dialectical means that the two articulated terms—here individual and collective—mutually presuppose each other and therefore cannot be separated analytically. It is not that individuals and the collective they constitute *inter*act, as the collective exists only *in* its individuals, but the individuals are explicitly oriented toward the collective. Each individual participant in a cogenerative dialogue group is a constituent of the group as a whole; but his or her actions are such that it produces and reproduces *this* form of social situation (cogenerative dialogue) rather than another form of social situation (including anarchy).

Two rules assist in keeping the individual|collective relationships a part of conscious practice within the field of cogenerative dialogues. First, within each cogenerative dialogue we insist that the group ask: "what have we cogenerated?" Second, we also insist that the group is explicit about adopting a shared responsibility for enacting agreed-to changes in subsequent classes. That is agreements from a cogenerative dialogue become objects for changing culture in the classroom; agreements to "have one another's backs" as efforts are made to enact changes with shared responsibility for success and failure. Hence, the teacher (or coteachers as the case might be) is not held solely responsible for the quality of teaching; and students (or a student) are not held solely responsible for learning. The collective responsibility for agreed-to changes from the cogenerative dialogue transfer to the classroom field and, in subsequent cogenerative dialogues, the extent to which collective agency occurred in the classroom can be a focus for critical dialogue.

CRITICAL PEDAGOGY

Within the context of coteaching, cogenerative dialogues are conversations about shared experiences of participating in the field. A cogenerative dialogue group might consist of one resident teacher, two new teachers, a head of department, two students selected for their differences from one another, and a university supervisor. An example of the roles of participants in cogenerative dialogues is typified in the following analysis in which the participants were the coteachers (Lisa and Jeannie), a researcher (Ken), and two students (Abdul and Cassandra). The two students were asked to participate because they were different from one another in terms of gender, ethnicity, level of success in the class, and career goals. Abdul, a male, was an immigrant from Pakistan, who was high achieving, wanted to pursue science at university, and headed toward a science-related career. Cassandra, an African American female, was a conscientious student who was frequently distracted by peers and struggled for success in science. Like Abdul she planned to attend university with the purpose of following a profession in the health sciences. Since the cogenerative dialogue occurred immediately after a lesson on protein synthesis, the students had to obtain permission to miss their physical education class in order to participate.

Shared Experiences

After an introductory discussion about what makes an effective teacher Ken focuses dialogue with the question "What about this class?" The students then assume central roles and in their contributions freely discuss peers, parents and other classes. Abdul refers to the value of labs in this class and his appreciation of the class being taught by coteachers. As one of the best science students in the school, Abdul makes clear his expectation for a demanding curriculum from which he can learn. Cassandra also comments on the relevance of the curriculum, how different it is from the science her mother studied at school, and how much of what she is learning is new and so much better taught than her other classes. During this dialogue the teachers are attentive to what the students say and they interact with them as equals. There is no hint of any of the participants having a privileged voice. Ken's role is that of an active listener and it is only when the dialogue seems to be too distant from the patterns of coherence and contradictions arising from the teaching and learning in this class that Ken asks: "So what are the next steps in this class? I really like the learning environment . . . but things could be better. So how could they be better?"

Possible Improvements

A highly interactive dialogue between the coteachers and the two students then unfolds. The conversation addresses the limited chalkboard space and below par computer resources and restricted access to them. The proportions of teacher and student talk in this part of the cogenerative dialogue are virtually equal. As possible solutions to these problems the group discusses the projection of images from a computer to a screen hung from the ceiling, an idea that is rejected because of violations of the fire code if screens are hung from the ceiling. Lisa then asks about the value of the handouts the coteachers are preparing to obviate the need for students to copy notes from the chalkboards. Both students agree that the handouts are of great value and a commitment is made to continue to prepare notes and worksheets for each class period. The associated problem of limited chalkboards also is discussed. The dialogue among the participants acknowledges that the physical layout of the classroom precludes an easy solution. Ken suggests that in an effort to resolve this problem we meet with the principal and charter coordinator. Quickly the group arrives at a consensus to request more chairs, a decision that prompts the coteachers to identify a potential problem of long transitions when students move from the chairs to the laboratory workstations. During this discussion there is an acknowledgement that the duration of transitions is now much shorter since the coteachers recently changed the composition of the work groups. The changing of work groups then emerges as a point of contention in the cogenerative dialogue.

Resolving Disadvantage

Jeannie queries, "How are the new groupings going?" Abdul immediately takes a turn at talk, beginning with a statement about how disadvantaged he is by his new group assignment. He shows in his explanations a deep understanding about himself as a learner and the ways in which he could learn from peers in productive groups. He describes his small group as dysfunctional, necessitating that he work alone. Cassandra quickly points out that the regroupings are necessary and work in her favor since she is now participating more consistently and learning more. After a highly interactive conversation a consensus is reached that the learning environments are better overall, but some group assignments, including Abdul's, need to change. The conversation flows from a discussion of groups to one of management and a comment that one day "it was as quiet as a mouse." Jeannie then quips, "there was a mouse!" The students and teachers laugh together at this allusion to the appalling conditions of the classroom, noting that rodents are too often seen scurrying across the floor. The quip segues to a lively discussion on the students' interests in dissection and an agreement to do dissections in the near future.

Fairness

The dialogue also addresses the reasons for students not consistently doing their homework in a satisfactory and timely fashion, even though their grades count on homework being completed. Both students are insistent that the coteachers create and enforce more stringent rules about doing homework. Such enforcement actions therefore are requested as structures that students request to better deal with the homework question, both constraining them to act in a certain way while also increasing their resources for timely completion. During the interactions it is clear that failure to do the assigned homework is regarded by the coteachers as a major issue on which they want help. The teachers and students interact continuously and Ken also contributes to a possible solution. There is a consensus that some students develop bad habits when rules are set and are not enforced. The extensive nature of the conversations is an indication that the coteachers welcome the suggestions of others and that students want a fair system that discourages their peers from doing homework in advisory period instead of at home, especially on the weekends. Associated issues that arise in the dialogue include students getting extra credit to make up for missed homework assignments, calling parents and guardians of students who do not do homework, and how to deal with as many as a quarter of the class who are failing because they have not done their homework on time. An agreement is reached that the students concerned will be invited to participate in a cogenerative dialogue in an endeavor to resolve this problem.

REACHING CONSENSUS

When Ken moved to a university in New York, a group of teacher researchers joined him in undertaking research on cogenerative dialogues in their own classes. Briefly, we describe some of the most salient aspects of what we have learned from these ongoing studies. In this and the following sections we explore what we have learned about the uses of cogenerative dialogues in these different structural arrangements and of course in a city in which ethnic and social diversity are more pronounced than in Philadelphia where we initiated and developed this practice.

Gillian Bayne, a teacher researcher in a high achieving school in New York City has used cogenerative dialogues as a way to reach out to ethnic minorities, who often times have not performed as well as white students in her classes (and the school). In her second year of using cogenerative dialogues, Gillian has seen spectacular changes in varying levels of participation and achievement within several aspect of the two student researchers she involved in cogenerative dialogues in her first year. Theo, native Spanish speaking student of immigrant descent, has excelled as a high-performing student, and has shown leadership as a peer teacher, curriculum planner for after school clubs, including a Hispanic Culture Club, and has been a youth advocate in and out of school, including participation in a lobbying visit to Albany to address politicians on issues relating to second language learners. The evidence is compelling in the sense that Theo expanded his action possibilities and therefore control over his life conditions and he attributes much of his change in roles to his participation in cogenerative dialogues. Jazz, an African American female student, continues to make great strides both inside and outside of her current science classroom. The greatest evidence of Jazz's benefits from participating in cogenerative dialogues rest in her increased sense of self, voice and actions, all resulting from an increased awareness of individual agency.

Gillian regards cogenerative dialogues as a way of improving the quality of teaching and learning. Typical of these is a cogenerative dialogue intended to address Ray's failure to participate in group activities and his tendencies to disrupt others in the class. The participants are Ray, Gillian, Riah, and Pearl. All are black: Gillian Caribbean American, two of her students African American an one a combination of Caribbean and African American. The three minute vignette we analyze involved the four of them meeting over lunch. They were grouped as shown in Figure 4.1. They also had eye contact with one another and ample table space to place and eat their lunch.

In the entire cogenerative dialogue the talk is shared equally among the four participants in terms of turns and duration of utterances. However, in the selected vignette Riah, Ray, and Gillian have more turns at talk, and Pearl only speaks once, as she overlaps Riah and Gillian. Riah and Ray each have nine utterances, with an average duration of about eight seconds—reasonable for developing ideas and lis-

Figure 4.2. The participants in this cogenerative dialogue are, from left to right, Riah, Pearl, Gillian, and Ray.

tening attentively. The pattern reflects sensitivity to the goal of sharing talk and reaching collective outcomes.

Gillian begins the vignette with a critique of Ray's participation in class and says it is not satisfactory. She expects the group to cogenerate a solution that involves Ray being more collaborative with others in the class. Riah then initiates interactions with Ray, querying him about what he does and also making suggestions related to what he might try. This proves to be both a significant and ironic act, as Riah was personally invited by Ray to join the cogenerative dialogues, so as facilitate better understanding between students and teachers and to create concrete strategies which would result in improved learning experiences for students. Ray shows lots of body movements, swaying back and forth and from side to side and speaks emotively. He explains that he likes to work by himself and when he is told this is not an option he says that he doesn't like working with others and getting constructive criticism from them. As he explains his preference to be told when he is right and wrong he raises his voice to be emphatic. Gillian gets involved on five occasions and in each case she makes suggestions of what is possible and what is not, on one occasion reminding Ray that he needs to improve his collaboration in order to achieve at a higher level.

BUILDING SOLIDARITY

Ed Lehner is a teacher researcher at Liberty High School, one of twelve suspension centers in New York City. Suspension centers are alternative high schools where students attend classes after receiving a suspension that precludes them from returning to their home school for an entire academic year. All Liberty High School students are identified as non-White minorities, have been suspended, and attend the school because they committed a violent offense against another student or staff. The student racial profile is 60 percent African American, 36 percent Hispanic, and 4 percent Asian.

"I got you. I'll take care of you." Ed's comment and a gesture down toward a person seated at the end of a rectangular table commenced a cogenerative dialogue with five students. The first few seconds of the vignette were punctuated by the metallic clicks and associated hissing of cans of soda being opened as Ed assured the students that he would talk to their professors if they were late for class, and he then asked the group about the rules for cogenerative dialogue. Dahlia, to Ed's right, was the first to make an attempt at articulating the rules. The following transcript provides an indication of the ways in which Ed and five of his students initiated a cogenerative dialogue.

```
01 Ed: So, here we are. Pretend a::::h (0.4) Who can tell us
       what the rules of cogenerative dialogue are? (5.9)
       How about the rules of cogenerative dialogue? How we
       set it up. How we do cogenerative dialogue?
02 Dahlia: How we::: (1.0) talk.
       (0.7)
03 Ed: Kay. Talking. (0.2) But the goal is what? To↓
       (0.7)
04 Dahlia: See what we have learned.
       (0.6)
05 Ed: See what we have learned.
06 Dahlia: =and?
07 Ed: =and possibly (1.3) improve
       (1.0)
08 Dahlia: Science
       (0.3)
09 Ed: That science and our science learning.
       (0.5)
10 Ed: Pass to you who are science.
11 Pierre: =[Bad.
12 Damien:  [So you learning science too (0.8) As we go
       along. (0.2) You know it but you're learning more
       about it.
       (0.1)
13 Ed: I'm learning more about it. But also, I'm somebody who
       wasn't good at science. (0.8) In college you only
       have to take one science course. (0.5) I took sort
       of a course called chemistry for poets. (0.6) It w's
       really simple. It's real easy ((laughs as he says
       the last two clauses)) (0.6) ((clears throat, 0.6))
       (0.5)
14 Ed: What I'm interested in my research with Sanford,
       Ronald and Dahlia (0.2) is how can we better (1.2)
       how can we better learn science and create the
       structures to make that happen?
```

A feature of this short excerpt is how Ed maintains a casual manner throughout while establishing a focus on the goals of cogenerative dialogue, all the time ensuring that interactions between the participants are synchronous and produced positive emotional energy. The conversation is light-hearted with laughter a prominent feature. Ed is relaxed and openly swigs from his can of coke as students contribute to the dialogue. Similarly, the students are relaxed and interact with one another and Ed. There are loud bursts of laughter, showing appreciation for one another's humor. It is evident in Ed's speech that, even though he speaks more than any other person in the above excerpt, he also pauses for periods in which others might have spoken and thereby could have taken a turn at talk. Any pause greater then 0.5 seconds is often associated with a change of speaker and hence it is apparent that Ed spoke in ways that provide structures for changing the speaker.

At turn 12 Damien comments that cogenerative dialogues also are forums in which Ed can learn more science. His comment shows an awareness of Ed teaching out of the field in which he is certified to teach and, at the same time, sensitivity to acknowledge that Ed knows some science and can learn even more in cogenerative dialogue. In turn 13 Ed builds on what Damien has said, and brings to light his limited background in college level science, even pointing out that he avoided science and intentionally selected the easiest course he could take. By laughing at his personal situation the students have a fine example of not taking offense when the conversation focuses on what might be regarded as a limitation in Ed's professional preparation.

Immediately prior to this excerpt the group has eaten a pizza lunch, a feature of the way Ed runs cogenerative dialogues. In his second year of doing research on the uses of cogenerative dialogues, Ed is aware of the importance of establishing and maintaining rapport with students, sustaining an environment in which there is a build-up of positive emotional energy. Hence, as the cogenerative dialogue commences with the opening of soda cans, the students frequently allude to the pizza, eating too much, and as the gas from the soda builds up in their bodies, some of the males in the group belch, catalyzing laughter, apologies (e.g., Ronaldo says, "my bad"), affirmations (e.g., Ed says, "no problem"), and resumption of the conversation. Although there were numerous instances of distracting events, there was not one instance of Ed making an effort to discipline any of the participants. Accordingly, the group was self-regulating. In a similar vein, topics that might be regarded as taboo surface as foci for brief interactions chains (e.g., comments on neo-Nazis; reactive comment from a participant; laughter from others) and wane without focused discussion as the dialogue returns to the issues being discussed prior to the perturbation.

Ed initiates a conversation on reviewing the rules for cogenerative dialogues. There are three and the students describe them as one person talks at a time, participants show respect for one another, and we have to come up with something. Ed then asks for a review of what they have accomplished cogeneratively so far. The group identifies three accomplishments and then discusses how they are working and additional changes that are desirable. In essence the conversations about how well the agreed-to changes have been enacted identifies claims and some contradictions. According to Ed the three points were: (a) We set up the smart board in the morning from 8:00–8:45 A.M. with the previous day's notes, so that students who had missed notes could come and get them. Students could also talk through their notes with us to ensure that they understood the material. (b) Students who could not get to class during the 8:00–8:45 A.M. time frame could also get one of the three master notebooks to check their notes against the teachers' notes. The master notebooks can be taken out of the classroom and are available all day long. (c) Important information, or new concepts were put on note cards to allow the students to talk through the concepts.

During a conversation on what could be done to improve the science class so that learning is enhanced, Pierre raises the issue of breaking it down better. This becomes a conversation that is wide ranging and focuses on the diversity of students in terms of their aptitude, pacing, and the difficulty teachers have in getting it "down for everyone" and moving on. With only forty-five minutes of class time the participants appreciated the contradictions of making sure everyone gets it and getting through what has been planned. Although there was not a resolution of how to resolve this contradiction there was evidence that all participants in the cogenerative dialogue understood the dimensions of the problem and did not see it as an example of bad teaching. In fact, during the discussion Dahlia raised the issue of order and it was apparent that the students regarded science as better managed than their other classes. When Ed probed about what Dahlia meant by order she explained that in a comparative sense science was more organized. At about that same time Ronaldo was emphatic that they are doing a better job in science, making it fun to learn and a class in which he did not sleep. His mention of sleep prompted Ed and Dahlia to interact about how this had been raised with the class as an issue and since they discussed it there has been "no sleeping in class."

There have been many examples of the participants in the cogenerative dialogues benefiting from their participation in the field. One that is worth mentioning involves the use of rap as a way to celebrate the successes of the class and participation in cogenerative dialogue. Ed adopted the practice of allowing students to do freestyle rap and to the students' delight he created and performed his own rap. Performing rap became a sign of belonging to a science class and celebrating success. In contrast to the ways in which Sarah-Kate LaVan and Jennifer Beers have used rap with female students in Jen's classes, where science was written into raps, the raps produced by Ed and his students were not associated with science—they were just done in relation to being in the science class. Just as, in the earlier example, the incident about the presence of a mouse in the class served as a mutual focus for collective effervescence, so too did the ritual practice of performing rap at the end of class and cogenerative dialogues. It seems as if the buildup of a positive emotional state, associated with participation in activities such as rap can become signs of the enjoyment of being together, thereby making a positive impact on belonging to this group and participating in the group's activities.

BEYOND SOLIDARITY

After a year as the sole teacher researcher at Marie Curie School, Chris Emdin invited three of his colleagues to join him as teacher researchers—studying the ways in which student learning opportunities were expanded through the use of cogenerative dialogues. Ed Lehner and his group from Liberty decided to collaborate in a project that transcended classes, schools and in the context of New York City, borough (since Marie Curie is in the Bronx and Liberty is in Brooklyn).

Like the students he teaches, Chris grew up in the Bronx, living in the housing projects and developing a pride in his neighborhood. After a year of cogenerative dialogues his focus, reflecting the awesome knowledge of his students, was to identify the rituals in which his students engaged in fields out of the classroom. Through cogenerative dialogues he and his students identified out-of-school rituals and then focused on whether or not they assisted or hurt the students' learning of science. The students then identified rituals that could be substituted for those that hurt the achievement of science to improve the learning of science. At the same time they explored how to bring rituals from out of the classroom into the classroom. Hence, based on these decisions, students altered their in- and out-of-school rituals and Chris agreed to do likewise. One important example was that Chris routinely broke up out-of-school friendship groups because of their disruptive potential in class. The students articulated how they knew how to collaborate with peers with whom they spent a lot of time out-of-school and could use their social networks to enhance their learning of science. Chris agreed and allowed them to choose with whom to work in class. The outcome appears to have been positive: increases in learning of science, a stronger identity with science, and feelings of affiliation with science and the school. As a teacher researcher Chris reports that the uses of cogenerative dialogue in multiple classes led to its diffusion throughout the school and a strong sense of affiliation that transcends grade level and teacher—which he describes as cosmopolitanism.

Chris undertook an analysis of the hip-hop culture and showed how within that culture there is not a hierarchical power organization and that participants have equal power and accept one another's culture. His analyses provide numerous examples of the deficit ways in which schools and schooling are represented in rap and in symmetrical ways, how schools view rap. As others have done in cogenerative dialogues in urban schools, Chris makes a strong case for the use of raps to present the possibilities of schooling and of science. At the same time, through the use of rap in cogenerative dialogues and classrooms, it is possible for students to use their social and symbolic resources from the hip-hop field to enhance their learning of science and success at school. Furthermore, as an out-of-school ritual in which most inner-city students participate, either by performing or listening, the inclusion of rap in cogenerative dialogues and the classroom also is a sign of respect that might well fuel the capital exchange cycle that leads to the production and hence reproduction and transformation of culture, including the learning of science.

SEEDBEDS FOR PRODUCING CULTURE: THE ROLE OF EMOTIONS

The outcomes from cogenerative dialogues suggest that they function as seedbeds in which new culture is produced—that is reproduced and transformed to allow participants to interact successfully in interaction chains associated with high levels of synchrony and the emergence of solidarity. A pleasing outcome has been that participants in cogenerative dialogues have been able to take their new culture back into the classroom and enact it in ways that have increased the quality of teaching and learning. The results from the schools in which we tried whole-class cogenerative dialogues suggest that in cogenerative dialogues students create forms of culture that are subsequently enacted in other fields. We have evidence that culture produced in cogenerative dialogues is enacted in other fields that include the science education curriculum, other subject areas, the hallways and lunchroom, and home. That is, cogenerative dialogues are regarded as sites for cultural production that can then be enacted in a variety of other fields as well. This realization led us to focus on our earlier decision to encourage cogenerative dialogues to include participants who are different from one another. Perhaps there are more important reasons for urban schools to employ cogenerative dialogues, as participants tend to learn how to successfully interact with others across the boundaries of age, gender, ethnicity, and class. For example, the small-group cogenerative dialogue is a relatively safe field in which students can learn to interact successfully with other students, adult teachers, and adults from different social classes. The converse is also the case, for example, when a middle-class, White female teacher has opportunities to successfully interact and show respect for the practices of poor, Black youth. Having built culture around successful interactions in small-group cogenerative dialogues the opportunities are then there for this culture to be enacted in different fields, for example, in the science classroom, throughout the school, and in the streets. Hence, we have learned to regard cogenerative dialogues as fields in which culture is produced, transformed, and reproduced, thereby increasing the likelihood that practices in other fields can be socially and culturally adaptive.

A key part of an evolving theoretical framework concerns the emotional aspects of being a participant in a field. Randall Collins (2004) examines interactions in many social settings and provides a framework that interconnects successful interactions with the generation of positive emotional energy, in which case an interaction chain can become a sign that is charged with positive emotional energy. A typical sign for positive emotional energy is when participants walk away from a meeting expressing how good it made them feel, how much they valued the interactions, and so forth. In contrast, when interaction chains are unsuccessful they can become invested with negative emotional energy. Relating this framework to our research on cogenerative dialogues, it is evident that as the incidence of successful interaction chains increases, positive emotional energy builds up, and student identities can be inscribed with affiliations that lead to solidarity within a group of participants. Conversely, a higher incidence of unsuccessful interaction chains can produce a buildup of negative emotional energy that can shatter solidarity and sow the seeds for the growth of solidarity built around counterculture. A requisite for successful interaction chains is shared focus, such as occurs when participants are aware of what is to be accomplished and know where others are situated with respect to their goals, roles, and responsibilities. Sharing videotapes for the express purpose of understanding some event to do something about preventing its recurrence constitutes an object around which a shared focus develops.

In urban classrooms, especially, there was ample evidence of teachers and students failing to interact successfully as curricula were enacted. The net effect of successive failed interactions was a build-up of negative emotions such as failure, frustration, disappointment, resentment, anger, boredom, and lack of interest. Negative emotions such as these can accumulate in an upwelling of negative emotional energy, which can manifest in resistance and identity inscriptions that are alienating with respect to science, the teacher, and school. Rather than building a community that has solidarity, a classroom can be fragmented with numerous contradictions associated with a basic inability of students and teachers being unable to adapt their capital to align with others' capital to produce chains of successful interactions, and the associated positive emotions and emotional energy. In such cases it appears as if teachers and students do not have the cultural resources to interact successfully in classrooms. More often than not interactions fail and produce negative emotional energy. It makes sense that teachers and students need a place to learn about one another's culture and how to adapt and align their own cultural resources with others' culture. Pleasingly, cogenerative dialogues appear to be a field in which new culture can be produced, allowing individuals who are quite different to successfully interact with one another. Relatively small groups are ideal for producing new culture to allow successful interactions to occur. In some instances it makes sense for one teacher to interact with just one student, allowing each to learn about the culture of the other and to learn how to adapt to produce successful interaction chains. However, we keep in mind the importance of students needing to learn to interact successfully not only with the teacher but also with peers who are "culturally other"—that is across boundaries of gender, race and language. Hence, the ways in which we structure cogenerative dialogues with the purpose of producing new culture is to vary the size, as necessary, from two participants (i.e., a teacher and a student) to three, four, and even five participants (i.e., a teacher with up to four students). In all instances we endeavor to create groups that consist of participants who differ from one another in terms of such characteristics as gender, race, class and native language.

Interactions that fail and events that generate negative emotional energy are ideal foci for cogenerative dialogues. For example, in our explorations of coteaching we have seen cases where one coteacher wanted to step in, but the coteacher who was teaching at the time did not provide the space for participation. Similarly, there have been instances of both teachers talking loudly at the same time, competing for the attention of students, talking over one another in an effort to seize control, and failing to teach when called on to participate. In such cases the evolving learning environment is not conducive to the learning of students or to the coteachers learning to teach. Occurrences such as these are ideal foci for dialogue and negotiated consensus on how to make improvements.

Sarah-Kate LaVan's research with Jennifer Beers, conducted in an urban high school in Philadelphia, was continuous over several years and involved coteaching with and without new teachers. Their research was part of a multi-year study of the teaching and learning of science in urban schools in which we were involved. Accordingly regular reporting of what was learned from the research occurred in weekly research meetings and day-by-day debriefing meetings. It was apparent from this study in particular that the students involved were changing in numerous ways that seemed highly desirable.

During the spring of 2003 we began to view cogenerative dialogues as seedbeds for the production of culture associated with successfully interacting across boundaries defined by factors such as age, race, social class and gender. For example, membership of a social group defined by an age range (e.g., 13 to 16 years of age), gender, race, and neighborhood affords the creation of distinctive patterns of coherence in schema and practices and simultaneously occurring contradictions to those patterns. We know that being is inherently singular plural, which means that all humans are positioned differently inherently and therefore also *dis*positioned. However, communication is possible when the differences between individuals are not too large. Some students, however, are placed so differently in this social space that they have difficulty in communicating effectively across the social boundaries, even though these boundaries are porous. Bringing these students together in cogenerative dialogues provides them with opportunities to produce new culture that affords successful interactions between the youth from different places in social space.

Adults face similar challenges. Our experience is that middle-class adults, especially those who are White, experience difficulty in seeing the capital of urban youth in a positive light. Differences in culture tend to be seen, at least initially, in terms of deficits, and often manifest in educators' feelings of sympathy and well-intended efforts to help disadvantaged youth. In a class that consists of many different youth cultures a teacher can fail to appropriate students' practices in ways that lead to the production of science culture, acting instead in ways that students do not appropriate in the intended ways. Instead students might experience the discomfort and frustration of their efforts failing to reap the intended outcomes and they may view what the teacher does as irrelevant to meeting their goals. Because of the ethnic diversity of many urban classrooms, it is not surprising that teachers and students have difficulty in producing synchrony and what happens is often experienced as asynchrony and in terms of associated negative feelings. In contrast, if teachers set up cogenerative dialogues with one or two students, the ethnic diversity can be managed more easily, and all participants can take advantage of opportunities to learn about one another's culture.

Within our research program there are numerous case studies in which students who participated in cogenerative dialogues expanded their agency in their science class, in other classes, at a school level, and in their homes and communities. Needless to say, we were very excited at the prospects of these examples of cultural reproduction and transformation—recognizing that the field of cogenerative dialogue might be central to the improvement of schools as learning places. However, there also were grounds for caution because students who participated in cogenerative dialogues developed levels of critical awareness that in some cases landed them in trouble. For example, in one of our studies there was a student named Ya-Meer; he also participated as a student researcher. One day, Ya-Meer challenged the way he was assessed by one of our teacher researchers and the challenge to the teacher's authority was seen as overstepping the boundaries of being a responsible student. With Ya-Meer and his coteachers at the time, we wrote a paper about how this problem was eventually resolved. However, Ya-Meer was able to make the participating university and school administrator researchers notice what was happening and to create structures to ameliorate the difficulties that were anticipated. Natasia, the student featured in chapter 2, had to work the contradictions out for herself.

Natasia was sensitive to the need for teachers to prevent students from disrupting the learning of others. Consistently, she connected this to the level of planning, the consistency of effort in class, and the demonstration of care for learning and welfare of students. She wondered how her mathematics teacher could stand the stress of teaching without a higher level of control.

> You don't get nothin' done in Miss Smith's class. Miss Smith has no control. She has no strategy. She has nothin'. I'm like how have you been a teacher for as long as you've been a teacher if you have no control, no organization? She loses everything. I'm like I don't understand how you've been a teacher for as long as you've been. And I be like Miss Smith, come here. And I tell her to watch what I'm watchin'. I be like don't say nothin', just watch. This one turned around. This one talkin'. This one eatin'. This one playin' with the calculators. I'm like, what is this? This make no sense.

Natasia approached Miss Smith during class to offer evidence of her ineffectiveness. Because of the way in which teaching and learning roles are conceptualized Natasia's move is risky for her and for her teacher and it is no surprise that Miss Smith does not welcome Natasia's analyses even though acceptance of shared responsibility for the classroom activity is laudable. Natasia's courage in venturing an analysis of her teacher's participation is a role that is not anticipated by Miss Smith and is unwelcome. However, creating a division of labor in which students accept shared responsibility for the collective activity and participate in activities in which contradictions are identified and resolved has the potential to catalyze desirable changes in the curricula enacted in urban high schools. Natasia's initiative in adopting this role is against the grain since the roles of students traditionally have been crafted as less powerful than those of the teacher and usually it is regarded as disrespectful for students to suggest to a teacher how to improve her teaching.

A CASE FOR ONE-ON-ONE COGENERATIVE DIALOGUES

Ashraf Shady, a teacher researcher, is an immigrant from Egypt who has English as a non-native language. Ethnically he designates himself as non-White. However, he is considered White in a political sense and his Black students also consider him to be White. Ashraf is struggling with the teaching of his middle school classes, especially a class in which a number of the students are classified as special education. Accordingly, he selected this class as the target for his research, anticipating that he would be able to dramatically improve the quality of learning through the uses of cogenerative dialogue. He identified two African Americans, a male and a female, to participate in the study as student researchers. During a cogenerative dialogue the group planned an inquiry lab that involved stacking water drops onto a one-cent coin. To Ashraf's dismay the lab disintegrated into a water fight, with both of his student researchers as central protagonists. The contradiction of the water fight and the key involvement of both of his student researchers, regarded by Ashraf as an act of betrayal, was then the focus of a cogenerative dialogue, which highlights several issues addressed below.

As our experiences with cogenerative dialogue have increased we have learned of the centrality of learning to successfully interact across cultural boundaries, usually defined by age, race, gender, and language. In this cogenerative dialogue the three participants differed in terms of age (Ashraf is much older than Star and Steve who are teenagers), race (the students are African American and regard Ashraf as White), gender (Star is female and Ashraf and Steve are male), and language (Ashraf has an accent based on English being a second language and the students share an African American dialect). These sociocultural differences create a scenario in which each of the three participants in the field possesses quite different culture and there is a high potential for each to misinterpret the cultural enactment of the others. Analyses of a transcript and videotape of the cogenerative dialogue confirm the presence of widespread asynchrony and also reveal some notable examples of synchrony.

The initial eight minutes of the transcript show that Ashraf has almost every other turn at talk, and the average length of each turn for Ashraf is greater than for Star and Steve. As Ashraf began to speak to the students it was apparent that they interacted with him asynchronously—not unlike the patterns he describes in his classroom. During these interactions in the cogenerative dialogue there is evidence of the students having one another's back when, for example, Ashraf identifies instances of inappropriate behavior from Steve and Star speaks up in Steve's defense. Another noteworthy pattern is both students mentioning the importance of showing respect to one another, peers, and Ashraf. However, initially this did not happen. Even in a small-group setting the allure of earning one another's respect by disrespecting an authority figure was great. As Ashraf spoke, the students showed signs of disinterest, disengagement, and disrespect. Also, by laughing *at* rather than *with* Ashraf, the students disrespected him and may have earned one another's respect. Within our research group, an interpretation we have discussed and reached consensus on is that the students are playing with Ashraf, using verbal and non-verbal codes that he does not understand and then laughing at him as a sign of their success in being disrespectful to him, in his presence, without his knowledge. His simultaneous laughter reinforces their success in being able to play with, and thereby disrespect, a person in an institutionally higher position with greater levels of agency without his awareness. One interpretation of why this happens is that Ashraf does not understand enough of the students' culture to successfully interact with them. Symmetrically, they do not understand his culture to the extent that they can interact successfully with him. Furthermore, there is a sense that Ashraf has deficit perspectives concerning these students and they interpret his willingness to help them as disrespectful. Similarly, both students likely regard

Ashraf's cultural differences through deficit lenses. The issues of how cultural otherness is perceived and appropriated are important foci for ongoing research.

After the first eight minutes of cogenerative dialogue the pattern of exchange between the participants changed in terms of the average length of utterances being about the same for Ashraf, Steve, and Star. As before, the most common pattern was for Ashraf to take every other turn at talk and only rarely did Steve and Star verbally interact with one another. There was a change in the focus of the conversations too. In response to a query from Ashraf about her failure to participate in class, Star shifted the focus of discussion onto issues of a highly personal nature. Interactions between Ashraf and Star were then synchronous and symmetrical. Chains of one-on-one interactions produced success, although Steve was not involved during these interactions. Ashraf showed that he was listening and he and Star maintained a focus on the personal circumstances of Star's home life. Ashraf was willing to listen and ask questions that allowed Star to provide additional information and fully describe situations about her relationships with the adults in her home. A possible cogenerated outcome is that Ashraf and Star learned to successfully interact with one another for an extended period of time in which active listening was apparent and each speaker was sincere and showed the other respect. Producing shared levels of power also was evident in the sharing of talk time and turns and the establishment of foci for conversation. The public nature of subsequent conversations raises ethical issues about whether or not the conversation should have been permitted to continue as it did in the presence of Steve who was marginalized during the conversation between Ashraf and Star. Steve seemed aware that he was not to interact in this segment of the conversation and showed signs of non-alignment and asynchrony by fiddling with a gas tap and enacting signs of disinterest. Occasionally the content of the interactions was of such interest that Steve turned his head to look and listen, and sometimes his facial expressions showed signs of empathy—possibly signs of shared experiences in the home.

Ashraf referred Star to the guidance counselor and eventually an appropriate agency was involved in providing her with support. We decided that the most effective cogenerative dialogues for Ashraf, Star, and Steve, were one-on-one meetings, with the goal of producing culture to afford them successfully interacting in fields characterized by cultural otherness. Ashraf made this structural adjustment, involving Star and Steve in one-on-one meetings and creating a new group with several different students from the same class. In so doing he began to build social and symbolic capital with a greater number of students and there was a greater incidence of successful interactions not only in the cogenerative dialogues but also in the classroom. At the same time Steve, Star, and a growing number of their peers learned to interact successfully with Ashraf.

PULLING OFF COGENERATIVE DIALOGUE: A METALOGUE

Michael: As with our other metalogues, I am going to attempt initiating a conversation that takes us further and leads us to learn from what we have learned, here about cogenerative dialogues. The first issue pertains to the nature of the rules a teacher and his students may generate: I see them as situational and therefore appropriate in one setting but possibly inappropriate in another setting. For example, the outcome of my own negotiations with students, according to which they could decide about how to achieve a particular government-imposed curriculum objective may not be transferable to the schools and settings that we feature here. That is, students and teachers may not be comfortable with a situation whereby one group of two or three eleventh-grade students learns about electricity by producing a comic strip for ten-year olds that contain the salient concepts whereas another group of four students designs and conducts a series of experiments involving regular, semi-, and super-conducting materials.

Ken: If I understand your point, I agree that the actual agreements reached will not be necessarily appropriate for other fields. The consensus that supports those agreements is the collective of participants in the cogenerative dialogue. When there are efforts to do what was agreed in another field, such as a classroom, the buy-in might not be sufficient to allow all that has been planned and agreed-to in cogenerative dialogue to be enacted as intended. However, efforts of the participants to enact agreed-to changes in a classroom will change the structure of the classroom and at the very least expand the agency of the others from the cogenerative dialogue, who can then also enact practices that cohere with the plan. However, to return to your point, what is anticipatory, appropriate, and timely in any field will depend on the structure of the field—including the participants and the capital they have to pursue individual and collective goals.

Michael: My second point pertains to the fact that we do not *make* others responsible for their actions and contributions to shared lessons and cogenerative dialogue sessions. Everyone in the situation *is* responsible in the sense that all social situations are coproduced—even in extreme cases where a teacher lectures and her students silently copy notes. Lessons and cogenerative dialogues involve collectives and not saying a word and silently sitting and listening are actions that constitute the events for what they are. Even silently sitting is an action, and precisely *because* students sit silently can the lecturer lecture. Thus, while taking courses both at the high school and university levels, I frequently intervened pointing out any errors in the lecture talk or chalkboard notes. The ensuing discussions with the teacher or professor changed the type of lesson enacted. Because a lesson or cogenerative dialogue session is the result of *collective* action each member is responsible for the outcome, the (collectively) enacted curriculum. "Taking responsibility" therefore is but another way of saying that a student contributes in a more active way to the constitution of cogenerative dialogues and therefore in the decision about practices that teacher and students want to collectively enact.

Ken: Having the rule that we will assume shared responsibility is a structure that can be appropriated to ensure that an individual has a commitment to what is agreed-to collectively. What is of interest to me is that the rule is an affordance for cultural production—cultural reproduction and transformation that include those resolutions that a group might have agreed have been cogenerated and much more—culture associated with praxis as it unfolded during the cogenerative dialogue, culture about which participants are not fully aware and yet may be enacted in other fields, expanding agency and affording an improved social life.

Michael: I agree, but also was pushing even further. It is not simply that we assume shared responsibility, if by *assume* one means to say that I have a choice over whether I am going to take responsibility for. I take it with Emmanuel Levinas (e.g., 1978/1998), who suggests that we are thrown into a condition of being responsible, which predates our existence as conscious beings—both at the level of cultural history and at the level of the individual born today. We can reject this responsibility or acknowledge and live up to it; in either case, it is a condition of our lives. We therefore are responsible for the actions of others; without attempting to recapitulate my argument, here the trajectory it takes. My action has an outcome, in which, according to G.W.F. Hegel and Karl Marx, I have externalized and estranged myself. This outcome is a resource in and for the action of others so that my externalized and estranged Self is implicated in the action of another, implicating me, in turn, in the outcome of his or her actions. It is in this deeper sense that I would like to theorize the concept of *responsibility*, which inherently comes with a degree of passivity, as I am no longer in control over what someone else does with the resources I nevertheless have created.

Ken: The responsibility I was thinking of points to cultural production, or enactment, in another field—the classroom. It is my experience that tradition cedes responsibility for the quality of teaching and learning to teachers. Unless specific attention is directed toward collective responsibility for enacting agreed-to changes in the classroom there was a tendency to expect the group to cogenerate recommendations for change and then to blame the teacher if it all did not turn out as agreed. However, when explicit attention is paid to collective responsibility for attempting to do what was agreed to, there is more evidence in the classroom of teachers and students from the cogenerative dialogue group acting in synchrony and showing solidarity.

Michael: A third pertinent issue is that about deciding who participates and, perhaps even preceding such decisions, the question about initiating cogenerative dialogues. A critic might suggest that a cogenerative dialogue practice initiated by a teacher preserves the institutional asymmetry between students and herself. The attendant theoretical difficulty lies in the idea and possibilities that we can empower others. For if we claim that we could empower someone else, this very act would not be one in which the "empowered" individual or group has power over. I tend to think about the initiation of cogenerative dialogue practice in terms of offering the possibility and resources for enacting schooling differently. It is then up to the students to decide if they want to take up this opportunity, and in responding positively, they act and empower themselves. Empowering here means that they expand their room to maneuver and they do so because they goals they set for themselves require new forms of actions. I therefore view teachers intending to introduce cogenerative dialoguing as making salient to students that there are other forms to enact schooling and one of these forms lies in making collective decisions about the content and form of the lessons in which they find themselves.

Ken: Absolutely. Students participate in cogenerative dialogues in numerous out of school fields and so do adults. Of course they do not call them that and may not call them anything at all. What we are doing here is intentionally articulating a field that has great potential for educators wanting to improve the quality of schooling. Initially a teacher might set them up and make it possible for students to learn about what a cogenerative dialogue is and what it is not. Then, just who can call them, decide who participates, and when to schedule them can be worked out to fit the school and its participants. If students benefit from being involved, then it is unfair to exclude students from being involved and it is more than an issue of allowing students to get involved if they want to. Structures should be created to expand the agency of all and I feel this should include getting all students involved in cogenerative dialogues as fields to support their getting the most from schooling. I am certain that at this point I do not know as much as I need to know about all the various forms of cogenerative dialogue and how to work them into the enactment of schooling.

Michael: Ultimately I understand cogenerative dialoguing as providing a forum in which teachers and their students can build trust and a sense of solidarity in the sense that both groups find themselves in situations that produce and reproduce the institution of schooling. Finding themselves in this situation involves a certain level of passivity, which they may deal with when they come to the understanding that they are *in this together*. Once a teacher and her students come to this understanding, that is, of their inherent and unavoidable responsibility for teaching and learning, they are in a situation where they actively expand their room to maneuver, that is, actively empower themselves, by participating in cogenerative dialoguing as a forum for making collective decisions about how they will maximally deal with the situation into which they are thrust.

COGENERATIVE DIALOGUES

Further Insights from and for Praxis

In this chapter we articulate the nature of cogenerative dialogues by examining in detail a cogenerative dialogue that followed the cotaught lesson presented in chapter 3. Our account shows that if given opportunities for doing so, students can be valuable contributors to the understanding of classroom events and participants in planning teaching strategies, learning approaches, and curriculum. Although cogenerative dialogues have evolved a great deal since this one took place, the analysis provides insights into the topics that arose and how they unfolded. Importantly, the transcripts provide insights into the ways in which the participants view classroom events and their personal roles in relation to the collective of the class. Both of the student participants have struggled with science in the recent past and could easily be regarded as students at risk of not proceeding with further education beyond high school; yet the ways in which they speak about complex topics show that they have deep insights into education and ways in which it can be changed to better serve their needs. They also show that they are cooperative with their teachers and resolute in making suggestions, especially when they feel enacted curricula are not challenging and therefore do not meet their needs.

Some of the general comments about the cogenerative dialogue are that the participants speak seriously to one another in focused interactions in which there is ample evidence of success: verbal and non verbal indicators that perspectives are valued and regarded as resources for learning from one another. There is a sense that participation in the cogenerative dialogue makes a difference to the subsequent enactment of science activities. Students—including those who might have been termed difficult, and frequently students in difficulties both in and out-of school—and coteachers show respect for one another by listening, not interrupting, taking what is said previously as a basis for issues of discussion, asking follow up questions, and listening actively and supportively. Nonverbal forms of support include head nods, smiles, eye gaze, gesturing, and occasional touching on the arm (though there are limits as to who may touch them, as shown in the exchange between Ken and one student during regular class time). Each participant experiences the respect of others, who listen to what they have to say, comment, and ask follow up questions. Also, each participant has at least one turn at talk that is prolonged and initiated discussion on a topic of importance.

Most interactions can be described as successful and when there is disagreement or the anticipation of disagreement each of the speakers is halting in the way she or he starts to speak. However, due to the support of the group, there are few interruptions and no instance of an unpleasant interaction. Participants create and maintain a shared focus and help one another to say what they want to say across boundaries of gender, ethnicity, class, and age. In the next section, we present a case study that exhibits many of the characteristic features of cogenerative dialogue praxis as it has evolved at City High School (Philadelphia) where we have conducted research on coteaching and cogenerative dialoguing over the course of a seven-year period.

CASE STUDY OF A COGENERATIVE DIALOGUE

The cogenerative dialogue occurred directly after class and Ken invited Darnell and Despina to participate because they had been closely involved in the lesson in interesting ways. Ken regarded Darnell as a solid chemistry student, highly motivated and a dependable person who assumed a high level of civic responsibility in the school. Despina had a recent history of failure in science and often was playful in class. Ken thought she had great potential to succeed, but represented a dialectical opposite for Darnell. Her role in the cogenerative dialogue was a great surprise for Ken in that she was articulate and showed maturity and knowledge of teaching that exceeded what might be expected of a teenager. Nine themes arose in the cogenerative dialogue and each of these is discussed below, some supported by transcriptions from the digital videotape. Many of these themes relate back to the coteaching described in chapter 3 and all have deep implications for the enacted curricula, including the activity on limiting reactions. The themes addressed in this section are grouping practices, peer teaching, characteristics of good science education, labs, compromise, laziness, identity of new teachers, coteaching, and shared responsibility for teaching and learning.

Grouping Practices

In many ways Alex taught differently to Victoria and Jessica and also to other teachers in the building. He put this down to epistemological differences, especially in regards to the type and amount of structure provided by the teacher. Not surprisingly the issue of structure emerged in many of the themes dealt with cogeneratively. In this case Victoria and Jessica had decided to enact a different way of grouping students, different that is to the way in which Alex allowed students to form their own groups in the cotaught activity discussed previously. Whereas Alex preferred students to assume responsibility for forming groups and making them productive, Victoria and Jessica decided to change the group membership, break down the amount of socializing, and increase the proportion of productive verbal interaction in groups. Participants discuss this issue in the following transcript from the first video vignette.

1   Jessica: All right. Just in general we want to know your honest opinions.
2   Despina: I think class today was fine because we had um more class participation than we usually do. People seemed more interested and trying to give answers or justify things or-

3 Victoria: Um. Did you guys find the, oh, moving of people
             to be part of that?
4 Despina: U:m.
5 Darnel: Yeah.
6 Victoria: Like. Coz we're grouped [different. Right?
7 Darnel: [There wasn't-
8 Victoria: Like. Because you asked me in class. I don't
             know. I was kinda smart about it and I'm sorry
             but because Carri asked me why we are moving
             desks and I said ah because we felt like it.
             ((Laughing)) ah ha ha. So she said, "Oh. So you
             felt like it." And I didn't mean for it to come
             off that way, but we had a bigger [agenda.
9 Darnel: [I think it's
             a really good thing. It really helped. Because
             the way that you all presented the lesson today
             it was more as though like you had to think
             about what you were gonna say first and then
             like how you take like ah um atomic radius and
             then apply it to the octet rules and to use that
             ah then you could u:m transfer it and say well,
             it's the same as saying like the d orbitals, I
             mean the d elements, how they come into play. It
             was more like today like you had to think about
             it a lot more than previous times because previ-
             ous it felt as though like everything was right
             there and needed to think about it and this
             since the seats and groups was moved and
             switched and not with their friends and a lot of
             people was not just talking to their partner
             they was talking uh they was talking to their
             partner, they was talking about the lesson today
             so not something else that didn't make sense. So
             a lot of it was a productive day. ((Segment was
             47.9 s in duration.))
10 Victoria: Did you feel the same way like about productive-
             ness?
11 Despina: Yes and I think that u:m that that's how we need
             to do when we do u:m when we get in our groups
             because I know a lot of times there's a whole
             group that knows something or knows part of
             something and then you have a group with two or
             three people who know everything about what was
             going on and you had this group getting what
             what they need to get done and then this group
             not so. This way, once we mix it up a lot of
             people have a chance to do the work. A lot of
             people have less chance to to slack like they
             normally do and there's more productivity with
             others. ((Segment was 35.3 seconds in dura-
             tion.))

Jessica initiated the cogenerative dialogue with a brief opening in which she invited the students' honest opinions. Her remarks carried a tone of assurance that they could be open without any fear of reprisals and her sincerity conveyed a sense of trust and respect. Her immediate attention to her pen and notepad were signs that she would be recording notes based on what they said. From then on Jessica spoke infrequently and was attentive throughout the duration of the cogenerative dialogue.

Despina began in a positive tone mentioning participation, interest and desirable forms of involvement. Her eleven-second response to Jessica's invitation was trailing off when Victoria jumped in, relating the benefits described by Despina to the way they had arranged groups, a change to past practices and especially to the ways in which Alex organized groups. Her question catalyzed immediate one word utterances from both students, indicative of their agreement and after a pause of more than a second, Victoria continued with turns 6 and 8, in which she laid out more information about the grouping practices, their rationale, and an apology for an unintentional bad attitude she demonstrated in class. The apology was a sign that she would review what she had done and if what she had done showed students disrespect, as her performance in this case did, she would apologize. As she came to the end of turn 8 her body movements were indicative of her being finished and the intensity of her speech diminished. Darnell was anxious to contribute and he overlapped Victoria's final word as he commenced turn 9.

Darnell spoke for approximately 48 seconds and began with a specific response to Victoria's question about the grouping practices, explaining why he thought it was a good thing. His justification for preferring this approach to grouping over allowing friendship groups was that in the latter the talk was not as focused as in the new approach which was more focused and productive. As he did later in the cogenerative dialogue, Darnell illustrated his position with examples drawn from today's lesson and he related the structures to his preference for learning to be meaningful.

After a pause of more than a second, longer than might have been expected, Victoria invited Despina to address the issue of productivity. In turn 11 Despina spoke for about 35 seconds, affirming what Darnell had said and supporting the new practice of arranging groups. Her argument, which was accepted by all participants with nods and smiles, focused on the distribution of students who could contribute to the issues being addressed by the small groups. She favored a system of grouping that fairly distributed knowledge of science across the groups. The new approach fostered desirable forms of participation and less "slacking off." Despina's comments about peers helping peers were a transition into another issue that was central to the ways in which the coteachers were teaching.

* * *

Ken: Both students appreciated the changes to grouping practices and related it to learning and staying focused.

Michael: During my first cogenerative dialogue sessions involving high school students from these inner-city schools, I had been quite surprised. I had expected that many of these students might not be able to express themselves in articulate ways about the classroom environment and the structures that mediate what and how they can learn. I expected even less that students would be interested in participating in these sessions, which from the outset had as their purpose the improvement of teaching and learning for the benefit of the students. But each time we had these sessions even before designing our heuristic for making them work, students made tremendous contributions in our effort of understanding what is at stake. Darnel and Despina are but two further students who are willing and able to express salient issues concerning their classroom.

Ken: The duration of student utterances is salient to this and other episodes. When they have the time to do so, both students talk cogently and at length.

Michael: What I learned from this and similar experiences is that we cannot make inferences from classroom behavior to the students' intentions; and we cannot make inferences about how they might contribute, as we have witnessed early on with the one student who though seldom at school and caught stealing video equipment from his school made considerable contributions to our understanding of the lessons he attended together with us.

Peer Teaching

Peer teaching occurred informally and formally in numerous ways in the cotaught class described in chapter 3. For example, in individualized activities it was common for students who had a good grasp of the subject matter or the exercise to be worked on to help those near to them who may have been in need of assistance. Similarly, those who finished quickly, like Darnell, were asked to assist those who needed more assistance than the coteachers could provide. Finally, through the use of the front whiteboard the coteachers introduced an idea they had picked up from a college chemistry class in which Victoria and Alex were students—to involve all students in producing answers to be reviewed by their peers. Hence students routinely wrote their answers and presented them to the whole class who often provided feedback and corrective suggestions. The following transcript provides insights into the positive dispositions of all participants in the cogenerative dialogues to the uses of peer teaching in the class.

| 1 | Victoria | Do you guys like the idea that u:m, you know, some people are stronger, like we know that both you are stronger in this work as opposed to your classmates. Do you like the opportunity to teach your classmates? It's not just like always us teaching you all, but like I think what we're trying to get out of this is having you guys take the initiative to teach each other. Like do you find that to be like intimidating, like are you scared of doing that or do you actually like the challenge? (0.7) |
| 2 | Darnell | I like the challenge personally because I just recently, like somebody told me, this is recent, |

that when you learn stuff in school you're only
going to walk away with thirty-three percent of
it or thirty percent of what you. What you gotta
do is you gotta take what you learn and apply it
and try to make common use and common sense of
it. So, when you do it that way you're gonna remember far more greater things. Just like with
that thing ((points at periodic table)) I said
is it is it indirectly proportional. So if you
know one unit give you more then if you knew
something else it's gonna give you less. So, if
you can remember that rule you can remember
about like atomic radius and stuff like that.

3 Victoria   =Like inverse?
4 Darnell   =Yeah. Inverse proportion.
5 Victoria   Inverse. [Right↓.
6 Darnell   [So. It's just that you gotta. You
gotta put things together to see how it work for
you. Like. I like teaching people you know, especially if I understand it or if I understand
it well enough that I can tell you because I'm
gonna try to tell it to you as though like how I
understand it and from a student to another student it's easier from a student to a teacher and
a teacher to a student. That's how I view it.
(0.6)

7 Despina   And u:m I agree because it was last year, because this is why I'm in this class, because I
didn't do so good in my other science class and
I was, I was bent on when I go to college, if I
go to college. Well, when I go to college sorry.
I'm ah I don't want anything to do with science.
Nothing. I don't want nothing. But after taking
this class I'm like maybe it wasn't me that was
the problem and now I see that once I apply myself, not sayin' I wasn't before, but this interaction, this class has made me think so many,
so much differently than I did before about science because before I wanted nuthin to do with
it. Well now I see that I mean there's things I
can understand. Concepts, there's things. I can
learn things. I can learn things and do good in
the science class and because before I was I'll
stick to math and English. I really did not like
science. (1.2) So, it's changed my understanding
and to think I can help other people, u:m with
this, when I came from hating science and not
doing well in it at all to bein' able to help
other people make me feel better about myself as
a student and a classmate.

In setting up a question about peer tutoring Victoria shows her respect to both students, an important sign within the youth culture to which Despina and Darnell both belong. After seeking her perspectives she reiterates that "we're" expecting students to initiate coteaching of peers. For a moment it appears as if Despina will quickly respond, however, she notices Darnell is leaning forward, turns to him and with a smile and a gesture, she signals that he may have the next turn at talk.

In turn 2, Darnell covers a lot of territory in 36 seconds of talk, interrupted briefly with a series of interactions with Victoria (turns 3–5) in which she affirms her understanding of a point about inverse proportion. Turn 6 then proceeds for an additional twenty seconds. Hence, Darnell's response to Victoria's question about peer tutoring was extensive in terms of duration and the issues on which he touched and elaborated.

In turn 2 Darnell addresses his preference for meaningful learning and being able to apply what he learns to his life and learning heuristics so that he can figure out other trends in science, such as using inverse proportion as a principle that allows him to describe certain trends associated with periodicity. As he frequently does in cogenerative dialogues, Darnell takes specifics from the previous class as an illustration of the points he is making. In turn 6 Darnell makes the point that peers can learn from one another a little easier than if they are interacting with a teacher. He goes further to affirm that he likes to tutor his peers, especially if he feels comfortable with the subject matter.

Victoria's interruption reflects her concern for being accurate in the use of terminology. Darnell says indirect instead of inverse proportion and even though it is probably a slip of the tongue, Victoria corrects him as soon as there is an opportunity to do so. Darnell accepts her correction in good spirit and without pause he moves on to turn 6. From the moment he begins to speak all participants in the cogenerative dialogue, including Ken, are leaning forward, nodding their heads in agreement with what he is saying and smiling. Jessica continues to take notes based on what he is saying. No wonder that when he concludes Darnell appears pleased with his contributions and looks expectantly toward Despina, showing interest in what she might say.

Despina does not speak until 0.6 seconds of silence has elapsed. This is consistent with earlier research on coteaching in which pauses of greater than 0.5 seconds are resources for fresh speakers to participate in an interaction. In this case there is no competition for a turn at talk, Despina knew it was her turn and she was ready to contribute, well aware of the intention of Victoria's initial request. Her turn at talk extends for seventy seconds and like Darnell, Despina first contextualizes what she has to say and appears comfortable in developing her point. She repairs her own inadvertent utterances as she constructs a lengthy response to the invitation about peer tutoring. Just as Darnell covers many topics he considers salient, Despina also touches on numerous issues including her level of success in science before and during this class, how her performance in science relates to her college aspirations, and how her success in science is related to the forms of teaching in this class. The opportunity to participate as a peer tutor is for Despina a sign of self worth and a contributor to a growing sense of communality and solidarity with others because she is able to help peers.

A characteristic of this vignette is just how articulate the students are in expressing their perspectives about learning, understanding, effective teaching and tutoring peers. There are few interruptions and ample evidence that a strong mutual focus existed and a willingness to allow others to speak, listen to them, and then build agreement around the interactions, in this case, consisting of eight turns at talk, three of which are of significant duration. The emotional energy is high, as can be taken from the speech parameters such as speech intensity and pitch levels, and each speaker uses gestures to emphasize points, depict shapes and occasionally point to an artifact such as the periodic table.

* * *

Ken: What strikes me in looking at the transcript is how insightful both students' comments are. If only the conversation had picked up on some of the points that were raised, for example, in relation to the roles of teachers and students had taken and possible changes they might have wanted to make therein. With this, I do not mean to take a deficit perspective but rather prospectively, reflect on the conversation to think how we might improve upon cogenerative dialoguing in future sessions.

Michael: As I said before, the level of articulation of which these students are capable has struck me; now I am no longer surprised. The students are highly sophisticated. Thus what really strikes me now is the difference between the deficit accounts some science educators construct concerning the knowledge of students in inner-city schools and the competencies that they display in face-to-face encounters about how to improve the teaching and learning situation in their classrooms.

Ken: In turn 2 Darnell was making a good point about the benefits a peer teacher can gain from teaching others. I was quite impressed with his idea of walking away with only a third of what was taught. Then he gave an example and made a slip, and Victoria picked up on it correcting the slip right then and there. As a general rule I think it would be preferred for Victoria to focus on the main point that Darnell was making—following through perhaps to the point that there is consensus on what is going to happen in the next class in relation to peer tutoring.

Michael: It would be interesting to bring this issue up in a conversation involving Victoria. I would be interested in finding out what her preferred action would be and whether she enacted it or whether the situation confronted her with resources that constrained what she could do. The other issue for me in your statement is the extent to which the preferences of others can or should become resources for a teacher to change—I guess this has been the approach research has taken in the past: creating policy or model curricula to be taught in their preferred way rather than in the preferred ways of the teacher.

Ken: There is also a take-away message in Darnell's comment in turn 6, raising the possibility that students can better learn from one another than from a teacher. Once again there are some avenues that would directly flow from that premise—for example more group work or more peer tutoring.

Michael: I remember that this very issue had come up early in our work involving Natasia, who already features in chapter 2. I think that we have not yet gotten sufficient mileage out of this realization. To create communities of learners, we need to set up contexts in which students decide what they need and draw on the available resources, which more frequently will be their peers rather than one of the few teachers in class.

Ken: Despina makes some critical points in terms of her own identity. I am most impressed with her willingness to assist others to learn and to see that her previous experiences with science are not necessarily a characteristic of science, but of enactment. I would hope that her comments would not just be left dangling as they move on to a fresh topic. It might reasonably be asked about this round of conversation—what did we cogenerate?

Michael: Sometimes we realize important issues only after the fact. Now that we see Despina at work and come to understand something important to her engagement, it would be interesting to have another cogenerative dialogue to push understanding further—as we have done it with Natasia, where we continued interacting with her in the course of coming to grips with Chuck's problematic presentation of the dihybrid cross, which took us nearly 16 months prior to completing our manuscript.

What is Good Science Education?

Ken uses Despina's clear explanation of her success in this class as an opportunity to ask her what it was about the previous class that she does not like. She elaborates without hesitation to the effect that her previous teacher in high school has focused on the subject and presents the material so fast that it is difficult to succeed and enjoy the class. She now realizes that it was the class not the subject that she did not enjoy. Her comments underline the centrality of teachers in how students position themselves with respect to subjects like science.

Darnell quickly follows on from Despina and in so doing communicates that in middle school he hated science because of the way it was taught. His comments also address the role of the teacher, forms of participation, and his growing awareness that science is relevant to life, interesting, and could involve investigations. It is apparent that he now loves science and especially likes to work out puzzles and problems, not only in laboratories but also through conversations with others. His mention of laboratories is an opportunity for Victoria to insert a "right" in one of the pauses between Darnell's words, thereby signaling an intention to speak. Darnell quickly finishes and without any pause Victoria asks about laboratories in the science course.

What emerges from this vignette of just over 100 seconds is an awareness that science is neither inherently good nor bad, and depending on how it is taught, students can either switch off or learn and build an interest. Fortunately, in the cases of Despina and Darnell, their histories portray a trajectory from failure to success and from hating science to being interested in it. For the teachers it is apparent that the students regard teaching as central to structuring science in ways to afford learning.

* * *

Ken: The students are quite consistent in their valuing of science that has relevance to their interests and lives outside of school. They also agree that science should be challenging—intellectually stimulating.

Michael: I think that this positive emotional valence with respect to science comes with the sense of control over the conditions in which they learn. Whenever humans have a say in what they want to do and how they want to do it, the sense of being in control and being able to define goals is associated with higher emotional valence than having to do as someone else wants. What bourgeois psychologists call "being motivated" really means doing on your own what someone else wants you to do (Holzkamp, 1993). Motivation, in this way, is a tool for the subjugation of students from lower classes to the ideology of the dominant middle-class culture that organizes school structures. As Penny Eckert (1989) has shown for working-class students in the American Midwest, school culture more closely matches the cultural values of the White middle class and is biased against the cultural practices of working-class students—including, for example, same-age versus cross-age relations, being a jock versus being a burnout, being motivated to do well in school versus being motivated to have good relations with your peers, and so on.

Ken: I couldn't agree more. As it is taught, and what is taught, in urban science classes is barely useful to urban youth—either in making sense of social life or gaining entry to prestigious schools and programs. Instead, failure to perform as well as suburban students on high-stakes tests encourages and reinforces deficit perspectives about what urban youth know and can do.

Laboratories in the Science Program

Darnell's mention of laboratories catalyzes a discussion that lasts for more than eight minutes. This vignette is salient to the entire cogenerative dialogue because it is the longest discussion, it involves all participants in lengthy explanations of their perspectives, and there is disagreement. As in the previous two vignettes, Victoria sets up the focus, building on an issue raised by Darnell in his comments about what constitutes good science education. Although they are long, the transcripts clearly show that although the students wanted less structure and a more challenging curriculum, Victoria had arguments as to why the status quo was desirable.

```
1  Victoria   I wanted to ask about u:m labs. Like when we do
              labs like we haven't really gotten to do many
              like we've done four. U:m. How do you guys feel
              like when we actually do them? Do you think we
              give enough time to prepare for them? Do you
              think we explain enough? Or do you get like, do
```

		you guys get the concept behind why we actually do the lab or is it more open ended? (1.5) U:m. Maybe I didn't ask it right. He. He. He-
2	Darnell	Me personally, I think that I get I get too much information. That's what I get.
3	Despina	Thank you ((reaches out to touch Darnell's right arm)).
4	Darnell	I think I get [too much information.
5	Despina	[I mean because you I think that u:m we need to . . . the rest of the class needs to . . . we need to be able to find out. Okay. This is the information. I need to figure out how to put this in a chart. You know because the last lab that we did (1.0) the, all we basically had to do for this lab we could have had to do the experiment but we put everything on the board. But if everybody put all their answers on the board then we go over it then we have charts and everything that's already prepared for us so we just follow the information. So, it wasn't much that we needed to do on our own if you didn't do anything in the experiment. So, I think that as far as labs go we need to do more things that we could figure out for ourselves, maybe one time. "Okay, here's information. You got this? You got the solutions. You got the reactions. Put it in a chart. Well you know you have, oh, you know how to make a chart, you have the columns, you read them all, and then you have the information. Put it in a chart (1.0) and then I want to see this, this and this in a chart." And then we can come up with our own, you know, things. And as far as the labs are concerned, I find, I find 'em, they're reasonable. U:m. Isn't that the traditional lab format? We don't have to write, you know, everything in the you know, scientific method. We just need to write the purpose, and kinda, like the cover letter, what each one was about, the procedure, conclusion. So, I don't, I'm not finding that hard at all. ((Approximately 101 seconds in duration.)) (0.2).
6	Darnell	I think as well like as the year progresses, and it's almost over give a prelab. Give a prelab like how we had to find solubility and different things. If we could have found different solubilities and what they're mixing with and what they're not mixing with. Then and you wouldn't have to give us procedures on what to do, just say, well we want you to react these different metals. I know over the summer time we didn't have a procedure, then we had to start from

scratch. The only thing is that: was this for-
maldehyde present in diet soft drinks? So you
could take that anywhere you wanted to take it.
So, I think if this is supposed to be preparing
us for college and then it's for the world of
work. If you do go on in science, if you go on
in science, it's not a big name where you say
the procedures for every scientific thing you
want to do. You've got to make up your own procedures. So, I think as the year's like almost
over, just say, arright, "You've got a prelab
that you're gonna do u:m a project on x, y, and
z. There's some information here and you're on
your own." You just sit back and if we've got
questions we like, well what do you think? You
know. Ask what we think first and then if you
see we're doing it wrong then you can intervene
and help us. ((63 seconds in duration.))

Although the vignette continues for several lengthy turns, it is convenient at this juncture to review how Despina and Darnell respond to an invitation to critique the approach taken to labs. Earlier discussions of what had been tried by the coteachers were very positive and the students and coteachers were aligned in their talk and stated preferences.

As Victoria sets up the issue in turn 1 it is evident that she anticipates some difference of opinion among group members. She takes the number of labs they have done off the floor for discussion when she explains that they have done only four and seems to offer an apology for the low number. She then focuses discussion on how students feel about what is done in laboratories, and in a sense her subsequent questions provide a roadmap for what the students address in turns 2 through 6. Before making a transition to the next speaker, Victoria allows a pause of 1.5 seconds (much longer than the maximum one-second silence that linguists have reported to be found in normal conversations), ample for someone else to have spoken. Her expectation appears to be that one of the students would have responded since her request for feedback was directed at them. Their failure to access the pause prompted a hedging sentence from Victoria on clarity and then a nervous laugh.

In turn 2 Darnell offers a critique by saying that he gets too much structure from the teachers. Despina offers her support for him by saying thank you in a way that indicates her agreement, and by reaching over to touch his arm, she provides Darnell with encouragement to continue. In turn 4 Darnell repeats his claim that there was too much structure. At this time Despina initiates turn 5, a monologue that continues for 101 seconds. The start to this turn suggests that Despina has not thought out what she wants to say. There are false starts as she tries several ways to get started. Then she pronounces, "Okay," and begins to lay out an approach that is characterized by her having more autonomy to figure out what to do and when to do it. In making a request for more autonomy she describes how recent approaches have made laboratories procedural and have even taken away the necessity for students to complete the laboratories to finish what the teachers want from students. Following her critique she does a role-play in which she shows the coteachers how they might address students with her suggested approach. Finally, she explores some aspects of writing a laboratory that she endorses, but then concludes that none of what is done is challenging to her.

In turn 6 Darnell speaks at length on much the same issues raised by Despina. He argues for less structure, illustrates with examples from a summer program he was in and from a recent laboratory, provides a role-play on how to present the approach to students, and justifies his request in terms of preparing them for college. At the heart of Darnell's turn is inquiry and learning, a theme he constantly advocated throughout the years of our research. Somewhat in contrast but also complementary was Despina's position that too much structure reduces the challenge and associated interest.

* * *

Ken: The students agree that the laboratory tasks should be more challenging and open-ended. What is of concern is the failure to explore why they think what they do and how class might be different of their ideas were enacted.

Michael: Perhaps part of the training of new teachers would be to assist them learning how to listen. Despite your research more than twenty years ago about wait time II, which I understand in terms of the teacher listening to as many students as possible during class, teachers generally still do not listen to students. They tend not to listen during class, where the object is student learning; and they tend not to listen to students' concerns. Perhaps a new metaphor, which you reported to be operating like a master switch, may assist teachers in changing their orientation towards teacher–student conversations. If they were to understand themselves as listeners and learners, perhaps the associated images of the teacher-as-learner-and-listener metaphor might be a resource that assists them in doing better justice to the intent of cogenerative dialogues.

* * *

Victoria's turn 7 is almost three minutes in duration, easily the longest monologue in the cogenerative dialogue. She addressed each point raised by the students, sometimes agreeing with their sentiments, but firmly illustrating why the open-ended, less teacher-structured approach the students advocated was not practical in the circumstances. Because of its length, we present turn 7 separately:

```
7   Victoria: Okay. U:m. I think we we may not be able to do
              that necessarily in our class because the dif-
              ferent levels of people in the class would, you
              know, that that the way that you guys, you know
              suggested that labs be more you know more more
              put towards you for the responsibility to get
              things organized, get things prepared and go.
              For some students we don't have a problem like
              we'll know you guys can do that, or you're very
```

independent, no problem. But for everyone, that person that's independent, there's another one that won't do the work if if it's not assigned. If it's not structured they won't even know where to begin and in college your laboratories for chemistry, for physics, for biology, they're very structured and Miss Rodriguez can attest to that. We get books, like huge books and they tell you step by step what to do. The analysis is not given to us. You have to take that on to your own. That's the next step. More of the thought behind why you would justify things, why you see one thing when you predicted another. Um, but in these type of, you know, well give us a project where we really don't know what to do that's what the science project is. It's independent, you can do it on your own time. You can do whatever you want with the topic. You're like "I wanna study you know how different plants grow based on the amount of sunlight I give them. Right?" You know, that's a whole other thing. That's a whole other subject. You can do it at your own time, at your own pace and you need to do it for this class. That's where open-ended research, like where we place responsibility completely on you guys. That's what the science project is and we're gonna go over that a little bit more in the coming weeks. Like in the next two. But I think in terms of laboratory, that's why we really can't do it ill-structured. It has to be very structured for this type of class where it is introductory. You guys haven't seen any of this before, you know. Like we want you guys to see "Oh, this does relate to this chemistry concept we just learned this week." Like reactivity is this because you see electrons being transferred. If we don't give you the background you guys'll be like "Oh, it's just another. Like see how that's cool. It changed color. It changed shape." You know, I think structure provides you like a view of what we should be looking at and it's chemistry. But I like the idea about ill-structured labs. We just can't do them. Ha ha. Like chem. Two. I think the next level of chemistry, when you have all this background information then we can build on that, right? If you have the basic knowledge let's go to the next step. What can we start doing? What can we start thinking about? And how can we show it in the lab? That's the stuff I love. That's what I want to do my PhD on.

From the outset Victoria rejects the idea that there would be less structure of the sort described by Despina and Darnell. She relates this position to the diversity in the class. She quickly excludes Darnell and Despina from her characterization of students as needing the structure. In so doing she confirms the high respect she has for these two students. Victoria states that without the structure some students will not be able to start an investigation. Her comments reflect deficit perspectives and might be a good example of the cautions Despina has urged throughout the cogenerative dialogue, to suspend judgment and search for the talent in students, creating structures to challenge and interest the class. Arguably, maintaining the status quo will maintain the perception that the course is easy and lacks challenge.

Victoria then characterizes college science in opposition to the optimistic way in which Darnell represents it. Darnell's optimistic image of science reflects his experiences in science summer camps while Victoria's accounts reflect her experiences as a science major and graduate student. Her call to a colleague (Miss Rodriguez), who has joined the cogenerative dialogue as an observer, to confirm her negative characterizations of college laboratories is a concern. Darnell's optimistic view and quest for inquiry is central to his goal of pursuing a college degree in science, becoming a research scientist, and one day competing for the Nobel Prize.

Victoria subsequently connects college science laboratories to Darnell's goal to pursue inquiry, explaining that the science project associated with their class is designed to meet inquiry goals. Even though Victoria's descriptions of what is involved in the science project would likely appeal to Darnell, the kernel of her argument is to keep things the way they are. She explains why inquiry approaches in the laboratory are not viable in this class and that without a toolkit of chemistry concepts the students will not see what they are supposed to see in the laboratory. Later she projects that students may have the necessary foundational knowledge to support inquiry-oriented laboratories by the time they take their second chemistry course. Interestingly, her argument here is central to her disagreements with Alex, disagreements that have made coteaching with him increasingly difficult.

In his own research on labs in urban science classrooms, Alex shows how the foundational knowledge needed to support serious inquiry-oriented investigations could be built simultaneously with on-going investigations (Carambo, 2005). One year earlier than the present cogenerative dialogue, in a study undertaken with ninth-grade students, Alex shows how deep learning may arise from lab investigations when text and electronic resources are available to support conceptual growth in the areas associated with the investigation.

* * *

Ken: Victoria seems to adhere to a view of structure that only acknowledges her own practices as structuring. I see this as a widespread problem that contributes to teachers failing to search for the students' capital and allowing them to use their agency to structure their own learning.

Michael: I see Victoria's way of approaching teaching as consistent with the dominant paradigm according to which teachers know and transfer this knowledge to students. Despite years of constructivism, this has not changed; even university professors of science education talk with a split tongue, simultaneously emphasizing knowledge as something constructed and producing papers about the responsibility of teachers to make sure students get the science right. So university teacher education continues to emphasize teachers' responsibilities for student outcomes.

Ken: It seems ironic to me that some of the earlier discussion about peer teaching can address Victoria's problem of some students not doing the work or not being able to do the work. The use of peer tutoring with the sorts of grouping arrangements discussed earlier seem to allow for exactly what Despina and Darnell are asking for.

Michael: What students appear to recognize is the need for having appropriate resources for learning and for being able to draw on those resources that they consider to be the best at the moment. Even if a teacher thinks she knows best, whether she currently addresses the learning needs of the students is an empirical matter and therefore needs to be solicited from students.

Ken: Victoria's lengthy monologue and perhaps the level of commitment she shows to inquiry effectively shuts down further input from the students on making the labs more open-ended. She is not just having dialogue about the ways in which laboratories are enacted; but explaining why laboratories have to be taught as they are presently taught. Calling on a colleague to support her descriptions of how it is at college also is a call for external authority—a structure that makes it less likely students would elaborate on their perspectives. Effectively the opportunity to cogenerate an outcome is truncated with Victoria's clear expression of intent to maintain the status quo.

Michael: Unfortunately, Virginia displays a pattern across situations of thinking she knows best and of being insensitive to the input of students and teachers alike. One would hope that she would begin listening to others, students and colleagues alike, and, in reflecting upon what she hears, learn about how situations are experienced and described by others.

Compromise

In the next vignette Ken endeavors to locate the middle ground with a suggestion to try to cater to the needs of all students, including those who want more autonomy and greater opportunities for inquiry. As a participant in the cogenerative dialogue he felt a need to legitimize the perspectives of the students while not disrespecting Victoria's perspectives. He would have preferred to remain silent, but Victoria's comments had effectively silenced the students. As soon as Ken begins to speak both Jessica and Victoria began to take notes. He feels that the power dynamics had shifted appreciably in the discussions of lab and there was little to be done about it here. The note taking was a sign to all participants that Victoria and Jessica were his students and would not likely disagree.

```
8   Ken:      So, let me say something over on the side here
              because I think you had a good idea then. U::m,
              I mean is it possible for the structured labs
```

and then those that finished the structured labs quickly and well could have u:m, additional open-ended activities ah that they could move on with. It seems to me that we don't want to have a structure that prevents people from going to where they can go. U::m. I mean it's just a thought because I think it's always good, ah to challenge the best while you pay attention to those that need additional structure as well. So, I mean it's a bit unusual in the sense that for the teachers you have to do a little bit of extra work and bring a few more materials or an extra little challenge. But I like the idea of encouraging the more able to get through perhaps a little more quickly and then have an open-ended lab that not everybody, but some can participate in. Everybody could do it potentially but they would have to earn their stripes.

Ken makes it clear that he sees merit in the ideas put forward by Darnell and Despina and he suggests something akin to the challenge activities enacted in the previous lesson (see chapter 3)—to cater to the needs of students who finished early. Having an inquiry component to laboratories, for those who earned the right to participate, seems consistent with the previous dialogue and with the necessity to cogenerate shared agreements on what would happen when the science curriculum was enacted in the future. Head nods and note taking suggest there is consensus even though Ken would have preferred additional conversation about the specifics for planning and enacting this change of direction in subsequent laboratories.

* * *

Ken: My participation was not effective in the sense that we now understand the purposes of cogenerative dialogues. If I had not spoken at all it might have been that Darnell or Despina would have countered Victoria's perspectives. My strong position truncated everybody's agency in that the stakes for expressing a different perspective were raised considerably. Both teachers beginning to take notes when I started speaking is a sign that the power differentials are not easily swept aside with rhetoric. It takes more to equalize power than simply having a rule that everybody's contribution counts the same in cogenerative dialogue. This vignette makes it clear that equalizing of power takes effort from all participants over time to speak for the benefit of others participating and bring their perspectives to the fore. Just as Victoria made her perspectives clear to all in the previous move, so did I when I responded.

Michael: Even if you now say that your participation has not been effective, we can learn from the situation. In other words, you can learn from the instances precisely because you now feel it has been inappropriate, which allows you to engage in an endeavor to produce a possible candidate explanation for what has happened and how you might have acted differently if you knew what you know today.

Ken: Yes. As readers think about setting up cogenerative dialogues they can plan to avoid the power issues that arose in this instance.

Michael: For me, it is not so much a question of equalizing power as it is a question of acting without drawing on your institutional position to assert yourself in ways that differ from the ways others have available. The question of power becomes irrelevant when all participants in cogenerative dialoguing sessions adhere to its principles, which means, that they all give as much as they take from the situation.

Laziness

As soon as Ken completes his comments about possible compromise Despina begins to talk, initiating a topic about some of her peers being lazy. Her remarks are a return to the comments about some students being slack during group work. Despina does not have a deficit perspective on the talent of her peers and describes many of them as bright but complacent, regarding this class as easy. Her comments about the class lacking challenge also reiterate what she and Darnell have said throughout the cogenerative dialogue. Despina notes a disturbing trend to reduce the requirements when students complain about the workload and urges the coteachers not to relax the requirements. In her comments Despina notes issues of peer pressure but encourages teachers to find out if there are students who could and would do the work before acceding to the requests of what might be a vocal minority.

The interactions around the topic of student laziness are somewhat more interactive than others in this cogenerative dialogue. In contrast to the others described earlier in this chapter, the interactions are relatively brief and at some stages there is overlapping talk among participants. This is an example of a student raising an issue for discussion and in this instance Jessica is the first of the coteachers to raise questions for further discussion, related to how to address the issue and how to know how far to push on these "lazy" students. Despina points out that the coteachers should take into account that the theme for their small learning community in which the course is being offered is science, engineering, and mathematics. Accordingly, she feels that the coteachers should not dilute the rigor of the courses by lowering expectations for lazy students.

* * *

Ken: The students repeatedly call for more challenge and what they appear to mean by this is intellectual rigor. It seems as if the coteachers, especially Victoria, are unwilling to change their approach to curriculum, but will consider taking actions to deal with lazy students. I think the deficit perspectives of students are powerful schemas that, on the one hand, justify the forms of structure the teachers seem committed to, and on the other hand, contribute to the truncation of student agency.

Michael: This again shows us how students both understand what is at issue and that they have possible solutions to the problems teachers identify. Working with the collective and allowing it to deal with issues such as laziness appear to me better strategies than the punitive measures teachers have been using for ages in their attempts to align students with their own intentions.

Identity of New Teachers

Victoria and Jessica are concerned that they did not enjoy the same status as their resident teacher, Alex. Darnell and Despina both assure the coteachers that they are effective in their roles and that they should not be concerned with Alex having more status with the students than either of them. They joke that he is responsible for the grades and hence will always have higher status. Victoria's examples seem to relate to management, that Alex gets the students' attention quicker than her even if she uses much the same approach. Darnell makes the point that in some ways the new teachers are treated like substitute teachers, but that this could change as they have an impact on the learning of students. Despina urges the coteachers to build their own pedagogy and not try to imitate Alex. She uses examples from her experiences with other new teachers and offers specific advice on the desirability of avoiding comparisons.

* * *

Ken: I am reminded by my own experiences as an urban science teacher, of the need to earn the status of being considered by these students as a teacher. Alex also had to struggle when he first came to the school.

Michael: In this episode, students' treatment of new and substitute teachers sticks out for me. With most of these types of teachers, students appear to be using the lower institutional position as a resource for treating these teachers differently, outsiders to their normal environment. Yet Victoria, in contrast to substitute teachers, has been spending much more time in the class. This makes me think that the teachers make available to students, as some research suggests, their lesser status and power through their prosody among other means. All of this occurs at levels not normally available to consciousness.

Ken: Jessica has spent much of her time in the class working in peripheral roles, doing one-on-one and small-group teaching. In contrast, Victoria quickly took up opportunities to coteach and solo teach the whole class. So, it is not surprising that students regard Jessica, Victoria, and Alex differently. Also, the differences between Alex and Victoria are strident, especially in making the curriculum challenging. It is no surprise that Jessica and Victoria experience identity issues. The issue is this: how can they begin to see their identities in relation to the conversations about the curriculum that emerge in this cogenerative dialogue?

Coteaching

The discussion of the identity of teachers evolves to address the effectiveness of coteachers. The following transcript captures the dialogue that unfolds.

1	Victoria	Does it help for you guys to see like, when trying to explain something and then you know, a lot of people will say: do you guys get it? And then one of the others will jump in and say, "Okay, it looks like this." Like to get two or more perspectives on the same subject, does that help you guys [see] the concept
2	Darnell	[Yeah.]
3	Victoria	more because I notice that with the three of us we have that ability to jump in and say wait, hold on?
4	Despina	=Hmm.
5	Victoria	I don't think they'll see it. Let me try it my way and I don't know if you guys see that in your other classes because I didn't, you know, I never even got to ask you guys do you have other new teachers in your class? Like how involved are they? Do they take over like we do on some days? Or do they coteach? Like do they teach together with the resident, the resident teacher, right? Like we don't even know the structure.
6	Darnell	=Right.
7	Victoria	=All we know is what we have in our classroom.
8	Darnell	In comparison to other new teachers they, it's like they try to do the same thing, but it's not like yours. Like you could be over there saying one thing and Miss Jessica'll be like why don't you try this right here. "Oh well, I understand this way. It's like they got to go on for a whole period of time. I don't understand. I don't understand. I don't understand." With you guys it don't have to be "I don't understand." If you feel as though it's a easier way, a better way, it's like when you use u:m ((looks at periodic table)) you use sodium, you can use chloride, chlorine. It was like, whoa, try to do this one, it's a little bit easier. I mean that's what you be saying instead of me. That'll make it so that they understand it when the reality they already went over it that way. So, I think it's better. Like they say, what, two heads is better than one, three heads is better than one you know. You'll always be able to clean up for somebody else. Like well Miss V put something out and it was good, but Miss Jessica contributes a little bit more and Mister Alex can come over and tie everything together. Like

> you can go in any order. Now so I like, I like
> how y'all teaching now.

In turns 1, 3, 5, and 7 Victoria sets up a context for obtaining student input on the nature and effectiveness of coteaching. Her setting of the stage invites a comparison with the ways in which Despina and Darnell have experienced other new teachers. Turns 2, 4 and 6 are brief utterances, signs of Darnell's and Despina's approval of coteaching and its effectiveness. In turn 8 Darnell explains that other new teachers do not coteach and they are less effective than the coteaching team involved in this study. Darnell's explanation is supported by his animated gestures and several examples drawn from recent shared experiences.

* * *

Ken: Here, Darnell focuses on his own learning and on the extent to which coteachers can expand his agency; hence, the focus is his learning of science.

Michael: This is a nice illustration of the opportunities cogenerative dialogues provides for expanding student agency.

Ken: It seems a pity that the conversation did not turn to one of how could we be better in what we do. So many of the conversations in this cogenerative dialogue lack a critical edge.

Michael: I would not focus so much on the missed opportunities, as we always find out later that there are other things that we could have talked about. In a way, it is with hindsight that we can say that opportunities have been missed. For me the important issue is not the missed opportunities but the design challenge these raise: how can we design cogenerative dialogue sessions such that we can learn from them as much as possible. For example, these sessions might become objects for the inquiry of all involved, such that teachers or students might choose to bring a clip from a previous session to a subsequent session.

Shared Responsibility

Ken initiated the final vignette that we selected from the cogenerative dialogue. He focuses on the acceptance of shared responsibility for the class. Ken identifies some students who have been disrespectful and disruptive and asks how the group might deal with similar practices in the future. Both students suggest that they could have a role in letting classmates know "when enough is enough." Despina once again addresses the responsibility to get the most from students. She uses examples of students she knows who could not earn respect for their scholarship and therefore adopts the roles of class clown. She urges the coteachers to listen to what students have to say and not to jump to judgment. A telling example she uses is that sometimes as students are explaining a teacher is thinking up his or her reaction and misses the opportunity to learn what the student knows or how to advance his or her learning. She emphasizes that classroom environments should support students' risk taking; assuring them it is all right to have wrong answers. Her advice is to be attentive listeners, suspend judgment, and emphasize inquiry learning.

Ken's intention in raising the issue of shared responsibility is to guide the dialogue towards some agreement on what the group has agreed to in the cogenerative dialogue and what responsibility they all have for enacting changes in the next lesson. He does not push when the participants decide to focus on further discussion of deficit perspectives and the way they play out in low expectations for some students and less than stimulating learning environments.

* * *

Ken: Despina knows that she and her peers have capital that can be a foundation for success. Throughout this dialogue she has cautioned against deficit perspectives and has exhorted teachers to listen and learn from the students. There is some distance to go since in the cogenerative dialogue there were questions, answers, and then movement toward the next topic.

Michael: This appears to me one of the important lessons from our work concerning cogenerative dialoguing. Teachers and other stakeholders have the opportunity to learn about what students experience as resources or constraints for their agency in learning science. The most important thing teachers can do is this: begin to listen rather than feeling the urge to push on with covering curriculum.

Ken: The students showed they have a good grasp of what they want in a science curriculum and how the roles of teachers and students might be changed to expand their agency and opportunities to learn. The cogenerative dialogue did not go to the next step to push for a consensus on how to catalyze desirable changes. The hard work of negotiating agreements did not occur.

Michael: This shows us again how important it is to include students in shaping the classroom learning environment and in producing resources that all can use for higher levels of achievement and, even more important, for better understanding of the science concepts at hand.

MOVING AWAY FROM DEFICIT PERSPECTIVES

This cogenerative dialogue provides stunning insights into the capacities of urban youth to analyze teaching and learning, to represent their own perspectives in articulate and extended ways, and to raise difficult issues across boundaries of class, ethnicity, gender and age. There is ample evidence in the cogenerative dialogues that the students can develop solid and extended arguments, listen attentively and when the time comes address salient issues that maintain focus to address group goals. The coteachers and the students show respect for one another, earn the respect of others, and rarely take the turn of others. There is awareness that each will have a turn at talk and that it is acceptable to be critical. Also, when critical comments are being advanced there is no attempt to shut down the speaker and responses are calm, reasoned, and cordial.

This research has not explored the extent to which one field is a seedbed for the growth of new culture, but it is evident that students like Darnell have enacted similar interaction patterns in the cogenerative dialogue and the classroom. He has enacted successful interactions in both fields and the features of those patterns are so similar in terms of what he says and does and how he does what he does to argue that this cultural capital transcended the two fields. There is every reason to expect that Darnell would enact much the same capital when he goes on to college.

The question of deficit perspectives and their dissemination through cogenerative dialogue is a concern that emerges from this study. A potential concern is Victoria's effort to address each point that Darnell has raised. Ken happens to agree with Darnell, that an appropriate preparation for college would be to prepare him to reason, raise questions and problem solve. Victoria, who has recently experienced science as a graduate and an undergraduate, speaks forcefully to convince Darnell that he had an incorrect perspective on what college science was like. Whereas she is close to the mark and probably represents her own experiences accurately in the course of the events, she may dampen Darnell's enthusiasm for pursuing a science-related career and college level studies in science. Perhaps Darnell would have responded that if college science is as Victoria depicts it then it too would have to change to have a greater emphasis on inquiry. What is interesting is that the perspectives put by Despina and Darnell are close to those of reform-minded science educators. Advocates of cogenerative dialogue must pay attention to the possibility that differentials in institutional positions associated with status will make certain arguments more acceptable than others during cogenerative dialogue. In this regard Ken has been haunted by the images of Victoria and Jessica taking notes when he has taken a position that was somewhat counter to their practices and justifications for not changing the laboratories. Even though the outcomes are consistent with his preferences, the spirit of cogenerative dialogues—i.e., all voices carry equal weight—is not in evidence throughout this episode, just as the asymmetries grounded in the different institutional positions of the participants are evident too when Victoria responds to Darnell and Despina about the need for less structure in the laboratory tasks.

LEARNING ABOUT LEARNING FROM COGENERATIVE DIALOGUES

Although Ken initially requested that cogenerative dialogues occur for a given class twice a week, they happened much less than that and eventually Ken set a rule that cogenerative dialogues should occur at least once a week. The problems were with scheduling. Because of the work schedules of the coteachers and the students it was difficult to find the extra time. An implication of this is that cogenerative dialogues should probably be scheduled in advance and should not be seen as the prerogative of the teacher to schedule or not. As is evident in Sonya Martin's doctoral study (Martin, 2005), when things get hectic for the teacher, cogenerative dialogues tend to occur less frequently, just when the students need them most. A second issue is getting representatives from each stakeholder group. For example, Alex has had a great deal of work to do and often has not participated in cogenerative dialogues (such as the one analyzed in this chapter). Even so, they should go on because the participants can benefit nonetheless. Finally, selecting the students can be an issue, especially how many of them should participate. We have found two to three students to be about the right number and to the extent possible a dialectical process should be used to select opposites. We have had most success when there is stability of the students in the cogenerative dialogues. In stable groups, over time, characteristic culture can emerge and the cogenerative dialogues can be fields in which the culture produced is potentially transformative for enacted curricula in classrooms.

One of the key features of cogenerative dialogue is the rule structure. As is evident from this study, differences in power can distort the focus of dialogue and the nature of the agreements reached. Accordingly, just as Jessica did in opening the cogenerative dialogue the rule of it being a place where participants are free to speak openly without fear of reprisal is essential. A complementary rule is that all participants must show one another respect, be sensitive listeners and respect the rights of others not only to speak but also to establish common foci for dialogue. Part of attentive listening is commenting on what others have said an not moving on without there first being a consensus on previous issues.

Establishing shared foci can be done in a number of ways. In the cogenerative dialogue analyzed in this chapter the foci are established in an unfolding way as the participants discussed a recent lesson in which all have participated. This is successful in that the issues identified are salient to the participants; but a weakness is that there have not been clear cogenerated outcomes. That is, there is no clear expectation that goals, roles, and rules would change and that this group has a shared responsibility for enacting the agreed to changes successfully. An alternative that has emerged after this cogenerative dialogue: to identify contradictions arising from enacted curricula and make these the foci for cogenerative dialogue.

A focus on identifying and resolving contradictions arises from a depiction of culture as being enacted as patterns having thin coherence alongside of contradictions to which the patterns of coherence are dialectically interconnected. One idea is to identify the contradictions and either minimize their occurrence or if the contradictions are desirable, increase their incidence. The most important aspect is not to brush contradictions under the carpet but use them as objects of inquiry and to learn from them as much as possible. Of course in doing so, enacting a change, additional contradictions will be introduced and these may also have to be foci for cogenerative dialogue. But these new contradictions can then become the new foci and common objects for subsequent discussions. That is, as all activity systems, cogenerative dialoguing sessions produce contradictions, which, when used as objects for focused inquiry, have the potential to become resources for learning and, therefore, for the improvement of the life conditions—here, coteaching and cogenerative dialoguing sessions. Participants in cogenerative dialogues might not always be aware of contradictions and it can be useful for one or more of the participants to select video vignettes having thirty seconds to two minutes duration. Participants can then review these vignettes and patterns and contradictions about which they were previously unaware. Through subsequent interactive dialogue agreements can be reached on whether or not changes need to be made. Whether video vignettes are used to establish a shared focus, a consensus should be reached on what is to be done, one that is collectively owned. In addition, all participants should consider their roles in enacting what has been agreed, the individual roles having a dialectical relationship to the collective roles of participants.

SHARING RESPONSIBILITY FOR EFFECTIVE TEACHING AND LEARNING

Professional development approaches and needs can be mediated, and perhaps contorted, by macrostructures such as high-stakes testing. In such circumstances well-intended educators, and especially people from funding agencies, might focus resources on improving the performance levels on high stakes tests. Perhaps it is partly this emphasis on external, high-stakes tests that leads scientists to look at what is happening in schools and cast the problems in terms of students and their teachers not knowing enough scientific concepts and theories. Assumptions about deficiencies of science subject matter can lead to approaches to enacting curricula and professional development of science teachers that fail to take into account sociocultural and cultural-historical factors: especially how to effectively communicate across borders defined by variables such as social class, economic status, native language, gender and race.

In this chapter we are explicit about issues inherent in planning and enacting effective professional development programs. As throughout this book our approach is theoretical and empirical. We opt to examine a professional development program planned to address the needs of disadvantaged high school youth in New York City. This context is salient because there is a significant focus on learning subject matter and holding students, teachers, and schools accountable for high levels of academic achievement through performance on state-level examinations referred to as *Regents* examinations.

The design for this project has many features that would be regarded as desirable by school districts and funding agencies. For example, faculty from university science departments collaborated with teachers, some identified as exemplary and others from low performing schools to provide an intensive course for students who were previously unsuccessful in a high-stakes examination. The rationale for the design of the project consisted on a number of taken for granted assumptions, including: (a) less is more, (b) there should be a strong alignment of what is taught with what is tested, (c) success is represented in test scores, (d) teachers from different institutions and at different points in their career can collaborate to improve their teaching, and (e) deep knowledge of subject matter is central to effective teaching. These assumptions, as a set of priorities, gave shape to a professional development project and served as referents for tweaking the roles of participants and the associated division of labor. At the same time, the absence of an explicit theoretical framework for students' learning of science, teachers' teaching science, and new teachers' learning to teach science fostered an approach to enacting and adjusting the project based on the commonsense rationale provided earlier and the status of the participants. Accordingly, the college professors who had a hand in designing the project turned out to have had the strongest voices regarding whether what was happening was appropriate and in need of change. Consistent with our theoretical framework, we understand this fact to be the result of interactions, in which the professors and others may have used institutional positions as resources for producing and reproducing societal and institutional differences.

HISTORICAL PERSPECTIVES ON EXTERNAL ASSESSMENT

In New York City there has been a long history of teaching to the test. The first Regents examinations were administered to eighth-grade students in 1865 and since that time they have been refined and remain a key part of an external assessment of the achievement of high school youth in a variety of school subjects. Success on the Regents examinations involves high stakes because, for students to graduate from high school, they must pass five Regents examinations, including at least one in science. Even though the Regents examinations are considered to be external measures of achievement, they are administered under the aegis of school principals and are scored by classroom teachers. Even so, for many, and perhaps even most educators in the state of New York, the Regents examinations are the gold standard for successful learning and teaching. Many stakeholders show an interest in how individuals perform on the Regents, the extent to which teachers succeed in getting their students through, and whether given schools compare favorably to those with similar demographic indicators.

Relatively low levels of success on the Regents examinations in the subjects living environment, chemistry, and mathematics were among the indicators that led a group of mathematics and science educators to select Franklin High School in the city of New York as a low performing school that would benefit from an intensive professional development program. Along with Orchard High School, a low performing school from the South Bronx, science and mathematics teachers from Franklin High were invited to participate in a range of professional development activities that included an intensive summer program for them and selected students from their school—those who had either failed, or had not yet passed, a Regents examination in one of the three selected subjects.

In this chapter, we focus on four chemistry teachers from the two schools and students who had failed ($N = 13$) or had not yet passed ($N = 6$) the Regents examination in chemistry. The students were taught by a group of teachers consisting of the chemistry teachers from the two high schools, three chemistry teachers from other schools, two undergraduate cadets, four prospective chemistry teachers, and three college chemistry professors.

As pointed out, the plan for the professional development part of this project did not have an explicit theoretical rationale for learning to teach through participation in the project. Accordingly, the activities for the summer were planned on the basis of the wisdom of the principals and their advisors, based on what they assumed to be best practices for improving the achievement of urban youth. It was assumed that teachers would learn from the experience of working together, especially from collaborating to improve student achievement. Accordingly, a range of activities was planned to utilize the teacher participants as (social, societal) resources to mediate student learning and thereby benefit them with respect to their knowledge and achievement in chemistry.

The group planned a curriculum and an associated division of labor so that students participated in lectures, laboratory tasks, and tutorial sessions. The division of labor perhaps reflects a hierarchy in which college professors and high school teachers were assigned to teach the subject matter that was regarded as most central for succeeding on the Regents examinations. A lecture theater was obtained for whole-class teaching and each morning session was planned for a college professor and a high school teacher to divide the available time to teach designated subject matter, allow time for students to complete specified exercises, and then to work through the solutions to some of these exercises.

Other teachers would participate in coplanning activities in a separate venue and then join the lecture in progress, presumably to learn through the experience of what was done and how it was done. Although we do not analyze the teaching of laboratory tasks here—mainly the prospective teachers and undergraduate cadets taught them with assistance from a college professor and teachers when the labs were sophisticated (e.g., such as in a nylon production lab)—we provide some information that serves as background against which all the other events played out. Thus, one of the classroom teachers from an "other" high school coordinated the labs and provided oversight for the allocation of teaching resources to them. Similarly, one of the "other" teachers coordinated the tutoring activities and rostered teacher resources to students so as to provide the latter with the help they needed and ensure that they worked with a variety of teachers during the five weeks of the program.

Initially there was not a conscious decision to coteach, however, as the summer program progressed there was more of an effort for teachers to coordinate their activities with the learning of students as a goal. As the five weeks progressed, however, the incidence of coteaching increased and one-on-one and small-group interactions had many of the characteristics of cogenerative dialogues. From the outset the goal of the summer program was very explicit, to focus on the students' achievement on the Regents examinations in chemistry. The unambiguous goals were to get all students through the Regents examination with a passing score of more than 65 percent. The following excerpt from Ken's fieldnotes captures some of the priorities of the summer program.

> "Three absences and you're out." The rigid criteria for participation and success in the summer program were laid out by the project leader as rules that would shape the activities for a five-week, four-days-a-week program that combined professional development and academic achievement for students who had previously been unsuccessful on the New York Regents examinations in chemistry, living environment, or mathematics. During a meeting attended by college professors, schoolteachers, and college students who would be tutors in the project, the project principals discussed logistics and requirements in a no-nonsense manner that was accepted by the participants. A key

rule that was established is that the passing level on the Regents examinations to be administered at the end of the summer project was to be 65 percent, "don't even mention any other possibilities." Students participating in the course either had previously failed the Regents examination associated with the course for which they were enrolled in the summer or had not yet taken it.

THE PARTICIPANTS

Toward the end of the spring semester of 2005 we began an ethnographic study of learning to teach chemistry, involving a chemistry teacher from Franklin High, a large comprehensive school in Manhattan. The school has an enrollment of 2,600 students and a high degree of cultural and social diversity. For example the students are racially diverse, consisting of 67 percent Hispanic, 25 percent Black, 6 percent Asian, and 2 percent White students. About 22 percent are English language learners and 85 percent are from economically deprived families, which made them eligible for free lunch. The school is relatively low-performing, especially in science. In a given cohort, about 60 percent of the students graduate in four years, about 30 percent are still enrolled, and 10 percent drop out of school within the first four years. Of almost 300 students who sat for the Regents examination in chemistry only 120 obtained a passing score of more than 55 percent. Since Franklin High had many of the characteristics of a low performing high school it was selected with another school from the Bronx to participate in the professional development program described.

Xiao, a Chinese American teacher, and some of his colleagues from Franklin High, agreed to participate in and were selected for a professional development program in the summer. We identified Xiao as the principal focus for this research because he was struggling to succeed as a chemistry teacher even though he had a strong background in chemistry. Being Chinese American he was unlike most of his students and he had difficulty creating and sustaining learning environments that were conducive to learning science. Xiao chose a chemistry class for us to observe and with the permission of all participants we undertook an ethnographic study in the class to better understand the teaching and learning that occurred.

Students from the class who had failed the Regents examination in chemistry (or had not yet taken it) were invited to participate in a five-week summer session in which science teachers and university scientists collaborated to provide them with an intensive program leading to success on the examination they had recently failed. On any given day students attended a lecture, participated in tutoring activities and undertook lab investigations. Each Thursday the students took a trial Regents examination in chemistry. The teachers and students were given feedback on the scores and efforts were made to increase performance on the next occasion. Finally, at the end of the course all students remaining in the course took an official Regents examination in chemistry. Nineteen students took the final Regents examination, 18 of them gaining more than the cut-off for a pass (i.e., 55 percent) and 17 attaining more than the principal investigator's criterion (i.e., 65 percent, the official criterion for passing the Regents examinations for all students entering high school from 2006 onwards).

What follows is a vignette based on our analyses of the data resources (e.g., fieldnotes, videotape analysis, interviews of the teacher and students) obtained during an ethnography of Xiao's teaching at Franklin High. In subsequent sections we explore his teaching at the beginning of the summer session, and then toward the end of it. Also, we analyze Xiao's interactions with students in small-group tutoring sessions.

STIFF STANDING TEACHING

The students seemed restless as Xiao wrote notes onto the board. The background noise was not conducive to learning or teaching. For example, loud, disrespectful comments abounded and one student exclaimed "Oh shit!" Throughout the lesson the background noise was dominated by exaggerated laughter and disruption as students engaged in horseplay and interactions not related to chemistry. Xiao explained to the students that the work was very easy and encouraged them to get involved, however his Chinese-English dialect was different than those of his students and some of the more boisterous males mimicked him, seemingly to gain peer approval for their overt displays of disrespect. For many male students there was scant evidence of them copying the notes or otherwise getting involved in class activities.

When Xiao taught the whole class he usually did so from a central position, immediately in front of the first row of seats. He appeared tense, and this tenseness was expressed in his body movements, gestures, and oral expression. While interacting with students Xiao stood erect and stiff, appearing aloof and distant. He was distant (physically and emotionally) from his students, which can be inferred from the fact that he rarely lowered his head, crouched down, or leaned forward to interact with them.

As the amount of writing to be copied from the board grew there was increasing evidence of students becoming involved. Then, after the students finished copying the notes, Xiao asked them to solve problems from a worksheet related to likely questions on the Regents examination. He read aloud from the worksheet, gave instructions and, as necessary, worked typical examples on the board. As he did so, he posed questions focused on obtaining a correct solution and, when they occurred, student responses were delivered as a chorus. When students responded to a question Xiao explained and elaborated to provide insights into obtaining a correct answer. Eventually Xiao solved most of the problems he posed and students copied the solutions into their notes. Although some, mainly female students, were consistently involved there was widespread evidence of asynchrony with Xiao's practices, as students talked socially, put their heads down, fidgeted, and looked elsewhere. There was a pattern of sporadic engagement and disengagement, the background chatter being punctuated by comments intended to distract others.

Although Xiao had a good background in chemistry, the classroom environment produced structures that made it difficult for him to enact the curriculum in the way he preferred, to create structures to support the learning of most students. If his knowledge of chemistry were to make a difference to the learning of chemistry, Xiao and the students would have to successfully interact to produce structures that focused and sustained appropriate forms of participation.

LECTURING

From the outset there was no doubt that the summer program was set up to make sure that the participating students were successful on the Regents examination. Although a goal of the project was that the different teachers would improve their teaching as a result of being involved in the summer, the model for learning to teach from others was not explicated. Groups were formed with the intention of focusing the curriculum on science content most likely to be tested on the exam and ensuring that students were test wise. Indeed, when a prominent science educator was told about the design for the summer she commented, "How do you know you're doing any more than teaching them to take tests?" No doubt her remark referred to the design feature that each Thursday afternoon the students would sit for a Regents examination in chemistry. On the basis of their weekly performance the curriculum for the next week would be planned to address weaknesses and provide intensive opportunities for students who were failing to receive appropriate tutoring.

Although most of what we address in this report concerns Xiao, it is illustrative to examine briefly what happened during the summer program as far as learning to teach was concerned. As we describe at the beginning of this chapter, there were approximately sixteen teachers in the chemistry group. The teachers varied greatly in their experience of teaching (e.g., years of teaching, type of institution, levels of students)—especially with respect to the social and cultural characteristics of the students they had taught previously and would teach in the future. Initially the division of labor was for a college teacher to teach during the first part of the lecture and a high school teacher to teach the second part. The other teachers were expected to be present during the lecture as much as possible to experience what was taught and how it was taught. However, it turned out the lecture time was used as planning time, so that the coordinator of the tutoring element, for example, would discuss possible foci for the tutoring sessions and ways to interact with the students. Similarly, the laboratory coordinators often used part of the lecture time to interact with the prospective teachers, who had an active role in working with students during the laboratory tasks. However, as is evident in the following example of a lecture, the roles of the other teachers who were in attendance were restricted to observing and only occasionally getting involved, perhaps to correct "slips of the tongue."

Stand and Deliver Teaching

The following excerpts from our fieldnotes capture some of the essence of the teaching that occurred during lectures held in the first week of the summer program. Anne, an assistant professor in the chemistry department of a university, taught this lesson.

The lesson begins with Anne blowing up a balloon, asking the students "What happened?" once she has it inflated. There is a rapid series of questions and responses as Anne endeavors to get the students involved. Students like Alison offer suggestions and when she does so Anne probes to get her to elaborate. Terms such as pressure and expansion are volunteered and Anne encourages others to make suggestions. Soon she asks, "What is in air?" Fred volunteers the word "nitrogen," and Anne returns to the chalkboard to list the constituents of air. She writes a list consisting of "nitrogen, oxygen, carbon dioxide and other things." Having created the list Anne then writes the answer to her question about the balloon: "I am pushing air into the balloon and this makes it expand. Creates pressure by pushing on the inside."

One of the few examples of other teachers collaborating with Anne occurs when Roslyn hands out folders to the students as Anne continues to teach about particles and the spaces between them. During this time Dan responds to a question and Anne repeats his answer and comments, "We'll think about that in a second." Within a short time Anne offers Dan a chance to elaborate before opening the issue to the whole class. Alison responds, and then Michael follows providing another response. The issue concerns the question of whether volume is largely occupied by the particles or the spaces between the particles. Anne calls for a vote by getting students to raise their hands and then she calls on two students who have not raised their hands, asking them to explain what they have voted for—to show that they understand the issues.

The lecture is teacher centered and the pace is slow and methodical. Anne uses a style in which she asks questions, seeks responses, and evaluates the adequacy of the responses. The questions are clear and carefully stated and Anne probes to get responses. The student responses consist of few words and occupy little time, when they do occur at all. That is, the average duration of student responses is short. When students do not respond, and this occurs frequently, Anne speaks and her responses are relatively long in terms of words per speaking turn and time taken. Evaluations usually come from Anne and are relatively lengthy, usually consisting of elaborations of the content.

Anne mainly teaches from a central position in front of the first row of seats. She is directly in front of the projection screen, which is not being used at that time. Her oral delivery is supported with iconic gestures and delivery is slow. The questions she asks are such that students focus their thinking on the nature of gases and the interactions between the particles and the walls of the container. Inscriptions on chalkboards, mainly key words or answers to questions Anne poses, support verbal interactions. In fact, when students or the teacher provided a correct response, Anne writes a summary of the key points on the chalkboard so that it becomes a record that students can refer to and copy into their notes.

Throughout the thirty-minute lecture other teachers in the room sit together and follow the lesson, sometimes taking a time-out to interact with one another and read material that is unrelated to the lecture. From our perspective the division of labor used in this lecture and others that occurred in the first week probably reinforce the types of teaching we have observe from Xiao, that is, stiff-standing teaching. Anne's ways of teaching perhaps are not as conducive as envisioned for learning to teach in ways that are engaging for learners and did not get students as involved as might have been possible if more coteaching occurred.

With an expectation that our ethnography would be educative for the participants and catalytic in terms of affording the project's goals, the following questions and comments were provided to the principals of the summer project and Anne, the teacher in this lecture.

Query: To what extent did the students access the verbal utterances of the teacher?

Discussion: Although I have not undertaken an analysis of the audio recording of this lesson my impression from being in the room is that the delivery was clear and focused. There was very little interaction and those examples of interaction involved only a small number of students. Are there target students in the class? That is, do a small number of students get involved in interactions with the teacher a disproportionate number of times? In this initial activity two or three of the students appeared to be involved more than others who were relatively less involved in an overt way (i.e., by interacting verbally).

In terms of the types of verbal involvement the teacher employed a full range of verbal moves (questions, responses, explanations, evaluations, speculations etc). Also, the teacher spoke for lengthy periods of time and took successive turns at talk. When students did speak it was difficult for others to hear them due to the geography of the room and the air conditioner noise. Accordingly, frequently Anne had to repeat student responses so that others could benefit from them.

Query: To what extent did students have access to teacher resources to support their learning?

Discussion: The seating arrangements were not conducive to students easily talking to one of the many teachers in the room; to share their thoughts on the questions Anne posed or to test their current understandings with someone who already knew the chemistry. What are the roles of the many teachers during activities such as these? There is a plethora of research that suggests that achievement rises significantly when students can systematically review what has happened in lectures and whole-class interactive teaching. For example, in the 1980s Mary Budd Rowe did her work in college chemistry classes where college students were asked to discuss for two minutes what had happened in the previous ten minutes of instruction. In Rowe's study, students interacted with their nearest neighbors and achievement increases were substantial. Is it possible that the teachers or tutors in the room could be seated among the students so that they could interact with them periodically throughout the lesson? In the first twenty-seven minutes of the lesson most teachers in the room were not involved in teaching the students, nor were they available as resources to support the learning of students who may not have understood a key concept and may have been in need of help then and there. Is there a reason to preclude the use of teacher resources in activities such as these? Is there a way for students to signal a need for on the spot assistance during whole-class teaching?

Query: If teachers are to learn new ways to teach by being in classrooms as others teach—how did today's activity afford the learning of teachers?

Discussion: Summing across the teachers several observations are salient for discussion. Some arrived on time—others were late. Some were occupied with other tasks (reading books and newspapers and speaking to others). What is the model used for teacher learning? In the first twenty-seven minutes the teachers participated mainly as observers. They watched and listened. Is this the best way for teachers to learn to teach by being with others?

Commentary: The goal for students was to understand a model for gas pressure. The arbiter for what was acceptable in the initial twenty-seven minutes was the teacher. Students could recall from their previous studies or they could guess, but they did not have opportunities to build and test their own models. Essentially they were to understand the canonical model for gas behavior. A question then would concern the opportunities students had to put their own understandings to the test, either in writing or orally. Perhaps this is where other teachers could have had a role, by interacting with students around their understandings. Although students may have been actively involved in a cognitive sense, in the initial activity there is not much evidence to support such an assertion. For the most part there were few successful interactions around which students can build understandings and a sense of success and belonging. How were students involved in the lesson, and how were their ways of participation related to learning?

More Stiff Standing Teaching

During a lecture taught by Xiao, about three weeks after we watched him teach chemistry at Franklin High, there were twelve teachers in the lecture theater, consisting of college professors and instructors, prospective teachers, high school teachers, and undergraduate cadets. Seventeen high school students were seated in the front four rows, mainly adjacent to other students. Two undergraduate cadets sat in the fourth row and the teachers, with few exceptions, were seated in rows five, six, and seven.

Figure 6.1. Xiao writes on the chalkboard while continuing to talk to the class.

As Xiao taught the lesson on energy transfer, in a lecture theater, he situated himself at the front, right of the classroom and remained relatively fixed, standing upright and stiff. His body movements consisted of pointing and occasional rotation of his upper body to look at the chalkboard. As necessary he walked briskly to the board, usually talking to the class as he moved and then, as he wrote, he spoke with his face to the board and his back to the class (Figure 6.1). Speaking to the board certainly was possible without the inevitable consequences of student misbehavior because there were so many teachers present in the class. Hence, for the short periods in which Xiao taught in this way he did not communicate as well as he might have otherwise. Also, it might be argued that Xiao was using teaching practices that would not serve him well in a regular classroom in which he was the sole teacher.

For approximately ten minutes Xiao engaged students in whole-class interactive teaching. In two vignettes selected from this lesson he used his voice and the chalkboard as resources and to a more limited extent, the talk of students and other teachers. During whole-class interactive teaching episodes Xiao maintained lengthy turns at talk through the use of short pauses of less than 0.3 seconds in question chains and longer pauses within explanations of science, such as energy transfer. Control also was maintained, even across longer pauses, when he asked (perhaps overly ambiguous) questions that took time for potential respondents to relate the question to the topic under consideration (e.g., "If you die, what's going to happen?"). In such cases Xiao asked the question, paused for one or two seconds, and then connected the question to the particulars of science: in this case energy transfer. As he provided explanations he often interspersed more specific questions that established a focus for the thinking of students but rarely resulted in a change of speaker. The following transcript illustrates some of these patterns.

```
1 Xiao: Ah. Heat. Heat. Heat.
2 Xiao: We've been talking about heat all the time. What is
        heat?
```

```
           (0.9)
 3 Xiao:   Do you see a pattern?
           (4.9)
 4 Xiao:   Do you see a pattern?
           (3.6)
 5 Xiao:   Did I say you think?
           (0.4)
 6 Students: He he. ((Chorus of laughs; 0.4 s duration.))
 7 Student: =I dunno.
           (0.9)
 8 Xiao:   No!
           (0.4)
 9 Xiao:   Nor does he.
           (0.8)
10 Student: °Energy.°
           (0.1)
11 Student: °Energy.°
           (0.4)
12 Xiao:   It's energy. Good.
           (0.3)
13 Xiao:   Maybe we'll leave it at that.
(0.3)
14 Xiao:   I think we have it.
15 Xiao:   =A good sense of what heat is. Yes? Now. At the end
           of the first lesson I hope if I give you a simple
           situation what I want you to be able to do is to
           trace the flow of heat or give a direction of the
           flow it's not very complicated. Okay? How do we de-
           termine the direction of heat flow? We have to start
           with something. This is a very simple rule. It's not
           hard to understand. It is very powerful. ((Walks to
           the chalkboard.))
16 Xiao:   The direction of heat transfer ((begins to write on
           chalkboard)).
           (24.7)
17 Xiao:   Heat always flows spontaneously (3.6) from an object
           of high temperature ((continues to write on the
           board)). Somebody to read it? Or all together all?
           (0.3)
18 Student: I will.
           (1.4)
19 Xiao:   Thanks. ((Finishes writing on the chalkboard.))
           (13.3)
20 Xiao:   What does spontaneously mean?
```

The above transcript is extracted from a whole-class interaction in which Xiao began at the front right of the lecture theater, occasionally pointing to a chalkboard on which he had written the schedule for the day. In turn 1 Xiao asked what is heat? He paused for almost two seconds and when he did not get a response he asked whether the students had seen a pattern, presumably in earlier conversations about heat. The question about seeing a pattern was asked twice, and after the second time, a pause of almost four seconds was provided for students to formulate a response. Getting no response, Xiao smiled, quickly glanced out the open door, and then implied that the students to his left did not think (turn 5). There was a short burst of giggling; some rapid interactions, and then two students volunteered a response: "energy." Xiao looked pleased, affirmed the answer, and decided to leave it at that, stating that the students had a good sense of what heat is. However, based on verbal interactions, there was no evidence to support the decision that students understand what heat is, even though Xiao moved on to discuss heat transfer.

During this vignette Xiao was the central teacher, the other teachers and tutors sat at the side of the class, frequently interacting with one another socially and for the most part not interacting with students. With this arrangement the students did not have access to additional teaching resources. Hence, in turn 15 Xiao assumed that students knew what heat is and began to explain heat transfer there were no discernible checks on understanding, except for each student judging his or her own understanding.

The lesson proceeded with some questions about cold, whether or not it was a form of energy. Xiao also stressed that energy flows from high temperature to low temperature. Consistent with Xiao's statement of goals (turn 15), he wrote some situations on the chalkboard (see Figure 6.1) that required students to apply the rule about energy transfer. Some of the examples Xiao chose to illustrate energy flowing from high to low temperature were not easy for students to follow. For example, he discussed how a person whose body temperature at death was 37 °C slowly loses energy until it reaches room temperature at 20 °C. He may have chosen this example to make the point that when a person is living, the body uses energy to maintain a constant body temperature even though the surrounding temperature is less than body temperature. During a preliminary discussion of these situations, Xiao asked questions without an apparent effort of obtaining answers from the students. His pattern was to ask a question and then provide a partial answer, leaving students to complete one or two words. For example, Xiao might ask, where's the energy coming from? Before any answers were provided he would then say, "the energy's coming from the . . . ?"

Xiao wrote four situations on the board and students copied them into their notebooks. As was the case whenever he wrote on the board, Xiao turned his back to the class and spoke directly in the direction of the chalkboard. This practice is an example of a division of labor that reflects solo teaching. In other examples of coteaching we have seen that writing on the chalkboard—e.g., summaries, definitions, sketches, and diagrams—was often done by a coteacher while the central teacher interacted orally with the class. The coordination of effort among coteachers thereby effectively utilized time, maintained focus, and, with the added information on the chalkboard, expanded the agency of students and the teachers. Under the arrangements in the present class, the students had two periods of down time: as they moved to create groups of two, and as Xiao wrote the situations on to the chalkboards at the front of the class.

As Xiao wrote on the chalkboard the teachers joked with one another and students copied the situations into their notebooks. Only once was there input from a

Figure 6.2. Synchronous interactions involve coteachers and students in small groups. (The photo has been blurred to mask identities.)

teacher that meaningfully structured the class—when Xiao drew a diagram of a house and labeled the temperature as 70 °C. As Xiao explained the diagram to the class, Anne corrected him and he changed 70 °C to 70 °F. Although this appeared to be a simple slip, the same error reoccurred later in the lesson.

After about eighteen minutes of class time some of the coteachers began to interact with the students as they worked in groups to explain energy transfer in the four situations that focused this part of the lesson. However, most of the coteachers remained seated and conversed with one another, leaving students to work at their own pace and without access to additional teacher resources (unless they requested them). The teachers who interacted with the students got close to them, either sitting down adjacent to them or crouching down to look over their shoulders from the row behind them (Figure 6.2). This was the first instance of tutoring in a whole-class lecture. Later in the project the practice of coteachers tutoring students during lectures became more prevalent.

Throughout the room coteachers leaned forward and interacted synchronously with students. In the specific instance depicted in Figure 6.2 the students differed from one another in terms of race and there were two girls and a boy. Hence, in this case, successful interactions occurred across potential barriers of race, gender, and language (first languages of participants in the group were Spanish, Chinese, and English). Age might have been a potential barrier as well, although in this lesson many of the coteachers were close in age to the students. This group was typical of others in terms of its diversity. As the lesson unfolded in this way, evidence of synchrony was head orientation and movements, body lean, eye contact, and oral acknowledgements of agreement (e.g., uh huh, right, yea). Throughout the room there was no evidence of resistance, frustration, or disapproval. Instead there was a working buzz characterized by chemistry talk and sounds of agreement.

Interactions also occurred among the coteachers and these took several forms. Some concerned what was happening in the class as it unfolded and others were about the tasks and how to illustrate them with demonstrations. For example, one of the college professors brought in some liquid nitrogen as a way to illustrate energy transfer from an object at room temperature (a thermometer) to a very cold substance (liquid nitrogen). Such interactions served a planning function and also expanded the classroom teacher's repertoire of suitable demonstrations and the associated scientific explanations. In this present arrangement of coteachers from different institutions and with different backgrounds in education and science, there were opportunities for all to learn from their ongoing interactions with one another.

After about ten minutes of small-group activity Xiao interrupted the group and began to present solutions to the first situation. He did not request any of the groups to stop work or to look his way, he simply began to address the class—some groups paid attention and others did not. Xiao accepted the structure of some groups attending mainly to him and others continuing with highly focused interactions within the small group. That is, coteachers continued to interact successfully with students about their solutions to situations within a framework of whole-class interactions led by one solo teacher. These patterns of interaction were distinctive of coteaching and quite different from what happens during solo teaching.

The small-group interactions were analogous to cogenerative dialogues as small groups of teachers and students interacted successfully across boundaries, such as race and gender, which frequently militated against science learning. In contrast, the interactions in these groups were appropriate, timely, and anticipatory, leading to high levels of synchrony and success. In many respects the learning environments that emerged were reminiscent of those described in Mary Budd Rowe's ten-two method according to which there should be two minutes of debriefing for every ten minutes of direct teaching. The difference in this setting is that students benefited from a disproportionate number of teachers and forms of scaffolding that were tailored to the learning potential of students. Given our earlier sense that the lectures of Xiao and Anne were not optimal for most learners for most of the time, the uses of tutoring within an umbrella of a whole-class lecture has appeal in situations structured in similar ways to this summer program. Although such arrangements lead to situations where not everybody is aligned to a single focus, it does make available many more resources for learning as those "in the know" interact with learners and thereby scaffold their attempts at understanding the concepts at hand. The available (social) resources are thereby actively used to maximize learning.

By the time Xiao had almost completed his explanation of the first situation all participants were focused on his explanations that were enacted in much the same way as the earlier part of the lesson (and in his lesson at Franklin High School described previously). After thirty-one minutes Xiao began to discuss a fourth situation. The following transcript illustrates a reoccurrence of the patterns seen earlier in the lesson and while Xiao taught at Franklin High.

```
1 Xiao: How does the A-C work (1.5) in the fourth situation?
        (0.6) If my house is, (0.3) it's at 80 degrees Fahr-
        enheit. (0.2) Okay? (0.3) Outside temperature a hun-
```

```
        dred degrees. (1.2) So you want your house to get
        seventy degrees centigrade. That's what you said and
        total's half that-
        (0.6)
 2 Anne: Seventy Fahrenheit.
 3 Xiao: = Seventy Fahrenheit. (1.7) Always getting the two
        confused. (3.3) I won't spend a lot of money so I
        set it at seventy. Others will find it not so
        comfortable. So how does the A-C work? You don't do
        things with the cold. You do things with the heat.
        So, what's the A-C doing? Think of it that way. It's
        doing something with the heat right? What is it do-
        ing?
        (2.6)
 4 Xiao: Karina?
        (0.3)
 5 Karina: What's the name for the outside to bring it in?
        (1.4)
 6 Xiao: A::H, again you're talking about cold
            [and bringing the hot in.
 7 Chorus: [We didn't hear, we didn't hear her back here.
        (1.1)
 8 Professor: What did you say Karina? What did you say
        again?
        (0.4)
 9 Karina: Oh that what if the A-C moved the hotness from
        outside to convert it to the cold on the inside.
        (0.3)
10 Professor: How does it do that?
        (1.8)
11 Xiao: You think of it in terms of energy conversion again
        or (1.6) getting the heat and getting it somewhere
        else.
        (0.7)
12 Xiao: What does the A-C do? It get rid of the heat right?
        (0.2) What does it need to do?
        (2.6)
13 Xiao: That's why you're paying a lot of money. That's why
        the A-C wastes a lot of electricity, uses a lot of
        electricity. Why? Because it's up a hill. (1.1)
        First of all, if there's no A-C what's going to hap-
        pen? (0.6) Where's the heat transfer?
        (1.7)
14 Student: From outside.
15 Xiao: =The heat is going to go from the outside into the
        house (0.9). The A-C prevents that from happening
        but not only does that do that it gets rid of the
        heat from the house and dumps it outside. So, that
        goes against the natural course of things. This is
        eighty and this is a hundred and yet your A-C has to
        remove the heat from the lower temperature and dump
```

> it into a source with a higher temperature. (0.8) Is
> that going up hill or down hill?
> (0.4)

16 Student: Downhill.
> (0.5)

17 Xiao: You're going up. You're working hard. You're battle.
> That's all. You're paying a lot of money that's all.
> An A-C has to use a lot of electricity. (2.1) Since
> you're going up hill it's going against the sponta-
> neous sort of thing. It's got to go from the lower
> temperature to a higher temperature.
> (2.2)

18 Xiao: We're talking about it.
> (0.7)

19 Rosalie: Why?
> (1.2)

20 Xiao: I don't know. You're opening a can of worms. (0.2)
> What do you think it is? Go ahead.

21 Professor: =The heat from the house boils the freon.
> (1.0)

22 Professor: [It's a great process.   ]

23 Rosalie: [They have a gas in there.] Right?
> [That expands.

24 Professor: [It's under pressure. That's why. That's why.
> It follows the gas laws. We'll talk about that
> later.

25 Xiao: Yea. It's pretty complicated solution. But, that's
> going to be the example for some things.

As Xiao explained the fourth situation, he set the scene in an explanation that was punctuated with pauses of more than a second as he gathered his thoughts and posed a series of questions separated by pauses of 0.2 and 0.3 seconds. The questions were not to be answered, but served as a means of focusing on the salient issues of the situation. However, Xiao made a mistake in describing the tempera- ture of the house as 70 °C instead of 70 °F. Anne, an organic chemist, quietly cor- rected him, grinning broadly as she did so. He apologized and continued to set the stage for the situation, once again asking a series of four questions before calling on Karina to respond.

Karina's response was quiet and took the form of a query that was not heard by others and a chorus of voices let Xiao know that they did not hear Karina. The voices were from the other teachers in the room, and one of them, Jim, asked Karina to repeat what she had said. With the benefit of having another turn at talk Karina did a better job of explaining that she was thinking, "The A-C takes the hotness from outside and converts it to cold on the inside." Jim asked Karina how this is done and Xiao commenced an explanation of how to address problems of this type.

It is evident from the transcript provided in the second vignette that the patterns seen in the first example were repeated. Xiao gave explanations that were punctu- ated by longer pauses and when he asked questions he tended to ask them in chains, each question separated from the next with quite short pauses on the order of 0.2 seconds. From the perspective of wait time research, this is insufficient time for students to reflect and engage with the problem framed in the question; long pauses between question and the first response and substantial (temporal) engagement with any particular problem have shown to lead to more learning (Tobin, 1987). Primarily, Xiao's concern appeared to be to articulate the subject matter in ways that were intelligible to the students without actually ascertaining whether the subject matter as articulated *actually* made sense to students. He did not engage students in verbal interactions and did not use the tutors and teachers in the room to facilitate the learning of others. As our research in Australian classrooms had shown, without such interactions, students make sense of what they see and hear in a lecture in many different ways, frequently incompatible with the standard ways of understanding science (Roth, McRobbie, Lucas, & Boutonné, 1997). As a result, students and teacher come to inhabit different conceptual and social worlds, essentially misunderstanding science content and how others know it.

Cogenerative Dialogues in Tutoring

Xiao was involved in tutoring sessions with students four days a week for an extended period. In a tutorial session undertaken one month into the summer program Xiao was seated with three students; and they were working through some problems involving oxidation-reduction ("redox") reactions and balancing ionic equations. The group consisted of two females (including Karina) and one male differing from Xiao and one another in terms of race, native language, and gender. What was most apparent in the small-group interaction is that all participants talked and did science continuously. Exchanges were fluent and there was a sense of purpose in the group. Xiao was accepted as the teacher and turns at talk were shared. There was little down time as the students worked together and independently on exercises that were written on a sheet. When he was working with the whole group Xiao selected an exercise from a sheet and the whole group worked on it together. The following transcript provides insights into the nature of the interactions in the group.

```
1 Xiao: Karina did you get that?
        (0.3)
2 Karina: °Yes. I get it.°
        (0.9)
3 Xiao: Whenever the oxidation number goes up in your number
        line (1.1) that's when you're losing electrons actu-
        ally. That's when it's oxidation. Reduction is (0.3)
        Hm:m↓? ((Directed to Jamal.))
        (0.6)
4 Karina: So:o is it like C-u plus.
        (0.5)
5 Xiao: C-u zero to C-u plus two. (0.3) Where do you put the
        electrons? You're losing electrons. You're losing
6 Karina: =So, you put them over here.
```

Figure 6.3. Xiao interacts with Karina, using pen, gesture, worksheet and voice to establish and sustain mutual focus. (The photo has been blurred to mask identities.)

7 Xiao: =Yes. Your electrons are always on the side of the
     ion side.
8 Karina: They always, always on the side of the ions?
9 Xiao: Okay. Here's your ions so your electrons are here.
     You're losing the electrons.
10 Karina: Okay, and-
11 Xiao: =Or you can write it this way to better understand
     C-u minus two electrons will give you C-u plus two.
     When it's minus here, when you move it over, it be-
     comes plus just like in algebra.
12 Karina: Oh. You're right.
13 Xiao: Because you're losing electrons here. See it's eas-
     ier [to understand.
14 Karina: [Yea. I see. Yea. You're right.
15 Xiao: Okay.
16 Karina: And reduction goes-
17 Xiao: and reduction is gain of electrons. LEO makes GER.
     Right? Grr that's the lion. Gain of electrons is re-
     duction. When you gain electrons the oxidation num-
     ber goes down. That's why it's so confusing. When
     you gain electrons where do you put the electrons?
     You're gaining electrons.
18 Karina: Actually, you're putting it on the other side of-
19 Xiao: =here. So, first of all you have a positive charge.
20 Karina: Right.
21 Xiao: You can see what's happening. Where do you put the
     electrons?
     ((As he finishes his final utterance Xiao flings the
     pen toward Karina, indicating that she is on her
     own. He then grabs Jamal's worksheet.))
22 Xiao: You know this already by now. Wonderful. You got it.
     You got it. Now do number twenty-one and twenty-two.
23 Jamal: It's easy.

Table 6.1. Relative achievement of Karina on the Regents Chemistry Examinations

Student	Test 1	Test 2	Test 3	Test 4	Test 5	Final test
Karina	34	55	61	67	70	72
Mean	43	57	60	65	69	72
SD	9	7	8	10	8	8

```
24 Karina: Is this correct Doctor Xiao?
25 Xiao: ((Oriented toward Jamal)) You're going ahead. So do
        it.
```

The small-group tutoring session was extremely productive. Xiao interacted successfully with each of the students, one-on-one, and in pairs and threes. Also, the students remained focused either on the verbal interaction or the completion of exercises from the worksheet for the entire session. During the above interactions with Karina, Xiao was very animated with his gestures, which were synchronized with other actions (including writing on Karina's worksheet), talk (including variation in prosody), and body movements (including head nods). The interactions were conversational and evidence of synchrony was widespread. Xiao encouraged the students to remain engaged and showed delight when they were successful. The students accepted Xiao's verbal accolades as well deserved. What is evident from the tutoring sessions is that Xiao gradually has learned to interact in ways that were acceptable to students, provided them with spaces to participate and learn, and allowed him to earn social and symbolic capital through successful interactions with students (as expressed in students' acceptance of him as a teacher and resource for learning). The patterns evident in the interactions in tutorials were distinctly different than those observed in Xiao's classroom at Franklin and his initial teaching in the summer program.

The pattern used within the chemistry group was for a teacher to remain with a tutoring group for a week. However, this was the only week in which Xiao was involved with tutoring. What seems plausible is that Xiao learned how to interact successfully with these students and then employed similar ways of interacting in his whole-class teaching in the lecture theater. In this regard the tutoring sessions were very much like cogenerative dialogues. Although we do not attribute causation between activities in different fields, it is clear that the students steadily improved their test scores from the first to the sixth testing occasion. Our Table 6.1 shows that Karina, who was quite involved in her interactions with Xiao, has improved her achievement in week 3 by about 0.8 standard deviations, which was more than the improvement in the mean score of the class as a whole. In fact, the table shows that Karina not only improved relative to the participants in this course but also was on a trajectory of more than doubling her score on the Regents examination.

The Emergence of Coteaching

Two weeks after the lesson on energy transfer Xiao cotaught a lesson with Anne on the half-life of decaying substances. There were visible signs of change in his dress—e.g., his dress was more casual, wearing a T-shirt without a tie—and manner of interacting with students and other teachers. In addition, the teachers were distributed around the room and close to students so that they could interact with them routinely as whole-class interactions occurred. Hence, as Xiao taught from the front of the class, there were numerous teacher student interactions occurring in the class. This was a continuous process throughout this lesson. Also striking was that Xiao no longer taught in ways that were stiff and stationary. He used the chalkboard and moved from it toward the class to elicit responses from students. Also he used student responses as a basis for entries on the chalkboard or for his own subsequent talk.

After working an initial example there was a prolonged period in which the students worked within groups, usually interacting with a coteacher and peers. Xiao monitored the interactions and from time to time drew attention to issues that needed attention of a group. Prior to commencing work on a subsequent example, Xiao and Anne huddled at the chalkboard and, with considerable guidance from Anne, set up a table for the data to be displayed in attempting to solve this exercise. Their interactions were evidence of synchrony between the two and the interactions were successful. Xiao accepted Anne's suggestions and as she returned to sit with a student he signaled his readiness to assume a lead role in the lecture. There is some evidence in the literature that such alignment is the result of the interactional resolution of power–status issues, a resolution that is mediated by attendant emotional alignments and a sense that interactions with others are non-threatening (Kemper & Collins, 1990).

Two weeks later Xiao was teaching in ways that were almost unrecognizable compared to how he had taught previously in his high school, mainly due to the differences in the structure of the class. When he stood to lead whole-class interactions they were very brief in duration and tutoring activities predominated. Xiao's role seemed to be to respond to questions and manage the time allocated for different tasks. Xiao interacted fluently with coteachers and students and provided them with resources to support tutoring in small groups, consisting of one to two students and a coteacher.

Because coteachers were distributed among the students throughout the lecture theater, they often represented the students' perspectives for them or encouraged students to get involved overtly in the lecture. On one occasion several of the teachers felt that Xiao's approach was unnecessarily cumbersome and engaged him in a whole-class interaction. Most readers will have had experience that when experts get involved in discussing details of the subject matter that they know, outsiders often do not know what is going on. That is, although experts might think that others are able to learn from their talking through the finer issues of the subject matter, such talk frequently sounds to outsiders like gibberish. The following transcript shows the verbal interaction that unfolded between Xiao and a number of teachers.

```
0 1 Xiao: Five over two. Two and a half. Thank you everything
          is okay. So the answer is one point five. (3.4) Any
          questions? (0.9) If you follow this procedure you
          will be able to solve all of these problems. No ex-
          ceptions ((Allan, a teacher, raises his hand.))(0.3)
          Yes?
          (1.3)
  2 Allan: Instead of putting the coefficients in front of the
           x under the coefficients you can use the coeffi-
           cients and put the x on top of them.
           (0.3)
  3 Jim: Think the math [would be easier?
  4 Xiao:                [Well, this needs one way. I don't
          think about that. That would put-
  5 Allan: =Wouldn't math be easier?
  6 Matt: =Yes.
  7 Xiao: If you put what?
          (0.7)
  8 Allan: This x above
           (0.4)
  9 Matt: The x above instead of below.
  10 Rosalie: =It's in the ratio.
  11 Xiao: =It doesn't matter to me. I mean if
          [you put the x above
  12 Matt: [the reason I go for that is 'cause of the math-
  13 Xiao: =remember to put the coefficients below.
          (1.1)
  14 Matt: Yes. That's what I'm saying. Put the x above instead
           of below it then it's ah.
  15 Xiao: =I'm teaching one method so I would say just follow
           what I am doing and if not you can do it in your
           head you do it.
           (0.8)
  16 Matt: Oh, that's okay ((nods his head)).
  17 Xiao: [So this is just-
  18 Matt: [We're talking about fractions.
```

This transcription and the associated vignette is a contradiction. Public interactions between teachers were rare at any time and disagreements among the three chemistry teachers from the same school (Xiao, Matt, and Allan) were unique. Rosalie also was a chemistry teacher and it was unusual for Xiao to "stick to his guns" while acknowledging that others could opt for different approaches. In a sense, the solution offered by Xiao was formal acknowledgment of the equality of the teachers distributed throughout the room. Earlier, especially in the first two weeks, power was more centralized with a single teacher who assumed responsibility for whole-class interactions while other teachers in the room took a more passive role of spectators.

Expanding the Roles of Students

In this study the roles of students were limited by tradition. From the outset most of the students were selected for their deficits and there was a sense that success would be measured in terms of overcoming the deficits and obtaining an outcome of 100 percent of the students exceeding a pre-specified criterion of 65 percent on the Regents chemistry examination. Even though there were no visible plans for teachers to learn to teach from one another, there was an increasing tendency for coteaching among teachers to occur as the five weeks unfolded. There was also some evidence of students acting as peer teachers (or cadets as they were called) for one another. Probably because of the high ratio of teachers to students—almost one to one—there was a lower incidence of peer teaching than we frequently see in our studies in which cogenerative dialogues occur.

This case study of Xiao's teaching draws our attention to cogenerative dialogues as seedbeds for the growth of new culture. Whenever teachers and students interact possibilities arise for interactions in which new forms of culture (e.g., chemistry) are produced; and these new forms subsequently can be enacted in the classroom field and improve achievement. In the case of tutoring, a shared goal was to increase the achievement of students. Within this context, mainly as an unconscious process, all participants learned how to interact successfully with the others in the group. We do not suggest that Xiao built new culture in his tutoring sessions with students and then enacted this new culture in his subsequent teaching. However, we regard this assertion as worthy of further consideration. The uses of tutoring appeal as sites for scaffolding the students' doing, hence achieving of chemistry and sites for learning how to interact successfully with cultural and social others. Hence tutoring appeals as a field that is highly appropriate in the various ways in which it emerged in this five-week program—appropriate that is for becoming a better teacher and a better learner.

The potential value of tutoring sessions in which every participant has a role in teaching others "how to interact successfully with people like me" focuses our attention on the absence in this program of cogenerative dialogues as a means for identifying and resolving contradictions with respect to the experienced and preferred learning environments. Rarely did students have a chance to speak to their teachers about their learning and to advise on "how to better teach kids like me," which our research in inner-city schools in Philadelphia has shown to be a powerful means for addressing the learning needs of students. More importantly, the onus on teaching was assumed to reside with the teachers and there were no discernible efforts to create collective responsibility for teaching. Based on our previous experiences, we tend to think that if cogenerative dialogues had been formally scheduled to involve teachers and students then solidarity might have been quick to emerge and the levels of achievement may well have been much higher and what was thought of as success may have been expanded considerably.

There are two complementary goal areas accomplished through cogenerative dialogues. In alignment with Paulo Freire's *conscientization*, participants in cogenerative dialogues can raise consciousness of all to practices that are enacted without awareness and relate to the disadvantage of others. By identifying such practices they become objectified and can be taken into account when the curriculum is enacted. Going through video collectively allows such practices to be noticed and to be turned into objects of reflection, that is, to be objectified. As such, the participants could then attempt to explain and theorize their practices and thereby enhance their understanding of them in the course of building on the *practical understanding|explaining dialectic*. That is, learning occurs as participants draw on their practical understanding to explain the (objectified) practices, thereby enhancing their practical understanding (Ricœur, 1991). In the process, participants in cogenerative dialogue also can assume collective responsibility for enacting agreed to changes and provide support to attain collective goals and outcomes.

In our previous research and derivative studies we have focused on identifying and resolving contradictions, once again making conscious and collective decisions about possible changes in goals, roles, rules, and resource distribution. Via the conscious route agreed to changes can be accomplished.

The idea of seedbeds for the production of new culture operates unconsciously in that new ways of producing synchrony and success can be produced and learned without an awareness of what has been learned—by means of the processes of *mimesis* or *entrainment*. In this instance production is associated with interacting with social and cultural others in a context of the participants sharing turns and carefully attending to others' actions. Focused efforts to produce success and maintain synchrony produce novel structures, expanding collective agency and sustaining a field in which new forms of culture are produced as well as reproducing received cultural forms. Accordingly, participants add to their capital and capacity to be agential in other fields, such as in subsequent chemistry lectures. It is possible that through tutoring activities all students and teachers expanded their social and symbolic capital that afforded successful interactions across borders defined by factors such as social class, gender, and first language. We note that, consistent with the notion of *cultural lag* (Swidler, 1986), capital produced in the cogenerative dialogue field may not be enacted in the field of science education for some time—until the structures of that field resonate with the new forms of culture, supporting its enactment, possibly/often without conscious awareness.

Enacting Coteaching from the Outset

The different types of teacher recruited to participate in this project lead to a potentially very rich learning environment staked with resources and there is a high potential for significant learning to occur from coteaching. With the wisdom of hindsight the principals of this summer program might have established a plan for each lecture and laboratories to include two main coteachers with other teachers being dispersed throughout the class, prepared to step forward as the need arises to interact with students to afford their learning. The coteaching model would be one in which all but two coteachers enact peripheral roles and have the autonomy to interact with small groups of students with their interests as primary foci. As coteachers teach at one another's elbows they experience dynamic structures that continuously change their agencies and opportunities to learn to teach while focusing on the learning of others. Structuring all activities so that the available teachers can serve as resources to support the learning of the students and expand the variety of ways in which teachers interact with students and thereby teach them, seems to be in everybody's interests.

Beyond the Gold Standard

Offering students opportunities to learn about science by expanding their access to human and material resources seems like a highly desirable thing to do. In this case the students who were invited to participate in the program were those who had failed on the Regents examination and those who could not take it because at Franklin High School there was no laboratory available and hence students could not do laboratory work. This is an inherent contradiction, because New York State requires each student to complete and write satisfactory laboratory reports for a minimum of twelve hundred minutes of laboratory work. From a learning perspective it makes sense to retain the structuring of the daily schedule, to allow for learning of content, tutoring in small-group settings or in one-on-one situations, and laboratory activities. However, the ways in which students could access the teacher resource were limited in the laboratory and lecture. Furthermore, lectures were highly focused on what would likely be tested and the teachers and students were restricted in what they felt they could do to follow topics that had personal relevance and interest to students. However, the focus on the test, regarded by the principals as essential, might have constrained what participants wanted or desired to do. At the time of the first Regents examination none of the students had reached the criterion required to pass the test. However, three of sixteen students exceeded the criterion of 65 percent after one week. What is the justification then for continuing to focus these students' experiences on passing the test? With the vast array of teachers available to tailor curriculum to the needs of students it might be that more could be done to recruit these students to science rather than persist with an intense focus on exceeding the criterion.

At the end of the project all but two of the students passed at criterion level or above. One of the two failures was between 55 and 65 percent and the other failed with a score of less than 55 percent. We acknowledge that all but two of the youth involved in this project, all racial minorities and from economically challenging circumstances, are on a pathway toward high school graduation for which a successful Regents examination in science is a prerequisite. However, there is more to education than merely getting through. How has participation in this five-week program added to the youths' capital in ways that expand their agencies, equipping them to address macrostructures that tend to oppress them, truncate their opportunities for advancement, and reproduce disadvantage? The jury is out on how participants expanded their agencies and can overcome macrostructures. We do know, however, that students requested more laboratory tasks and this might be a sign of an interest in *doing* science, perhaps as a basis for building interests and capacities for improving the quality of social life. If cogenerative dialogues had been included as a regular feature of the summer program the schedule might have been more responsive to a broader range of students' perspectives and capacities.

In terms of learning to teach, the set up was questionable from the outset. As we mention throughout this chapter, the gradual evolution toward the use of coteaching provides glimpses into the potential for effective forms of pedagogy as students have greater access to varied forms of teaching. Similarly, as the amount of coteaching increases, all teachers increase opportunities to experience more forms of teaching and to expand their repertoire of teaching capital. A question that arises concerns the reasons for the incidence of coteaching increasing. Some of the principals in the project suggested that there was a conscious effort to increase coteaching and some of the feedback from the research group suggested coteaching as a potential way to resolve some of the contradictions we identified in our fieldnotes. It is also probable that as the students and teachers got to know one another better there was less of a sense of intrusion in stepping forward to teach in peripheral ways as central forms of teaching were ongoing. Hence, increases in social and symbolic capital were resources for increasing the extent that coteaching was happening.

What if coteaching had been considered from the outset as an optimal way to expand opportunities for students to learn and for teachers to learn to teach from one another? If this had been the case then the amount and nature of coteaching episodes would have been an indicator of the quality of the classroom environment. Teachers and students could have been made aware of the centrality of coteaching and their roles in creating greater access to teaching to support the learning of students and learning to teach. In this scenario coteachers would have been assigned throughout the five weeks, distributed across forms of activity (i.e., lectures, laboratories, tutorials). There would have been less tardiness from teachers, less evidence of teachers watching during lectures, fewer clumps of teachers sitting away from students, and reduced instances of teachers taking time outs when they might have been supporting students' learning. Coteaching provides an immediate rationale for the changes listed in the previous sentence. Furthermore, if there is to be a greater incidence of coteaching there is an obvious need to plan for the forms of coteaching that are most appropriate in lectures, labs and tutoring sessions. Hence, acceptance of coteaching in a program such as this invites planning around the division of labor among teachers, with a primary concern for maximizing the learning of the students.

EXPANDING PARTICIPANT AGENCY: A METALOGUE

Michael: During my first reading of your account of this summer program, two issues stand out. One pertains to the changes that we can observe not only in the way Xiao teaches but also in the way he dresses and interacts with others. This reminds me of my own experiences as a department head of science, where one chemistry teacher in particular resisted my attempts to involve teachers in professional development. Although he participated in observing other science teachers and in coteaching two or three lessons per year, he found my own classroom in particular "very messy" and an inappropriate learning environment—though the students in his class were silently copying notes from the chalkboard whereas mine were continually experimenting and there was never any whole-class lecture and direct teaching but only one-on-one and small-group interactions over conceptual and mathematical problems identified by students themselves. He also observed the classrooms of other teachers who had bought into my preferred approach and who felt comfortable with employing it in their own classrooms after they had spent some time in my classroom interacting with students as they went along designing and implementing their own investigations. Nevertheless, when I left the school after three years, the chemistry teacher approached me and said, "You know, I just hated how you were teaching and the kinds of approaches you were promoting while you were here—especially initially. Now, three years later, I find that my teaching has changed considerably and that I have become more like you and the other teachers in my approach." The point of this anecdote is that even though he was against changing teaching and even though he had resisted becoming involved, he did change over time. The atmosphere in his classroom was more relaxed and allowed students more space to become involved.

Ken: In the example you describe the teachers were together for a lengthy period of time and in many places and contexts. Hence they had numerous opportunities to become like the other by being together and to some extent, coparticipating. In the summer program the chemistry teachers were initially clumped and their proximity to one another and distance from the central teacher allowed them to monitor what was going on and in some senses pursue other goals. Though they sat together they tended to pursue individual goals. Later, when they were distributed throughout the classroom they were teachers for the students in their proximity. Hence their teaching was coordinated loosely with the ongoing flow of teaching and learning and over time there were widespread signs of synchrony. The teachers in the room were coteaching and this greatly increased the number and diversity of structures that could be appropriated to facilitate student learning and learning to teach.

Michael: The most difficult thing to do appears to be breaking with one's own habits. In part, it takes recognizing that we develop ideologies and that we need to break with our own habits of thinking and understanding. I personally feel that I have grown considerably precisely at the moment when I began to question my own thinking. This occurred, for example, during coteaching, during events when I privately viewed the action of a coteacher in a negative way. In my internal monologue, I might have described another teacher's actions as "this is stupid." But my next thought then turned onto my own thinking, making it an object of my personal inquiry. Why would I think that someone else's actions were stupid or wrong? Which presuppositions would make me think in this way? Such questions then led me to inquiries by means of which I came to understand the ideologies I had developed about teaching, learning, and so forth. I do understand that your teachers needed to be together for a while before they came to understand that coteaching would provide resources not only to their students but also to themselves for learning how to teach.

Ken: I want to emphasize the importance of the tutoring within a whole-class structure. Teachers working with one, two, or three students allowed all interaction participants to focus on success. Hence there was pervasive evidence of head nods to show understanding of one another, questions to seek clarification, and persistence in staying the course until confusions were resolved. Successful interactions occurred among participants who differed in sex, ethnicity, language resources, and culture. Hence, students and teachers became cultural brokers, learning how to adapt, and adjust and enact in ways that afforded others. In this way, what students and teachers learned were potential new roles for whole-class interaction—either as a teacher or as a learner.

Michael: I thought about the situation you described as one that affords many opportunities for learning, though some readers may find the situation with an almost one-to-one teacher–student ratio as idealistic. But this is a summer camp, and in this case we find opportunities for a community of practice in the way you hardly ever can find it in a classroom, where there is always one representative of the scientific community and twenty to thirty newcomers. From my perspective, any resource that leads to learning and development is good. This does not mean that we can reproduce a situation in some other context. But this is not the real issue. We need to think educational reform in terms of the resources and associated possibilities any local system can generate.

Ken: The realization that tutoring sessions were very much like cogenerative dialogues allowed us to treat them like cogenerative dialogues in a theoretical sense. Hence, the goals can be seen as much broader than just reproducing and transforming the culture of chemistry. As well, teachers and students are to learn how to interact successfully and in so doing produce new culture that will expand their agency in a diverse mainstream in which it is essential to interact across cultural borders. The goals act symmetrically, for all participants not just teachers or students—all need to learn to be cultural brokers.

Michael: I think that your articulation is very similar to the conceptualization of this situation in terms of the community of practice or perhaps better, a community of learners. Both teachers and students in this summer program are learners, and I think it is not too big a step to think that both types of participants come to increase their understanding of chemistry and how to teach it to others.

Ken: Teacher education programs in universities might look to the use of tutoring within whole-class structures, which undertaken together have enormous potential for learning to teach science, both in and out-of-field. This would have been a wonderful way for me to re-learn to teach in urban high schools—in lieu of the difficult alterative of solo teaching within whole-class structures. Jessica, one of the coteachers involved in chapter 3 opted to learn to teach mainly by tutoring individuals on an as-needed basis and participating peripherally for more than a semester. One day she stepped forward and started to teach in more central ways—another fine example of cultural lag. When the structures were conducive to her enacting particular culture she stepped forward and acted appropriately.

Michael: The other issue pertains to the situation where three teachers articulate different approaches to solve a certain problem. We do have a similar situation in chapter 2, where Natasia offers a solution to the difficulties that the biology teacher Chuck had gotten himself into. We, the coteachers, too, had different solutions to the problem. Yet we did not articulate these in and for the class as a whole—perhaps the fact that the lesson was coming to its end mediated this engagement. I also think that our understanding of the possibilities of coteaching and cogenerative dialoguing were not yet advanced enough for publicly enacting differences about how to resolve the problems Chuck had gotten into. For me the fundamental question pertains to the possibilities that the articulation of the differences might give rise to. On the one hand, if the goal is to teach to the test and if students want to know just the one right way, then articulating differences about how to do a dihybrid cross or how to solve the present chemistry problem may be experienced as a burden. But if the purpose of the lesson is to provide resources for understanding, articulating different approaches and their advantages and disadvantages may actually be experienced positively. More so, if students themselves get involved, much in the way Natasia had told us during the cogenerative dialogue that followed the lesson described in chapter 2, then each participant has the opportunity to develop a more profound understanding of the scientific concepts involved.

Ken: For conversations such as this to benefit learning there probably needs to be a consensus on motives. I am not sure this is the case with the teachers here. I regard this as a nice example of Xiao's agency in that he showed the students one way to do it, and then allowed the other teachers to offer alternatives they considered to be better for the students to obtain right answers. Xiao, did not resist and present his way as the right way, but presented the suggestions as alternatives, some of many ways to get a solution. He made it explicit that teachers could work with their students to find which approach worked best for them. The conversation had a successful outcome in that the final result expanded the collective agency in as much as the bottom line was whatever was best for student learning.

Michael: As I am thinking about what we can learn from the events in this chapter, I am wondering about the extent to which we can say that having a number of subject matter courses is a measure of how well a teacher is prepared to understand and teach a particular subject matter. Here, another anecdote comes to my mind. It involves one of my professors who made this remarkable statement: "Now, after teaching this introductory physical chemistry course for twenty years, I am beginning to truly understand what it is all about." And with his better understanding, he felt that he was becoming a better instructor. The lesson we can learn from this chapter and this anecdote is that subject matter preparation alone does not make a good chemistry teacher specifically or a teacher of any science generally. While taking courses and preparing to become teachers, these individuals themselves need to be involved in the kinds of experiences that we advocate, where they come face to face with their own understanding as they articulate it for others in small-group interactions with their peers all along their university preparation.

Ken: Xiao had a PhD in chemistry and so did many of the teachers in this class. However, unless a teacher is accepted as such, and knows how to successfully interact with would be learners it does not much matter what is to be communicated. Successful interactions are all about fluent interaction, minimizing breaches and acting in ways that expand the agency of others, while attaining individual and collective goals. Building functional collectives is at the heart of good teaching and learning and it cannot be seen as a responsibility of a teacher more so than a learner. As a statistician might say, knowing chemistry well is necessary but not sufficient.

COTEACHING AND COGENERATIVE DIALOGUES AS RESEARCH METHODS

As is evident from the earlier chapters, coteaching and cogenerative dialogues are more than methods for learning to teach and improving the quality of teaching and learning. Increasingly, researchers have employed coteaching and cogenerative dialogues as research methods, forms of participant observation that create opportunities for coteachers (as researchers) to experience directly the praxis of teachers and learners. As research method it is necessary for researchers to consider possible ethical implications of employing either of these fields in research involving human participants.

Following the creation of Federal law in 1974 to regulate research with human subjects in the USA, the *Belmont Report* was released in 1979—providing guidelines on the ethical principles of undertaking research with human subjects. The report contains a useful overview in which, among other things, there is a discussion of professional practice and research. There are several interesting insights including a statement to the effect that research seeks to contribute to generalizable knowledge through theories, principles and statements of relationships. The report notes that research and professional practice can occur together and that if there is any element of research—e.g., as defined by the intent to publish the results rather than doing quality improvement—then the relevant institutional ethics review board should be involved to protect the human subjects. If there is any doubt about whether an activity is research, a researcher should get approval from the local institutional review board responsible for research with human subjects.

The issues raised in the Belmont Report are relatively straightforward. In an application for approval the research is laid out in a formal protocol that contains the goals for the research and a description of the procedures to be followed in pursuing the goals. Then a researcher has to make the case that three ethical principles are addressed in the conduct of the research—respect for the autonomy of participants in research, beneficence, and social justice. Since approval to undertake research with human subjects has to be obtained in advance, ethical conduct has to be planned to show respect of persons, beneficence, and justice. In the following sections we address how to write a proposal in which coteaching and cogenerative dialogues are used as methods in research in schools. Personal pronouns are used to represent Ken's voice throughout this chapter.

COMPONENTS OF PROFESSIONAL PRACTICE

Before proposing research with coteaching and cogenerative dialogues as methods it is important to resolve some issues about professional practice. The primary goal for each method is to improve the quality of the learning of all students. Hence, it can be considered a professional judgment for a teacher to decide to use coteaching and cogenerative dialogues as an integral part of the ongoing curriculum—a feature that would occur irrespective of whether or not research was to occur. Just as other innovative practices might have to be cleared with teachers and school administrators, and even school district personnel, we expect that site-specific clearances would be necessary and parents probably would be advised. However, consent would not be needed from parents to use either coteaching or cogenerative dialogues as methods to improve the learning of students. If the school district and school give the go-ahead then coteaching and cogenerative dialogues can be regarded as part of normal professional practice—part of the enacted curriculum. There are, however, different perspectives that may vary even within the same IRB. Thus, at the University of Victoria, for example, research conducted by graduate students from the Department of Public Administration concerning the practices in companies interested in quality improvement may receive a waiver from ethics review, *because* their study is classified as quality improvement. At the same time, social studies teachers wanting to conduct research concerning their own practices—e.g., concerning coteaching—would have to go through a full review. The IRB argues that what matters are the intents underlying the studies—in the first instance, the *companies* want the quality improvement study to be done whereas in the second instance, teachers want to get graduate degrees. At present, there appears to be a shift and the IRB begins to recognize that with respect to the teacher practices, the work is done for the improvement of professional practices so that the case is not unlike that in quality improvement studies.

Setting the Stage

As we have shown in the earlier chapters in this book there are good reasons to include coteaching and cogenerative dialogues as part of everyday practice. There is now a growing international literature that suggests that students and coteachers benefit from coteaching and that learning environments can be substantially improved through the uses of cogenerative dialogue. If a comparable amount of research was produced in the medical sciences, general practitioners might be seen as less than professional if they were unaware of the research and failed to practice medicine in ways that cohere with the latest research—especially research that produced positive outcomes with few, if any harmful side effects. Hence, based on what we know already the case is strong to employ coteaching and cogenerative dialogues as part of good professional practice (i.e., for quality improvement). Because the goal of using coteaching and cogenerative dialogues is to benefit the students and the coteachers, the use is consistent with how the Belmont Report regards practice and it is quite different from the ways in which they relate research to the production of generalizable knowledge. So, even though the uses of coteaching and cogenerative dialogue might be thought of as innovative, experimental, and perhaps on trial—the goal is to use them to produce improved learning for students and hence an evaluation would be focused not so much on producing generalizable knowledge, but on evaluating the methods (i.e., coteaching and cogenerative dialogues) to see whether or not tinkering was needed and whether their uses should be continued. Accordingly, in these circumstances coteaching and cogenerative dialoguing can be regarded as part of professional practice and not part of research.

As illustrated in chapter 4, Ashraf, Ed, Chris and Gillian used cogenerative dialogues as part of professional practice in the research we described in New York City—a method for examining the ways in which cultural production affords successful interactions across the boundaries of fields such as gender, ethnicity and class. Here the goals are at least twofold, to produce improved student learning and also to produce generalizable knowledge about the benefits of cogenerative dialogues as fields for cultural production—reproduction and transformation of culture and its uses in fields away from the cogenerative dialogue—and including the science classroom. It is clear therefore that the research part of the project needs approval of the institutional ethics review board (IRB); not to use coteaching and cogenerative dialogues—which are used to benefit teacher and student learning— but to get their approval of the research methods involving human participants. Hence, an application to the IRB would describe how professional practice does not have to be changed appreciably to allow the research to be undertaken in an ethical way and that prevailing professional practice sets the stage for the research for which approval is sought.

As university professors we require the permission of school district and school personnel to be a coteacher and participate in cogenerative dialogues. Notably, because of the attendant *power-over* issues, it is easier for professors to receive approval if they are *not* involved in grading and giving grades. In fact, at the University of Victoria, it is easier therefore to receive IRB approval for a study on coteaching and cogenerative dialoguing—if he or she is not involved in grading— than for two teachers, who do such a study to obtain graduate degrees. At City High, coteaching became part of the standard approach to science teaching— routinely involving new teachers, university mentors, and researchers. In our case, a regional coordinator gave Ken permission to ask the school principal to coteach with a science teacher in a small learning community (SLC—a school-within-a-school). The principal was enthusiastic and after clearing it with the coordinator and faculty of the SLC she gave her approval with an understanding that we would also seek approval to undertake ongoing research in the school. When details of the collaborative research were worked out, at the beginning of a longitudinal multi-year study, we sought the approval from the school and then the IRBs of the school district and university.

When Michael came to Philadelphia, the principal readily agreed for him to participate as a coteacher in science classes in the school and also to be a researcher (since by that time we had the approval of the school district and university IRBs). Ken then added Michael's name to the IRB approvals from his university and the school district. If Michael had been at a university in the USA, he would also have made an application at his own university to undertake this research with human subjects. The IRB protocol numbers issued from each university would be cross-referenced. The same is the case for studies conducted within Canada. Frequently, a study passes first the IRB in one institution and a copy of its approval is provided as attachment to the request in the second institution.

Applying to the IRB

The focus of an application to an IRB is communicating the purpose and methods to be employed in research with human subjects so that colleagues on the committee have sufficient information to make a decision regarding the ethical treatment of human subjects. Although the IRB at Ken's university provides a structure in terms of seven questions to be answered, Ken generally re-reads the Belmont Report to be conscious of the meanings given to respect, beneficence and justice. Similarly, in the Canadian context, three funding councils (science and engineering, social sciences and humanities, and health) produced a common policy document (http://www.pre.ethics.gc.ca/english/index.cfm) that binds researchers working with human subjects. Ken then responds to the questions making sure that these three issues are addressed explicitly and fully. In contrast to the approach at Ken's university, Michael's university provides a form with very specific questions concerning all aspects of the research to be conducted.

There are two parts to an application, informing the IRB members about the design of the study and responding to their questions and then ensuring that participants are fully informed about all aspects of the research and their rights as participants, including their right to withdraw at any time without the need for providing reasons or penalties. In the Canadian context, these two aspects are embodied in two documents, the application for ethics review and the consent form subsequently used with the participants and provided to the IRB as an appendix. The Victoria IRB will also request school and school board approvals. If the latter require the university review to be conducted beforehand, then the IRB will do with copies of the application letters subsequently submitted to the two institutional levels of the school system. The IRB also requires copies of the letters informing the parents about the research and the consent letters they have to sign—if applicable.

AN IRB PROPOSAL TO UNDERTAKE RESEARCH IN URBAN SCIENCE

At Ken's university an application to the IRB consists of the responses to six questions and the provision of the protocols he plans to use to recruit participants to the planned study and, if they are over 18 years of age, ensure that they consent to participate with full knowledge of what is involved (see Figure 7.2). If they are minors they give their assent—in which case a parent or legal guardian gives consent (see Figure 7.1). In the Canadian context, participants of all ages are asked to provide consent. For students under 16, the parents (guardians) also provide consent but, should there be a discrepancy, the child's consent may override the one provided by the parent (guardian). For students between 16 and 18, parents (guardians) receive a letter informing them of their child's participation; for students 18 and above parents do not need to be informed. In the following subsections, we articulate typical responses Ken would construct to answer the questions provided by the IRB to obtain the information they need to decide whether or not to approve research with human subjects. We chose to exemplify the IRB application in Ken's context, as it requires much more narrative text than an application at the University of Victoria, where researchers mostly check boxes. (Two IRB-approved examples of applications for teachers doing research in their classrooms can be found at the URL: http://www.educ.uvic.ca/Ethics/cases/cases.php.)

1. *State the purpose of the research. Include major hypotheses and research design. If the study is part of a larger study, briefly describe that larger study and indicate whether it has received IRB approval from another institution.*

Purpose The purpose of this research is to study middle school science education to ascertain the extent to which the cultures enacted by students and teachers are adaptive and to investigate how the use of cogenerative dialogues leads to improved teaching and learning. Because coteaching occurs in the classroom we also will investigate learning to teach and changes in teaching.

Two contexts are of interest in the study: in-class lessons (e.g., whole-class, small-group, individualized, demonstrations, labs) and cogenerative dialogues (in and out of class time). Coteaching is a context for teachers to learn from one another, consciously and unconsciously. Also, because coteaching involves interactions between teachers we will study the extent to which interactions are successful and describe and seek to understand how teachers adapt to one another's cultural enactment to produce new forms of teaching. Cogenerative dialogues—which involve students, teachers, researchers, and sometimes administrators in discussions over shared experiences of teaching and learning—can address the extent to which teaching benefits learners, the roles of the teacher and students, what appears to work and what does not, and the associated divisions of labor and power relationships.

Participants convene as equals with the goal of identifying contradictions and patterns of coherence that occur in the classroom practices so that we can reach collective understandings on how to resolve contradictions that are identified. Agreement can be reached on patterns that ought to be strengthened and others regarded as deleterious and in need of elimination. Similarly, environments can be enhanced by eliminating some contradictions and strengthening others; making patterns of coherence by increasing the frequency of contradictory practices. By actively involving students in cogenerative dialogues there is a potential for them to identify maladaptive practices and schema such as rules that may be oppressive and lead to alienation.

Hypotheses Ethnography allows for research questions and associated assertions and contradictions to emerge from the ongoing research. The design of this study allows for the participants to immediately change their practices to take advantage

169

of what is learned from the research. Five broad hypotheses associated with this study are:

- Different forms of cultural enactment are associated with the teachers' and students' ethnicity, gender, social class and native language. These differences are associated with contradictions that often appear as resistance and lead to unsuccessful interactions between participants.
- The teachers and students have difficulty in anticipating others' cultural enactment and interacting in ways that are appropriate and timely. The result is a high incidence of unsuccessful interactions associated with an accumulation of negative emotions such as frustration and disinterest in learning.
- One-on-one cogenerative dialogues allow a teacher and a student to learn to interact successfully. What is learned is then enacted in the classroom to improve the quality of teaching and learning.
- Small-group cogenerative dialogues containing coteachers and students are sites for interacting successfully and synchronously, and cogenerating outcomes and shared responsibilities for enacting them. An outcome of participating in cogenerative dialogues is solidarity, which can then be enacted in the classroom to increase the responsibility that agreed to changes are successfully enacted—thereby transforming learning environments through the resolution of contradictions.
- Whole-class cogenerative dialogues increase the incidence of collective responsibility for learning and support for enacting agreed to changes in the classroom. Hence whole-class cogenerative dialogues afford the improvement of classroom learning environments.
- Coteachers produce new forms of teaching culture that afford improved learning environments for students.

There are other very important outcomes likely from participation in cogenerative dialogues. All participants learn, in a relatively safe context, how to discuss and reach agreement with others who differ in terms of age, sex, ethnicity and class. It is important for teachers and students to learn to communicate across such boundaries and what is learned about cogenerative dialogues can then be the basis for culturally adaptive teaching and learning in a classroom context. Hence it is important in cogenerative dialogues to "cogenerate" a collective responsibility for enacting agreed upon changes in the science classroom. The shared responsibility distributed across students and the teacher can break down the model of teacher as lone hero who alone is accountable for the quality of science education. The collective responsibility raises the possibility of creating communities of learners in which the learning of science can thrive and identities can be honed that are connected with success in science and enjoyment of doing science.

Cogenerative dialogues have been catalysts for changing the nature of learning environments. In this study we expect small-group cogenerative dialogues to occur at least once and preferably twice a week. Any of the researchers can raise issues for discussion and "cogenerated" solutions, including issues, impressions, raw data, analyses and interpretations. Based on our experience in urban schools we will conduct cogenerative dialogues at lunchtime and after school. Whole-class cogenerative dialogues will occur in class time. One-on-one cogenerative dialogues will occur on an as-needed basis, in and out of class time.

Research Design The study is situated in one science class of a low performing public middle school in New York City. The study is ethnographic and involves three researchers (including the resident teacher) as participant observers. The orientation in the research is phenomenological/hermeneutic—that is we endeavor to learn from the participants by finding out about their experiences, as they live and describe them, in urban science classes. The participants in this study will be the coteachers (the resident teacher, Ken and Michael), students from one class selected by the resident teacher, and school administrators.

Like so many teachers in urban schools, the regular science teacher for the class is an immigrant, a scientist who opted to become certified to teach science when he came to the USA. The teacher differs ethnically from all of his students most of whom are Black and either African American or Hispanic. English is not his native language and, although he regards himself as African American, he is light skinned and his Black students do not regard him as "one of them." The teacher also belongs to a different social class than his students, all of whom are from homes where poverty is a factor. Differences in social class, ethnicity, gender, and native language are associated with differences in the cultural resources of the students and the teacher and within the students there is also significant diversity in the culture they can enact.

Researchers will observe, videotape, and converse with participants. We do not want the research to be too obtrusive or time consuming and to the extent possible we will study normal life in urban science classes and learn from it. We will employ a variety of qualitative data resources (e.g., videotape, field notes, transcripts of conversations, artifacts used/produced by participants in their normal work, email exchanges between researchers and other participants). We will ensure that participants are aware of which data resources are being used in the study, how they are being used, and how we interpret the data. We will routinely communicate with stakeholders about our interpretations and their perspectives on our interpretations will be seriously considered.

Cogenerative dialogues will vary in their size ranging from one teacher with one student through to all coteachers with the entire class. The most common size will be five to six participants—all coteachers from a given lesson and two to three of the students (selected for their differences from one another).

Commentary The coteaching and cogenerative dialogues are presented as part of professional practice. Hence, the IRB is not being asked for permission to use coteaching and cogenerative dialogues and the students' participation in cogenerative dialogues is part of what happens in the classroom, irrespective of whether or not research is approved.

The six hypotheses require access to videotape, analytic memoranda, and artifacts such as digital recordings of student work products.

2. Describe the source(s) of subjects and the selection criteria. Selection of subjects must be equitable and, in the case of protected populations such as children, prisoners, pregnant women, the mentally disabled, etc. should address their special needs. Include number of subjects.

A teacher who wanted to use research to improve the quality of teaching and learning in an urban school initiated this study. In collaboration with administrators at the school he selected a low track eighth-grade class he was teaching. The decision reflects the school's goal for this class to benefit from participating in the study. The class contains 32 students, equal numbers of males and females; all from ethnic minority groups and economic conditions that are challenging. English is not a native language for 60 percent of the students in this class.

Ken Tobin will attend a class session in which students are asked to be involved in the study. He will explain the purposes of the study and ask students to sign an assent form if they are willing to participate. The resident teacher will not be present, thereby avoiding students feeling coerced to participate as a sign of allegiance to the resident teacher. All students who assent will be given a consent form to be signed by a parent (guardian). Completed forms will be returned in an envelope addressed to Ken Tobin and left with personnel at the main office. Copies of the signed assent and consent protocols will be mailed to the parent/guardian. (Sample consent and assent forms are provided in Figures 7.1–7.3.)

Commentary In studies such as these we employ authenticity criteria in which the research is intended to catalyze changes to improve the quality of the institutions being studied—in this instance schools, especially science classes. Also, the research intends to help those who cannot help themselves to benefit from what is learned in the research. Accordingly, it makes sense in a study such as the one proposed here to allow the teacher researcher and school administrators to decide which classes can be involved in the research—so that those who need to benefit from the research most urgently can be selected.

In this study the most contentious part is the video- and audio-taping. It needs to be clear that students can be involved in the study and decline to be videotaped and audiotaped. The consent and assent protocols are designed to allow these preferences to be exercised. Several contingencies may have to be clarified for the IRB. What happens if a student cannot participate because there is not a signed assent and consent form on file? What happens if a student or parent/guardian opts to be involved but not to be videotaped and/or audiotaped?

To the extent possible normal practices should not be disrupted by a study. Hence, it is not a good idea to change seating arrangements to accommodate those who opt not to be involved, or decline to be videotaped and/or audiotaped. The assurance we provide is that we will attempt not to capture their images or voices and we seek their cooperation in avoiding being recorded. In addition, we guarantee that if we inadvertently record them we will not analyze the video and audio. In this way it is not necessary to get a one hundred percent return rate for participation.

CONSENT FOR MINOR TO PARTICIPATE IN RESEARCH

Title of the Study: Use of research to improve the quality of science education in an urban middle school.

Invitation to Participate: Your child is being asked to participate in this research because he/she is a student in a school that has agreed to participate in a study of the teaching and learning of science in an urban middle school.

Purpose: This study seeks to enhance science education in urban schools. The study will explore how students' learning of science is affected by teaching and the ways in which your child and other students participate in the class.

Procedures: During this study your child may be videotaped or audiotaped. He/she may be asked to take part in interviews. In addition, test scores and school records may be accessed. Selected excerpts from the videotapes will be used in the dissemination of what is learned from this study.

Risks: Except for the embarrassment of seeing him- or herself on videotape segments shown to the class there are no potentially harmful risks related to participating in this study. Your child's images will not be shown to the whole class without first obtaining his or her permission.

Benefits: As a result of participation, your child's awareness about school and learning may be increased, particularly in science. The study provides students with valuable insights into different approaches and practices in teaching and learning science.

Withdrawal: Participation in the study is voluntary and if your child decides to participate, he or she can withdraw without any penalty at any time. Participation in the study is not a factor in determining your child's grade or standing in any course.

Alternatives: You may choose not to allow your child to participate in this study. If so, he/she will not be videotaped, audiotaped, or interviewed, and no references to him/her will be made in the reporting of this study.

Compensation: Your child receives no financial compensation for his/her participation.

Confidentiality: All information collected in this study will be kept private and your child will not be identified by name. The researcher will keep the audio- and videotapes from this study in a locked filing cabinet. Only the researchers will have access to these tapes.

Subject Rights: If you have questions about your child's rights as a participant in this study, you can contact the IRB Administrator, Gotham City University, (367) 373-2724, IRB@gcu.edu.

Conclusion: You have been given the opportunity to ask questions and have had them answered to your satisfaction. You have read and understand the consent form. You agree to allow _____ to participate in this research. Upon signing below, you will receive a copy of the consent form.

I agree for my child to be videotaped	Yes	No
_____ (Initial)		
I agree for my child to be audiotaped	Yes	No
_____ (Initial)		

Name Parent/Guardian	Signature	Date	

Figure 7.1. Sample consent form for the participation of minors.

ASSENT TO PARTICIPATE IN RESEARCH

Title of the Study: Use of research to improve the quality of science education in an urban middle school.

Description of the Study: You are being asked to participate in this research because you are a student in a school that has agreed to participate in a study that seeks to understand how to better teach and learn science in urban schools. During this study, you will be audiotaped or video-taped and you may be asked to take part in interviews. Selected clips from the videotapes will be used in telling others about what is learned from this study.

Risks: Except for the embarrassment of seeing yourself on videotape segments shown to the class there are no potentially harmful risks related to your participation in this study. Your images will not be shown to the whole class without first obtaining your permission.

Benefits: As a result of participation, your own awareness about school, communication, and learning may be increased, particularly in science. The study will provide urban schools and the university with valuable insight into different approaches and practices in teaching and learning science.

Confidentiality: All information collected in this study will be kept private and you will not be identified by name. The researcher will keep the audio and videotapes from this study in a locked filing cabinet. Only the researchers will have access to these tapes.

Subject Rights: If you have questions about your about your rights as a participant in this study, you can contact the IRB Administrator, Gotham City University, (367) 373-2724, IRB@gcu.edu.

Disclaimer/Withdrawal: Participation in the study is voluntary and if you decide to participate you can withdraw without any penalty at any time. If you decide not to participate there is no penalty. Participation in the study will not be a factor in determining your grade or standing in any course.

Voluntary Assent: I have read this form. Any questions I have concerning this study and my participation have been answered. I agree to participate in this research.

_____	_____
Name of Subject	Signature of Subject Date

I agree to be video taped	Yes	No	_____	(Initial)
I agree to be audio taped	Yes	No	_____	(Initial)

Child Assent Documentation
I certify that the study and the procedures involved have been explained to _____
in terms that he/she could understand and that he/she freely assented to participate in the study.

_____	_____	_____
Name of person obtaining consent	Signature-person obtaining consent	Date

Figure 7.2. Sample assent to participate in research

3. Provide a description of the procedure to be followed. If available, include copies of questionnaires and/or interview protocol, or a sufficiently detailed description of the measures to allow the IRB to understand the nature of subjects' involvement.

The researchers will coteach with the primary goal of enhancing the students' learning using established school practices, including cogenerative dialogues, approved by the school district, school administrators, and the resident teacher. The coteachers will not write field notes in the class, their primary roles being to teach the students, observe, and videotape what is happening. As high school science teachers for many years, Tobin and Roth are well qualified to teach middle school science.

Videotapes of science lessons will be made for sequences of two to three consecutive lessons at intervals of three weeks. As a lesson unfolds, the coteachers will videotape what happens, making sure only to capture the images of students who have agreed to be videotaped. Students who have declined to be videotaped will not be videotaped intentionally. If the image of a person who has not agreed to be videotaped were inadvertently captured, his or her image would not be used in the analysis or interpretation. The teacher researchers will create seating options for students not wanting to be videotaped and discuss these options with them. If a sizable number of students do not wish to be videotaped it is unlikely the class will be involved in the study. For example, in a class of thirty, if more than five students declined to be videotaped (that is if assent/consent forms were not returned from five or more students) we would identify another class to participate.

All students will be invited to provide their perspectives on what is happening and why it is happening. Usually these perspectives will be shared informally as the lesson progresses and in cogenerative dialogues convened out of class time. If an interesting event involves a particular student then arrangements might be made to converse with the student about the event. When this occurs a video-clip that incorporates the event can be identified and the conversation can take place after the student and researchers have reviewed the video-clip. Any student wanting to participate in conversations about the class or other aspects of the research can request a meeting with the teacher researchers and provide his or her perspectives on what is happening and why it is happening in regards to the teaching and learning of science in the classroom. The request can be informal (by just asking) or a form can be completed and left in a box at the rear of the class (see protocol in Figure 7.4).

Any student also can volunteer to be a student researcher. All students who volunteer will be involved in tasks such as reviewing and editing videotapes of the teaching and learning in the class, selecting short, edited video vignettes that show typical classroom practices and contradictions they consider worthy of discussion with the teacher and other researchers. Student researchers will be involved in discussions with the teacher and other students about the video vignettes and other shared experiences they consider salient to the quality of teaching and learning in the class.

Because the research method is ethnography there are no pre-planned interviews or questionnaires to be used. During cogenerative dialogues issues from the class will arise and questions will be asked about them as part of the flow of conversation. Questions are as likely to be asked by students as teacher-researchers. The hypotheses provided in response to Question 1 are the best indication of the likely focus of emergent questions.

4. Describe any potential harms or benefits to be derived by subjects, with a discussion of the risk/benefit ratio. For approval of any study with more than a mini-

175

CONSENT TO USE VIDEO TAPE

I am Ken Tobin, a professor in Urban Education at the University of New York. I am doing research in Gotham City public schools in an effort to learn more about how to improve the quality of teaching and learning science. I can be reached at (737) 327-2437. Alternatively you can email me at ktobin@gcu.edu.

You have previously agreed to be involved in a study of the uses of coteaching and co-generative dialogue at the school. As part of this research I have used videotape to explore how learning happens as the teacher and students interact with one another and materials from the classroom. I want to use short segments of the video to educate others about what I have learned from the research. Your image is included in one or more of the short excerpts I want to use in meetings with science teachers and researchers at professional meetings throughout the world.

I am requesting permission to use your image for the purposes of professional development for teachers and disseminating what I have learned from the research. You can view the videotape at the school or request a compact disk or digital videodisk containing the images for which I am requesting your permission.

Your name: _____

If you have questions about your about your rights as a participant in this study, you can contact the IRB Administrator, Gotham City University, (212) 817-7525, IRB@gcu.edu.

Please read the following and if you agree, select Yes or No to indicate your preference, and sign below.

Circle Yes or No as appropriate:

I allow you to use the video segments that contain my images:		Yes	No
I would like to view the video segments at school:	Yes	No
I would like a CD or DVD containing the video segments:	Yes	No

I give permission for you to use video-clips that include my image in professional development activities with teachers and meetings of researchers to let others know what has been learned from the research.

Yes: _____ No: _____

Signature: _____ Print name: _____

Figure 7.3. Sample consent to use videotape.

mal risk, the benefits must clearly outweigh the risk. Describe how the study may expose participants to stress, physical, psychological or interpersonal hazard, including the possibility of pain, injury, disease, discomfort, embarrassment, worry or anxiety.

To our knowledge, there are no known harmful effects from participating in the study. The benefits are a heightened awareness of learning and teaching and, as we know from nearly a decade of research on coteaching and cogenerative dialoguing, increases in academic achievement are likely to occur. In addition, all students will have opportunities to learn about video editing, compression of video data, and analysis of audio files in terms of amplitude, frequency and pause duration.

Anyone in the class will have an opportunity to view the videotape and collaborate with the teacher researchers in the analyses of videotape. This allows students to satisfy their curiosity about what we are videotaping and in so doing they can learn more about the teaching and learning of science in their class and become more aware of their own roles as learners. Also, in after-school activities all participants will be offered the chance to learn to use software to edit and produce movies using iMovie3 and QuickTime Pro, save movies on to CD and DVD, and use audio analysis software such as PRAAT.

Student researchers will be invited to attend seminars in which they are taught relevant methods and theory associated with the research. The researchers will teach the seminars at the school at times that are outside of the official school hours. When student researchers are in class their roles are not different from any other student in the class. They are not required to videotape if attending to the camera in any way is deleterious to their learning.

If we want to show a video-clip to the whole class or to a section of the class—for dissemination of what is being learned from the research, we will ask the permission of the individuals captured in the video-clip to show the clip to the entire class. Video-clips typically vary from 30 seconds to 2 minutes in duration. In this instance there is a potential for those individuals depicted in a video-clip to experience mild embarrassment even though they agreed that we could show the video-clip to the class. At the same time the use of video-clips in this way has been catalytic in other studies and the benefits to all students far outweigh moments of embarrassment experienced by individuals. It is probable that the moments of embarrassment decrease as the use of video-clips with the whole class increases. Hence the greatest risk of harm occurs in the early stages of the study.

If we want to show a video-clip or digital offprints from the videotape in contexts of educating other teachers or disseminating what we have learned from the study, written permission will be obtained from all participants whose images appear in the video-clips to be used. Alternatively, we will assure confidentiality by blurring images or using sketches based on the digital images.

Commentary A common problem contained in many applications to an IRB is failure to identify the benefits of being involved in research. If there are no benefits then a serious question can be raised about the relative weight of benefits to harms (i.e., beneficence). Obviously a researcher would want to argue that the benefits of research far exceed the harms. Hence, in any application to the IRB an effort should be made to identify sensible benefits and harms and ensure the balance is in favor of getting the research approved. If there are no benefits identified it is possible for an IRB to decline to approve the study as proposed.

5. Describe the specific methods by which confidentiality and anonymity will be protected, including the use of data coding systems, how and where data will be stored and who will have access to it, and what will happen to data after the study is completed.

REQUEST TO PARTICIPATE

Name: _____   Email address: _____

Please check any that apply and put your request in the box at the back of the room.

☐   I would like to participate in a cogenerative dialogue on _____
       (write the day or date).

☐   I would like to discuss what generally happens in my science classroom.

☐   I would like to discuss my participation in science.

☐   I would like to discuss the teaching of science.

☐   I would like to discuss why we do science and what science might be like.

Figure 7.4. Sample consent to use videotape.

The researchers will know the identities of the participants and hence anonymity is not possible in this study. However, participants will be guaranteed complete confidentiality: real names are not used in the analysis, interpretation, and dissemination of what is learned from these case studies. Pseudonyms will be used for people and places. All data resources, including field notes, videotapes, audiotapes, transcriptions and interpretive documents will be kept in locked filing cabinets or password protected databases in the researcher's office.

Commentary Participating in research should not harm participants and researchers should plan to protect them from harm. In the research proposed here the greatest problems come from inadvertently using actual names and using videotapes and offprints that can reveal the actual identity of participants. Hence assurances regarding the uses of video and audio recordings are provided in the informed consent and assent protocols and additional approvals are obtained for the uses of videotape and offprint images in dissemination and professional development.

6. If applicable, provide the following: (1) a description of the debriefing procedures to be used where deception has occurred (2) a statement describing what action you will take should the research reveal the possibility of a medical or other potentially troubling condition.

No deception is involved in this research.

COTEACHING AS A RESEARCH METHOD

In the early 1990s, coteaching began for us as a research method when teachers interested in introducing constructivist approaches to science education in their classrooms but felt uncomfortable in teaching in an open-ended way because of what they felt to be a lack of knowledge in science. In the course of several studies, Michael recognized the possibilities in coteaching to be not just a way to enhance the learning of students but as a research method in its own right. Through the participation in teaching, the researcher actually becomes part of the culture; in many respects, coteaching is a form of apprenticeship for a researcher new to a school. In ethnographic research, there is a tradition of using apprenticeship in this way, where researchers learned about the culture by apprenticing, for example, to become a blacksmith in an African country or an amateur boxer in New York (Wacquant, 2004). Why would coteaching, as apprenticeship, provide ethnographers with a unique perspective?

On the grounds of different theories—including practice theory or cultural historical activity theory—what is salient as resource for action at any moment is a function of the intentions and projected outcomes of our actions. Participative thinking, that is, how we are attuned to a situation and what we note or take for granted, is mediated by our purposes. If we go into a science classroom to observe and take notes then what we are attuned to and the temporality of the events are very different than when we go into the same classroom with the intent to teach chemistry, biology, or physics. Early in his career, while still teaching high school physics, Michael found out quickly that he could either be a teacher or a researcher but not both at the same time. As a teacher, he did not have the time or orientation to also ascertain the continuous function of the camera in his classroom—every now and then, therefore, it turned out at the end of a lesson that there was a malfunction and so the video was lost.

Coteaching, therefore, is a special method for doing research in classrooms. In this section we present a study in which coteaching was employed as a research method. The roles of Ken, Michael, a resident teacher, and a new teacher are explored in the analysis and associated metalogue.

Sticking to her Guns: A Research Scenario

For many years Alex has been a coresearcher with us. A teacher at City High, Alex began teaching in a low track school-within-a-school, known as Science, Education and Technology. After a few years he was moved to a college track school-within-a-school with much the same name, Science Engineering and Technology. Ken cotaught with him regularly over a number of years and when Michael came to Philadelphia Alex, Michael, and Ken undertook collaborative research, often about coteaching. In the following vignette Ken and Alex were among the coteachers, although Alex does not feature prominently in the chosen vignette.

Victoria, a new teacher, was coteaching during a review of chemical valence. The other principal teachers on this occasion were Jessica, and Alex. Ken and Rowhea Elmesky were there as researchers and Sonya Martin was in attendance as the university person supervising student teaching. Also, Ken and Sonya were coteaching the science methods course, a two-semester sequence of courses that focused on the teaching and learning of science in urban high schools. Hence, the

Figure 7.5. Victoria teaches while standing next to the whiteboard and the periodic table of the elements. In the far background, Jessica stands next to a student.

lesson involved six coteachers, each primarily concerned with affording the learning needs of students. For most of the lesson Jessica, Rowhea, Sonya, and Ken were coteaching mainly in peripheral ways, interacting with small groups and individuals, though occasionally using the whiteboards at the front of the room and the periodic table, which was adjacent to the whiteboards (the configuration can be seen in Figure 7.5). As I taught I carried a small digital videocamera in my hand, occasionally placing it on the desk when I needed both hands to teach. Victoria and Alex were more likely than any of the other coteachers to teach to the whole class during this lesson. In this lesson I tended to teach in a region of the class that was close to the periodic table, although in the 96 minutes of class time I traversed the entire classroom, interacting with students in all parts of it.

The research goals associated with Victoria, Jessica and Alex coteaching in an urban science class were clustered in two areas. We were interested in finding out more about learning to teach through coteaching, especially about what did and did not work well. At the same time there were many questions we had about teaching and learning, mainly about identifying the cultural resources used by urban youth as a foundation for building science fluency and the ways in which teachers and students adapted and aligned their culture as teaching and learning were enacted.

Victoria stepped forward to teach the whole class how to use the periodic table to obtain the valence of an element—using a "trick" to figure out the number of valence electrons for an atom of a specific element (Figure 7.5). As Victoria explained that she had a trick for students to figure out the valence, Mirabelle raised her hand and volunteered that she knew another way to get the valence. As a coteacher I sensed that Mirabelle's actions disrupted the flow of Victoria's teaching. Though I was pleased to see her initiate this interaction, I sensed that Victoria would not relinquish control of the discussion to Mirabelle on how to use the periodic table to obtain information on valence. Victoria reiterated that the placement in the table determines the valence, but Mirabelle countered that this is not what she is talking about. Then Victoria pointed out that what she has said *"is* the trick." By emphasizing the verb *"is,"* she indicated that there is only one correct way for figuring out valence, and this one way is the one she has been articulating for the class. The transcript below picks up at this point.

```
Episode 7.1
a   01 M:    <<p>there's another way you can figure it
             'out>
    02       (0.96)
b   03 V:    this ˄IS the way to do 'this
    04 A:    <<p>I hope so.>
    05       (0.34) ((Sasha and Tracy turn their heads to-
             ward Mirabelle))
    06 Ta:   [.hh h[h
             [((turns, smiles at Mirabelle))
c   07 M:    [arright ((smiles))
```

Microanalyses of the videotape reveal that in turn 01 Mirabelle speaks in a quieter voice than before. She restates that there is another way to figure "it" (valence) out. After a lengthy pause of almost one-second Victoria exclaims in a determined fashion, "this IS the way to do this." The word "is" is stressed through a heightened frequency and amplitude and the final word in the sentence, "this", also is stressed through the use of an increased frequency. The statement may have been intended to convey that Victoria's way is the only way to find valence from the periodic table. As soon as Victoria emphasized "*is*," I began to move forward toward Mirabelle. My concern at that point was that an argument could develop and spin out of control. I had a sense that Mirabelle might respond explosively and create a dispute that would lead to her being removed from the class. Hence, I moved closer to Mirabelle, about ten feet to her right, to be in a position to intervene, should my intervention be desirable. Because I had been coteaching in this class continuously, I knew that Mirabelle would not back down, would say what was on her mind, and would not want to be put down by Victoria in front of her peers. Being an accomplished basketball player, her peers regarded Mirabelle as a leader, with tendencies to get her way through the use of verbal and physical aggression. Many weeks after this event, one of the student researchers from this class who also was a basketball player, described Mirabelle as a bully who is sometimes "crazy."

Video analysis reveals that in the background, Alex supports Victoria's position with a low-intensity comment, "I hope so." His remark increases the likelihood of conflict since Mirabelle might consider that the teachers were ganging up on her. However, Mirabelle's peers interact to provide support for her. First Tracy and Sasha, then Tasha turn their bodies and heads while Mirabelle is in the process of orienting herself to present her account of the method. Figure 7.6 shows the seating arrangement of these and several other key students during this episode. There is eye contact among several of the students just prior to Mirabelle announcing the intention to articulate her method uttering "arright" (turn 07), and then explaining

Figure 7.6. Seating arrangement of students salient in our analysis.

how subtracting two from the atomic number of the first row of elements generates the valences of the associated atoms. With the utterance of "arright," Mirabelle moves her body right to left and her hand into a forward position, and then erects the body again as if taking a position from which to launch the articulation of her method of recalling and remembering chemical valences.

As a teacher-researcher my concern was for Mirabelle in the sense that I did not want her to be disadvantaged by sticking to her guns. I valued students getting involved and I enjoyed the passion that Mirabelle was showing during this sequence of interactions. However, I knew that Victoria wanted to be sure that all students in the class knew how to use the periodic table to extract any relevant information they needed and I recognized her practices as efforts to shut down Mirabelle's attempts to present a counter perspective. At the same time, Victoria was a student and a friend. I did not want her to feel lack of support in the event that problems arose. Although I moved closer to Mirabelle, my role remained peripheral in that I listened and watched as the camera captured Mirabelle and the students in her vicinity.

What is salient from this vignette is that eventually Mirabelle presented her alternative model and recognized its limitations. Victoria was able to reinforce her trick for using the periodic table to find the valence of an element, and many students followed both arguments attentively and noticed that Mirabelle's method of subtracting two from the atomic number didn't work for all elements. There were times in the short sequence of interactions when the emotional climate seemed overheated, and yet events did not spin out of control. As I experienced it as a teacher and researcher, the interactions heated up for a short time and then cooled down again. Microanalyses reveal that students interacted verbally and non-verbally to show their support for Mirabelle, providing structures to encourage her to proceed with her argument—as if to reassure her that they "had her back."

My recollections about the lesson are very much focused on this vignette, because we have spent hundreds of hours analyzing and interpreting what happened. However, immediately after the lesson I had a number of pressing concerns including how to recognize the capital that students brought with them from out of school fields and that might reasonably be used as a basis for building science learning. This concern pointed directly to the scenario we have described here. In addition, I was anxious to know more about how to create positive learning environments for excellent students like Darnell and Katrina who seemed not to be challenged by curriculum. I also wanted to know at the same time how to get other students to participate in ways that were sustained. In terms of teacher learning I was concerned about the deteriorating relationship between Alex and Victoria, fueled by different epistemologies, ontologies, and axiologies. The interactions with Mirabelle raised a question of how different teachers might view Mirabelle's efforts to be involved and, for that matter, Victoria's roles in the vignette.

Did my moves toward Mirabelle reflect an unconscious manifestation of deficit perspectives? I worry about this because as it happened the students kept the heat out of the interactions even though my feeling at the time was that the tone and emotional content might become inappropriate. As a researcher I am delighted that what happened did happen, because it allowed us to see how middle class, ethnically-other teachers can misunderstand the ways in which urban youth interact and act in ways that are intended to shut them down. Mirabelle stuck to her guns, yet she was aware of my presence and as I moved closer toward her the videotape shows her quick eye movement to take notice of where I was situated. So it is not just Victoria through her verbal interactions but also Alex through his verbal support for Victoria, and me through my proximity move who apparently coordinated actions to maintain environments that were more comfortable for us. The lack of comfort I felt was emotionally laden. I wanted to avoid conflict, I was afraid that verbal aggression would spiral out of control and result in physical conflict, and I doubted Mirabelle's ability to keep a lid on her emotions. With the benefit of hindsight I can at least consider that my feelings and non-verbal interactions during this vignette were grounded in deficit perspectives of urban youth and an inability to notice the positive aspects of Mirabelle's arguing practices.

Immediately after the lesson I clipped and used the above vignette in a discussion with a colleague in teacher education—as an example of an effective learning environment. My colleague was appalled with the quality of teaching and learning and was highly critical of Victoria and her resistance to Mirabelle. She argued that Mirabelle should have been encouraged to calmly explain her model and participate in a rational discussion of the strengths and weaknesses of each approach. My position was that Victoria asking Mirabelle for a justification (turn 01 in episode 7.2) acted as an emotional trigger that created structures to support an argument ritual associated with interacting with peers in her social life in her neighborhood and especially on the basketball court. Victoria appropriated Mirabelle's practices and Mirabelle responded with emotion and in so doing provided a rationale that allowed Tracey and then Victoria to judge that her model has limitations. What makes that bad teaching? Is it the emotional climate that is judged to be inappropriate—because of middle class White discomfort with emotionally laden interactions?

The interactions were certainly much more emotional than they had been. Just prior to the transcribed text in episode 7.2, Tracey asks Mirabelle in a low pitched

*Figure 7.7. Mirabelle launches her body forward, throws her arm and hand forward, ges-
ticulates toward the periodic table of elements, and raises her the volume and pitch voice as
she utters, "I'm just saying, just use the number two."*

and low intensity voice, where the two was coming from—the two Mirabelle was
subtracting from the atomic numbers. Episode 7.2 begins (turn 01) with Victoria
repeating Tracey's question with the pitch of her voice rising near to 300 Hz and
the intensity increasing above normal levels, especially as she utters "two". There
is a brief pause, interrupted by Tasha's "from" uttered at low speech intensity. At
this point, Mirabelle launches her body forward, raises her voice and her pitch repeatedly moves to 500 Hertz and beyond as she utters, "I'm just saying, just use the
number two" (Figure 7.7). Her frustration is apparent. Mirabelle then speaks in an
accusatory way that her teacher does not want her to copy text, with a possible implication that what she (Mirabelle) searches for is understanding and having a sure-
fire way to remember valence. The frustration is also apparent from the way she
uses her body to direct others' attention, for example, to a particular place in the
periodic table. At this stage, her speech rate has increased from an average of five
syllables per second to over eight syllables per second.

Episode 7.2
```
d     01  V:    Where is the 'twO coming from.
      02         (0.52)
      03  Ta:   <<p>from.>
      04         (0.19)
e     05  M:    <<f>I'M JUST SAYing just use the number 'TWO:
                (0.14) ─i: ─you=don=t=wan=me=da copy text from
                noWHERe, or yOU can take t=the two come from
                the (0.16) the 'rOW,> I mean
      06         (0.42)
f     07  Tr:   <<p>that won't wORK f'r (0.57) for=ALL=of
                them.>
      08         (0.42)
      09  V:    it=doesn't=work for=ALL of them.
g     10  M:    'well 'what. you <<f>want> then the <<f>─'TWO>-
```

11   (0.30)

The discussion with the colleague from teacher education bothered me because of the very clear deficit perspectives she had for the culture enacted by Mirabelle and for the ways in which she thought about effective teaching. Although she had not cotaught in this lesson she felt qualified to judge what was and what was not appropriate about Victoria's teaching. She was willing to say what Victoria should have done in each instance of the unfolding vignette. As a coteacher I certainly did not have that sense. I was there and could have intervened at any time had I felt a need. Also, there were six coteachers in total, all of whom allowed events to unfold as they did. My present feeling is that if I had been teaching in a more central role I would have allowed Mirabelle to fully explain her position as soon as she raised her hand. I have no way to know what such an approach would have allowed or how the students in the class would have participated. There are implications here for the assessment of teaching and the roles different stakeholders can and should play. These are taken up again in chapter 8. Here we focus closely on our roles as teacher researchers involved in coteaching.

As a coteacher my role as researcher is to focus on the learning of students in an unambiguous way. I do not feel role conflict and if I need to put the camera down I do so. If a student picks up the camera while I have it down I allow that to happen, too, so that mystification and glamorization of videotaping is minimized. I rarely take notes and if I want to make an analytic memorandum I use my iPod to create an audio file. In such cases I put the videocamera on a desk and move away to record the audio message as a discrete file. During the lesson I ask questions and talk informally to students and coteachers and the interactions are captured on videotape. As a coteacher I have a sense of the game, which allows me to anticipate unfolding structures and enact teaching in ways that are timely and appropriate (what Michael has described as *Spielraum*, room to maneuver as sensed by the participant in the "game," and what we have also discussed as teaching fluently).

Coteaching as a research method provides a first person experience with the teaching and learning as it unfolds. I find the videotape an essential resource because so much of what happens is missed as I coteach, yet I also feel way ahead of what it was like taking fieldnotes from the front or side of the class or behind a videocamera stationed on a tripod. As soon as possible after a lesson I like to review the videotape as I import it into iMovie (video processing software that comes with the Macintosh operating system). I simply watch and take notes as I do. Later I can use the digital file to move back and forth and change the speed of replay in a search for patterns, contradictions and salient events. The replay and review can be thought of as writing field notes, though I think of what I do as writing analytic memoranda. The replay stimulates recall of points I want to expand in narrative form at a later time and other events that I want to get more information about and possibly revisit using video analysis. On the initial review of the tape I identify the segments I will explore in greater depth and transcribe.

I identified the vignette involving Mirabelle as a contradiction to a pattern of role enactment when a coteacher teaches from the front of the room. Most often there is question and answer and it is quite unusual for a student with a counter idea to the teacher to get more than one turn at talk. Hence, I wanted to know more about the event, especially because I remembered it as a heated moment. Independently, one of the student researchers identified the same vignette as an example of effective student learning. She saw Mirabelle's argument as an example of inquiry.

Michael frequently came to Philadelphia to experience first hand what it was like to coteach in urban high school science classes. Routinely we used coteaching as a research method to learn more about learning to teach, teaching and learning by experiencing the praxis of others as coparticipants. As such we experienced the dynamic structures of the classroom fields in which we did research, felt the dispositions to act in certain ways and learned to anticipate the unfolding praxis of others and enact appropriate practices that expanded the agency of other coparticipants. Examples are provided throughout this book, but especially in chapter 2. Accordingly, we were able to study (a) teaching as Chuck and Andrea enacted it, (b) learning as students like Natasia practiced it, (c) the limitations of Ken and Michael coteaching science in a field in which a teacher has limited subject matter knowledge, and (d) the emergence of conflict and its resolution as these relate to identity construction in teachers (Alex) and students (Ya-Meer).

These experiences of coteaching science to urban youth allowed Michael to develop a sense of the game and a framework for making sense of videotape of urban science classes in the school in which he had taught. Hence, even though he was not a coteacher in the lesson in which Mirabelle presented her explanation for chemical valence, he had cotaught in the same school-within-a-school and several of the students in the class were in classes cotaught by Michael. I approached Michael to participate in the research, to provide a third-person perspective and to employ micro-analytic techniques that I had not yet developed, involving the use of PRAAT in the analysis of prosody, that is, the analysis of voice parameters such as speech intensity, pitch, and speech rates. Because these parameters are expressions of a person's current emotion, they are of theoretical interest from the perspective of the sociology of emotions concerned with understanding social phenomena in terms of interaction rituals (Collins, 2004). In PRAAT, we found a tool that allowed us to reliably construct data as evidence in support of our theoretically founded analyses.

The vignette was contained in a video-clip that was less than four minutes duration. We divided the clip into three parts and began intensive analyses of each in which we transcribed and analyzed salient interactions over a period of two weeks, collaborating for three to five hours a day and working independently in between periods in which we worked together. The focus of the analyses was to make sense of the interactions in terms of emotions, using our ethnographic based knowledge to augment what we could see happening at the micro level, where interactions occur without the participants being fully aware of what is happening and why it is happening. That is, the microanalysis afforded us developing an understanding of the agency|structure relationships being enacted as praxis.

1: Cristobal stands on the side; Chris moves more toward the center position and teaches. Some students begin to become restless.

2: At this point, Cristobal moves his body forward, getting closer to the center, as if he was getting ready to act.

3: Chris does not give up the lead, students quiet down, and Cristobal moves back to his preferred position "in the wings."

Figure 7.8. Sample video-ethnographic data for an article on how coteachers become like one another.

VIDEO-ANALYSES OF COTEACHING

As part of our research, we draw on a variety of qualitative research methods appropriate in school contexts, including ethnography, discourse analysis, and microanalytic approaches to studying social practices. In addition to writing the usual observational, method-related, and theoretical field notes, we videotape lessons and cogenerative dialogue sessions, interview students and (new) teachers, audiotape interviews conducted by high school student research assistants among their peers, and collect the teaching-related discussions new teachers held using an online internet forum. Teachers sometimes are equipped with recorders to ensure that their talk is captured at all times and recorders are placed on various student desks to assure that all contributions to whole-class conversations are recorded and available for analysis.

Working with the Video Images

All relevant videotapes are digitized to make them available for analysis using iMovie (Macintosh OS X), which allows slowing down and speeding up the playing and moving through the recording image by image to capture phenomena at the micro level, where we observe patterned actions that the speed of everyday activity does not allow us to observe in real time. The recorded events are transcribed and enhanced by salient video frames. The audiotapes of classroom events, interview sessions, and cogenerative dialoguing meetings are also transcribed and made available for analysis. The first transcriptions are often completed by the high school research assistants, because of the high fidelity with which they capture student contributions to the conversations in the science lessons.

We sometimes prepare video ethnographic data, especially when the phenomena of interest can be observed but not heard. For example, for an article on how coteachers come to be like one another coauthored by the four coteachers in the

187

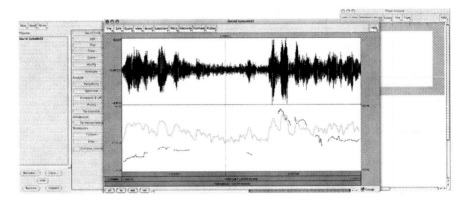

Figure 7.9. Screen print of the PRAAT interface with three windows open: main window for file management (left); sound analysis window (center) with soundwave (top) and intensity and pitch (bottom); and graphing window for producing and exporting high quality images. The sound track represents the exchange between Victoria and Mirabelle in Episode 7.2 from turn 01 through the word "number" in the first line of turn 05.

room, we annotated sequences of images from the lesson (e.g., Figure 7.8). The episode clearly shows how the teacher in the background gets ready to address trouble in the classroom but then backs off when students quiet down as the lead teacher (Chris) gains control. When we have not had the opportunity to ask for permission to use video images or want to hide the identity of the participant, we may construct drawings such as those featured in Figures 7.5 through 7.7. Drawings also have another advantage: those aspects can be made visible that are relevant to the analysis while leaving out all of the gratuitous detail that a photograph displays and thereby distracts readers' attention to what really matters to the analysis. For example, the comparison of Figures 7.7 and 7.8 easily reveals that the former shows precisely Mirabelle's body position and orientation relevant in the analysis whereas the change in the position of the teacher in the background is not as readily available from the photographs we had used in our article (Figure 7.8).

To construct drawings, we use the following process. From the video display, we make a screenprint, which is imported to painting software such as Photoshop. Because the screenprint has a pixel density of 72 points per inch, the density of the image is changed to at least 300 points per inch—the standard requirement made by journal and book publishers. The image is cropped and then sized to correspond to the desired measures (e.g., the photograph underlying Figure 7.7 was sized to 2.5 inches width). In the next step, we create a new layer on top of the photograph and then use a black "pen" to draw the outlines of the desired persons and features. As Photoshop allows hiding layers individually, the image to be published is produced by saving the drawing separately in JPG format. This image can then be imported into the article or book chapter.

Working with the Soundtrack

The transcripts of selected lessons are then enhanced to contain information regarding sequencing (overlap/latching), timed intervals, characteristics of speech production (stress, lengthening of phoneme, intonation, loudness), and comments. The transcriptions available in Episodes 7.1 and 7.2 are good examples for the way in which the transcripts appear. At this stage, the software packages Peak DV and PRAAT are used to work with the soundtrack, for increasing the gain to amplify the volume, which improved the hearing of doubtful words, for measuring the pauses using the waveform display of the sound, and for establishing pitch levels and contours, which were clearly visible in the display of a particular sound.

PRAAT is a freely available piece of software used by linguists around the world that exists for Macintosh, Windows, Linux, SG, Solaris, and HPUX platforms (http://www.praat.org). It handles a number of different sound file formats, which we save directly from the iMovie program. When imported and displayed, the sound track of the following excerpt from Episode 7.2 looks like what can be seen in the central panel of Figure 7.9:

```
Episode 7.2 (repeated)
d    01  V:      Where is the 'twO coming from.
     02          (0.52)
     03  Ta:     <<p>from.>
     04          (0.19)
e 05   M:        <<f>I'M JUST SAYing just use the number
```

Readers clearly see how the pitch of Victoria's voice moves upward and has a peak (as indicated by the diacritical sign "´" preceding the word "two" in the transcript). One can easily distinguish the very softly (piano) and on falling pitch spoken "from" (<<p> from.>) transcribed in turn 03. Finally, one can see the high-intensity and high-pitch utterance of "I'm just saying." In the transcript, the increased loudness is denoted by "<<f>" for "forte," and the increased pitch by the capitalization of the letters. The pauses, as transcribed in turns 02 and 04, are measured and displayed by dragging the cursor from the beginning to the end of a valley in the intensity and sound wave displays.

There are different ways of proceeding to produce a high-quality output of sound wave, intensity, and pitch. We have used both of the following methods. First, PRAAT already has a plotting feature (right-most panel in Figure 7.9) that can be used to create figures and export them into several graphic formats. Second, because we also write the text into the diagram and because we may want different symbols and other graphical features, we sometimes make a screenprint of the display. This screenprint is imported into a graphics program (e.g., Illustrator), where the interesting features are reproduced as a diagram in a second layer, similar to the production of drawings. By using back and forth between PRAAT and the drawing program, the words are then matched to the intensity and pitch display. Once the drawing is finished, the imported screenprint is deleted and the figure is exported into an appropriate format. An example from the lesson in which Mirabelle and

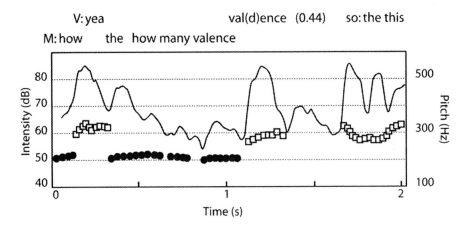

Figure 7.10. A part of the Mirabelle–Victoria interaction produced for an article concerning prosody as resource in and for social interaction.

Victoria argued over the right method to find the valence of an element is displayed in Figure 7.10.

Why Go through the Trouble of Doing Microanalysis?

Some science educators may ask us why we go through so much trouble to do analyses that may, on the surface, have little to do with science education. The answer is rather easy. Throughout this book, readers find us using concepts such as alignment, synchrony, mutuality, emotional energy, and verve. It turns out that all of these theoretical concepts find their equivalents in the way human beings generally and the coteachers and students specifically speak. Thus, emotional energy is directly expressed in speech intensity; higher emotional states also are expressed in higher pitch such that when people argue, especially when they are angry, pitch levels tend to go up, sometimes doubling and tripling in value. People also tend to speak faster when they become excited and angry—such as can be seen from the increase in Mirabelle's speech rate when Victoria questioned the suitability of the former's method for calculating valence.

Other examples for the use of PRAAT to support theoretical concepts include alignment and synchrony. It turns out that synchrony expresses itself in the alignment of the pitch levels with which people speak. Thus, when Alex responded to a student, his pitch begins by matching that of the student and then returns to his own preferred pitch levels. Most of the new teachers coteaching with him fell in line and also matched their pitch levels both with those of students and Alex's. Victoria, on the other hand, does not match her pitch level with others, which parallels the conflictual relations she has had both with Alex and with students. Figure 7.10 presents a clear example of this divergence in the pitch levels: Victoria speaks with a pitch about 80 to 100 Hertz above Mirabelle, whereas it would be typical for Alex to match that of the student.

COGENERATIVE DIALOGUES AS A RESEARCH METHOD

As a research method, cogenerative dialogues provide interesting insights into many aspects of the social lives of the participants, not only what is said, but also non-verbal interactions and into the emotional content of the interactions between participants. It is a way of constructing meaning subsequently to be reported to fellow teachers and peers. A key intention is to provide for a method in which the traditionally strong and overpowering voices of researchers are treated on an equal footing with the voices of those that have been underprivileged in educational research: teachers and students.

Constructing Meaning

To construct meaning, we enact a dialectic process consisting of two movements: understanding and explaining. Immediate understanding of the praxis situation is primary and constitutes the necessary prerequisite of any other form of understanding (e.g., theory). This practical and existential understanding precedes, accompanies, and concludes explanation; it completely envelops it. However, this primary understanding has to be expanded through a second, explanation-seeking (critical) hermeneutic analysis lest teachers and researchers are to remain stuck in the ideologies of their immediate understanding. This explanation-seeking form of analysis develops primary understanding. Such analysis is required to detect any structural contradictions that are of a societal nature; we become conscious of the fundamental conflicts on the level of ideology through an analysis of structures.

In our research, this movement from primary to theoretical understanding is initiated during cogenerative dialogue sessions where we began by talking about shared events, which we often made present again by replaying salient moments recorded on video. These conversations allow us to arrive at better and deeper understandings or simply to raise salient issues that we identified as needing further inquiry, which we subsequently conducted individually or in groups. An important part of the analyses were additional meetings in which we replayed the episodes, stopping whenever one individual identified an issue as salient. We then talk about the issue until all participants feel that the event has been sufficiently discussed. These intensive discussions allow students, teachers, researchers, and other stakeholders to learn about their practices in ways that their normal orientation to the classroom does not usually permit, as is evident from the following excerpt in which Michael and a new teacher reflect on this form of analysis.

> Chris: It's really, really interesting to me that I'm having ideas now in this cogenerative dialoguing session that I really haven't thought about, not on the level at which we think them now, although they've been in there.

191

Michael: Like the kind of things we have been talking about watching the video?

Chris: Yeah, and so for me seeing him [Alex] use some sort of technique that has to do with some sort of theory or suggest something about how he is teaching, this is interesting.

The initial purpose of the cogenerative dialogue is to change the teaching and learning environment. But during these meetings, we also make explicit attempts to "ratchet up" our conversation, to move from our immediate experience and *emic* discourse to explaining experience and the use of *etic* discourse; that is, we began to articulate more general and site-independent, general categories. We revisit the discussed events both in further face-to-face meetings and email exchanges among participants. The descriptions of classroom events and associated analyses, as we provide them throughout this book, emerge from these recursive discussions that originally begin with the cogenerative dialoguing and that are subsequently revisited until we feel that we understand and have an explanation for them. But cogenerative dialoguing is not the necessary starting point for reflecting on teaching. In some instances, one or more individuals take a particular clip and repeatedly view it. They then meet and discuss their individual analyses and in fact deepen these through their collective analysis.

Once we have written our initial analyses, we cycle them in draft form among other stakeholders (authors), who change them by adding, cutting, or by highlighting parts that require further discussion. We meet to discuss or electronically communicate to identify what we have learned during the previous stages of the analysis. This makes our research a recursive process, where later discussions take contents and processes of earlier ones as their topic. Such recursive processes allow us to develop even deeper understandings.

Archeology of Ontology and Ideology

As method, we have used cogenerative dialogues as places for making visible different ontologies, that is, different ways in which stakeholders experience social life in the places we are studying, such as classrooms. These can emerge as contradictions identified in the dialogue as such or as differences in perspective, arising in the cogenerative dialogue. For example, differences in perspectives on how well new grouping arrangements are working, between teachers and students, can be an indication of different ontological positions of the coteachers and students. Coteachers might judge the effectiveness of work groups on the incidence of social chatter whereas students may judge them on the extent to which they can contribute meaningfully and learn. Similarly, a vignette selected to show effective teaching, between Alex and Victoria shows Alex asking a question about the tendency of zinc to form positive or negative ions. He pauses and begins to scan the class with his eyes. After 0.8 s Victoria rephrases the question to a more convergent form, the first part requiring a yes or a no response (Is zinc a metal?). Underlying the look of frustration on Alex's face is a possibility that his preferred environment is one in which students leave the class with questions, whereas Victoria values students knowing correct information and being able to recall it. This difference in perspective, unlike the ones about the functioning and effectiveness of groups was not resolved through cogenerative dialogue, even though it was identified in cogenerative dialogue as an issue.

Any of the participants in a cogenerative dialogue could edit videotapes of their classroom to obtain examples of contradictions that might be resolved cogeneratively and improve the quality of teaching and learning. The vignette involving the interactions associated with the Mirabelle vignette would be a good example of a contradiction, given the differing perspectives of teacher educators, researchers like me and the students who identified this vignette as an example of good learning. We have adopted the practice of asking participants to watch the videotapes and to select any vignettes to show contradictions, good or bad learning, good or bad teaching, or events that are salient to the quality of the class. The participants were asked to edit them to be between 30 seconds and 3 minutes duration. During the cogenerative dialogue they were either projected using a digital projector connected to the computer or were viewed on a large screen monitor. The vignettes thereby became foci for dialogues that educated participants about one another's perspectives, thereby creating interactions leading to educative authenticity.

Cogenerative dialogues also are sites for creating consensus on what to do differently in other fields, such as the school and classroom. As we explain in chapters 4 and 5, the consensus is to be generated as one that all participants can support. Discussions about what happened, for example, in a class, become concrete objects that can be manipulated in terms of possibilities, creating agreements to enact changes, for example within the class, school or home. Hence, cogenerative dialogues are potentially catalytic and if the changes catalyzed reduce oppression then they are also sites for critical conversations and the consensuses can lead to more equitable classrooms. Discussions that identify forms of oppression and ways to minimize inequities are part of critical pedagogy and are a central part of critical ethnography.

Cogenerative Dialoguing and Writing the Research: Metalogue

Michael: Cogenerative dialogues have been an important context for making sense of the events in urban high schools not only for bringing about change but also as a method for generating data and interpretations on which subsequent publications in very different communities of practices were based. Because we wanted to be consistent with our understanding of theory generation as a collective process that did not privilege any one voice, there were consequences to the way in which we wrote research. Metalogues, a term first that was introduced and used, to the best to of my knowledge, by Gregory Bateson (1972), became to us an important genre for many reasons. It preserved the voices of individual authors, high school students and teachers alike; it was a way of "ratcheting up," that is, a way of moving from data

presentation and description to theory; and it was a way of introducing reflexivity into our research—its written product took the form of the process.

Ken: As well as moving from experience to theory about experience metalogue
allows moves to policy, practice and research concerns. Hence, based on
what was learned in a study, the authors can explore different realms of
applicability for them. The power of metalogue is that each author can
present his or her own perspectives and there is no obligation for co-authors
to sign on and agree. In this way the unfolding text, as a form of culture can
have its coherences and contradictions and readers can anticipate learning
from all of what is written. It is important to show multi-authored texts in an
authentic way that benefits from the diversity among authors. Unfolding text
is a structure, not only for readers, but also for authors and metalogue and
voiceover are ways for authors to be agential with respect to this dynamic
structure. For example, it is an opportunity to interpret interpretations and
thereby learn more about oneself and the other authors and it is also a way to
look at the practices in other fields, such as teaching and learning science in
other schools, formulating policy at local, district, state and national levels,
and doing research in the future.

Michael: For me, this reflexive nature of the metalogue was always very important:
it is not just a genre for preserving voice and presenting multiple perspectives
on some issue that we have experienced in different ways. Rather, at the level
of writing research, it reflected the same kinds of processes that we were part
of in the field. And then, it became reflexive of learning at the writing stage,
when we learned again from our previous learning.

Ken: My use of metalogue stemmed from a long history of co-authoring texts with
participants. It always bothered me that co-authored pieces tended to reflect
the most powerful voices on the team, usually mine. Although we worked
hard to reach consensus usually I persuaded my co-authors to a different
point of view. In a study involving Gale Seiler, who was a doctoral student at
the time and MacKenzie (Mac) Smith, who was a student teacher in a master's degree program at my university, we wanted to write a paper that addressed the challenges of teaching science methods courses that prepared
teachers for their student teaching assignments in urban high schools and
thereafter for careers as high school science teachers. Mac was critical of the
course I was responsible for; so we decided to use metalogue as a way to preserve the voices of the three different researchers and bring into contrast the
areas of agreement and disagreement.

Michael: Interestingly enough, for me, too, the metalogues—as the cogenerative
dialogues—arose from a concern for the voice of participants. In 1992, I was
still a high school teacher when I wanted to do a study on students' epistemology and talk about the nature of science. As I was doing the interviews,
one of the students, Todd Alexander, asked me whether he could work with
me, collect data, and write. While working on the text, it became clear to me
that we had to preserve our respective voices, and so we experimented with
personal voices within stretches of collective voice. Later on, I worked on ar-

ticles reviewing the literature in the social studies of science, and argued, among others, for the use of different genres in science education. Reading a number of books on epistemology that used dialogue as genre inspired me; the history of writing in dialogic form probably begins with Plato's Socratic dialogues and has continued to the present day. A key publication for me was an article entirely written in dialogue form entitled "Four dialogues and metalogues about the nature of science." Initially, there are two levels of conversation: at one level, four high school students talk about the nature of science; at the other level, a researcher and a journalist talk about the students' conversation, sometimes even talking to the students. When we drew conclusions, we ratcheted up within the conversation to look at what we had learned in the study, which therefore constituted another level. For me, this publication was central for its reflexive nature: it argued that scientific knowledge was discursively constituted and did so in a discursive way. Then, of course, you and I began to work together more closely when you moved to Philadelphia, and when we worked at City High School, where we had similar concerns.

Ken: At the time you and I were in regular email contact and I knew of your concern for voicing and privilege and I was impressed by the potential of conversations among participants—to reflect different perspectives. Several years before I was an external examiner on a doctoral thesis written by Mark Williams in which he had created a dream sequence in which three philosophers participated with him about his research, social theory and the salience of dreams. The effectiveness of these dialogues in juxtaposing contrasting points of view struck me and it was only a matter of time before we began to use metalogue as a regular feature of our research. In a study of urban science teaching, in which I was the teacher, Edward Walls an African American student researcher and Gale Seiler a participant observer who undertook research in my class, we once again used metalogue to represent our very different positioning as educators and scholars.

Michael: I think it was also at the time that Jacques Désautels began criticizing us for not implementing metalogues in the spirit of its inventor Gregory Bateson. This ultimately led me to use the expression "ratcheting it up," meaning that metalogues are not just dialogues but moments of second- and third-order learning, that is, instances of learning about learning. So we began using metalogues to go back over terrain that we had covered, seeing what we have learned and attempting to learn from our own learning processes.

Ken: In this way, you and I have used metalogue effectively in numerous articles and books. Our approach has been somewhat the same each time we have participated in metalogue, whether we are seated in the same room in Philadelphia or Victoria or interacting on email. Having identified a topic, one of us usually identifies up to three issues considered to be salient and writes up to three paragraphs about each of those issues. The other then joins the conversation, addressing each of the paragraphs by inserting text after them or breaking paragraphs to insert relevant dialogue. Over successive sweeps from

195

one participant to the other the depth of the interaction can be increased and we ratchet up from descriptive analysis to increasingly theoretical discussions about the emergent constructs that we have addressed. In our case the different perspectives tend to be complementary and reflect our different programs of research. In other cases, such as the edited book with Peter Taylor and Penny Gilmer the different perspectives may have addressed somewhat different issues, thereby giving the metalogues a broader scope than would otherwise have been the case. For example, as a chemist, Penny's perspective often reflected that of a scientist who is now focusing on education, Peter's tended to reflect his tradition of research using narrative, and I brought a perspective of a science teacher educator with recent experience in urban schools.

Michael: With the metalogues, we really blurred the boundaries that some people experience between doing research and analyzing data and writing the research studies. Doing (writing) a metalogue is part of the data analyses, it is another pass over the data but now concerning our own learning in the process of doing the study. However, we often engage in this only after having produced some text intended for publication. So in a sense we begin working with the data again not only to write the research but also to engage in further learning.

Ken: I find metalogue to be an ideal method for edited volumes, allowing the editors to engage in interactive dialogues that add significantly to the text of a chapter, allowing the editors to add their perspectives and also to connect to other works in the same volume. Similarly, in coauthored books such as this we can also get to deeper levels of meaning through the use of metalogue.

COTEACHING AND COGENERATIVE DIALOGUES AS ASSESSMENT AND EVALUATION METHODS

Teaching is evaluated in numerous ways and, depending on the purposes of evaluation, the validity of the performance measures on which decisions are made may be crucial to the teacher and the institution in which the teacher practices. Cases in which valid measures are essential include those in which legislatures and school systems have decided to assess teaching for purposes such as earning tenure, promotion along a career ladder, merit pay, and holding teachers accountable for pupil achievement. Teacher evaluation is also important in teacher education. The internship experience is a critical component of teacher education programs and valid assessments are needed to guide decisions on whether individuals can teach effectively and thereby earn a degree and certification to teach. Accordingly, in inservice and preservice contexts there is a significant amount of teacher assessment occurring and important decisions are made on the basis of the measures obtained. In this chapter, we describe and explain how coteaching and cogenerative dialoguing are forms of assessment and evaluation praxis that differ from the received ways of doing assessment and evaluation. We are concerned with questions such as, "Are measures of teaching performance dependable for the purposes of their intended use?" "Are the data on the basis of which decisions are made trustworthy, credible and dependable?" "Can the measures be used to differentiate individuals for decision-making purposes?" "Can the performance of individuals be dependably compared to given criteria and judged to have surpassed or fallen short of given benchmarks?"

WHAT IS BEING MEASURED?

"Take this manual and take these tapes and don't come out of there until you can score it the same as the answer key." I (Ken) had just met my major professor and he was putting me to work. The Teacher Performance Assessment Instruments (TPAI) were in a pilot form and I was assigned to the research team that would do the validity and reliability studies on the quality of the measures obtained when they were used with beginning teachers. As an Australian science teacher educator I had been involved in teacher education at college level for about five years and prior to that I had supervised student teachers for many years. Even though I accepted my assignment with enthusiasm I had a sense of disquiet that stayed with me for all the years I worked on teacher assessment systems. Setting my feelings aside I entered a small dark room, put the tape in the VCR and set it running.

Getting it right was no slam-dunk! The TPAI consisted of statements about teaching, known as indicators, and I was to consider a lesson and then make a rating based on the fit between my judgments about the teaching and the description on an anchored rating scale. Each indicator consisted of a medium inference stem supported with five levels of competence, written at what was described as a medium level of inference. The descriptions provided a basis for rating each indicator from a low of one to a high of five. There were more than fifty indicators comprising the TPAI and each of these was to be assessed. The indicators clustered into what were known as teaching competencies, such as classroom management, planning, communication, relationships and professionalism. Numerous indicators provided a measure of each of the teaching competencies and my job eventually was to statistically identify the optimal cut scores for each competency.

Raters were trained to use the TPAI to produce uniform ratings and for a short time in the 1980s states like Georgia mandated the use of such instruments, which were refined and used for the purposes of teacher certification and for progression along the career ladder. Through factor analysis we explored the internal structure of the measures and undertook criterion related validity studies in which measures of teacher assessment were correlated with valued criteria such as achievement and student perceptions of the learning environment. Through the uses of generalizability theory we explored the extent to which measures were stable across facets such as rater, occasion of measurement, and class. The generalizability coefficients were then used to adapt indicators and competencies so that more dependable data were obtained—that is data that cohered and provided generalizability coefficients greater than a cutoff of 0.8, for example. The idea was to develop a system that provided data in which individuals could be ranked with confidence on the basis of their scores. Since hiring and firing would be associated with their teaching performance scores it was important that the scores were sufficiently dependable to withstand a court challenge to decisions.

* * *

To understand the fundamental difference that exists between coteaching and cogenerative dialoguing as assessment and evaluation methods, on the one hand, and traditional methods of assessment and evaluation, on the other hand, we require a model or theory about the processes by means of which the lived experience of teaching comes to be expressed in narrative descriptions and numbers. Here we provide such a model that allows us to understand not only the reduction of lived experience to qualitative, narrative accounts of the events in a classroom but also the use of instruments and quantitative measures followed by statistical analysis.

To distinguish the lived experience of actual teaching from denotations and descriptions of patterned practical actions, we use the terms praxis and practices, respectively. Praxis denotes the lived experience of being in the classroom, which we have tried to capture (obliquely nevertheless) in our account of coteaching the monohybrid and dihybrid cross (chapter 2). Undoubtedly, our account already is a reduction and it will be impossible for readers to get back to how it felt for Michael and Ken to be there. But the richness of the description—including the anxieties, uncertainties, and feelings of being exposed—provide a different image of teaching than if it had been done in terms of *strategies, skills, pedagogical (content) knowl-*

edge, content knowledge, or any other theoretical concept available today in the educational literature. The term *practices*, too, are abstractions from what people do, because they express events in terms of repeated and repeatable patterns. These patterns are the results of observing and comparing across observations, and therefore structures that are apparent to observers who stand back. Practitioners, however, even the most knowledgeable of scientists, do not know what they have done *until after they are done, when they see the outcomes of their actions and can make these actions present again in some form* (Roth, 2006).

Philosophers and sociologically oriented practice theorists concerned with knowledge and the ethico-moral dimensions involved in knowledgeable action identify the singular, once-occurrent act itself as the locus of knowledge (Bourdieu, 1990). Thus, participatory thinking only is enacted and available in the process of the action. In other words, what distinguishes the accomplished practitioner from a novice is that the practical wisdom of the former "consists in inventing conduct that will best satisfy the exception required by solicitude, by betraying the rule to the smallest extent possible. . . . Practical wisdom consists here in inventing just behavior suited to the singular nature of the case" (Ricœur, 1992, p. 269). That is, "the man [sic] of wise judgment determines at the same time the rule and the case, by grasping the situation in its singularity" (p. 175). Our question now is this: "How do assessment and evaluation capture the degree of wisdom that expresses itself in the singularity of the act, which can be grasped in and through the demands of the situation?" To answer this question, we require a theory that allows us to understand the relationship between praxis and practical action, in its singularity, and the various forms in which it is made present again to support judgments about the quality of teaching that has occurred.

We have a starting point for an answer in chapter 2, where we present a model (Figure 2.1) that allows us to understand the relationship between the singularity of lived experience in and during which our practical knowledgeability articulates itself and the different forms in which the events are captured and presented again for the purposes of constructing and supporting statements about the quality of the teacher's knowledgeability. Because of the centrality of the relationship between the singularity of praxis and the way in which it is captured in different types of documents, we reproduce the model in expanded form in Figure 8.1 focusing on the relationship between lived experience and structure, on the one hand, and on the nature of the assessment and evaluation processes that are intended to account for the lived experience and the knowledge it expresses, on the other.

The model is based on an iterated matrix expressing the relationship between the subject (generalized human being) and the generalized other, that is, the material world (Müller, 1972). The subject–other relationship can be viewed from the perspective of the possible encounters, as expressed in the left matrix of Figure 8.1a, leading us to a symbol matrix; or the subject–object relationship can be investigated under the aspect of form, as expressed in the right matrix of Figure 8.1a, leading us to a structure matrix. Human praxis is expressed in the left matrix, whereas its structural accounts are expressed in the right matrix.

Among the different types of encounters possible involving subject and object, the meeting of subject and subject, teacher and student, is the most important in teaching, as it is precisely here in this meeting that teaching|learning occurs. It is the quality of this encounter between subject and subject that mediates the quality of student learning and teacher teaching; more so, teachers learn to teach in the encounter with the student, so that students also can be seen as teachers and teachers as students.

The material and social constraints teachers and students experience in the classroom find their expression in the lower left cell of the matrix: what is other meets the subject, constraining the latter, defining the conditions, taking various forms of influence, and constraining the subject (student, teacher) by drawing on institu-

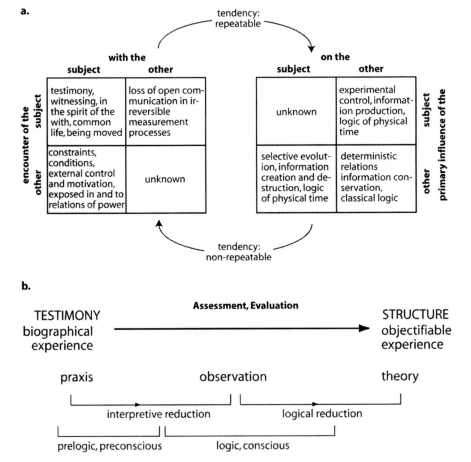

Figure 8.1. a. Relationship between lived experience and structure; experience can be reduced to structure repeatedly, but experience cannot be recovered from structure. b. Assessment and evaluation reduce lived experience to structure.

tional position as a resource. The encounter of coteachers working together in the same classroom also is of the subject–subject type.

The encounter of the subject with the other, for example in the form of a measurement instrument, a video camera, is experienced as loss of communication and an irreversible measurement process. It is no wonder that teachers initially are hesitant to have observers who take notes, cameras, or questionnaires and other documents used to evaluate what they are doing.

Viewed from a structural perspective, the relations involving subject and object present themselves very differently. Thus, the structure of the subject–subject encounter is inherently impossible within a structural perspective, because of the singularity of each encounter. Thus, even couples who have lived together for half a century cannot with certainty predict what the respective other will do in all situations that they experience together. A frequently raised question pertains to the fact that interactions can be studied in a variety of ways as this is done, for example, in the experimental procedures of social psychologists or, to return to the example of Ken rating the relationship between teachers and students as available on the videotapes, by means of observation and coding of naturalistic studies. But in each of these situations, we are dealing with some form of preparation, which makes two or more subjects the object of the study, and thereby objectifies the subjects. In its very etymology and definition, the object is the other (the Latin root *ob-* means "in front"), other than the self, which is close, a relation captured in the prefix *sub-*, Latin for "close."

When the primary influence is that of a subject on an object, we deal with experimental control (upper right cell of the right-hand matrix [Figure 8.1a]) and the production of information, which leads us to the logic of linear physical time. When Ken coded the tapes according to the TPAI coding protocol, he first reduced the observable events—already reduced because they are taped from an unacknowledged viewpoint—to categories and rated behaviors according to an assigned scale. That is, he produced numbers that captured some (very limited) aspects of teacher–student interactions. These numbers could subsequently be used to build mathematical or statistical models that either did not take into account the temporal unfolding of the events, thereby flattening time altogether into pure structure or related them to produce causal models (knowledge → action, action → effect) that inherently are linear in time.

When the influence of the generalized other on the subject is considered, we obtain structural models of how the actions of a subject are *determined* from the outside. Causal models of achievement, for example, as sociologists and social psychologists construct them, are typical examples that fit into the lower-left cell of the structure matrix.

The possibilities for moving between the two matrices are asymmetrical. The process of going from the experience matrix to the structure matrix is repeatable; this is just what Ken did in repeating the coding for tapes featuring the same or different teachers. The actions of every teacher he observed thereby came to be reduced qualitatively onto the other categories and, within each category, to a quantitative determination of more or less, higher or lower. The reverse process, however, is non-repeatable. Even for the same teacher, a particular code is insufficient to get the researcher back to a specific event. This is much like the uncertainty and impossibility to unequivocally determine the shape of a three-dimensional object if only its shadow projection on a wall can be seen. That is, assessment and evaluation provide us experience in an objectifiable form, but in this form, it cannot be mapped back onto a specific biographical experience and the knowledgeability it expresses.

The processes of assessment and evaluation are represented in Figure 8.1b. In a first reduction, Ken perceived the events reducing them to description. This first reduction—how and as what we see something—occurs at a pre-logic and preconscious level. It is precisely here that ideology operates, almost inaccessible to our everyday experience. We can understand ideology, a condition for subsequently changing it in a conscious manner, by exercising radical doubt and deconstructing our constructive processes (Bourdieu, 1992). In a second interpretive reduction, Ken associated a particular moment on the tape with a theoretically driven category of the TPAI. In a third reduction (drawing on an operational definition of levels of performance within a category), he then assigned a numerical score. Subsequent reductions led from the many numbers available in the datasets to structures expressed in terms of a few factors that result from a factor analysis. All of these subsequent reductions are conscious and therefore subject to explicit logic (Figure 8.1b).

The important feature of this model is that it recognizes the non-repeatable nature in the movement from structural aspects of experience to the experience of praxis itself. That is, we cannot take a structural account (even if it exists in more narrative terms) and unequivocally relate it to a particular moment in and of praxis. That is, in a strong sense, knowledgeability and the appropriateness of practical action, which only is available from within praxis, is neither captured in nor recoverable from any form of structural account. More so, the further assessment and evaluation move away from the richness of praxis to theoretically driven (numerical) accounts—e.g., scores on a rating sheet—the less likely it is that the account captures the true nature of participative thinking and the appropriateness of the actions that are determined at the same time as the rule (e.g., desired practice) and the singularity of the situation. That is, the impossibility of the reverse trajectory from structured account of praxis reveals the limitations of attempting to capture the practical wisdom in lived experience by means of external observation and structured accounts that result by logical reduction.

Attentive readers might already expect us to suggest that assessment and evaluation in coteaching and cogenerative dialoguing bear a very different relation to lived praxis. Throughout this book we provide descriptions of coteaching that show how one or the other coteacher moves to address a situation recognized—not as a result of reflection but based on participative thinking and a sense of the game, which do not (have to) involve reflective thinking at all—as warranting some action. In a sense, then, participative thinking allows a coteacher—supervising teacher, university supervisor, methods professor—to evaluate the situation without explicitly drawing on (evaluation) theories and theories of teaching and redress it with an appropriate action. More so, the moment constitutes an experiment, in which the supervisor tests his or her practical knowledge with respect to the situation at hand. The success or failure of the action and the situation itself subsequently can become objects of reflection in a conversation involving all stakeholders present. In the following sections we return to several episodes described in other chapters to make them objects of reflection from the perspectives of assessment and evaluation. These sections then become moments for reflecting on the different nature assessment and evaluation practices take in coteaching and cogenerative dialoguing.

DOES VICTORIA'S TEACHING DO JUSTICE TO MIRABELLE?

When I (Ken) first met Victoria she was attracted to Penn's teacher education program because she could earn two master's degrees en route to gaining her certification to teach. She had a strong background in biochemistry and biology and the allure was compelling to gain a master's degree in chemistry education, in which eight of the courses were in chemistry. Victoria valued science subject matter and regarded knowledge of science as a central part of her teaching toolkit. She taught accordingly and regarded her role as a dispenser of accurate facts and procedures as most important. When she taught, her tendency was to create structures that portrayed correct facts and procedures as a priority. Throughout the time in which she cotaught with Alex, Jessica, and me, Victoria enacted practices to interact with students to efficiently represent facts and procedures accurately.

In her articulations of teaching and planning Victoria showed a deep understanding of the value of inquiry, laboratory tasks, and teacher demonstrations. When she was conscious of her teaching she showed she could structure active student participation. However, when she "got into the game," as occurred in the vignette involving Mirabelle, her practices seemed to cohere with an ontology of science consisting of facts and procedures, that is, as truths to be memorized. The patterns of interaction we described in the previous chapter need to be interpreted in terms of Victoria's goals of all students learning how to use the periodic table to find the valence of a given element.

As a coparticipant I sensed trouble as Victoria showed reluctance for Mirabelle to explain how to find valence from the periodic table. Without conscious awareness I moved closer to Mirabelle, allowing me to intervene should that be desirable (i.e., expanding my agency through my positioning with respect to Mirabelle). With the benefit of hindsight, my purpose in moving was to protect Mirabelle from acting out to such an extent that she would be thrown out of the class. However, intervention was not necessary and the class did not spin out of control. Even though there were undoubtedly some students who "knew" the trick from the outset, the time spent and the extent of student interactions pointed to a productive learning environment for most students. Furthermore, Mirabelle was actively involved, presented her model, realized its inadequacies and, in the end, knew what Victoria wanted her to know. In the process all students had a chance to learn the correct procedures while understanding that subtracting two from the atomic number would not work for all elements.

Being part of the game allowed me to experience praxis of the key participants and to use my agency as it changed within the dynamic structures of the classroom. My concern, like Victoria's, was for the learning of the students, including Mirabelle. That I did not take a turn at talk suggests that I felt that what was unfolding was appropriate. If my intervention could have enhanced learning, I would have participated accordingly. The outcomes depicted in the vignette were not produced only by the practices of Mirabelle and Victoria—neither of these protagonists can be held solely responsible for what happened. All participants contributed to producing the outcomes and have collective responsibility for what happened. Thus, by standing back and by refraining from interacting with the two, I also contributed to making the classroom episode what it became.

Any judgment on the quality of the teaching and learning needs to take account of the practices of all participants in the field and collective agency, not only the agency of individuals. *Should-haves* and *could-haves* need to be referenced to collective agency and objective structure and the impossibility of knowing what would have happened in different structural configurations. Cogenerative discussions among the participants can yield insights into the alternative ways in which culturally "othered" participants make sense of a vignette, like the one involving Mirabelle. The field is ideal for identifying examples of inequity, sources of oppression, and affordances to promote science fluency.

In chapter 7 I noted that soon after the lesson I clipped the vignette involving Mirabelle and, in a discussion with a colleague, used it as an example of effective teaching and learning. In so doing I was consciously making trouble. It bothered me that the rationale underlying much of what was done in teacher education at my university was built around reflection in and on action. There was a tendency to regard teacher change in terms of conceptual change—i.e., some form of structural change between someone's ears and underneath her scull—and to set up fields in which new teachers learned from highly expert resident teachers, by observing them teach, writing and speaking about what they experienced, and then trying to emulate their practices in solo episodes of teaching in which they received feedback on their teaching strengths and weaknesses. The feedback was received regularly from the resident teacher, administrators in the school, and university-based mentors—usually former teachers hired to coach new teachers and provide them with the resources needed to become increasingly expert.

Over time the field experiences evolved to incorporate critical analyses in which the new teacher, resident teacher, university mentors and school administrators met to discuss the new teacher's teaching, her reflective and other written products that included a descriptive profile of the school, the students, and relevant contextual analyses. In some senses these discussions might be regarded as precursors for cogenerative dialogues—were it not for the fact that the teaching that was the focus of discussion was that of the novice, the new teacher, who was assumed to have much to learn from the experts who were assembled to share their perspectives, regarded as the kernels from which improved practices would eventually emerge.

The participants in the conversations had experienced what happened as observers, except for the resident teacher, who had taught the same students and usually had been involved in coplanning with the new teacher. Hence, the topics for discussion emerged from discussions about the new teacher's first-person experiences of teaching and others' third-person experiences of the new teacher's teaching, based on observing and reading. Discussions were asymmetrical in that narratives encapsulating nuggets of teaching wisdom and exhortations referenced to theory and empirical research trumped other claims about what is best to do. The goal of the discussions is to afford improved teaching of the new teacher.

I knew that there was a high likelihood that showing the vignette to my colleague would elicit from her a deficit-laden judgment about what was wrong with the teacher and student practices. My goal was to establish a context for a discussion about theories of knowing (epistemology), theories of Being (ontology), and theories of values (axiology) in relation to teaching. Quickly our discussion became an argument in which each of us endeavored to convince the other about the best way to learn to teach in urban schools. On the one hand, my colleague advocated an approach in which new teachers were placed with the best resident teachers in the city. After a period of observation the new teacher began to teach and assignments were closely monitored with more classes being assigned until, eventually the new teacher assumed the resident teacher's full teaching assignment. Success was evident—within this perspective—when the resident teacher could leave the classroom and the noise level would remain the same and work output would not decrease.

Enacting my colleague's model for teacher education had several immediate consequences. First, the quest for excellent urban teachers often resulted in precious few hits, these being dispersed across large urban areas. Second, the excellent teachers often had the "best" (most cooperative, most subjected and self-subjecting) classes and were reluctant to give them up to new teachers, whom they regarded as an inconvenience that would disrupt the learning of their students. Hence, there was a sense of having to make do with less than optimal placements and a preference to place new teachers in suburban schools where the better teachers were assumed to teach. Accordingly, plans were made to allow for a period of teaching in an urban school and a similar period of teaching in a suburban school.

On the other hand and in contrast to my colleagues, the revised model for teacher education was to place new teachers in schools where they could make a positive difference to the learning of their students. My goal was to place them in sufficient numbers where they could learn from one another by being together and teaching together. The idea is that as culture, teaching is produced as it is enacted, in a process of affording the learning of others. What is enacted as teaching—that is, the culture that is produced—depends on the dynamic structures that support the practices of teachers and learners. Hence, I maintained that the best place to learn to teach is in an urban school, where diverse student groups produce forms of culture that new teachers may not have encountered previously. For example, Victoria may not have previously encountered an argument like the one Mirabelle presented during the lesson. The argument and its associated interactions were affordances for all coteachers to reproduce and transform teaching culture as we cotaught in a context that was unique.

What happened can be judged against many benchmarks, each carrying sets of assumptions that may or may not hold. For example, my colleague held Victoria accountable for the events that unfolded. Why not me? Why was I not considered accountable for what unfolded? An assumption made in many programs is that after a certain period of time, say five weeks, a new teacher assumes full control for the classes she teaches. This assumption has no place in our coteaching model, in which all coteachers share responsibility for what happens, including the university supervisors and methods teachers present, not only among themselves, but also among the students. Hence, even if there were only one teacher in the room, we would not regard it as useful to think of the teacher as having responsibility independently of the students. Hence, just as Victoria cannot be held solely responsible for the quality of the teaching, nor can I. The responsibility for the quality of teaching resides in a dialectic relation linking individual and collective. "Good," "bad," and normal, everyday, so-so lessons all are the result of the collective actions of teachers and students. Both teaching and learning are collective processes that presuppose individual actions that realize them; but the individual actions are produced in view of the ongoing collective process.

My thoughts on the vignette and what to discuss in cogenerative dialogues, that is, the topics I would bring to the table would include: deficit perspectives on urban youth and the ways in which they manifest themselves verbally and nonverbally; baton exchanges between coteachers; and the ways in which students cool down overheated interaction chains. Other issues one might want to raise are the value of discussions about alternative ways of solving subject-matter-oriented problems (e.g., figuring out valence), how the discussion between Victoria and Mirabelle mediates (enhances, interferes with) the learning of other students, or the role being open to such discussions plays in building teacher-student rapport. Today, we can only wonder what issues Victoria and Mirabelle might have raised if we had sat down to have a cogenerative dialogue. My sense of things is that my colleague would have commenced with a description of what she liked about the vignette and then would have asked Victoria for a critique, opening doors for others to share their *could-haves* and *should-haves*.

As I am thinking about assessment and evaluation of teaching in the context of the Victoria-Mirabelle exchange, my thoughts take me back to my earliest teaching experiences. In my first years of teaching science in Western Australia, I received a visit from a superintendent of science, who assessed my effectiveness based on a classroom visit, usually lasting one day. Whatever happened during the day ended in an assessment in the form of a grade attributed to the quality of the teacher. That is, although the day consisted of a complexity of interlinked events—observations of classrooms, conversations—the ultimate result was a number. In terms of our model (Figure 8.1), the lived experiences and collective productions of many individuals present in the school on that day were reduced in several steps and by means of multiple processes made to yield a number. Of course before assigning a grade the superintendent spoke to school administrators and took into account what they told him. The system was complex and focused on teachers getting the right grade to support the decisions of administrators, such as the superintendent. To retain a position as a teacher, a certain numerical score was needed, say a 71. This numerical value might be derived from qualitative assessments of general teaching ability, teaching of subject matter, and professionalism. A written report would be provided in each of these categories with a rating, such as "good," "very good," or "excellent." The system seemed to be set up to get the score needed to progress, in turn, to the next level in the institutional hierarchy. For example, if it took an 81 to progress to head-of-department status, the assessment produced an 81 after the teacher had taught for the requisite number of years and those who were more senior had attained their appointments. An 81 might equate to a "very good" in a number of areas evaluated. The system was highly subjective and reflected a highly bureaucratic system of education that persisted in Australia into the 1960s.

The first big high school I taught at was Applecross High in the suburbs of Perth, Australia. The principal would wander through the corridors of the school, stopping from time to time to listen outside of classes. On the basis of his eavesdropping he knew whether or not to enter the classroom as a sign to teacher and students that he was always listening. Except for the day when I intentionally started a fire on the front bench to show students that oil floated on water, he never came into my class. Interestingly though, on that day at least he was outside, eavesdropping and when he sensed I had made an error he was at the doorway as I demonstrated how to use sand to extinguish the blaze. This principal always maintained he could discern a working noise from a "zoo" and could decide which teachers to retain and which to let go based on his daily surveillance of the school. But this does not appear to be a useful method neither for doing valid assessment nor for creating forms of evidence that support an assessment decision. Our coteaching arrangement involving Victoria and her peers provided an alternative even in a situation where the institutional configuration demanded that the university supervisor enact interpretive and logical reductions to produce a grade that "summarized" Victoria's teaching.

As a graduate student in science education Victoria was continuously involved in coteaching for a year. Sonya, her university mentor, was required to give her a grade (an institutional requirement), however, her roles as mentor were enacted through coteaching and participation in cogenerative dialogues. Accordingly, she experienced teaching and learning science as a coteacher with Victoria and developed a sense of what Victoria could and would do as a teacher. Furthermore, as a result of her participation in cogenerative dialogues she experienced the changes that were agreed to and subsequently enacted in the classroom. These experiences allowed Sonya to write narrative accounts about Victoria's teaching, accounts that could be sent to potential employers, attesting to what Victoria had done as a teacher.

As science teacher educators Sonya and I suggested that all new teachers create a digital portfolio to capture many facets of their teaching, including changes, throughout the year. These digital portfolios were part of a summative evaluation, consisting of video vignettes selected to show teaching and learning in many contexts, digital images of student work, and examples of curriculum resources used in the course. On the scale in our model, these videos, although some readers might be tempted to think that they are praxis, actually constitute a first reduction. The camera is pointed somewhere, and its direction therefore chosen; also, the level of zooming selects a particular aspect, and therefore constitutes a reduction of the lived situation. Nevertheless, the video clips provide a richer account of salient moments in the teaching and therefore constitute a re-presentation of events, however limited, which exceeds in richness the limitations of a grade, which has little to no relation with the events that they are said to stand for. More so, in selecting the video clips, the new teachers have a certain level of control over the artifacts that are to stand in for them when they apply for a job, for example. These artifacts even allow, within certain limits, to make the backward trajectory from structure to praxis, whereas from a grade, say a 71 or C, the recovery of the original moment of praxis is hopeless.

Video excerpts selected from cogenerative dialogues also were produced as examples of the ways in which Victoria considered multiple voices in planning and enacting science curricula. A feature of the digital portfolio was a section that highlighted the research undertaken by Victoria in her own classroom. Hence, the uses of technology allowed Victoria to re-present teaching and learning over the different contexts that applied to her teacher education in ways that would provide potential employers with insights into what she knows and can do.

According to institutional requirements, Sonya had to submit a grade each semester to reflect Victoria's participation in the field experience and an associated seminar. The requirements for earning an A were outlined in a course outline and for the most part if all requirements were met the student earned an A for each semester. These requirements specified the necessity to coteach at least one class a day in a block schedule and assume full responsibility for another. Other requirements were the minimum number of cogenerative dialogues a week, the need to undertake research on teaching and learning in at least one of the classes taught, and the necessity to produce a digital portfolio as a summative evaluation of the field experience—providing evidence for student learning and learning to teach.

There is no arguing against the political necessity for assessing teaching performance. The institutional requirement that regards field experience as a graded course has a long history and the practice is pervasive. However, given the individual|collective dialectic it is not possible to separate the practices of any individual from the collective participants of the field in which the teaching was enacted. Hence the agency of a teacher and her enacted practices are interconnected with the structures of the field. Individuals cannot be held solely responsible for what did and did not happen in a classroom. However, over a period of time, through coteaching and cogenerative dialogues, it should be possible for agreed-to forms of teaching and learning to be enacted consistently. Also, by recording the descriptions of what happened and why it happened, accounts from different stakeholders can be included in the re-presentations of enacted curricula in ways that are potentially meaningful to potential employers—more so than a pair of grades on a transcript.

ASSESSMENT RELATING TO THE MONO- AND DIHYBRID LESSON

In this section, we return to the episode featured in chapter 2 where we coteach a biology lesson with Andrea and Chuck. As in chapter 2, this account is provided from Michael's perspective and written in his voice. The account has three elements that take us through the issues of assessment and evaluation. The first element concerns a critical episode that became transformative in our praxis, because it constituted a fall-back to older ways of thinking about assessment; when we became conscious of it in and through dialogue, it radically changed how we were thinking about the relationship between individual and collective responsibility in coteaching and about the role of assessment. In the second element of the account, we return to the moment when Michael took the lead for a moment after having the sense that the lesson was taking students through the monohybrid case in a manner that might not lead to deep understanding. In the third situation, Chuck recognized that he had bungled the teaching of the Punnett square while attempting to show how to figure out the genotypes and phenotypes resulting from a dihybrid cross; this episode led to an extended, eighteen-month conversation involving the four coteachers and Natasia, the target student in this class on that day.

A Transformative Moment for Thinking about Assessment

In this book, we repeatedly point out and describe how coteaching and cogenerative dialoguing evolved as forms of praxis from the contextual particulars in which we found ourselves respectively. That is, the two forms of praxis each began at some critical moment in our careers, responding to some problem we faced. We did not make up and theorize how teachers should teach and then asked schools and teachers to implement what we had theorized (dreamed up) beforehand. The reverse was the case. As coteaching and cogenerative dialoguing unfolded, we began to think about how to understand what we were doing knowing that if we were to interpret and reflect about our actions to seek explanations for why events were unfolding in the way they were, our practical understanding also would unfold. For this reason, it does not come as a surprise when we initially acted in ways that we subsequently abandoned because we recognized that these actions were incompatible with our unfolding understanding of the praxis. One major transformative moment that mediated our concrete praxis of coteaching and cogenerative dialoguing occurred in the lesson of the monohybrid and dihybrid cross.

Initially I had not been aware of an exchange between Andrea and Ken, which occurred while we were waiting for the student whom Andrea had sent to wash the only overhead transparency sheet that existed in this classroom. I do no longer recall how I experienced this period of transition, though I remember quite well that there was a moment in which we just waited. But the wait did not stand out for me sufficiently to have a negative reaction to it so that I could make it an object of my internal monologue in the way other aspects and actions in the lesson had become an object.

209

The issue, however, came up during our cogenerative dialogue session. At one moment during the session the videotape shows Ken saying to Andrea, "You said that you overheard what I said when you were walking to the door today?" She simply laughs, and Ken pursues, "What did I say?" This time Andrea responds.
– "I am falling asleep, keep going."
– That's right, I said, "Come on, come on, come on, you are driving me nuts. If I was a student in this class, I would be falling asleep." How can you work your way through periods like that? I know you had plan A, which was to do whatever. And you didn't have time left to do plan A, whatever-
– Right.
– and so you had to switch to plan B, but the transition was-
– was long.
– was really long. And I was next door to someone who was battling. Maybe she is one of those who go to sleep in every period. Who knows? But she was battling to show any interest at all. So what she needed, I would say, is a fire lit under her. How could we have? I mean, I don't have any answer. But we didn't need a long transition there. Because the kids had done the jelly, they were moving into something else, you had to wash the transparencies.

In response to Ken's evaluative assessment, Andrea then accepts responsibility for the classroom event, denotes the long transition as a problem. She responds to Ken by saying, "Well that was the problem. I mean the problem was, I had to decide. Like I had planned that we make mobiles and stuff, with the scientific method. And I realized that there would not be enough time. And I had all that stuff laid out. So I thought we get into genetics and do dihybrid cross. And a student had written all over, as they were supposed to, and we had to wash them all off. Ken allays her concerns by accepting the explanation, "That's good, but . . . so?" and then follows with another descriptor, "It was downtime."

As Andrea's response shows, she hears the descriptor as a negative evaluation and responds by providing an alternative, something she *could have* done instead, "Maybe get discussion going, like have a question or something like that." Natasia chimes in with a comment that both allays and critiques moments of downtime, which can become too long: "Sometimes she lets us, well just to sit and relax for a few minutes. But you can't- like sometimes it is too long, and like." She stops, and a visitor from the university, who had joined the session, offered yet another *could-have* type of advice, "During that time period, you could have put on, like teaching. Like you could have used to say, do you like what I am doing today? You could have time to start, more like relationship between . . . like it doesn't have to be waste time, but it can be part of the learning time."

During this entire episode, I listen. I have not overheard Ken's comment. But I am talking to myself, "Why has Ken not done anything if he has felt that there was a pause?" At this moment, we have not had a lot of experience in cogenerative dialoguing, which is perhaps why I do not feel comfortable in making a critical comment about where this is taking us. I have a strong sense that we need to transform what we are doing in the classroom so that everyone is responsible for everything that is happening. I know I have to talk this through with Ken, but I have met Andrea and Chuck for the first time on this day. I do not want to sound as if I am making snide remarks, and do not know how addressing the issue would mediate the relationship between Ken, who is the university supervisor, and Andrea, who is the intern under Ken's supervision. I let the moment pass, but do address it with Ken when we have a private moment.

During that moment, knowing that he will not be upset when I address the issue I say, "Why have you not done something if you felt the transition was too long? Do you not think that all of us need to contribute to make the lesson the best we can and then address any issue in our cogenerative dialogues?" My intent is not to complain or to blame Ken, but to lead us to the next stage in our coteaching praxis and in our understanding of what we are doing. I do not recall how our conversation unfolds from there, but I know today that it was a critical moment in the development of my own understanding and praxis of collective responsibility in coteaching.

At this early stage in our coteaching praxis, Ken has acted in the old ways, which we were in the process of abandoning. Although already coteaching, in this moment he observed, then in an interpretive reduction (see Figure 8.1) assessed the moment as a shortcoming in Andrea's teaching, and then articulates the issue in evaluative terms after the lesson is completed. Now there is nothing wrong in talking about a critical incident after the fact, when the circumstances provide time for reflecting, but as Ken recognizes during our private conversation, at the moment he evaluates a moment in coteaching as a shortcoming, *he* has to address it, because those who do not recognize the shortcoming *cannot* address it.

The moment during the cogenerative dialogue session shows that Andrea accepts this traditional format of evaluation by taking responsibility for what has happened. But of course, all the *should-haves* and *could-haves* articulated in the session do not take us back to the lesson: the movement from objectified experience to praxis has the tendency to be non-repeatable (Figure 8.1). At the critical moment, Ken appears to be the only one making a negative evaluation; and he does not act to see whether what he does in fact bridges between the two lesson segments, the laboratory investigation and the review session that has become the solution to the time problem that emerges because the first task has taken longer than planned—for good reasons, as it has allowed students to build better understanding.

This moment during the cogenerative dialogue session shows us precisely the repeatable tendency of evaluative assessment, during which a moment of lived praxis is reduced to an objectified experience. Andrea, the subject, has been confronted with the other and, without being able to respond in the classroom situation, has become subject to an irreversible assessment measurement process, which in fact objectified what she has done. It projected on to Andrea what we—students and coteachers—have experienced and we held Andrea accountable for it. In fact, by not speaking up during the coteaching episode, I allowed Andrea to become stuck with the responsibility for the long transition although I had a different view and understanding of it. For her getting stuck with blame, I am responsible.

In this form of assessment, experiences are subject to a different temporal mode—the nature of lessons to unfold without time-out has been replaced by re-presentations that can be played through over and over again. The situation is articulated, that is, re-presented and then, alternatives are proposed for what *should have* or *could have* been done. However, we do not know whether the suggested solutions *actually* could have been done—we cannot know whether hypothetical solutions actually have any relevance to the moment that has irretrievably passed, that has occurred only once, and the actions (including doing nothing) have left their historical (because once-occurrent) mark. All actions in this transitional moment in the classroom have been enacted—waiting, watching, or evaluating—and we are ethico-morally (and should be from an institutional perspective) accountable for what we have done. Different actions develop the situation differently, but again, we all are not just neutral, indifferent elements in the situation and are in fact constitutive participants. As human beings, we always have the *choice* to act differently and therefore are responsible for the situation. In the next subsection, I return to the moment when I ask to contribute actively by asking students to answer my riddles.

Evaluation is Testing Alternatives

In the traditional approach to evaluative assessment, praxis is taken through a series of interpretive and logical reductions (Figure 8.1). In the previous episode, Ken has made an interpretive reduction that leads us to a description, followed by a first logical reduction in which the observation comes to be evaluated against an unstated referent, and then is categorized and accepted as a weakness in Andrea's teaching. In the introductory episode to this chapter, Ken is hired as a graduate research assistant to take the assessment even further to express teaching in terms of categories and scores that subsequently are subjected to statistical analysis to find patterns in the numbers. But how do these narrative assessments or the statistical patterns relate to moments of praxis? We see in the cogenerative dialogue session that various participants offer a series of *should-haves* and *could-haves*. But would these *should-haves* and *could-haves* emerging with the negative evaluation really be suitable alternatives? What evidence is there to support that *in this situation*, exactly when the long transition occurred, *any* of the *should-haves* and *could-haves* would have led to something better, whatever the something might have been? Perhaps waiting was the best option, at least from the perspective of three coteachers who simply waited; similarly, the students appeared to be content with the situation of having a break after a long investigation in which they conducted several experiments? Only when we enact a solution to a problem we identify can we know whether our "solution" really is a solution. Coteaching offers such a possibility of addressing something that a participant evaluates to be an issue. In terms of our model (Figure 8.1), rather than making an evaluative assessment and waiting to scold someone for it later, the person immediately acts upon the assessment. Rather than generating *could-haves* and *should-haves*, the person enacts a possibility he or she actually does-have in the *here and now*. This keeps the communication between different participating subjects open, in the spirit of the being-*with*-others, the common life, and being emotionally moved by the need of the collective situation (Figure 8.1a, top-left cell). I draw on my experience of acting in situation described in chapter 2 for articulating a different way of thinking about evaluative assessment.

In chapter 2, I describe the beginning of the monohybrid episode as one in which I am attuned to the lesson as it unfolds. When Chuck articulates for students a device for remembering the words phenotype and genotype and the sense of these two words, I make an evaluative comment in the privacy of my inner monologue. I do not have a possibility to enter the unfolding lesson until after Ken points to me, alerting Andrea and Chuck to the fact that I have signaled wanting to speak by raising my hand. Because I have attempted to remain in tune with the lesson, I have not pre-formulated what I want to say or the puzzle I want to pose. It is but a sense of the game that a puzzle allowing students to think through a situation as if they were solving a genetics puzzle relating to students' experiences—I am flooded by momentary flashes from the TV show CSI, the O. J. Simpson trial, and many other actual or literary criminal cases involve genetic testing. Invited by Andrea, I get to ask my question, "So I have blue eyes, and my wife has blue eyes. I wonder if anyone can figure out what my son Niels' eyes are?" There is a pause—the students did not seem to have understood. "Why would they be . . .?" From there, the lesson takes a new trajectory, because I, heretofore not having talked, now take the lead in interacting with the students. After my intervention, I step back and Andrea takes over using what I have said and done as a resource in her own actions. She now is in charge—developing the lesson further, on a trajectory that my action has set up.

In this episode, evaluative assessment and lesson are one. In the course of the events, fleeting thoughts of memorization and a pons asinorum emerge into my consciousness; and these framings are implicitly value-laden evaluative assessments. My professional sense leads me to want to teach differently, through puzzles and problems that students recognize as relevant. But rather than waiting until after the lesson, making an evaluative assessment and telling Andrea and Chuck about the *could-have-dones* and *should-have-dones* that I have in mind, I enact a possibility then and there: a puzzle requiring a solution in which the genotype of the protagonists in my story are derived on the basis of their phenotypes. At the same time, my solution to the situation is being tested, thereby becoming available to be experienced and subject to evaluative assessment. The puzzle does not have a *could-have* or *should-have* nature but is becoming an event. In this situation, what I do appears to be successful. The students actively engage, and Andrea picks up from my question and integrates her own approach with it. It is a demonstration about how one can teach differently that no longer distinguishes itself from the lesson. We continue to be confronted as subjects, in a situation of testimony in the spirit of being-*with*, our common life and purpose, and we are affectively moved by our commitment to a common cause, student learning.

In this situation, evaluative assessment and lesson are no longer distinct. The others in the classroom do not have access to my private thoughts. The lesson may unfold on a similar trajectory even if I do not have an explicit private thought about the shortcoming of rote learning versus true understanding and competent participation. In the subsequent cogenerative dialogue session, we do not come back to this issue at all; other aspects of this lesson specifically and of the biology course generally are more salient and pressing issues. We have taken the different trajectory that the lesson has taken in and with my intervention as a matter of course, which, as all matters of course, goes without saying. Nevertheless, everyone has participated in it and has experienced the use of puzzles in the teaching of genetics; but we no longer need to make it a point of discussion unless someone really were to have felt the need of bringing it up.

Here, evaluation is an integral part of praxis, the encounter of subject with subject. My intervention that emerges with the evaluation immediately is tested, and we all experience it as a success in the sense that the new trajectory does not come to be an addressable issue. My intervention does not involve the *could-have* or *should-have* structure, the relationship of which to praxis we do not know. However, we do know that even when teachers intend to change their praxis, frame *could-haves* and *should-haves* following explicit reflection and planning, they may do not enact them the next time they are in a similar situation; they continue enacting the same practices that they themselves intend to abandon. And this may be the case even in coteaching, where both teachers are committed to change.

In this example, evaluation and acting upon it have become one, even indistinguishable; this new form of evaluation has become possible in coteaching where the evaluator (researcher, supervisor) is part of the setting such that he contributes to the trajectory. The traditional move from praxis to objectified praxis followed by recommendations for change in practice has been replaced. Because the evaluating researcher contributes to making this a better classroom learning environment, none of the other participants feels to be confronted by the *other*, accompanied by a loss of open communication in an irreversible measurement process (Figure 8.1a). They do not feel that their once-occurrent actions are reduced to the same plane as the untested *could-haves* and *should-haves*, which do not know past, present, or future because they can be run and re-run ad lib and ad infinitum. They no longer experience themselves to be subjected, as an objectified other, to the experimental control of the researcher (also a subject) for the purpose of information production (Figure 8.1a, structure matrix, top right cell). With this change in the approach to evaluative assessment comes a change in the way the differently positioned subjects—new teacher, teacher, researcher, supervisor, methods teacher, student—relate to one another. There is room for a sense of solidarity to emerge.

A "Bungle" becomes a Learning Experience for Evaluators

Evaluators of teaching are human. As humans, they are subject to making decisions that they cannot fully account for. It lies in the nature of actions and language that they are grounded in a fundamentally inarticulate and unexplainable experience and understanding of how the world works. But this aspect of human nature leads us to the fact that evaluative assessment *cannot* be objective in the sense that the term has been used historically. Evaluators, too, are neither perfect nor know everything. In fact, it is generally unacknowledged that evaluation, too, is a form of praxis; inherently, therefore, doing evaluations allows evaluators to learn to evaluate. In the process, they come to better understand the content of their evaluations as well. In this final episode, I exemplify this aspect of learning on the part of a university supervisor (Ken) and a researcher (I) interested in evaluating coteaching.

The episode for my reflections about evaluative assessment of teaching (and learning) comes from the second part of the lesson on genetics, when Chuck has taken over the lead from Andrea. There is some more time before we reach the end of the lesson, and as the most expert on the dihybrid cross, it makes sense for him to take the lead. It turns out, as I describe in chapter 2, that he "bungles;" but we are all overtaken by the unfolding event, as we do not have a sufficient understanding of the different ways of approaching the task and the bell forces an end to the lesson. (In terms of Figure 8.1a, this is an encounter of the other [bell] with the subject [coteachers, students] represented in the lower left cell in the encounter matrix. We are constrained by outside forces to end the lesson even if all of us had preferred it to continue.) However, we begin by dealing with the problematic issue at the end of the lesson in a conversation Ken and I start, and then take it up again in the cogenerative dialogue session.

Initially, Ken and I talk, as we walk to the room designated for our session. I explain to Ken how his solution exchanges rows and columns. Andrea and Chuck disagree and I explain to Ken that his method makes little sense from a biologist's viewpoint, although it works out mathematically. I say, "Ken's right. It works because you put in all the genes. It just mirrors the genes rather than . . ." Andrea makes use of the pause my unfinished sentence leaves, "You get the combinations but not the cross. You get the two effective combinations, but not the cross." Chuck chimes in, which begins a brief exchange between him and me.

– You know you're right on this when it comes down here that you get the two . . . You can't do it . . .

– You're right. Mathematically it will come out the same . . .

– Oh, will it?

– You know why? Because what he does he just transposes the two genes.

At this point, Ken comments, "I told you it is mathematically correct. I didn't know if it made any sense scientifically . . ." The session then takes on a different trajectory as a participant raises an issue not concerning the dihybrid cross, but returns to it when Chuck engages Natasia in an interaction over the same issue. He wants to know from Natasia and Shawan how to better teach the topic. He is genuinely concerned about understanding what he could have done in the situation that both students identify as having involved "mistakes."

– Basically when I did that dihybrid cross, what would you have done? How would you have changed that?

– The way you made the dihybrid, with the mistakes?

– Yeah, with mistakes.

– Well that's good. I been . . . the easiest way is to make four boxes of four . . . One big Punnett square and make four individual Punnett squares in it. Simple!

– Oh, then you would have recombined all the blocks from the four different Punnett squares? Yes. Okay. That's one way.

The dihybrid episode is sufficiently problematic and raises many questions so that we continue to talk about it over the next eighteen months involving different combinations of the original participants in face-to-face conversations and email exchanges. Some of our exchanges focus on the content, some on the form of representations, some on other ways of presenting the lesson. As a result, it turns out that we all end up with a better understanding of the dihybrid cross and with different ways of teaching it—including the involvement of students such as Natasia in assisting her peers to learn.

In this situation, none of us has a solution to the problem in the cotaught lesson. There have been some initial exchanges about how to do the dihybrid cross, but as pointed out, the events are overtaking us. The situation, which all of us in fact coproduce, has taken on a life of its own; but we come to grapple with its implications for a long period of time. Although we do not provide a solution in the way I describe in the previous subsection, it turns out that we do not objectify one or the other person, though we objectify the lesson and its content. In the course of our discussion about the dihybrid cross, sustained by Ken and my sense that we can continue to learn from the episode, we engage the others to come to grips at a deep level with the content—in part deriving mathematical representations that allow us to understand why apparently different approaches yield the same result—and with alternative ways of how to teach the dihybrid cross, including the opportunities for students such as Natasia to support other students in their learning of doing the cross.

We cannot go back to test our understanding in the original lesson. We therefore do not make suggestions for what we *should-have* or *could-have* done. We do know that we have learned a lot as a result of this extended eighteen-month cogenerative dialogue—which we also captured in an article that all of us (Ken, Chuck, Andrea, Natasia, and I) coauthored. We know that our new understanding provides us with a greater range of action possibilities, a greater room to maneuver, which will be available to us in future lessons. Whether we do act upon or deploy these resources is an empirical matter and depends on whether the contextual particulars in fact allow these resources to be salient and deployed.

As an outcome of this extended inquiry, and especially in the comparison between the second and third elements in my reflection, I come to the conclusion that the two arcs in the evaluation model (Figure 8.1a), the repeatable and nonrepeatable tendencies, are related in a dialectical way when they are enacted as we have done in joining coteaching and cogenerative dialoguing. We do need the experience of encountering one another, teachers with other teachers and students, which provides us with a common referent or object, the lesson, which we, because of our biographical and institutional differences, experience in different ways. Together we can articulate and objectify these different experiences for one another. From these attempts at explaining the events and the contents, we enhance our understanding of both. But without our initial understandings, which arise from having encountered one another in a common life situation, we would not have been in the position to seek participant-based explanations. Our evaluative assessments all refer to the same moments of praxis that we experienced subject to the same temporal mode to which no outside observer has access. Although the results of our collective investigations are non-repeatable—we do not know where our a-posteriori solutions and teaching strategies would have taken the lesson. But we do have an expanded set of action possibilities (i.e., agency) by understanding not only ourselves but also the way other individuals understand.

In the process of objectifying our mutual experiences, we come to better understand; but our practical understanding of the events is the condition for the explanation-seeking interpretive reduction. The practical understanding—arising from the biographical experience of encountering another person in the lesson—therefore precedes, accompanies, and concludes the explanation-seeking interpretive reduction, but by returning with this explanation to the practical situation, we have been able to expand our understanding. The evaluative assessment of the events, rather than attributing success and failure to individuals, leads us to an increased understanding and an expansion of our professional competencies. It is in this sense and form that I believe evaluative assessment to be a true contribution to teacher development.

Conducting the evaluation in an open face-to-face meeting actually puts us into a new situation where we meet as subjects, a situation of testimony in the spirit of *being-with* an other, related through a one-for-the-other structure. The "evaluator" no longer is external to the life of the evaluated, but implicated with her in a common life. For development and growth, they do need to objectify their experiences, but they do so in the spirit of the one-for-the-other, in which evaluator and evaluated take symmetrical roles—my own action of presenting the genetics puzzle are as much subject to collective scrutiny and evaluative assessment as those of any other individual, including Ken, Andrea's university supervisor in the situation, or Chuck, who served as the supervising mentor teacher.

METALOGUES ON ASSESSMENT AND EVALUATION

In the two previous sections, we return to previously described classroom episodes with the express purpose of raising issues concerning assessment and evaluation. In particular, the episodes exemplify to us why coteaching and cogenerative dialoguing offer many advantages over other approaches to assessing and evaluating teaching. In this section, we use the metalogue genre to work through three main issues that have emerged from us considering coteaching and cogenerative dialoguing as forms of assessment and evaluation praxis.

In Coteaching, Recommendations are Tested Prior to Collective Evaluation

Ken: With three or four coteachers teaching together the teaching that unfolds consists of a collective "what is best for the class." Hence the mentors will do what they consider is best in the unfolding circumstances, sometimes consciously and usually without conscious awareness. Of course experience of a master teacher in action may be conscious even if the "master in action" is enacting most of what she does without being aware of the salient particulars.

Michael: Because a mentor teacher or university supervisor may step in and contribute, his or her action *is* immediately tested. This is where coteaching as praxis of evaluation offers advantages over other methods, as the teaching intern can see an alternative in situ rather than being confronted with a *you-should-have* or a number of *you-could-haves*. Just now I am remembering one of your first teaching interns at Penn, who was livid in his personal reflections about you telling him what he ought to have done—Cam was his name.

Ken: Exactly. Cam took exception to being told to do this and to do that. He wanted me to show him not to tell him. He had a solid point—but coteaching with me would have been a better solution than me showing him as he sat on the side. If something is tried and produces unexpected or undesirable consequences, the repairs can be enacted immediately and in a coteaching set up it might be other coteachers who repair a bungle. Hence, the testing of teaching practices is experienced as unfolding structure, expanding the agency for all teachers and students in a field.

Michael: This means that teaching, evaluation, and recommendation become inextricably linked in the moment of praxis, and interpretive reduction occurs only after the lesson has been completed. Because the evaluator and the evaluated both have participated in the lesson, they have a shared object, a lesson that they have experienced under the same auspices, that is, driven by the same motive, learning of students, and under the same temporal constraints that come from a non-indifferent participation in the teaching of students. The lesson is not set apart, often explained beforehand to students by one or the other participant as a special moment in the life of the person evaluated, and therefore a special show rather than normal, everyday teaching. And then, in and by cogenerative dialoguing, salient issues can be brought to light all the while knowing that the different institutional positions and biographies lead us to experience this shared moment in different ways yet without privileging any one of those experiences.

Ken: Cogenerative dialogues are an important part of looking again at what happened in a cotaught lesson to pick up on what actually happened—to objectify the teaching that seemed particularly useful. In instances where this happens consciously a brief huddle can bring other coteachers' attention to what happened so that it becomes noteworthy and an object for later study. Alternatively, much can be gleaned from analyses of videotape, clipping vignettes for discussion during cogenerative dialogues held after the class.

Michael: Yes. We could ask the students to select salient clips from time to time. We do involve students in cogenerative dialoguing, but we have not yet discussed in an explicit way the role or roles that they could play in and for evaluative assessment. At the university level, the students are contributing to the evaluation of teaching performance. I doubt, however, that the use of anonymous questionnaires and ratings allows us to come anywhere near a *just* evaluation, especially because the evaluators are not accountable for their actions. In cogenerative dialoguing, however, especially if recorded, everyone is accountable and there is a record that subsequently can be used should there ever be a question about the results of the evaluation process. In fact, in my teaching portfolio constructed during the earlier parts of my university career, I did involve students in discussions of my teaching—using clips that I had selected. Subsequently, I watched clips of my teaching and clips from the session with the student/s together with a colleague, whom I invited to evaluate my teaching and efforts at learning to teach.

Ken: The teaching portfolio is a good idea and usually is thought of as a re-presentation put together by an individual—usually a teacher. This dialogue raises the possibilities of expanding the roles of students (and all other stakeholders) to include their participation in creating a digital portfolio to represent the enacted curriculum.

A Digital Portfolio Provides Useful Information for Potential Employers

Michael: The digital portfolio rather than a university transcript may be a much better and richer form of evidence that employers may want to use prior to selecting potential candidates for teaching jobs in their district. When I go through the records submitted with an application for a position, I am always struck by the "flatness" of what I come to know about the person. I often think about the "patience of paper" with respect to what is written on it, and with the gap between what is on paper and what I experience once I meet those that have been invited for an interview.

Ken: A chief concern with radical ideas like these is to have any meaningful uptake. Discontinuing grades, politically, may be regarded by conservatives as another example of there being no rigor in teacher education. Even though we can argue intellectually that a grade for teaching is meaningless, powerful others will insist it must be done.

Michael: *My* concern would be different. As a superintendent or principal I would want to have a better way for preselecting candidates for teaching positions. A grade represents so little. If I had a few clips of the teaching of the person, and perhaps a narrative account about what the person wants to achieve, I would be happier. The numbers on paper, especially if different people at different universities produced them, tell us virtually nothing about the teacher.

Ken: Of course it is not a case of either this argument or that argument. Teacher educators will experience pressure to do both. I expect almost everybody to endorse the use of a digital portfolio that, as we describe it here, contains re-presentations that reflect many aspects of teaching and learning and also can embody the perspectives of different stakeholders. I also expect a consensus on it being more useful to potential employers than grades for what is usually referred to as student teaching. However, I do not see grades vanishing or being rejected as worthless.

Michael: I think that those who insist on the numbers do so for administrative ease—you can make a quick decision without really getting to know the person—rather than because you know something about him or her.

Ken: I am afraid it is probably deeper than this. My fear is that quantification is attached to rigor and high standards—especially if the candidates are ranked. If everyone gets an "A" then it is just another sign of educators having low standards.

Michael: This association between rigor and high standards, on the one hand, and quantification, on the other hand, is unfortunate and misrepresents the real issues at hand, as Kadriye Ercikan, a statistician colleague at the University of British Columbia, and I substantiate in an upcoming article of the *Educational Researcher*. Some qualitative research and evaluation is much more rigorous and more apt to generalization than a lot of so-called quantitative research and evaluation. To use another example, some of my colleagues on tenure and promotion committees count papers and page numbers, whereas I tend to read articles to establish the quality; they look at summary ratings, which conflate student judgments of professor knowledge, preparedness, responsiveness and the likes, rather than at observing the professor teach. Thus I believe in the greater value of allowing others to access the video clips in my teaching portfolios than the numerical scores—which I can proudly say are among the highest in my faculty. Thus, when I recently sent an application to another university, I put a digital clip online so that anyone interested in my teaching could watch; my teaching portfolio included a link so that my statement of philosophy and my statements about how I work with graduate students had a video clip as a parallel representation so that those interested in doing more than looking at my teaching scores could do so. If the clips were restricted to a certain length, going through the portfolio submitted would not take more than a few minutes of additional time.

Ken: The digital portfolio could also have other components, such as personal research. Teachers being researchers of their own teaching and the extent of the learning in their classroom, including their own learning as teachers is a central part of effective teaching, and hence a digital re-presentation of teaching and learning in a particular time interval.

Michael: This is *precisely* what I have done for supporting my requests for tenure and promotion and then for my promotion to full professor. It was perhaps this richness of my portfolio that allowed the unanimous decisions at various institutional levels despite the warning that my department head at the time had uttered with respect to there being insufficient evidence with respect to the quality of my teaching.

Cogenerative Dialogues are Fields for Producing New Culture to be Enacted in the Classroom

Ken: Conventionally cogenerative dialogues are fields in which coteachers and other adult stakeholders participate in critical dialogue for the purposes of improving the quality of classroom learning environments. That is, cogenerative dialogues are seedbeds for producing culture that has the potential to improve the quality of learning. I suggest that a key part of coalescing curriculum enactment and assessment/evaluation is to have cogenerative dialogues in which coteachers interact with students who are culturally other, with the goal of learning how to interact effectively—producing new culture that allows teachers and students to interact successfully. Hence, it is not necessary to analyze a lesson, identify all of the unsuccessful interactions, and figure out how to do a better job of aligning cultures (of students and teachers) in the next lesson. An alternative is to bring together participants representing the cultural diversity and allow them to interact in small cogenerative dialogues. In so doing all participants learn to adapt and align culture and can then enact the new culture in the classroom as structures unfold to permit them to do so.

Michael: Here, evaluative assessment involves students who, in the interest of making the next lesson better, contribute in ways that must be experienced as productive. So really, evaluation becomes a form of professional development rather than an endpoint. It integrates evaluation and professional development rather than serializing them: an evaluation is produced and a principal or superintendent recommends professional development—if in fact such is necessary. This is precisely what I was thinking as a department head nearly twenty years ago—make evaluation a central aspect of professional development. There is potential in the four-pronged approach mentioned in chapter 1—reflection on teaching, observing teaching, coteaching, and department head observation. I thought at the time that all of these together have a much greater potential as an evaluation method than the department head's observations alone; *precisely* because reflecting on one's teaching, having a colleague observe one's teaching, observing someone else's teaching, and coteaching *in addition to* my department head evaluation would already constitute a form of professional development. This is what I was after, assessment as development rather than assessment for its own sake.

Ken: Coteaching and cogenerative dialogues as methods afford forms of improvement that serve the goals of individuals and the collective. Based on our ongoing research this is accomplished to a greater extent than is possible with traditional forms of assessment where experts produce lists of strengths (which ring as insincere) along with longer lists of *could-haves* and *should-haves* (which are received with overt enthusiasm as a mask to smoldering resentment).

Michael: And the evaluators, too, would be developing not only as evaluators but also as teachers. For university professors, this would be an especially interesting way of staying in touch with the classroom, and mediating any claims by teacher education students about the degree to which the professor is out of touch with the real world of teaching.

Ken: These are good reasons for using coteaching and cogenerative dialogues as an evaluation method. The schemas produced in cogenerative dialogue extend beyond the objects that participants agree to change. For example, suppose there is agreement that in the next lesson small groups will be used to produce collective group solutions to problems, to be written on a small chalkboard for peer review of the whole class. What might not be so apparent is that in the process of producing an agreed-to outcome, there also may be a greater sense of solidarity and of the emotions associated with being with the others in the group and doing what this group does. The emotional aspects of participating in cogenerative dialogues and the possibilities for individual and group identity changes may be as important as the agreed-to changes to be enacted.

Michael: More so, solidarity is fostered not only among peers, for example, those who are enrolled to receive a degree and certification as teachers, but also among all participants and stakeholders. Ultimately, for me, education is something that we, society, are responsible for collectively. Evaluation as a form of praxis that allows teachers to develop appears to me as having greater potential than producing scores that someone else in the institutional hierarchy uses to make decisions that are harmful to the persons involved. Our lives and work sustain society; our real contribution lies in the fact that we sustain society into the future through our work that allows others, students and new teachers, to participate in sustaining and developing our collective forms of life. But here we also have to be cautious, because I do not want to see inequities reproduced but want us to work towards overcoming existing forms of oppression and hegemony.

Ken: Cogenerative dialogues allow for the possibility of identifying sources of hegemony, addressing them in the classroom, and producing new roles that lead to more equitable learning environments. In this way, the evaluation that occurs can produce tangible forms of social justice.

ON ASSESSMENT AND EVALUATION: PERSONAL JOURNEYS

Ken: I feel that after writing this chapter we have progressed a long way from where we were prior to the writing. In fact there are some issues swirling in my head, which I want to present so as to highlight some points that are salient to me in regards to the issues of this chapter. I invite you to join me in my musings over these issues and then perhaps we can take a similar approach to the issues you find salient.

Michael: I too sense that we have come a long way from where we have been when we wrote *At the Elbow of Another*, the first book on coteaching. My thinking with respect to and praxis of assessment and evaluation, however, has become both more radical and better grounded philosophically.

Ken: On the Nature of Good Teaching

After I returned the suburbs of Perth after two years of teaching in a rural community I had a great deal to learn about science teaching and the subject matter I was to teach. It did not take me long to demonstrate success. In many respects the students from Applecross were just like the kids I grew up and went to school with. But after two years there, when I was teaching about as well as I have taught anywhere, at the top of my game so to speak, there was a perturbation created by an influx of youth from a housing development project that opened up a few miles from the high school. This was low-income housing and the youth from this development were working-class. For the most part these youth were streamed into the lower tracks, coming to populate the bulk of the lower two tracks in what was then a ten-track system (i.e., 8-9 and 8-10 in eighth-grade). By that time I was acknowledged as a pretty good teacher and had mainly upper level students; but I believed in having continuing involvement with lower track students and requested to teach 8-10, the lowest track in the eighth grade. Phew. What a nightmare. These students were simply vulgar in comparison to the others I taught. From my middle-class perspective they lacked manners and knew little of how to "be a student" either at school or at home. My point in raising this is to note that my teaching, which was so fluent and easy in most of my classes, lacked fluency—teaching was hard work in 8-10. If any of the administrators were to assess the quality of my teaching please let it be with any of my classes, but surely not 8-10.

Of course not all of the working-class youth ended up in the lowest track and some of those in the highest track commanded attention because of their irrepressive expressive individualism. As with 8-10, it took a while for my teaching to adapt to unfolding circumstances that I did not anticipate—due to the presence of working-class youth and their different ways of getting involved. They had to learn to successfully interact with me and other students; and we (the middle-class teacher and students) had to learn to successfully interact with them. Anyone watching from the side would have been presented with a ready list of *should-haves* and *could-haves*. Imagine if I had been transferred to teach in a school in which all students were from working-class homes?

I use the term "vulgar" despite its deficit ridden connotations because this was the language my colleagues and I used to discuss the infusion of working-class youth into our school—we did regard the school as ours and in some ways the students were regarded through deficit lenses. For some time my teaching was not adaptable to the learning needs of all of my students and until I learned how to provide forms of teaching to support their agency the teaching and learning roles in some of my classes were less fluent than in others. Hence, the patterns of teaching in one class in particular (i.e., 8-10) differed dramatically from the others. Outside evaluation and assessment therefore would have been quite different had it been done across a range of classes.

Even though school administrators and policy makers like to consider teaching as generalizable over time of day, school, and class within school, there are tales comparable to the one above to illustrate that claims to generalizability are simply ill-founded. In Georgia the team responsible for developing an assessment system for assessing the performance had to use all of the data for the indicators and competencies to support a "Yes" or a "No" decision. A "Yes" decision implied that the teaching candidate could teach effectively in ways that generalized across teaching competencies, time of day, class, and school. Despite the statistical claims about the validity and reliability of the performance data the basic assumptions that teachers are independently responsible for the quality of the teaching and that contextual matters are irrelevant are simply not supported theoretically and especially by the narratives of any teacher who has taught in different sorts of schools.

***

Why would a dean ignore the evidence in this book as research? The analyses provided in this chapter are compelling to me. Having been a science teacher educator for several decades, I am convinced that coteaching and cogenerative dialogues provide pathways around many of the problems that policy makers have complained about for years. For example, a person gets an "A" for her field internship, a good reference from the teachers and administrators where she taught, and a strong letter of support from her college professors. Then, she struggles mightily after having been employed on the basis of her grades and recommendations. What does the grade represent? Not much it seems. Some people who get an "A" teach well and others with an "A" teach less well. Essentially a grade offers a sign that is suspect at best. Yet, as Michael points out in the previous section, an electronic portfolio can provide evidence from coteaching and cogenerative dialogues as well as insights into myriad forms of professional practice and the perspectives of many stakeholders, over a period of time. I regard this an acceptable form of reductionism that provides insights into whether or not what this teacher can do fits with the needs of the employer. Hence, what we have advocated in this chapter should have broad appeal to school and school district people and also to accrediting agencies who would see that what we propose addresses the performative aspects of teaching and learning, while avoiding over-reduction and over-generalization.

Two of my international colleagues, with a long history of using coteaching, were highly skeptical about their chances of convincing colleagues that coteaching and cogenerative dialogues could serve as viable forms of assessment. I believe their concern is that if assessment coalesced into enactment it would be invisible and policy makers would simply insist on a system in which there were more visible signs of its occurrence. Based on what we have presented here, a question for our colleagues to put to other stakeholders is what more is needed? If others' perspectives are needed then let them coteach and participate in cogenerative dialogues. If they do not have the time for such forms of involvement then their perspectives may not be worth having in the first place. Perhaps what I am most conscious of at the moment of writing is that *could-haves, would-haves,* and *should-haves* have little relevance if they take the form of third-person judgments about an objectified other who is assumed to have individual control over teaching. On the other hand, if the *could-haves, would-haves,* and *should-haves* are first-person accounts focused on we, all participants in a field, they may well be the seeds for curricular improvement, including enhanced roles for teachers and learners.

Michael: Evaluative Assessment—The Possibility of Impossibility

Niemand / zeugt für den / Zeugen
(No one / bears witness for the / witness)
–Paul Celan, Aschenglorie

Over the years, my thinking about the role of assessment and evaluation has become increasingly radical, associated with an increasingly radical praxis of undermining the very intention and power of assessment to create difference where democratic values suggest we maintain an open dialogue. As a high school teacher, where assessment in the form of giving grades is a prerequisite for being in the particular institutional position, my approach was for 65 percent of a student's term mark to be derived from self- and peer evaluation—using criteria the students set for themselves. As a department head of science at the same school, I moved teacher assessment from the traditional observation, scoring, and report-writing model to one that involved the teachers themselves such that evaluative assessment became, as described, conflated with professional development. As a university professor, working with graduate students, I commence my courses by announcing that all students will receive an A grade, allowing us to focus on learning and getting all participants beyond the goals that they had set for themselves before and in joining the course.

Central to my rationale is the generally unacknowledged history of grades and grading, which emerged at nearly the same time as institutions such as the prisons, schools, and hospitals (Foucault, 1979). The intention was clear: grades, associated with an entire economy of exchanging, losing, and gaining points, allowed for differentiation and ranking within a group of cadets. Those with more points were promoted into higher ranks and those with lower scores came to be foot soldiers. It turns out that the members of a rising middle class benefited from the system: in fact, the rise of the middle class is inseparable from the use of assessment and evaluation. School grades became the main tool for stratification, not only of the military but also of society. In so doing grades became a significant resource for individual and collective coercion and subjugation. Here is not the place to provide a detailed analysis of the function of assessment in producing and reproducing an inequitable society, based on an ideology of representation according to which grades, such as "71" or "A," can take the place of, stand in for, and therefore represent and be a representation of an individual (e.g., Roth & McGinn, 1998). That is, grades and grading are legitimate only if we presuppose that the "71" or the "A" are representative of (identical to) some aspect of an individual.

An interesting and eye-opening case with respect to the limitations of teacher assessment is evident for me in the evaluation of the competencies of individuals aspiring to enter a certification program for future French teachers at the University of British Columbia and Simon Fraser University (both in Vancouver). An entire team is involved in making the evaluation—which includes both written and oral examinations—as accountable as possible. Even after nearly twenty years, and involving several members of the team that constructed and continuously revised the scoring rubrics to which the candidates are subjected, there are instances when the examiners—all of whom are native French speakers—do not know whether a particular word, expression, or grammatical form is correct. With the help of a variety of dictionaries and tools, the team makes a decision as to the correctness of the candidate's verbal or written production. That is, even though the examiners themselves do not know whether an expression is correct, they will score against a candidate if they decide an expression is wrong. In the limiting case, such an assessment may lead to a candidate not being admitted to a teacher education program for teaching French. This case shows that in evaluation and assessment, there are not only questions about the validity and informative nature of scores and grades, but also ethical questions concerning the effect these practices have on the lives of real people.

Over the past several years, I have become interested in ethical issues, including that involving the use of grades to reproduce inequities. To better understand issues of equity and the production of inequities as well as issues of social justice and the finality of assessments, I have deeply involved myself in the philosophy of difference, which, through the works of philosophers such as Emmanuel Levinas, Jacques Derrida, Jean-Luc Nancy, and Gilles Deleuze, has come to define what is known as postmodernism. This philosophy presupposes the idea that anything we can think of simultaneously is particular and general, which in classical philosophy is an inadmissible contradiction. In the following four takes, I articulate my concerns regarding the ethico-moral dimension of evaluative assessment.

Take 1: The positioned nature of evaluative assessment Traditional assessment and evaluation are highly asymmetrical, "top down," as they affirm the sovereignty and indeed "authority" of the person constructing the evaluative statement, whether this takes the form of a narrative, letter grade, number, or percentage. The process legitimizes the knowledge/power of the person who "authors" the evaluation, and in authoring, reaffirms his or her authority. My comments about evaluation in the praxis of coteaching—where the person who, after consciously evaluating a situation as requiring a change in trajectory or because of a nonconscious sense of the game, requests and steps in to take the lead—entices us to think of evaluation without power, which is at once necessary and impossible. It is precisely this incompossibility—external evaluation without power that is at once necessary and impossible—that directs us to a solution. We recognize that any evaluation requires a decision, inherently perspectival, positioned and therefore *dis*positioned—in the dual sense of different in position and disposition and therefore contingent. Thus, no two individuals can take up the same physical position, forcing them to have different physical positions and therefore points of view: Andrea and Chuck or Victoria and Sonya inherently cannot have the same perspectives on the events. But being positioned differently means being dispositioned differently, that is, gives rise to the activation of different habitus or schema. If Andrea and I had exchanged our physical positions, there is a great likelihood that the lesson would have had a different trajectory due to the different ways in which we would have perceived the events.

Take 2: Veracity and justice in assessment decisions To elaborate and articulate a philosophy of *just* and *ethical* assessment, I draw on and elaborate a philosophical discourse concerned with judgment and witnessing (e.g., Ricœur, 2000). To begin with, assessing means making a decision. This decision expresses preference, evaluation, and approbation. The approbative nature of assessments requires data, which in coteaching, as in courts of law, is provided by those who have witnessed certain events. But, as we know from the legal system, witnesses frequently do not agree as to the nature of what has happened, who has done what. In fact, as the case of Rodney King—an African American beaten by several policy officers with their clubs—showed, even when an event has been recorded on videotape, witnesses of the original event and those watching the tapes may disagree as to the nature of what has happened. Although the tape shows several police officers beating up on Rodney King, the court saw itself confronted this question: Has this been an instance of police beating or an instance of police officers subduing an unruly and violent person? The nature of the process of witnessing events and the veracity of the accounts provided in a setting other than where the original event has taken place is at stake.

I begin with the idea that coteaching situates any individual charged with evaluating in praxis, and therefore in a position where he or she can witness the enacted curriculum. In this situation, the new teacher(s) and those in charge of evaluating meet each other in a common life, in the pursuit of a common motive: teaching to afford the learning of the students in their charge. All those present are witnesses, but because of their different institutional, experiential, and physical positions, likely differ as to how they make sense of what happens in a lesson.

During cogenerative dialoguing sessions, the participants in coteaching interpretively reduce the events in accounts of what has happened. In this process, they are both actors in the events described and they are witnesses of what has happened. However, although the two dimensions of actor and witness are conflated, participants in cogenerative dialoguing have no access to their own original participatory thinking because, as Figure 8.1 shows, this original testimony associated with the biographical experience is irreducible: there is always a loss, a reduction, however detailed an account and however many videotapes are used to document, attest to, the original event. This insurmountable singularity of the once-occurrent teaching act in particular and the historical event of the lesson in general introduces us to the enigmatic nature of the process of witnessing an event. This irreducible singularity of praxis underscores the significance of the irreducible nature of attesting to what really has happened. Such true attestation, if such is at all possible, comes with being a coteacher rather than an onlooker and the responsibility that comes with the once-occurrent nature of each act of teaching. The coteacher in the process of teaching is a privileged witness, who subsequently testifies (i.e., bears witness), articulating the autobiographical experience and thereby reducing it to a form that makes the event present again. For example, to truly understand the unfolding of my coteaching with Andrea, an observer has to be in my precise place, experientially, biographically, and with respect to all other participants in the situation. As participant I therefore have a privileged position with respect to understanding the nature of my involvement as the lesson unfolds. I am a privileged witness in this situation; and what I can attest to is mediated by the particular (physical, social, institutional) position I am taking at the moment, which, as the photographs in chapter 2 show, is one of the front corners. What I see and how I see it cannot be abstracted from this particular position.

As soon as I talk after the fact about this participation, I already see and provide an account of it from a different position. Making the event present again, therefore, leads to something different. When I talk about the experience of coteaching with Andrea, Chuck, and Ken in chapter 2, it is not coteaching itself. Any form chosen to bring some moment of praxis back to life irremediably and inherently is different. Even in the most detailed of accounts, participating coteachers cannot make a claim that is identical to any aspect of praxis. These accounts, bearing witness as they do to previous acts of teaching, are subject to the constraints on any form of functioning as a witness—they are necessarily reductions, descriptive accounts of what is considered salient at the moment of telling. As Figure 8.1a shows, any form of evaluation or assessment, constructed by means of interpretive reduction, no longer can assure its relevance and truth to the moment of praxis it is intended to be evidence of. That is, in the act of coteaching with Andrea, Chuck, the supervising and mentor teacher, and Ken, the supervising university professor, have come closest to evaluation in the true sense of the word in and through their interventions while we were teaching the biology lesson on monohybrid and dihybrid crosses. This experience, their witnessing-in-situation, is untranslatable into any genre that attempts to bear witness of the lesson to other parties (future employers, principals). Any decision about the form or content of the account requires a decision, which, as the term indicates, involves interruption. In this decision, the person making an assessment also takes a stand.

Take 3: The legal judgment as analogy To understand the nature of the decision-making in evaluative assessment, it helps me to use the judicial judgment as an analogy. In court cases, the decision about what has happened, who has done what, and who has to bear the responsibility, the decision is not based on a number system. Rather, the system is set up to consider a wide variety of evidence, most important and convincing among which are the descriptions witnesses provide. The ultimate decision of a case is made based on *all* documentations, even if this requires the considerations of thousands of pages. Turning to the evaluative assessment of teaching, I find it absurd, therefore, to assign one number to the multiplicity that such an experience constitutes for others and myself. There are so many dimensions of knowledgeability enacted in any single episode by any single teacher that a single number cannot ever aspire to capture. More so, assigning one number or letter grade means reducing the multiplicity inherent in teaching competence, quintessentially amounting to a process of adding dissimilar things (like adding apples and oranges). As another example, in my faculty, the quality of a professor's teaching is expressed in a summary score, which is the average of eleven scores on items such as "clarity of course objectives," "clarification of course objectives," "stimulation of student thinking," "instructor's enthusiasm," and "overall rating of instructor." (It is true, the overall rating of the instructor is averaged in with other items to yield the summary score for each of my courses, which the tenure and promotion and salary committees use for making their decisions.) It would be ridiculous to reduce the work of a judge to the addition or averaging of numbers assigned to each document. If it is not done presuming that it would make juridical judgments more "objective," then this has a reason precisely in the fact that it would not allow justice generally and equitable social justice specifically to emerge. It is equally ridiculous and really unethical to reduce evaluative assessment of teaching competencies to one or more numbers.

Cogenerative dialogue sessions can be thought of in terms of a legal analogy as well. They are like a group of jurors, all of whom also have been witnesses. During cogenerative dialogue sessions, the participants in a prior lesson, coteachers and students, engage in interpretive reduction as they articulate their positioned observations and function as witnesses of their previous biographical experience. There is a difference between cogenerative dialoguing and other situations in which the participants may bear witness to what has happened in the classroom: In cogenerative dialoguing, the participants do not have to prove to each other that they have been witness to the events that they now evaluate, they do not have to swear that what they have experienced is true, which is required in other situations where someone bears witness (e.g., a court of law). In cogenerative dialoguing, all participants know what they are witness of, and for, and whether there are other witnesses. This is where the strength of cogenerative dialoguing over other methods of evaluation derives from. In other forms of evaluative assessment, those for whom the assessment and evaluative statements (narrative, grades) designed, did not have immediate access to the original moments of praxis in which the knowledgeability of teaching was enacted, and therefore cannot bear witness for the witness—i.e., the person writing the evaluation or constructing assessment. Teachers have to trust that whatever evaluative statement or grade they receive relates to what they have done and developed the competence to do. They have to trust that the reduction is repeatable, as indicated in Figure 8.1a. The participants in cogenerative dialoguing, however, are positioned differently—even though they, too, no longer are present at the moment that they are bearing witness of while talking about what has happened. But each participant in cogenerative dialoguing who becomes witness of a past event is present to his or her testimony, thereby attesting the veracity of the evaluation. "Whoever bears witness does not provide a proof. It is someone whose experience, in principle singular and irreplaceable, comes to attest, justly, that 'something' has been present to him" (Derrida, 2005, p. 35). Despite all the differences that may exist between the different forms and contents of the individual commentaries (i.e., testimonies), cogenerative dialoguing offers greater possibility to evaluation and assessment than those constructed by and for third-parties because it is not subject to questions concerning the veracity of what is being said.

Coteaching confounds (tacit or explicit) evaluation and professional development; but it provides opportunities for forms of learning that inherently and irrevocably occur in the background that constitutes the very possibility of and for practical understanding of how the world generally and classrooms in particular work.

Cogenerative dialoguing provides opportunities for articulating the different forms of testimony, which are tied to our inherently different biographies without the necessity of proving what we say, as all participants have witnessed the once-occurrent events that they choose as topics of dialogue. But precisely in the differences between the individual testimonies lies the possibility for explication and therefore understanding to emerge and evolve. Both forms of assessment and evaluation praxis involve the encounter of the other, subject meeting subject, with all the possibilities that understanding the other provides to understanding oneself.

Take 4: Constructing a case and interviewing for a position Where do we go from here? In outlining the difficult nature of evaluative assessment, I am not arguing for abandoning this practice. Evaluative assessment is a way of intervening in social practice, which can be used to transform this practice. Thus, I ask myself how would I change, for example, the hiring process for a new teacher at my school to find out who might be the most suited among the available candidates? As I ponder this question, I am thinking again about the legal system, which operates in terms of cases. Each judgment not only constitutes a realization of current law, but also a case to be used as precedent in subsequent trials. A case, inherently, is a complex collection of diverse pieces of evidence, testimonies, artifacts, and transcribed court proceedings. It is not an average of ratings. I think of evaluative assessment and evidence for teaching in terms of building a case, which, in analogy of a court case, consists of an assembly of diverse elements. A *just* legal decision emerges from the judicious taking-into-account of the complete documentation. To exemplify, take my experience of how interviewing for my present position imposes itself in my consciousness.

My application contained a teaching portfolio, including a three-part video showing me teaching, then talking to students about teaching, and then talking with a professor colleague about my teaching and efforts of improving by engaging in the dialogues with students. As part of the process I had been asked to teach a lesson to future elementary teachers. Although the committee thought that I did an outstanding job, a number of constraints limited my performance—what I did and could do, therefore limiting the learning of the students, whose professor had "given up" his class so that the hiring committee could evaluate my teaching. Today, if I were again the department head of science in a high school—having already practiced coteaching as part of the assessment and evaluation process I am responsible for—I would ask all invited candidates to coteach with me and other science teachers at the school. In cogenerative dialoguing sessions following the lessons, we could then find out more about how each of us viewed, including the applicant, the suitability of a candidate for the particular job we are seeking to fill.

Readers may wonder how I would make the initial selection reducing the entire list of applicants to a few that would be invited. In answer, I return to the analogy of court decisions: I want the applicant to build a case for his or her suitability for the advertised position. I would request an extended portfolio similar to the one that I have constructed as part of my university teaching. This involves, besides curricula, statements of philosophy and epistemology, and video clips featuring my teaching and interactions with students and peers in other relevant professional situations. Today, these sessions would be cogenerative dialogues, themselves based on cotaught classes. Such a portfolio is rich, diverse, and produces a poetic expression of who I am; and poetic expressions, as Jacques Derrida suggests, are characteristic of any *responsible* act of bearing witness. We cannot make just evaluative assessment unless we have a sufficiently complex set of evidence; and we can come to just decisions about whom to hire, who to recommend for professional development, or whether to support a tenure decision without having to reduce teaching competencies to single numbers.

COTEACHING AND COGENERATIVE DIALOGUING

From the Past to Future Prospects

In this final chapter of our book on the various aspects of coteaching and cogenerative dialoguing, we articulate what we have learned from our studies, including the analyses presented here. Throughout this book we have used metalogues, which originally denoted speeches between delivered between scenes of a play, but which, introduced by Gregory Bateson, also are used to denote explanatory dialogues that have structures fitted to the problems they discuss. We view learning as dialogical, beginning with cogenerative dialogues the results of which are "ratcheted up" in metalogues to learn from the learning that has occurred in the former. Fittingly, therefore, this epilogue—which literally denotes the final part of a speech—also takes the form of metalogues. As we re-read the book to this point and prior to the existence of the epilogue, six themes emerge: the changing faces of coteaching as teachers and researchers continuously adapt the method to address the emerging problems at hand; the alternative forms that cogenerative dialoguing praxis may take; the role of agreement and contradiction in learning through coteaching and cogenerative dialoguing; the possibilities for realizing the potential in collective activity; using coteaching and cogenerative dialogues as research methods; and assessing teaching through the uses of coteaching and cogenerative dialogues.

CHANGING FACES OF COTEACHING

Ken: In the Philadelphia work, our first foci on coteaching tended to be situations in which two coteachers taught from the front of the room. What seemed most critical was that we had a heuristic to communicate with potential coteachers how the baton might be exchanged as teachers taught together, taking turns at being central in interactions with the whole class. This was a priority for us because we had enacted coteaching without research and theory to guide the different ways in which it might be productively enacted.

Michael: In my work in British Columbia, and already during the teacher development model at Appleby College, we used a mixed approach where coteaching occurred both during whole-class interactive lessons and small-group work during which students engaged in open-inquiry. Both types of situations allowed teachers to work on each other's elbow and therefore learn, for example, to ask productive questions. I have to admit, I had no idea about learning in tacit modes; I had begun with a sense that there may be one teacher who has a solid science background who models questioning; and the other might have a solid understanding of the students or general pedagogy, and she might model good interactions with the students. Perhaps the best way of doing and describing what I was doing and thinking way back then is captured in the notion of *modeling*, which derived from the literature on coaching. Modeling was then followed by a process of *scaffolding*, where the coach provides supporting structures that allowed, for example, a new teacher to ask better questions. The final stage would have been *fading*, which actually meant that one coteacher, the *coach*, withdrew into the background of the lessons.

Ken: I am glad you mentioned coaching. We too did a number of years of research on peer coaching, back in the mid 1980s, but in our case the model did not use coteaching in any conscious way and when researchers like me "took over" a class to teach it solo, we struggled mightily. When we began to use coteaching in Philadelphia the coteachers taught together in every imaginable way, including small-group and individualized settings. However, since we had gone program-wide in terms of implementing it, we focused our research initially on the ways in which it was going to work in whole-class interactions—so that we could provide guidelines on the sharing of control. Over time our focus on learning to teach allowed us to identify ways in which coteaching could be enacted during whole-class settings and when students were arranged in small groups or to work somewhat independently of others. By focusing on interactions we could undertake research and enact different forms of coteaching. Hence, the roles of coteachers began to have a fine structure that expanded its applicability.

Michael: By the time we worked together in Philadelphia, I had already begun to theorize coteaching in terms of practice theory, cultural fields, and the sense of the game that the players develop when they work together. As in other "games," those participating in coteaching would take roles that sometimes paralleled each other, alternated from one to the other, or complemented one another.

Ken: The notion of central and peripheral roles seemed salient in as much as my initial concern was to push "reluctant" coteachers into central roles in which they dealt with the whole class well before they were equipped to do so. I see this as a pressure that came from traditional beliefs that teachers had to learn to teach solo and show that they could as soon as possible.

Michael: This was my concern, too, when I initially thought about coteaching as requiring a phase of *fading*, where the more experienced teacher eventually fades into the background to allow the new or less experienced teacher to teach solo.

Ken: Now I regard this as an error. Coteachers can legitimately coteach in peripheral roles, perhaps teaching individuals while colleagues assume more central roles of interacting with larger groups of students. In the process of teaching peripherally, a coteacher produces forms of culture that are appropriate and over time a sense of the game of teaching builds by teaching with others in the particular setting. When a coteacher has the repertoire of culture needed to teach in more central ways she will likely step forward and teach in those ways—perhaps not even consciously. I have learned above all to allow the coteachers to decide when to step forward and when to step back—and as a teacher educator, to be patient as different teachers find their own ways of successfully interacting with students in different grouping configurations.

Michael: This works when the coteachers are attuned not only to the science content and to students but also to other coteachers in the sense that requests to step in both are made and recognized as having been made. It is at that point that the baton can pass back and forth as needed; and precisely then do the teachers learn from each other because they make the best of lessons happen that they are able to.

Ken: When there is a fit between a coteacher's goals, the culture in her teaching toolkit, and the structures of a classroom, then she may step forward and enact teaching fluently; that is, in ways that are timely, anticipatory, and appropriate. Structures that push a teacher to step forward may or may not elicit appropriate and timely forms of teaching.

Michael: In this sense, I like to use an analogy with other activities that both require a precise sense of timing participation, which one learns by participating in these activities. One learns to be a good at jazz improvisations and jam sessions by participating in these forms of musical events; but the participation in such events generally requires at least the willingness to be attuned to the play of others. Similarly, one learns to be an excellent player in team sports that require precise timing by participating in such events; yet the participation itself requires a sense for precise timing.

Ken: Another awakening for me is that there can be value in a coteacher "shadowing" another—following closely on the heels, watching another coteacher intently, and in the process, making the sense of how she goes about her teaching. I recall you doing this to me on the first occasion you had been in Philadelphian high schools. This was not watching from the side, and you were able to track for a while and teach peripherally as occasions unfolded.

Michael: Intermittently shadowing or trailing an individual who is more familiar with the context appears to me a good way for getting a sense of the game precisely for starting up the chicken-and-egg kind of situation I just outlined—to participate, you need to have a sense of the game and of timing, but you participate because you have a sense for the game and of timing. So shadowing can then unfold into participation, much as I have done at City High School, where after a while I began to interact precisely with those students that I had seen you interact with.

Ken: As you describe it, this seems like an ideal way for new teachers to begin coteaching with a resident teacher. Initially at least it is easy to envision oscillation between trailing and coteaching peripherally.

Michael: Most important to me is the fact that more teachers in a class means more resources (i.e., structures) for learning—both learning to teach and learning to teach science, or mathematics, history, and so forth.

Ken: Increasing the number of teachers in a classroom makes sense in many ways. Of course, even when there are no new teachers available the number of teachers in a class can be increased by mobilizing students as coteachers—that is, students participate as coteachers as well as colearners.

Michael: The potential value of students as coteachers became salient to me particularly in the discussions we had with Natasia and Shawan following the lesson on the monohybrid and dihybrid cross. Perhaps they suggested the praxis of peer teaching because of their personal experiences in the African American culture, where collectivity plays a much larger role than in the Anglo-Saxon culture so focused on individualism. Peer teaching is not valued as much in a culture that values competition as a central element. But I believe that once students recognize the extent to which they learn when they assist peers, those currently reluctant will participate in peer teaching to a much greater degree.

Ken: You make a strong point here; one I had not considered. This may be a fruitful area on which to focus research. I'd imagine that without intervention forms of peer coteaching might emerge more frequently in settings with African American and Latina/o students than in those with mainly Caucasian youth. On the other hand, following participation in cogenerative dialogues, Caucasian youth might also increase their participation in and learning via peer coteaching.

ALTERNATIVE FORMS OF COGENERATIVE DIALOGUES

Ken: The research in this book has really expanded our ways of thinking about cogenerative dialogues. Initially we regarded cogenerative dialogues as opportunities for a small group of stakeholders to discuss shared experiences and negotiate changes to improve the quality of learning and teaching. Key outcomes were cogenerated—including changes in roles, rules, and resource usage and availability. The acceptance of shared responsibility for enacting agreed to changes was an essential piece of the initial formulation of cogenerative dialogue.

Michael: Here, too, we learned about and improved our praxis as we went along; and we came to theorize what we were doing only *after* we had some experience. It initially was a way of getting teachers to articulate their sense of the events for the purpose of getting them to think how they could improve upon their practice. Then we added students based on the idea that students are important resources for understanding how to teach students, especially those who are culturally very different than the teachers teaching them. And then we recognized the potential for theorizing teaching, learning to teach, and the production and reproduction of culture in the classroom and school.

Ken: Gradually increasing the number of students to participate in cogenerative dialogues seemed like a sensible progression—first to half classes and then to whole classes. However, soon it was evident that, depending on the size of the group, different outcomes were possible from cogenerative dialogues. In seeking collective buy-in for agreed-to changes, we did not want to give up on the smaller-sized cogenerative dialogues that allowed for more active forms of participation—because there were fewer participants.

Michael: The issue of number of participants revolves for me around the notion situational appropriateness. The questions "Who participates?" and "How many individuals (students) participate?" depend on the nature of the issue that needs to be talked about. The important point is that of dialogue—we want to open up communication to articulate and deal with problematic issues rather than allowing them to be internalized and becoming sources for conflict and violence. Thus, it would have been important to invite Mirabelle and one or more peers to have a cogenerative dialogue with Alex and Victoria to find out how they experienced the situation. This would then have allowed for all participants to reflect upon their actions and learn from them. Victoria may have come to value the role of alternative ways of thinking about and doing chemical problems; and Mirabelle may have come to learn about how her aggressive ways of dealing with difference are experienced emotionally and perceived consciously by various stakeholders—participant versus observer, student versus teacher. Cogenerative dialoguing sessions thereby become seedbeds not so much of cultural reproduction but more so seedbeds of cultural transformation.

Ken: That is a very salient point. The metaphor of the seedbed for cultural production opened a number of doors for imagining different forms of cogenerative dialogues. Initially it just involved a change of focus—examining how participants produced new culture through their interactions in the cogenerative dialogues and then looking to see if they enacted those new forms of culture in other fields—especially the classroom. However, we then realized that reducing the number of participants in a cogenerative dialogue might provide opportunities for participants to create culture needed to successfully interact across cultural borders defined by such factors as ethnicity, gender, and English proficiency. It was then that we realized two new powerful forms of cogenerative dialogue: one-on-one cogenerative dialogues and two-teachers-with-one-student cogenerative dialogues. In the latter case, a teacher with a history of interacting successfully with a student or group of students meets with a teacher who is struggling to interact with given students and a representative of the students with whom the other teacher is having difficulties. In an important sense this is a form of coteaching (in this instance with one student)—one teacher learns from the other by being with the other and coparticipating with her.

Michael: Considering these alternatives or rather, picking an appropriate form of cogenerative dialoguing itself requires a sense of the game, a sense that you learn by participating in the game, here cogenerative dialoguing. New teachers are enabled to participate in cogenerative dialoguing when they participate in this form of praxis. I envision that in the future we will have new teachers who participated in cogenerative dialoguing already as students. And

237

from such a perspective we transform not only schooling specifically but also society more generally.

Ken: If cogenerative dialogues are fields in which culture is produced (reproduced and transformed) then why not science culture? It was apparent that from this perspective tutoring was a form of cogenerative dialogue in which a small group of participants interacted with the purpose of improving their knowledge of science. Adoption of the rules of cogenerative dialogue raises the potential of structuring them in ways in which greater attention is focused on equitable participation and collective goals, accomplishments, and responsibilities.

Michael: It is interesting in this context that in computer clubs, youngsters learned by talking together through problems so that they arrived at levels of competence that exceeded what any one individual had come with to the club. I agree with you, why should this not be possible in science?

Ken: Once we see tutoring as a form of cogenerative dialogue we can plan for tutoring to occur as other coteachers teach the whole class or small groups. This may be especially salient when new teachers are involved in their very initial teaching experiences. A form of legitimate peripheral participation might be to participate in various forms of cogenerative dialogue as others coteach the whole class. These could include tutoring and huddles with other coteachers.

CONTRADICTIONS, AGREEMENTS, AND DIALOGUE

Michael: When talking to teachers and teacher educators, I often get the sense that contradictions and alternative perspectives are not valued. This became clear to me again with great force, when I recently articulated alternative perspectives on a teacher enhancement project though not until after I had pointed out its laudable features. The project leader, after reading what I had written, exploded and slammed the door to the dialogue, for which I had called both in my critique and in my message to which I had attached my analysis. I believe that this cultural form—allowing only agreement and not seeking out contradictions—is an impediment to learning. I value, with G.W.F. Hegel and Karl Marx, the role of contradictions as resources for identifying starting points for inquiry.

Ken: This is a good point. When I first read William Sewell's critique of Clifford Geertz's perspectives on culture the greatest implication for our research in urban science education was to regard cultural enactment as a dialectic of schema and practices—experienced as patterns of coherence and associated contradictions—which also are dialectically related. Hence, contradictions are a normal part of social life. As you do, we search for contradictions and seek to understand them. Also, they become seeds for the possible transformation of a field. So, to return to your experience with our colleague—it is a shame that she was not on the look out for contradictions and did not regard your third party identification of contradictions to consider as the best possible result from having an outside expert review what happened in her project.

Michael: Our coteaching model may be interpreted to mean that we only emphasize the tacit modes of teaching and learning. But we would limit ourselves if we were to rely solely on the tacit modes of learning. With my graduate students, I sometimes use the example of family problems to explicate that problems and contradictions do not *inherently* lead to understanding and development. There are couples and families who remain together for years despite violence, conflict, argumentation, and misunderstanding. They reproduce these unhealthy forms of praxis even though they and their relationship suffer from them. Here, a mediator or counselor may be able to assist the couple to locate an inner contradiction that arises from the employment situation of the husband or the particular form of life that comes from their working-class or welfare status. For me this shows that experiencing conflict does not itself lead us out of conflict. We require an explanation for why we do what we do, that is, a theoretical understanding of the situation that allows us to understand where the conflict is coming from.

Ken: A good example of this occurred with the coteaching relationship between Alex and Victoria. The contradictions in their interactions were evident and efforts to resolve them led to a build up of negative emotions, initially in the forms of frustration and disappointment, later evolving to stronger expressions of annoyance and anger. The partnership effectively disintegrated and the two teachers no longer cotaught or participated in cogenerative dialogues. Had we known more about cogenerative dialogues the relationship may have been transformed with Alex, Victoria, and me discussing their interactions and exploring why the unsuccessful interactions and the intensity of associated emotions escalated so rapidly.

Michael: In trying to come to grips with contradictions, or to frame problems as expressions of inner contradictions, we need to draw on our practical understanding that we have developed in the situation and through our praxis. This practical understanding, as Paul Ricœur has shown in such a convincing way, precedes, accompanies, and concludes explanation-seeking interpretation. But, precisely these explanations allow us to develop our practical understanding.

Ken: Exactly. Teacher educators cannot figure it all out by sitting in their offices and planning on their computers. For example, consider the roles of participants in cogenerative dialogues. We can plan a priori that the turns at talk are to be shared among participants, no speaker will speak for too long, interactions will be respectful, and all utterances will remain on topic until an agreement has been reached among participants. However, when I interact with Andrea in the cogenerative dialogue associated with the dihybrid cross, my praxis reflected a long experience as a university supervisor of new teachers. When I pointed out to her that a transition was too long, I was genuinely trying to be a good supervisor—offering suggestions that would in the future lead to improved teaching. My goal and associated praxis were at odds with the collective goals and intended outcomes of producing a commitment to how we could collectively improve the quality of learning next time we cotaught. Unless you had mentioned the contradiction to me—that I should have acted if I had thought the transition to be too long—I would probably have even been unaware that enacting my supervisor habitus was at odds with the goals of cogenerative dialogue and coteaching.

Michael: Radical commitment to dialogue is my personal answer to the question about how to coordinate problematic issues arising from individual|collective life. That is, I am not wishing away difference and conflict but I am favoring commitment to dialogue, which allows us not to come to agreements all of the time, but to an understanding. This then provides us with a resource for deciding at which points we require agreement to continue and at which points we only require understanding but not agreement. Thus, teachers and students have to come to some form of agreement about how to construct the context of their collective praxis, even if this means that they make arrangements for learning in small groups where certain differences and conflicts may not arise.

Ken: Let me see if I understand your point here. In cogenerative dialogues we usually seek to cogenerate agreements at a collective level—that is (and for example) we agree to try changes in roles, rules, and resource allocation in the next lesson. This agreement is reached through discussions of shared experiences in an earlier lesson and in the current cogenerative dialogue.

Michael: Precisely, we need agreement for a decision about what to do next, but we do not need agreement about our personal experiences of events. Because of our different backgrounds, experiences, and institutional positions, we will perceive and experience classroom events in different ways. But to be able to plan the next lesson, we need to come to an agreement if it is better to have a lecture or small-group work, whether we have more or fewer laboratory experiments, and so on.

Ken: The essence of what you are saying is that all participants should understand the dialogue, including the perspectives of each of the participants, and what the collective outcomes are to be. However, the individuals might retain their own convictions about what to do and why to do it—these may differ from what they agree should be done collectively.

Michael: Yes, precisely. Cogenerative dialoguing fundamentally is a different way of relating to the other, to difference, with the ultimate goal to reach agreement where agreement is necessary for continuing a form of praxis or to reach understanding of the other.

Ken: It helps if participants realize that they can act not only to reach personal goals, but also to reach collective goals and to afford other's meeting their personal goals. That is, having a functional understanding of the agency|structure dialectic, can greatly increase the productivity of cogenerative dialogues.

REALIZING THE POTENTIAL OF NEW TEACHERS FOR THE COLLECTIVE

Michael: I see in coteaching particularly great potential for realizing a greater degree of collective responsibility and the unleashing of heretofore-unused collective capacity. Rather than making those on a trajectory to become certified teachers spend so much time in university lecture halls and seminar rooms, they could participate in coteaching. All participants would be provided with resources for learning and development: there are more teachers in the classroom as resources for students; the new teachers learn in tacit and explicit modes from their mentors; and the mentors learn by becoming more aware of teaching practices.

Ken: I would much prefer to see teacher education done this way. I could envision coteaching occurring for the purposes of initial certification and professional development in much the way you imply. Imagine coteaching setups in the most needy of schools, university professors coteaching with new and resident teachers for a series of lessons. These sessions could be followed by opportunities to review, analyze and interpret videotape and other artifacts from the lessons and then in cogenerative dialogues there could be opportunities to identify and resolve contradictions in the ways in which we have discussed in the book. Larger cogenerative dialogues could then be forums for connecting theory and research to what has been learned from the coteaching and cogenerative dialoguing. If this process were followed coteaching and cogenerative dialogues would be central methodologies in teacher education programs.

Michael: In a sense, we are currently far away from realizing the potential in the collective for learning of individuals. Students can be learning resources for one another, as they already are when interacting at home or in the street. I see how they assist each other in learning new moves on the skateboard, both through modeling these moves and by analyzing the moves with them. Why should this form of collective learning not be possible in the classroom as well?

Ken: Of course in this book we have shown that it is possible and when it happens the ripple effects might even extend beyond one classroom to include the school and even a cluster of schools. I think the revolution that needs to occur has to be to critically address the ideology of individualism that supports solo teaching and models of accountability that hold individuals responsible for outcomes independently of the collectives in which they live their lives.

Michael: And this is where I see cogenerative dialogues playing an important role, because using them is a democratic way of changing an institution. In the process, we, too, will change; and to me, this is an exciting prospect, as it minimizes the possibilities for deleterious forms of social and cultural reproduction—increasing the possibilities for improving social life and for a life never to be in a rut.

COTEACHING AND COGENERATIVE DIALOGUES AS RESEARCH METHODS

Ken: It is pleasing to see colleagues from around the world beginning to employ coteaching and cogenerative dialogues together and separately in their research methods. Within my research groups coteaching and cogenerative dialogues have become central research methods in a relatively short time. The insights gleaned from the experience of coparticipation allows for different possibilities to be explored. Your earlier points about the individual|collective dialectic are very important here as well. There is less of a possibility for studies of teaching that incorporate deficit perspectives on teachers and since the responsibility for learning also is collective a tendency to "blame the victim" may not be as apparent in research that employs coteaching and cogenerative dialogues.

Michael: The mention of deficit perspective is interesting, as I have come to realize that it may be part of the ethos in science education to think about students' and teachers' knowledge in terms of the distance with some acknowledged or unacknowledged reference. Thus, we used to have and perhaps still do have the entire field of research on misconceptions, alternative conceptions, worldviews, and the many other terms that have denoted the fact that there are many individuals on this planet who use words such as "atom," "force," or "velocity" differently than scientists do. Similarly with science teachers, there has been a lot of research on teaching that explicitly or implicitly compared teaching, which has occurred in the contingency of some everyday setting—*these* students, at *this* time, with *this* curriculum—against *could-haves*, and *should-haves*. I have learned a lot from ethnomethodological research, which insists that we describe what happens precisely *because* it is praxis that concretizes one of the *real* possibilities for acting in *this* situation. This is why the coteaching method is so powerful: because researchers are in the situation where they are subject to the same constraints as others and have the opportunity to act on the real possibilities that exist at the moment. They thereby come to understand the *whys* and *hows* of the praxis in this situation they want to understand. I think that it would be interesting to theorize the relationship between a researcher's participative thinking while in a coteaching situation and her ethnographic account that she writes up once she has left the classroom.

Ken: Yes. That would be an interesting avenue to pursue in future research. Also, I can see considerable potential in examining the roles of coteachers and colearners as symmetrical. That is, the coteachers also are colearners and the students, who can be coteachers and participate as such in the research, are also colearners in the classroom and coparticipants in cogenerative dialogues. Hence, when coteaching and cogenerative dialogues are considered as research methods it is apparent that the student participants are also coresearchers. Thinking of the student participants as coresearchers likely adds significant value to a study.

Michael: In a way, it is reflexive praxis taken to a new level, where those inhabiting a particular lifeworld—e.g., the members of a small learning community at City High School—do not just enter a context like a box someone else prepared for them but in fact participate in shaping and reshaping the very conditions of their participation. The reshaping efforts—i.e., the science education *reform*—are based on their cogenerative dialogue praxis, where they achieve agreement on what to do next and how to do it. Cogenerative dialogues as research methods provides them with a tool to go about producing the resources they need for achieving agreements and plans for the future. As reflective practice, cogenerative dialogues allow participants to get at the determinations of their social life that come from the outside of their lifeworlds and therefore normally are hidden. These determinations come from the macrolevel conditions of society.

Ken: Within our own research squad we have felt a need to explore social life at macro-, meso-, and microscopic levels using a range of methods, some of which incorporate microanalysis of videotapes—as we showed in our research involving the interactions between Mirabelle and Victoria, for example. Coteaching and cogenerative dialogues can provide complementary perspectives to what can be learned from discourse and conversation analyses undertaken in microanalyses of videotapes. Together, richer insights can be obtained from research in schools and science classrooms.

Michael: Perhaps it is not so much that there is a difference, especially between cogenerative dialoguing and discourse and conversation analyses, as the latter can be conducted in cogenerative dialogue sessions, but that we generally choose different objects for the dialogue sessions than we do for discourse and conversations analyses.

Ken: This is a timely reminder. We have tended to use cogenerative dialogues primarily in classrooms and schools. I am curious about the ways in which you have employed cogenerative dialogues in fields other than education research.

Michael: We have used cogenerative dialogue, for example, in our ethnographic research on knowing and learning in fish hatcheries. Together with graduate students and a research associate trained as a biologist and anthropologist, we spent a day, interviewing, observing, or in fact co-participating in the daily chores. (We use apprenticeship as ethnographic field method.) In the evening, staying in a residence on the grounds of the hatchery, we met to make sense of the day's events. We articulated first understandings from the different perspectives that come with our prior experiences and with the different ways in which we have experienced the day, sometimes involving events in which we co-participated together with the fish culturists and workers to make sense of events that we have experienced together. In both types of situation, the participants dialogued to cogenerate understandings for the purpose of making decisions about what to do, in terms of research, on the next day. A similar situation exists in our research lab, where we engage in cogenerative dialogues for making sense of events shown on videotapes that one or more individuals have collected in the field. For example, a mathematics education colleague, a postdoctoral fellow whom we co-supervise, and I collected data in mathematics classrooms, cotaught by the colleague and a resident teacher. In our laboratory, we engaged in cogenerative dialogue for the purpose of producing interpretations, also involving the other researchers in my research group, who work on very different projects, like a marine college instructor, a dentist, a teacher educator, and an environmentalist. We find that cogenerative dialogue sessions not only produce many interpretive starting points but also generate solidarity within the research group.

NEW APPROACHES TO TEACHER ASSESSMENT

Michael: As we are completing this book, I am thinking that it would be exciting to be a department head of science again—or perhaps a principal or superintendent—so that I could do more about developing new approaches to teacher assessment. Our research on coteaching and cogenerative dialoguing has provided me with insights and theoretical frameworks that I have not had during my humble beginnings of using a more democratic approach to evaluative assessment of teaching performance. My experience in the early 1990s showed that it is possible to move from a traditional praxis, where a department head observes a lesson and then writes a report, to a way of doing evaluative assessment collectively and in a way that embodies different modes of learning.

Ken: You certainly introduced many innovative practices in your days as a department head—even at that stage you were making sense of science education and learning to teach through novel theoretical lenses.

Michael: Back then, we practiced reflection on our own practice, observed someone else teach, cotaught with other teachers, and had the department head do coteaching and observations and write a summary report. Today, I would emphasize coteaching and cogenerative dialoguing as methods for teacher evaluation and assessment. I would also push the use of video—which some of my colleagues, following my own examples, already used—as a way of generating objects for discussion during cogenerative dialoguing and as a way of producing portfolios that not only exhibit evaluation but also, over the years, growth as a teacher.

Ken: The development of electronic portfolios to represent teaching and learning has enormous potential to change the ways in which teacher assessment not only includes the teacher's voice, but also the voices of other key stakeholders.

Michael: This is precisely where I would be moving, as we had not done this back then, when the easy-to-use video-editing capabilities did not yet exist. Nowadays it is so easy to digitize video, to rapidly scan the videotape of a lesson, and to pick salient episodes without have to move at a much lower rate through a videotape to be able to copy some episode—in the way I had done my own professional development to build a video portfolio during the 1990s at the university level.

Ken: Doing these things opens the door to include students, colleague teachers and school administrators in coteaching and cogenerative dialogues and, in so doing, in assessment of teaching (and learning) as well. There also is scope to include participants from the community, including parents, in coteaching, cogenerative dialogues, and teacher assessment. As we have pointed out previously, the coalescing of teacher assessment with the enactment of curricula draws attention to their continuous nature.

Michael: When schools choose to do coteaching and cogenerative dialoguing, then evaluative assessment no longer is a one-off process but becomes indistinguishable from the praxis of schooling. It is a way of instituting continuous growth and development by both implicit—e.g., in coteaching—and explicit means—e.g., cogenerative dialoguing. It is a way of actively expanding the action possibilities and actively taking control over one's life conditions. It is a way of transforming a societal activity—i.e., schooling—in the very process of reproducing it.

CODA

Ken: We have come such a long way in a relatively short time. I am sure we will never forget the tough time we received in peer review. What have we learned that others might benefit from?

Michael: For me, those experiences taught me a lot about the conservative aspects of cultures, more directed to reproduction and preserving the status quo rather than attempting to change culture by developing new lenses and new forms of research. I also learned about the crucial roles editors play in the reproduction and transformative production of a field because of the institutional position they take, stabilized by tenure and promotion processes that use publications and peer review as resource.

Ken: The editors took a harsh stance and I wonder how they decided to whom to send the manuscripts? Irrespective, the reviewers and editors spoke with one voice, to the effect that we had not done anything new. There was a tendency for reviewers to feel this is just what they had been doing all along, dressed up (and obscured) with jargon. There was almost a sense that in submitting this work we were disrespecting their efforts in teacher education. Our manuscript was a source of symbolic violence to the editors and the reviewers they selected.

Michael: I had not thought about it in this way, but you are right, in proposing a radically new way of enacting teacher education and doing research— coteaching and cogenerative dialoguing—we were challenging the reproduction of culture and the status quo. But it does not have to be that way, because as editors of *Cultural Studies of Science Education*, we value and encourage authors to use and articulate new ways of doing and writing research. Having a multiplicity of lenses, producing something like a kaleidoscopic view, allows us to interrogate not only our research objects but also our very own ideologies.

Ken: You and I adhere to a bricolage approach to the uses of theory in research—in that, we do not see our own perspectives as privileged and are well aware that in illuminating in special ways selected theories also obscure in equally salient ways. Hence, in advocating coteaching and cogenerative dialogues, then and now, and theorizing them in the ways we do—we are not arguing that these are the only methods and the only frameworks that are salient.

Michael: That is right. And more so, we practice—and likewise encourage others to do so—a continual transformation of these forms of praxis to make them appropriate for dealing with the issues at hand and for making them contextually appropriate. What remains constant, therefore, are the terms we use to denote the forms of praxis, but what we actually do continues to evolve and change. I am envisioning the relationship between the terms coteaching and cogenerative dialoguing and what they denote to evolve in ways not unlike a signifier such as "atom" has stayed the same all the while its signified has changed continuously throughout its 2,500-year history. That is, the concept of *atom* has changed.

Ken: Conceptual change theories have been dominant in science education and so many science educators have been schooled in that way of thinking about learning science and learning to teach science. Back in the early 1980s Ernst von Glasersfeld was concerned by the ways in which the conceptual change group appropriated constructivism—implying this is how they had been thinking about science learning for many years and it was just the words that were new. He coined the term *trivial constructivists* to characterize their uses of just a few limited ideas from constructivism. The reactions of reviewers to our work seem like déjà vu (all over again). Of course it is not too clear what it is that some of our critics claim to have done previously because it is not in the literature and never made it through peer review.

Michael: After I heard this claim, I went to check in the ISI database, the one that sociologists use to construct claims about knowledge generation, disciplines, and the ways scholarly networks evolve over time. It turns out that there was only one article that came up when I used the term coteaching. That is, despite the claims some editors made that they had used coteaching for decades, there was nothing in the published literature about this work. There were no theories about coteaching or how it distinguished itself from other forms of working together on teaching-related issues, such as team-teaching.

Ken: Although we have an impressive literature to describe the evolution of coteaching and cogenerative dialogues and to expand their applicability, there are many in the policy realm who will not accept what we have done as research. Getting acceptance for the impressive studies that are annotated in the appendix is a challenge we address through this book and will continue through dissemination in journals and presentations at local, national and international meetings. The research agenda also will be ongoing and expansive.

Michael: There once was a baseball umpire who supposedly said, "It's nothing until I call it [a ball, strike]." I want to add, there is nothing to be called when

the pitch has not been made. If there are no studies and other forms of dis-
seminations of coteaching, it simply does not exist within the community.

Ken: Just yesterday one of my former doctoral students was discussing cogenerative dialogues and the impressive volume of studies to support their use. In so
doing she lamented that they do not appear to work in our research meetings.
I found myself disagreeing before I had fully considered whether or not she
had a point. The essence of my remarks to her was that cogenerative dialogues would be used regularly in research group meetings—but not all the
time. I want a field in which my expertise can mold what happens and take a
lead in structuring to expand the agency of the individuals and the collective.
I want a vertical structure in which the more senior postdoctoral fellows and
senior doctoral students proactively teach the newer researchers about theory
and methods and doing research. Funnily, I am haunted by her question.
Should our research meetings always be cogenerative dialogues? What do
you think about this issue?

Michael: It turns out that I have written about solidarity in my research group and
the horizontal structure that exists among its members in terms of who mentors whom. Sometimes it is a masters-level student who mentors a postdoctoral fellow, at other times it is a doctoral student. We consider knowledgeability and expertise to be distributed across the group; most important for us
is the provision of a structure that allows the expertise to become salient so
that those who feel they can learn actually do use them and enhance their
learning.

Ken: Though we have come a long way there still is much to be accomplished and
heavy activity is underway. It is to be hoped that we have caste many pebbles
into an ocean so that the ripple effects will be pervasive and self-
perpetuating. As we look ahead to our fourth book on coteaching and cogenerative dialogue my expectation is that we will have much to learn from
global studies that show the benefits of multigenerational applications of
coteaching and cogenerative dialogues. Though we do not see our methods as
panacea, we do expect the yield from using these methods to enrich social
life, not to enhance the economic and military advantages of our sectors of
the globe, but in ways that increase equity in education and open the gates for
social transformation throughout what is at present a troubled world. I am
buoyed by your characterizing these methods as democratic and regard them
as central in critical pedagogy and prime movers in discerning and defeating
hegemonies—wherever they persist.

Michael: And being democratic means that one may be called upon to share one's
expertise, which means that the participants collaborate in recognizing differences in expertise but use them to enhance their mutual learning. I do not
have general precepts about how this can be made to work everywhere. One
has to experience it in person and learn, by being open to learning, to allow a
research group to emerge in this way. But based on other experiences with
other facets of culture I have had, I am quite certain that local adaptations are
essential for any method to work globally. A statement I read last night about

understanding appears to be the fitting statement for ending: Grasping something does not mean being able to subsume it to some general concept; grasping is the movement of mind between the singularity of the case and the ideality (generality) of the concept (Nancy, 2002). The generalization of coteaching and cogenerative dialoguing means developing as many concrete singular applications as there are practitioners and practicing collectives.

ANNOTATED BIBLIOGRAPHY OF COTEACHING AND COGENERATIVE DIALOGUING RESEARCH

Over the years, we have conducted extensive research on coteaching and thereby established a field of research that did not exist—despite the claims of some reviewers of our early work. Our work also has produced ripple effects as others have commenced their own research programs. Research on coteaching and cogenerative dialogues us now firmly established in many countries and throughout the North America. This historical bibliography with brief descriptions reflects many of the studies conducted and published by our colleagues and us—giving readers an idea about the ground that this now extensive research agenda has prepared and covered. The publications are presented in two categories, books and refereed research articles and chapters, within each of which the publications are order by publication date.

BOOKS

Roth, W.-M., & Tobin, K. G. (2002). *At the elbow of another: Learning to teach by coteaching.* New York: Peter Lang.

> This book is about teaching and learning to teach, written from the perspectives and experiences of two educators who teach and, in so doing, learn to teach. Teaching and learning to teach at the elbows of other teachers (including ourselves) provide us with new and different understandings and allow us to describe a different epistemology of teaching. We adopt a first-person perspective on teaching, sometimes our own and at other times that of peers but through the eyes of coparticipants engaged in an activity with the same primary intention of assisting students to learn. Throughout the book we focus on teaching and learning to teach at different stages of the career ladder and explore different ways of conceiving the roles of researchers, supervisors, evaluators, cooperating teachers, and "new teachers."

Roth, W.-M. (2002). *Being and becoming in the classroom.* Westport, CT: Ablex.

> In this book, Michael develops a discourse about teaching that is deeply grounded in praxis, both his own and that of fellow coteachers. This discourse shaped much of our early work on coteaching and cogenerative dialoguing, prior to our adoption of the structure|agency dialectic as central framework. In Part I, "Being in the Classroom," he develops the experience-based praxeological concepts introduced in this preface. One chapter is devoted to each concept, including "temporality of teaching," "being in and being with," "habitus," "Spielraum," and "relationality." In Part II of this book, "Becoming in the Classroom," Michael presents coteaching and cogenerative dialoguing as a viable practice for teaching and learning to teach grounded in the phenomenological concepts introduced earlier. Chapter 6 sets the stage for a more in-depth presentation of "coteaching" in Chapter 7 and "cogenerative dialoguing" in Chapter 8. Coteaching and cogenerative dialoguing allow teachers to develop both implicit knowledge of, and explicit knowledge about teaching, factors that stand in a dialectical rela-

tion. The contradictions embedded in this dialectical relation and the opportunities for growth such that contradictions present are the topic of the final chapter.

Roth, W.-M., & Tobin, K. (Eds.). (2005). *Teaching together, learning together.* New York: Peter Lang.

This edited volume brings together authors from three continents (Australia, America, Europe) and four countries (Australia, Canada, Ireland, USA) who describe and theorize coteaching or cogenerative dialoguing as these practices have been implemented and evolved in response to problems and contradictions. Our introductions to the three parts of the book and our introduction and epilogue articulate similarities, differences, and salient issues between the different chapters. All studies also share sociocultural and cultural-historical underpinnings, which allows us to present a cohesive set of studies that improve our understanding of the coteaching and cogenerative dialoguing practices, and the constraints and contradictions they may face when implemented in various settings.

Wassell, B., & Stith, I. (2006). *Infinite potential: Becoming an urban physics and mathematics teacher.* Dordrecht, The Netherlands: Springer.

Beth and Ian undertake a longitudinal study of Ian learning to teach and transforming classroom learning environments through the uses of coteaching and cogenerative dialogues during a year in which he completed a master's degree, earned certification to teach physics and mathematics, and taught for a year in a neighborhood high school in inner-city Philadelphia. The study then continued for two years, exploring Ian's struggles to gain employment in an urban school and then his first two years of teaching in urban schools. The research includes multiple voices, especially those of Ian's students and Ian's voice as a teacher researcher. Accordingly, first-person and third-person accounts of teaching and learning are presented in a compelling ethnography of the uses of cogenerative dialogues to support a new teacher become more accomplished in meeting the needs of his students and building on their strengths. This is one of just a few studies that undertook detailed research of learning to teach in an initial teacher education program and then studied the subsequent years in which what was learned in training was used as a foundation for becoming a fluent teacher who could enact practices that were anticipatory, appropriate and timely.

REFEREED JOURNAL ARTICLES AND CHAPTERS

Roth, W.-M. (1998). Teaching and learning as everyday activity. In K. Tobin & B. Fraser (Ed.), *International handbook of science education* (pp. 169–181). Dordrecht, Netherlands: Kluwer Academic Publishing.

In this chapter, a practice perspective is developed along the lines of Pierre Bourdieu's work, including the nonconscious dimensions of learning while participating with others in a community of practice. The chapter uses the term collaborative practice and presents it as a context for learning to teach while teaching for newcomers and old-timers alike.

Roth, W.-M. (1998). Science teaching as knowledgeability: a case study of knowing and learning during coteaching . *Science Education*, 82, 357–377.

It is a common lore among teachers that teaching (as it happens in their classrooms) and talk about teaching (as it happens in universities) are incommensurable. This study was designed to learn about teaching as practice by investigating what two teachers learned from each other as they engaged over a period of three months in co-teaching an engineering curriculum to a Grade 4-5 class. The data sources for this interpretive study included ethnographic and video-taped records of lessons, planning and debriefing meetings, and staff development efforts. This study provides direct and indirect evidence for teachers' knowledgeability, that is, their knowing and learning in and about practice, including tacit and explicit aspects of teaching practice. Co-teaching afforded experiences that have been shown to arise from coparticipation in other domains. There is evidence that science content and content pedagogical knowledge fully unfolded only when embedded in and supported by appropriate practical pedagogical knowledge (which often resisted teachers' own efforts in formalizing it).

Roth, W.-M., & Boyd, N. (1999). Coteaching, as colearning, in practice. *Research in Science Education, 29*, 51–67.

In this study, we report on our learning as we engaged in a four-month experience of coteaching a water unit in a seventh grade classroom. Working at each other's elbows, in praxis, provided many opportunities to learn together: teaching and about teaching. We use two examples, learning to ask productive questions and struggling to enact an orderly curriculum to show how coteaching affords colearning, and how the lack of coteaching leads to struggling. Our work also suggests that coteaching allows for a mode of learning that is not captured by Donald Schön's notions of reflection-in-practice and reflection-on-practice. We conclude that coteaching, as colearning, is praxis.

Roth, W.-M., Masciotra, D., & Boyd, N. (1999). Becoming-in-the-classroom: a case study of teacher development through coteaching. *Teaching and Teacher Education, 17*, 771–784.

Although Schön's reflection-in-action and reflection-on-action have been important advances in understanding teaching, they do not capture important, tacit dimensions of the experience of teaching and being-in-the-classroom. These tacit dimensions of teaching cannot be acquired through didactic methods, but have to be enacted in lived experience. Teacher development can therefore be viewed as a becoming-in-the-classroom. In this paper, we show how coteaching provides a context in which novice teachers can come to embody this dimension of teaching that is essential to mastery.

Roth, W.-M., Lawless, D., & Tobin, K. (2000). {Coteaching|cogenerative dialoguing} as praxis of dialectic method. *Forum Qualitative Sozialforschung/ Forum Qualitative Social Research, 1*(3).

We present our {coteaching|cogenerative dialoguing} model in which historically existing boundaries between academic research and everyday teaching are considered. In coteaching, all individuals (teachers, teachers in training, supervisors, and researchers) participate in assisting students to learn; sitting on the sidelines and watching (objectifying) others is not permitted. In cogenerative dialoguing, these individuals and student representatives talk about their experience of teaching and learning in order to develop generalizations that open new possibilities for future action. On the basis of these generalizations and new action possibilities, changes are brought about in the environment to further enhance students' learning. Thus, {coteaching|cogenerative dialoguing} serves multiple purposes: besides the obvious context for teaching in a collective manner, it provides a context to research teaching, induct new teachers, supervise new and practicing teachers, assist teachers in development (that is, learning to teach). The structure of the {coteaching|cogenerative dialoguing} model is parallel to two dialectical pairs of concepts, {praxis|praxeology} and {understanding|explanation}, central to our epistemology and methodology, respectively.

Roth, W.-M., Lawless, D., & Tobin, K. (2000). Time to teach: Towards a praxeology of teaching. *Canadian Journal of Education, 25*, 1–15.

Despite much research on teaching, both preservice and seasoned teachers still experience a considerable gap between theory and the prescriptions for teaching and their own day-to-day practice. We conceptualize this gap in terms of the difference between descriptions of practice and practice itself. Descriptions are problematic because they cannot include the tacit understanding (background, practical sense) against which specific acts of teaching become meaningful and are inherently out of synchrony with unfolding practice. Using vignettes from a video database documenting our own and our collaborators' teaching, we illustrate how

> Bourdieu's notion of *habitus* (a set of dispositions) accounts for the generation of appropriate actions in situations where there is no "time out" for deliberation and how coteaching can support (preservice) teachers' development of this habitus.

Roth, W.-M. (2001). Becoming-in-the-classroom: Learning to teach in/as praxis. In D. R. Lavoie & W.-M. Roth (Eds.), *Models for science teacher preparation: Bridging the gap between research and practice* (pp. 11–30). Dordrecht, Netherlands: Kluwer Academic Publishers.

> In this chapter, I present our experiences with coteaching as a model of science teacher preparation. As I have outlined it here, coteaching requires a radical break with traditional notions of what makes a competent science teacher. Coteaching requires among others that faculty walk the walk about science teaching and coparticipate in the daily work of teaching children. Being-there and being-with another teacher allows them to see teaching as it is, what possibilities for action a particular moment in classroom life affords and so on. Being-there in the classroom and being-with another teacher and students is the primary place for understandings to emerge. This requires commitment to change that will take different trajectories depending on where you currently are.

Roth, W.-M., Lawless, D., & Masciotra, D. (2001). Spielraum and teaching. *Curriculum Inquiry, 31*(2), 183–207.

> In recent years, reflection-in-action has been a major concept for taking account of the craft and practical aspects of teaching. Yet in the everyday teaching praxis, reflection is largely absent for most of the time. In this paper, we argue that this absence is due to the fact that reflection requires objects of thought which have to be constructed. Both the construction and manipulation of these objects requires "time-out" from acting in real time. Taking time-out is frequently impossible in the praxis of teaching, unless we want to miss the "teachable moments." We propose *Spielraum*, room to maneuver, as a concept that describes the reality of teaching much better than reflection-in-action especially when there is no time-out for reflection. We use two extended classroom episodes to exemplify situations that are better described by the notion of *Spielraum* than by reflection-in-action.

Roth, W.-M., & Tobin, K. (2001). The implications of coteaching/cogenerative dialogue for teacher evaluation: Learning from multiple perspectives of everyday practice. *Journal of Personnel Evaluation in Education, 15*, 7–29.

> In this article, personnel evaluation is reconceptualized in terms of coteaching, an epistemology and methodology for teaching and learning to teach that is grounded in the collective (societal) motivation of preparing the next generation of citizens. Coteaching engages all participants (teachers, student teachers, supervisors, evaluators, and researchers) in the effort of helping students to learn. Central to coteaching are cogenerative learning sessions in which those who share a classroom experience (teachers and students) collectively construct local theory with the intent of improving the learning of students. Because our studies have been conducted in urban schools, in which often the least qualified teachers end up teaching, our work is particularly relevant to improving teaching in these most needy contexts.

Roth, W.-M., & Tobin, K. (2001). Learning to teach science as praxis. *Teaching and Teacher Education, 17*(7), 741–762.

> In this article, we propose *coteaching* as a viable model for teacher preparation. Coteaching, working at the elbows of someone else, allows beginning teachers to experience appropriate action at the right time. Coteaching provides beginning teachers with shared experiences that become the topic of their professional conversations with other coteachers (including peers, cooperating teacher, and university supervisors). We articulate our model within a phenomenological framework and exemplify each concept with vignettes from our ongoing research

on coteaching. A teacher preparation program that is situated in two urban schools provides the context for our research.

Tobin, K., Roth, W.-M., & Zimmermann, A. (2001). Learning to teach science in urban schools. *Journal of Research in Science Teaching, 38*, 941–964.

Teaching in urban schools, with their problems of violence, lack of resources, and inadequate funding is difficult. It is even more difficult to learn to teach in urban schools. Yet learning in those situations where one subsequently works has been shown to be the best preparation. In this article, we propose *coteaching* as a viable model for teacher preparation and professional development of urban science teachers. Coteaching, working at the elbow of someone else, allows new teachers to experience appropriate action at the right time by providing them with shared experiences that become the topic of their professional conversations with other coteachers (including peers, cooperating teacher, university supervisors, and high school students). The paper describes an ethnography in which a new teacher assigned for a field experience in an urban high school enacted a curriculum that was culturally relevant for her African American students, acknowledged their minority status in respect of science, and enabled them to pursue the school district standards. Even though coteaching affords learning to teach and the reform of curricula we raise doubts about whether or not our approaches to teacher education and enacting science curricula are hegemonic and oppressive to the students we seek to emancipate through education.

Roth, W.-M., Tobin, K., & Zimmermann, A. (2002). Coteaching: Learning environments research as aspect of classroom praxis. *Learning Environments Research, 5* (1), 1–28.

Critical educators have leveled a methodological critique against traditional forms of classroom research because they both objectify teachers and students and lead to results that do not enhance praxis. Over the past decade, we have developed coteaching as a context for learning to teach and supervising teaching, on the one hand and, on the other, as a method for doing research on and evaluating teaching. Coteaching involves an equitable inquiry into teaching and learning processes in which all members [or representatives thereof] of a classroom community participate—including students, teachers, student teachers, researchers, and supervisors. In this paper, we articulate coteaching in terms of activity theory and the associated first-person methodology for doing research on learning environments that is relevant to praxis because it constitutes an integral part of praxis. A detailed case study exemplifies coteaching and the associated research on learning environments.

Tobin, K., & Roth, W.-M. (2002). Evaluation of science teaching performance through coteaching and cogenerative dialoguing. In J. Altschuld & D. Kumar (Eds.), *Evaluation in science education in the 21st century* (pp. 187–217). Dordrecht, Netherlands: Kluwer Academic Press.

As we create new roles for assessing teaching performance, by coparticipating in classrooms and by making evaluation a collective responsibility of coteachers and students alike, we come ever closer to the tenets of Guba and Lincoln's (1989) fourth generation evaluation. As supervisors we learn from our evaluation in that our constructions vary over time, always seeking to be viable in changing contexts of learning and teaching. Collectively, we make every effort to ascertain what is happening and why it is happening from the perspectives of the key stakeholders and then to contribute to educate ourselves with respect to the perspectives of one another. As a result of what we learn through evaluation we seek to catalyze positive changes that are consistent with the goals of the teachers and students of the school; change is enabled because evaluation is a collective effort. Finally, we are tactical in our efforts to help those who have difficulty helping themselves in a school in which oppression is widespread and involves different stakeholder groups.

Roth, W.-M., Tobin, K., Zimmermann, A., Bryant, N., & Davis, C. (2002). Lessons on/from the dihybrid cross: An activity theoretical study of learning in coteaching. *Journal of Research in Science Teaching, 39*, 253–282.

> During their training, future teachers usually learn the subject matter of science. They are largely left on their own when it comes to figuring out how to teach this subject matter, that is, how to find appropriate pedagogical forms. In this article, we present a model of collective teaching and learning, which we term *coteaching/cogenerative dialoguing,* as a way to build deep learning of science concepts while learning about alternative ways to teach the same subject matter. As praxis, coteaching brings about a unity between teaching and learning to teach; cogenerative dialoguing brings about a unity between teaching and researching. Both are potential sites for deep learning. We articulate coteaching/cogenerative dialoguing in terms of activity theory and the associated first-person research methodology that has been developed by critical psychologists as a method of choice for dealing with the theory-praxis gap. Our detailed case study highlights opportunities of learning subject matter and pedagogy by university professors who participate in coteaching/cogenerative dialoguing in an urban high school.

Roth, W.-M., & Tobin, K. (2002). Redesigning an "urban" teacher education program: An activity theory perspective. *Mind, Culture, & Activity, 9* (2), 108–131.

> In this article, we use activity theory to frame the redesign of an urban teacher education program. Some of the contradictions that we had to deal with are endemic to traditional teacher education programs while others were particular to this program, which has as its goal to prepare teachers to work in urban (inner city) schools. Our intervention consisted of a change to coteaching, a collective form of teaching, and cogenerative dialoguing, a process of creating local theory involving coteachers and student representatives. Our coteaching/cogenerative-dialoguing paradigm makes salient the social, collective, rather than individual, psychological dimensions of learning to teach. As a result of the redesign process, new forms of relations between new teachers, cooperating (inservice) teachers, and supervisors emerged that are more participatory and democratic than they had been in the past.

Tobin, K., Zurbano, R., Ford, A., & Carambo, C. (2003). Learning to teach through coteaching and cogenerative dialogue. *Cybernetics & Human Knowing 10*(2), 51-73.

> This paper provides a theoretical and empirical analysis of the applications of coteaching and cogenerative dialogue as forms of practice that create opportunities for learning to teach science in urban high schools in which most students have very different cultural and social histories to the regular classroom teacher and two coteachers involved in a year long field experience. The authors employ cultural-historical activity theory and constructs from cultural sociology to highlight how coteaching and cogenerative dialogue create opportunities to learn to teach while teaching and at the same time allow for the development of collective responsibility for teaching and learning of science. They show how coteaching and cogenerative dialogue were enacted and evolved during the first semester of a two-semester field experience. A special focus is on identifying contradictions that arose, the manner in which they were addressed and resolved, and implications for future applications of coteaching in teacher education.

Eick, C. J., Ware, F. N., & Williams, P. G. (2003). Coteaching in a science methods course: A situated learning model of becoming a teacher. *Journal of Teacher Education, 54*, 74-85.

> A situated learning model of coteaching was implemented in the weekly field component of a secondary science methods course. Students cotaught by observing and assisting their teacher for one period followed by taking the lead in teaching the same lesson with their teachers' assistance during the following period. Students were peripheral participants, reflecting on both their teacher's practice and their own practice. Data supported four positive outcomes of this

model for the methods students: (a) comfort in learning to teach, (b) critical reflection in modeling the teacher's lesson, (c) development of confidence in teaching and managing students, and (d) positive effect of seeing and doing inquiry in practice.

Eick, C. J., Ware, F. N., & Jones, M. T. (2004). Coteaching in a secondary science methods course: Learning through a coteaching model that supports early teacher practice. *Journal of Science Teacher Education, 15*, 197 – 209.

Coteaching as a form of situated learning supports early induction into science teaching. The authors describe a coteaching model for secondary science methods students and what has been learned from this model. Secondary science methods students in pairs were placed with a science teacher to begin teaching as peripheral participants. A cooperative inquiry method was used to study this model. In-depth learning about the model and how to make it work effectively came from a process of research cycling over multiple semesters. This learning has been put in practical form as a primer for cooperating teachers and methods students participating in coteaching.

Murphy, C., Beggs, J. and Carlisle, K. (2004) Students as 'catalysts' in the classroom: the impact of coteaching between science student teachers and primary classroom teachers on children's enjoyment and learning of science. *International Journal of Science Education. 26*, 1023-1035.

This study is the first systematic investigation of the impact of collaborative teaching by student teachers and classroom teachers on children's enjoyment and learning of science. The authors describe findings from a project in which undergraduate science specialist student teachers were placed in primary schools where they 'co-taught' investigative science and technology with primary teachers. Students and teachers planned, taught and evaluated science lessons together. Almost six months after the student placement, a survey of children's attitudes to school science revealed that these children enjoyed science lessons more, and showed fewer gender or age differences in their attitudes to science than children who had not been involved in the project. The authors discuss how this model of collaborative planning, teaching and evaluation can both enhance teacher education and improve children's experience of science.

Roth, W.-M., & Tobin, K. (2004). Coteaching: From praxis to theory. *Teachers and Teaching: Theory and Practice, 10*, 161–179.

We evolved coteaching and cogenerative dialoguing to respond to the need of teachers inexperienced in one or another aspect of teaching to learn to teach at the elbow of another. As our praxis of coteaching and cogenerative dialoguing unfolded, we developed a theoretical framework. In this article, we present some core theoretical ideas that go with coteaching and cogenerative dialoguing. These ideas are rooted in our reading of cultural-historical activity theory and critical psychology. The resulting framework is particularly suited for analyzing and theorizing complex practices such as teaching and learning in schools for several reasons. First, it requires us to take a first-person perspective on the actions of individuals and groups. Second, it theorizes actions available to an individual as concrete cases of a generalized action available at the collective level. Third, we understand all actions to be mediated by the tools (language, curriculum theory), rules, community, and division of labor characteristic of the situation. Fourth, because this approach explicitly theorizes context, it is an excellent tool for articulating and removing structural contradictions. Fifth, the approach assists us in understanding the contradictions within a system in a positive way, namely as opportunities for change and growth. Finally, the framework explicitly focuses on the cultural-historical changes that individuals, their community and tools, and the reigning division of labor and rules undergo.

255

Roth, W.-M., Tobin, K., Elmesky, R., Carambo, C., McKnight, Y., & Beers, J. (2004). Re/making identities in the praxis of urban schooling: A cultural historical perspective. *Mind, Culture, & Activity, 11*, 48–69.

> In cultural historical activity theory, the entities that make a system are not conceived as independent but aspects of mediated relations. Consequently, an individual, a tool, or a community cannot be theorized in an independent manner but must be understood in terms of the historically changing, mediated relations in which they are integral and constitutive parts. Drawing on a case study that focuses on the identities of two of the authors, we show how, by participating in the activity system of schooling, the identities of students and teachers are continuously made and remade. A teacher changes from being "someone unable to control the class" to being respected and successful school staff; a student changes from being a street fighter to being an A student. Identity, we argue, should therefore not be thought of as a stable characteristic of individuals but as a contingent achievement of situated activity. Our case study suggests that cogenerative dialogues involving students and their teachers provide contexts for the reflexive elaboration of mutual understanding of the identities of individuals who occupy different social locations in the activity system.

Roth, W.-M., & Tobin, K. (2004). Co-generative dialoguing and metaloguing: Reflexivity of processes and genres. *Forum Qualitative Sozialforschung / Forum: Qualitative Social Research, 5* (3). http://www.qualitative-research.net/fqs-texte/3-04/04-3-7-e.htm

> In the course of our collaborative research we had evolved co-generative dialoguing and metaloguing as forms of doing and writing research. In this contribution, we exemplify these ways of being in the world of qualitative research, drawing on these forms as processes to construct our text and, reflexively, as forms of representing the products of these processes. They therefore also constitute a form of collective remembering in which the voices of participants endure on their own rather than disappearing in the voice of a collective author.

Roth, W.-M., Tobin, K., Carambo, C., & Dalland, C. (2004). Coteaching: Creating resources for learning and learning to teach chemistry in urban high schools. *Journal of Research in Science Teaching, 41* (9), 882–904.

> How do new teachers become confident and competent while they are interns in inner-city neighborhood schools challenged by many problems, often associated with economic shortfalls and cultural differences between the students and their teachers? Many science teacher education programs put a lot of emphasis on the planning stages of curriculum. But considerable discrepancies emerge between planned and lived curriculum, particularly in inner-city, comprehensive high schools, and especially in classrooms that honor student interests and culture as starting points for learning. Previous research showed that coteaching provides opportunities for learning to teach even though the lived curriculum emerges often in unpredictable ways from the dialectic of collective (teacher' and students') agency and structure. The present study allowed us to understand the underlying processes: the presence of a coteacher increases access to social and material resources, and thereby increases opportunities for actions that otherwise would not occur. Greater teaching opportunities provide newcomers with greater opportunities of learning to teach.

Roth, W.-M., Tobin, K., Carambo, C., & Dalland, C. (2005). Coordination in coteaching: Producing alignment in real time. *Science Education, 89*, 675–702.

> In coteaching, two or more teachers take collective responsibility for enacting a curriculum together with their students. Past research provided some indication that in the course of coteaching, not only the teaching practices of the partners become increasingly alike but also do unconsciously produced ways of moving about the classroom, hand gestures, and body movements. In this study, we investigate the possible sources of occurrence for the coordination of social and physical practices and provide exemplary episodes at a fine-grained level

from one coteaching pair. Drawing on key concepts from cultural sociology, we show how participants continuously create material and social resources that allow for new forms of agency in subsequent moments. Such resources include physical, temporal, and social spaces and meaning-making entities (language, inscriptions). We show how in productive coteaching, participants deploy and take advantage of these resources in synchronized and coordinated ways. The synchronization operates both at the temporal level, where coteachers work in concert like experienced jazz musicians in a jam session, and at a substantive level, where the practices of one look like those of the other. As coteachers generally are not aware that they adopt the ways of their partners as we articulate them here, there are considerable consequences, for better or worse, that arise from teaching with another person.

Tobin, K., & Roth, W.-M. (2005). Implementing coteaching / cogenerative dialoguing in urban science education. *School Science and Mathematics, 105,* 313–322.

Over the past seven years we have been involved in the development of a new model for the education of science teachers that has the potential to address teacher education in challenging urban settings characterized by problems such as teacher turnover and retention, low job satisfaction, and contradictions arising from cultural and ethnic diversity. An intensive research program accompanied the development effort; we used the research results as resources in redesigning the evolving model to make it more appropriate for the situations at hand. The science teacher education program at an urban university was built around a year-long field experience, during which all prospective teachers learned to teach in an urban high school while coteaching, that is, while teaching at the elbow of a mentor teacher or one or more peers. Over this period, we tried, tested, and investigated a number of different configurations of coteaching and the associated cogenerative dialoguing. In this paper, we describe the historical development of the different configurations of the model and the contradictions we faced that led us to enact changes to our approach. The central idea in our development effort was the creation of an environment that (a) best affords the learning of how to teach in urban high schools, (b) decreases teacher isolation, (c) mitigates turnover and retention, and (d) addresses contradictions arising from the cultural and ethnic diversity of students and teachers. Most importantly, this model of teacher education and enhancement simultaneously multiplies the resources and opportunities to support the learning of students.

Roth, W. -M. (2005). Organizational mediation of urban science. In K. Tobin, R. Elmesky, & G. Seiler (Eds.), *Maximizing the transformative potential of science education: Learning from research in inner city high schools* (pp. 91–115). Lanham, MD: Rowman & Littlefield.

Science educators usually deal with knowing and learning in classrooms as if one could usefully separate them out as a field (unit of analysis) that is not influenced by events and structures elsewhere in the larger organization. What and how students learn and what and how teachers teach are then problems of individuals or, at best, of the classroom as a collective. In the present study, I show that fields interact and the events and entities in and from one field have effects in other fields, where they come to structure actions, being deployed as resources and schema. More so, I show how some organizational features of school structure emerges from the interactions of people in particular fields, the interfaces between fields, or by attention to objects that move across boundaries and contribute to shaping events in fields other than that produced them. Cogenerative dialogues are shown to be important field that allow the temporally disjointed fields to interact and to be coordinated.

Eick, C. J., & Dias, M. (2005). Building the authority of experience in communities of practice: The development of preservice teachers' practical knowledge through coteaching in inquiry classrooms. *Science Education, 89,* 470-491.

Secondary science methods students' thinking on coteaching practice was studied for the development of conscious elements of practical teacher knowledge supporting the use of structured inquiry. Reflective dialogue on practice in an electronic forum was analyzed for elements of formal learning and biography (past and present) that informed thinking on practice. Changes in thinking over time were considered in light of observed practice, including methods students' thinking about inquiry through use of STC curriculum. Three concepts related to experience in learning to teach in this model emerged from the data: (a) movement from cultural acclimation to reflection on inquiry practice, (b) thinking through past educational knowledge and experience, and (c) integrating knowledge and experience in practice. Implications for preservice teacher education highlight the important aspects of learning to teach in practice in order to begin developing practical teacher knowledge for teaching using structured inquiry.

Wassell, B., & Stith, I. (2005). Becoming research collaborators in urban classrooms: Ethical considerations, contradictions and new understandings [40 paragraphs]. *Forum Qualitative Sozialforschung / Forum: Qualitative Social Research* [On-line Journal], *6*(1), Art. 18. Available at: http://www.qualitative-research.net/fqs-texte/1-05/05-1-18-e.htm [Date of Access: June 19, 2006].

In this paper, the authors outline several ethical considerations that arose in our collaborative research in urban classrooms. Specifically, Beth discusses the concerns she had as a beginning researcher with regard to the demands she placed on Ian, the subject of her research, during his first year of teaching. Together, they then discuss a sensitive issue that emerged in the data analysis and the implications of the decision to write about the issue. Finally, Beth outlines an argument for the misalignment between the theoretical framework used in her study and Ian's roles and participation in the research process.

Tobin, K. (2006). Learning to teach through coteaching and cogenerative dialogue. *Teaching Education, 17,* 133-142.

Ken presents theory and research associated with learning to teach science in inner city high schools on the east coast of the United States. He uses theories from cultural sociology as a framework to explore how coteaching is enacted in a science teacher education program in which coteachers collaborate with high school students in cogenerative dialogues, to study learning and teaching in their own classrooms. Ken presents an ethnographic case study of what is learned from coteaching and cogenerative dialogue in a setting in which coteaching involves a prospective teacher and a recently certified biology teacher in lesson on protein synthesis. Coteaching creates an expanded array of practices that afford the learning of students and for the coteachers to learn from one another. Cogenerative dialogues identify and resolve contradictions, creating a consensus among the coteachers and the participating students on how learning environments can be improved.

Scantlebury, K., & LaVan, S-K. (2006). Re-visioning cogenerative dialogues as feminist pedagogy|research [33 paragraphs]. Forum Qualitative Sozialforschung / Forum: Qualitative Social Research [On-line Journal], 7(2), Art. 41. Available at: http://www.qualitative-research.net/fqs-texte/2-06/06-2-41-e.htm [Date of Access: June 19, 2006].

Kate and Sarah-Kate discuss when cogenerative dialogues are a feminist pedagogy|research tool and also the circumstances when this is not the case. When viewed as a feminist pedagogy|research, cogenerative dialogues expose and discuss the unconscious and underlying structures that cause inequities both within and outside the classroom, particularly for girls and women. The authors raise ethical issues for researchers to consider how and when cogenerative dialogues may cause inequities by silencing students or reinforcing existing power differentials between teachers and students and offer suggestions for future research directions.

Stith, I., Scantlebury, K., LaVan, S-K., Emdin, C., Lehner, E., & Kim, M. (2006). The ethics of cogenerative dialogue: A cogenerative dialogue [17 paragraphs]. *Forum Qualitative Sozialforschung / Fo-*

rum: Qualitative Social Research [On-line Journal], *7*(2), Art. 44. Available at: http://www.qualitative-research.net/fqs-texte/2-06/06-2-44-e.htm [Date of Access: June 19, 2006].

The authors engage in a cogenerative dialogue about co-generative dialogue as qualitative research method and the associated ethics of using cogenerative dialogues. They conclude that cogenerative dialoguing constitutes an excellent starting point towards enacting equity in practice.

Stith, I., & Roth, W.-M. (2006). Who gets to ask the questions: The ethics in/of cogenerative dialogue praxis. *FQS: Forum Qualitative Sozialforschung/Forum Qualitative Social Research, 7*(2). Art. 38. http://www.qualitative-research.net/fqs-texte/a5b6c7/06-2-38-e.htm

We present cogenerative dialogue as an authentic research tool which, when conducted properly, can address some of the ethical issues inherent in classroom research. To begin with, there is the question of the participation of the researcher in the cogenerative dialogue. Next, we present cogenerative dialogue as an ideal tool to instigate interaction and participation among the participants in classroom research: students, teachers, and researcher. And finally we present cogenerative dialogue as tool to facilitate the discussion of the ethical issues that are part of the research setting (e.g., class).

Roth, W.-M. (2006). Une approche pratique dans la reforme de l'enseignement des sciences. In A. Hasni, Y. Lenoir, & Y. Cartonnet (Eds.), *La formation à l'enseignement des sciences et contexte des réformes par compétences* (pp. 157–191). Québec : Presses de l'Université du Québec.

There are gaps between the science students learn at school and what they do when science knowledge is called for out of school. A similar gap continues to be recognized in learning to teach between the knowledge future teachers acquire by taking university courses and the knowledge that they really need in the classroom. Despite many reforms in science education and science teaching, little has changed. Yet we already know—at least intuitively—what it takes to bridge both gaps. This knowledge exists in the old adage that states, "Practice makes perfect." The adage might be heard in the sense that one has to do something many times over before getting good at it. But one can also hear it in the sense of "learning in practice gives us perfect knowledge." In this chapter, I describe and theorize recent reform experiments in which both science students and future science teachers learn by engaging in the real thing—students contribute to the environmental knowledge of their community and in the process learn science; future teachers teach together with more experienced others and in doing so, learn to teach science even in the most dire circumstances such as inner-city schools. I use one concrete case where the two gaps were addressed simultaneously while I was teaching together with a teaching intern a unit on environmental science. I conclude by articulating why it makes sense to view middle and high school students as resources for knowledge-building in their community, and science-teachers-in-training as legitimate resources for assisting educational systems.

Emdin, C. & Lehner, E. (2006). Situating Cogenerative Dialogue in a Cosmopolitan Ethic [28 paragraphs]. *Forum Qualitative Sozialforschung / Forum: Qualitative Social Research* [On-line Journal], *7*(2), Art. 39. Available at: http://www.qualitative-research.net/fqs-texte/2-06/06-2-39-e.htm [Date of Access: June 19, 2006].

The authors acknowledge the transformative nature of cogenerative dialogues and focus on the ethical dimensions of the practice in order to move educational research, classrooms and schools beyond current conceptions of what is ethical. Utilizing a fusion of the Belmont Report with nuanced notions of fourth generation evaluation procedures, the authors ground cogenerative dialogues in a philosophical approach to cosmopolitanism that acknowledges the differences between multiple participants, multiple fields, and varying ways of knowing and being. First, the authors consider how grounding the character of the truly ethical research act in a cosmopolitan ideal can attain participant beneficence. Second, they consider how to

259

avoid the potential pitfalls of authenticity criteria in the practice of cogenerative dialogues by enacting practices that maximize tactical authenticity. Their approach to cogenerative dialogues serves as a method for critique and analysis that challenges current practice and considers the ethics of cogenerative dialogues in inner city schools in a new light.

Gallo-Fox, J, Wassell, B, Scantlebury, K. & Juck, M. (2006). Warts and all: An ethical struggle with disseminating research on coteaching [45 paragraphs]. Forum Qualitative Sozialforschung / Forum: Qualitative Social Research [On-line Journal],

The authors examine the ethical dilemmas that the researchers encountered between their philosophical perspectives and those of their colleagues from the field. We found that ethical issues emerged on three levels: during our enactment of the coteaching model, in our research endeavors on coteaching, and in discussing findings. Rather than reaching specific conclusions, this paper addresses the issues and their complexities. It is our intention that this metalogue will promote dialogue among teacher educators who plan to incorporate coteaching into existing traditional preservice programs.

Gleason, S., Fennemore, M., & Scantlebury, K. (2006). Choreographing teaching: Coteaching with special education/inclusion teachers in science classrooms. In K. Tobin. (Ed.), *Teaching and learning science: A handbook*. Praeger Publishing.

The authors explain how coteaching is employed in a science education for high school science teachers and a professional development program for their supervising teachers in a public high school. The use of a special education teacher in this study brings together the two fields in which research on coteaching is found—special education and science education.

Martin, S. (2006). Teachers as researchers. In K. Tobin [Ed.] *Teaching and Learning Science: A Handbook*, New York: Praeger Publishing.

Sonya provides insights into a process that brought research directly into her classroom, enabling her to make changes in her teaching while expanding learning opportunities for her students. Specifically this chapter details a collaborative research effort between high school chemistry students and their teacher as they used cogenerative dialogues to analyze video recordings and discuss their social interactions from their classroom.

Martin, S. (2006). Where practice and theory intersect in the chemistry classroom: Using cogenerative dialogue to identify the critical point in science education. *Cultural Studies of Science Education*.

Sonya argues for an inclusive model of science education practice that attempts to facilitate a relationship between "science and all" by paying particular attention to the development of the relationship between the teacher, students and science. This model hinges on the implementation of cogenerative dialogues between students and teachers. Cogenerative dialogues are a form of structured discourse in which teachers and students engage in a collaborative effort to help identify and implement positive changes in classroom teaching and learning practices. A primary goal is to introduce a methodological and theoretical framework for conducting cogenerative dialogue that is accessible to classroom teachers and their students. Sonya examines the relationships between teacher knowledge and researcher knowledge by exploring the practical application of cogenerative dialogues for classrooms teachers and the theoretical implications of using cogenerative dialogues for researchers.

Martin, S., Milne, C., & Scantlebury, K. (in press). Eye rollers, risk-takers, and turn sharks: Target Students in a professional science education program *Journal of Research in Science Teaching*.

Cogenerative dialogues are presented as tools to improve the learning environment in a college classroom in which there were problems with target students—those who monopolize material and human resources. The authors answer the following question: What strategies could help college science professors enact more equitable teaching structures in their class-rooms so that target students and cliques become less of an issue in classroom interactions?

Tobin, K. (in press). Learning to teach in diverse and dynamic classrooms. *Pedagogies: An international journal.*

Coteaching involves two or more teachers teaching together. Ken describes how to set up coteaching and the advantages for teachers and students associated with it. Cogenerative dialogues are conversations among participants about shared experiences—often in a classroom. The participants include teachers, two to three students and, when possible, representatives from other groups such as school administrators and teacher educators. Participants identify contradictions and negotiate agreements on how to resolve them, leading to changes to enact in future lessons and shared responsibility for improving the quality of teaching and learning.

Ritchie, S., Tobin, K., Roth, W-M. & Carambo, C. (2007). Transforming an academy through the enactment of collective curriculum leadership. *Journal of Curriculum Studies.*

Although the transformation of relevant curriculum experiences for African American youth from impoverished backgrounds in large urban high schools offers many leadership challenges for faculty, few studies have focused on the roles of students and teachers in the creation of distributed leadership practices to build and sustain improved learning environments. Through ethnography we explore the leadership dynamics in one academy within a large urban high school whose students are mostly African American. Students in some classes had opportunities to participate in cogenerative dialogues and, in so doing, learned how to interact successfully with others, including their teachers and peers, and build collective agreements for future classroom roles and shared responsibility for their enactment. The study highlights the centrality of successful interactions among participants and the extent to which co-respect and co-responsibility for goals occur. Initially, a lack of trust within the community undermined tendencies to build solidarity throughout the community despite a commitment of the academy's coordinator to be responsive to the goals of others, listen to colleagues and students, and strive for collective goals. We argue that all participants in a field need to take responsibility for accessing and appropriating structures to achieve positive emotional energy through collective curriculum leadership and climates that create and sustain educational accomplishments. Furthermore, we suggest that individual and collective actions should be studied dialectically in subsequent research on leadership dynamics in schools.

261

REFERENCES

Armstrong, D. G. (1977). Team teaching and academic achievement. *Review of Educational Research, 47*, 65–86.

Bakhtin, M. M. (1993). *Toward a philosophy of the act.* Austin: University of Texas Press.

Bateson, G. (1972). *Steps to an ecology of mind: A revolutionary approach to man's understanding of himself.* New York: Ballantine.

Bourdieu, P. (1990). *The logic of practice.* Cambridge, UK: Polity Press.

Bourdieu, P. (1992). The practice of reflexive sociology (The Paris workshop). In P. Bourdieu & L.J.D. Wacquant, *An invitation to reflexive sociology* (pp. 216–260). Chicago: University of Chicago Press.

Boykin, A. W. (1986). The triple quandary and the schooling of Afro-American children. In U. Neisser (Ed.), *The school achievement of minority children: New perspectives* (pp. 57–92). Hillsdale, NJ: Lawrence Erlbaum Associates.

Brown, A. L. (1992). Design experiments: Theoretical and methodological challenges in creating complex interventions in classroom settings. *Journal of the Learning Sciences, 2*, 141–178.

Collins, R. (2004). *Interaction ritual chains.* Princeton, NJ: Princeton University Press.

Deleuze, G. (1990) *The logic of sense* (C. V. Boundas, Ed.; M. Lester, Trans.). New York: Columbia University Press. (First published in 1969)

Deleuze, G. (1994). *Difference and repetition* (P. Patton, Trans.). New York: Columbia University Press. (First published in 1968)

Derrida, J. (2005). *Poétique et politique du témoignage.* Paris: L'Herne.

Eckert, P. (1989). *Jocks and burnouts: Social categories and identity in the high school.* New York: Teachers College Press.

Eldon, M., & Levin, M. (1991). Cogenerative learning: Bringing participation into action research. In W. F. Whyte (Ed.), *Participative action research* (pp. 127–142). Newbury Park, CA: Sage.

Emdin, C., & Lehner, E. (2006, May). Situating cogenerative dialogue in a cosmopolitan ethic. *Forum Qualitative Sozialforschung / Forum: Qualitative Social Research, 7*(2). Available at: http://www.qualitative-research.net/fqs-texte/2-06/06-2-39-e.htm [Date of access: March 21, 2006].

Foucault, M. (1975). *Surveiller et punir: Naissance de la prison.* Paris: Gallimard.

Guba, E., & Lincoln, Y. (1989). *Fourth generation evaluation.* Beverly Hills, CA: Sage.

Holzkamp, K. (1993). *Lernen: Subjektwissenschaftliche Grundlegung.* Frankfurt/M.: Campus.

Kemper, T. D., & Collins, R. (1990). Dimensions of microinteraction. *American Journal of Sociology 96*, 32–68.

Lave, J., & Wenger, E. (1991). *Situated learning: Legitimate peripheral participation.* Cambridge, England: Cambridge University Press.

Levinas, E. (1998). *Otherwise than being or Beyond essence* (A. Lingis, Trans.). Pittsburgh, PA: Duquesne University Press. (First published in 1978)

Martin, S. (2005). *The social and cultural dimensions of successful teaching and learning of science in an urban high school.* Unpublished doctoral dissertation. Curtin University, Perth, Australia.

Müller, A.M.K. (1972). *Die präparierte Zeit: Der Mensch in der Krise seiner eigenen Zielsetzung.* Stuttgart, Germany: Radius Verlag.

Nancy, J.-L. (2000). *Being singular plural.* Stanford, CA: Stanford University Press.

Nancy, J.-L. (2002). *Hegel: The restlessness of the negative.* Minneapolis: University of Minnesota Press.

Ricœur, P. (1991). *From text to action: Essays in hermeneutics, II.* Evanston, IL: Northwestern University Press.

REFERENCES

Ricœur, P. (1992). *Oneself as another*. Chicago: University of Chicago Press.

Ricœur, P. (2000). *The just*. Chicago: University of Chicago Press.

Roth, W.-M. (2006). Ontological ambiguity of practical action. *Submitted for publication*.

Roth, W.-M., Hwang, S., Lee, Y-J., & Goulart, M. (2005). *Participation, learning, and identity: Dialectical perspectives*. Berlin: Lehmanns Media.

Roth, W.-M., & McGinn, M. K. (1998). >unDELETE science education: /lives/work/voices. *Journal of Research in Science Teaching, 35,* 399–421.

Roth, W.-M., McRobbie, C., Lucas, K. B., & Boutonné, S. (1997). Why do students fail to learn from demonstrations? A social practice perspective on learning in physics. *Journal of Research in Science Teaching, 34,* 509–533.

Roth, W.-M., & Tobin, K. (2002). *At the elbow of another: Learning to teach by coteaching*. New York: Peter Lang.

Suchman, L. A. (1987). *Plans and situated actions: The problem of human-machine communication*. Cambridge: Cambridge University Press.

Swidler, A. (1986). Culture in action: Symbols and strategies. *American Sociological Review, 51,* 273–286.

Tobin, K. (1987). The role of wait time in higher cognitive level learning. *Review of Educational Research, 57,* 69–85.

Varela, F. J., & Depraz, N. (2005). At the source of time: Valence and the constitutional dynamics of affect: the question, the background: How affect originarily shapes time. *Journal of Consciousness Studies, 12,* 61–81.

Wacquant, L. (2004). *Body and soul: Notebooks of an apprentice boxer*. New York: Oxford University Press.

Wartofsky, M. (1979). *Models: Representations and scientific understanding*. Dordrecht, The Netherlands: Reidel.

INDEX OF NAMES

INDEX OF TERMS

J

Judgment: suspended, 123, 129
Justice: social, 165, 222, 226, 229

K

Knowledge: pedagogical, 77, 78, 251;
pedagogical content, 77; practical,
199, 203, 257; subject matter, 34, 186
Knowledgeability, vii, 3, 12, 19, 24, 34,
45, 68, 73, 75, 199, 202, 228, 229,
247, 250

L

Lag: cultural, 157, 162
Language, 4, 5, 34, 35, 36, 55, 94, 101,
103, 104, 135, 138, 147, 151, 157,
161, 170, 171, 172, 214, 223, 255,
257; of teaching, 34, 35
Latching, 189
Laughter, 96, 97, 104, 139
Learning: rote, 80, 214; tacit mode of,
239
Learning environment, 2, 3, 12, 15, 18,
20, 22, 81, 92, 93, 101, 130, 138, 148,
156, 157, 160, 166, 170, 183, 192,
198, 203, 222, 253, 258, 260, 261
Learning to teach, 1, 2, 7, 8, 9, 14, 16,
17, 18, 23, 24, 29, 30, 45, 52, 57, 81,
101, 107, 135, 136, 138, 140, 142,
159, 160, 161, 165, 169, 180, 186,
208, 219, 234, 235, 236, 244, 246,
249, 250, 251, 252, 253, 254, 255,
256, 258, 259, 275
Legitimate, 27, 28, 51, 54, 55, 79, 225,
238, 259
Limiting reagent, 63, 68, 72, 77
Listening: active, 105
Loudness, 189

M

Margin|center, 28, 54
Mentor (supervisor), 20, 207, 217, 218,
228, 257
Metalogue, 8, 179, 194, 195, 196, 217,
260

Mimesis, 62, 157
Modeling, 75, 234, 241, 255
Models: causal, 201
Monitoring, 58, 60
Monologue: inner, 213; internal, 160,
209
Motivation, 252
Motive, 13, 15, 29, 84, 89, 90, 91, 162

N

Narrative, 9, 30, 44, 45, 62, 169, 185,
196, 198, 202, 207, 212, 219, 226,
229; master, 30

O

Object, 23, 24, 31, 53, 55, 100, 121, 145,
148, 160, 200, 201, 202, 209, 216,
218
Ontology, 86, 203, 205
Oppression, 193, 204, 222, 253
Other, vii, 4, 5, 22, 33, 61, 137, 190, 206,
208
Outcome: cogenerated, 82, 132
Overlap, 189

P

Participation, viii, 6, 19, 22, 25, 27, 28,
44, 49, 52, 53, 54, 60, 61, 71, 81, 88,
89, 90, 91, 94, 95, 98, 101, 103, 109,
110, 112, 117, 125, 136, 137, 140,
143, 158, 168, 170, 171, 179, 203,
207, 208, 214, 218, 219, 228, 235,
236, 237, 238, 243, 258, 259, 263
Participative thinking, vii, 34, 44, 45, 47,
54, 56, 85, 202, 242
Passivity, 36, 46, 107, 108
Patterns: of coherence, 92, 102, 132,
169, 238
Pause, 12, 13, 40, 41, 42, 61, 97, 112,
115, 117, 120, 144, 146, 150, 176,
181, 184, 189, 192, 210, 213, 215
Peak DV, 189
Pedagogy, 20, 79, 127, 159, 234, 254,
258; critical, 193, 247
Peer: approval, 139; coaching, 234;
review, 65, 222, 245, 246; teaching,

U

Understanding, vii, 3, 4, 5, 6, 7, 8, 9, 11, 16, 23, 29, 30, 32, 44, 45, 48, 51, 54, 55, 59, 68, 71, 73, 77, 83, 85, 93, 95, 100, 108, 109, 113, 114, 115, 116, 117, 130, 146, 148, 151, 157, 160, 161, 162, 167, 184, 186, 191, 193, 203, 204, 209, 211, 214, 215, 216, 217, 227, 230, 234, 236, 239, 240, 248, 250, 251, 255, 256, 263, 264; existential, 191; practical, 4, 55, 157, 209, 217, 229, 239; primary, 191
Unsettled times, 15

V

Valence: emotional, 38, 87, 118

Validity, 8, 197, 198, 224, 226
Verve, 23, 59, 71, 72, 73, 190
Video: analysis, 23, 185; vignettes, 85, 90, 132, 175, 207
Violence: symbolic, 245

W

Wait time, 121, 151, 264
Waveform, 189
Wisdom: practical, 12, 199, 202
Witness, 225, 227, 228, 229, 231

Z

Zoning, 60, 65

ABOUT THE AUTHORS

Ken Tobin is Presidential Professor at the Graduate Center of the City University of New York. In 2004 he was recognized by the National Science Foundation as a *Distinguished Teaching Scholar* and by the Association for the Education of Teachers of Science as *Outstanding Science Teacher Educator of the Year.* Prior to commencing a career as a teacher educator, Ken taught high school science and mathematics in Australia and was involved in curriculum design. His research focuses on the teaching and learning of science in urban schools, which involve mainly African American students living in conditions of poverty. A parallel program of research focuses on coteaching as a way of learning to teach in urban high schools. Recently Ken edited a Handbook about *Teaching and Learning Science* (Praeger), *Doing Educational Research* (with Joe Kincheloe), and *Improving Urban Science Education* (with Rowhea Elmesky and Gale Seiler). In 2002 our book *At the Elbows of Another* received the Choice award in the category of *Outstanding Academic Titles.* With Michael, Ken is founding co-editor of *Cultural Studies of Science Education.*

Wolff-Michael Roth is Lansdowne Professor of Applied Cognitive Science at the University of Victoria, British Columbia, Canada. For most of the 1980–1992 period, he taught science, mathematics, and computer science at the middle and high school levels. From 1992 on, already working at the university, he taught science in British Columbia elementary schools at the fourth- through seventh-grade levels always associated with research on knowing and learning. More recently, he has conducted several ethnographic studies of scientific research, a variety of workplaces, and environmental activist movements. His research focuses on cultural-historical, linguistic, and embodied aspects of scientific and mathematical cognition and communication from elementary school to professional practice, including, among others, studies of scientists, technicians, and environmentalists at their work sites. His recent books include *Rethinking Scientific Literacy* (2004, with A. C. Barton), *Talking Science: Language and Learning in Science Classrooms* (2005), *Doing Qualitative Research: Praxis of Method* (2005), and *Learning Science: Singular Plural Perspectives* (2006).

NEW DIRECTIONS IN MATHEMATICS AND SCIENCE EDUCATION

Volume 1
Learning Science
A Singular Plural View
W.-M. Roth, *University of Victoria, Canada*
Paperback ISBN 90-77874-25-9 Hardback ISBN 90-77874-26-7

Volume 2
Theorems in School
From History, Epistemology, and Cognition to Classroom Practice
P. Boero, *Universidad de Valencia, Italy* (Ed.)
Paperback ISBN 90-77874-21-6 Hardback ISBN 90-77874-22-4

Volume 3
The Culture of Science Education
Historical and Biographical Perspectives
K. Tobin, *The Graduate Center, City University of New York, USA*
and
W.-M. Roth, *University of Victoria, Canada* (Eds.)
Paperback ISBN 90-77874-33-X Hardback ISBN 90-77874-35-6

Volume 4
Teaching to Learn
A View from the Field
K. Tobin, *The Graduate Center, City University of New York, USA*
and
W.-M. Roth, *University of Victoria, Canada*
Paperback ISBN 90-77874-81-X Hardback ISBN 90-77874-91-7

CPSIA information can be obtained at www.ICGtesting.com
Printed in the USA
BVOW030505250112

281328BV00004B/4/A